Reading Winnic

Reading Winnicott brings together a selection of papers by the psychoanalyst and paediatrician Donald Winnicott, providing an insight into his work and charting its impact on the well being of mothers, babies, children and families.

With individual introductions summarizing the key features of each of Winnicott's papers this book not only offers an overview of Winnicott's work but also links it with Freud and later theorists. Areas of discussion include:

- the relational environment and the place of infantile sexuality
- aggression and destructiveness
- illusion and traditional phenomena
- theory and practice of psychoanalysis of adults and children

As such, *Reading Winnicott* will be essential reading for all students wanting to learn more about Winnicott's theories and their impact on psychoanalysis and the wider field of mental health.

Lesley Caldwell is a psychoanalyst of the British Psychoanalytic Association. She has also worked as an academic, currently at UCL, for more than 30 years. She is the Chair of the Winnicott Trust and one of its editors.

Angela Joyce is a Training and Supervising Analyst of the British Psychoanalytical Society. She trained as a child analyst at the Anna Freud Centre where she has helped to pioneer psychoanalytic work with infants and parents, and is currently jointly leading the resurgence of child psychotherapy there. She also is an editor with the Winnicott Trust.

ALSO IN THIS SERIES

Psychoanalytic Understanding of Violence and Suicide Edited by Rosine Jozef
Perelberg

On Bearing Unbearable States of Mind Ruth Riesenberg-Malcolm. Edited by
Priscilla Roth

Psychoanalysis on the Move: The Work of Joseph Sandler Edited by Peter Fonagy,
Arnold M. Cooper and Robert S. Wallerstein

The Dead Mother: The Work of André Green Edited by Gregorio Kohon

The Fabric of Affect in the Psychoanalytic Discourse André Green

The Bi-Personal Field: Experiences of Child Analysis Antonino Ferro

*The Dove that Returns, the Dove that Vanishes: Paradox and Creativity in
Psychoanalysis* Michael Parsons

*Ordinary People, Extra-ordinary Protections: A Post-Kleinian Approach to the
Treatment of Primitive Mental States* Judith Mitrani

The Violence of Interpretation: From Pictogram to Statement Piera Aulagnier

The Importance of Fathers: A Psychoanalytic Re-Evaluation Judith Trowell and
Alicia Etchegoyen

Dreams That Turn Over a Page: Paradoxical Dreams in Psychoanalysis Jean-Michel
Quinodoz

The Couch and the Silver Screen: Psychoanalytic Reflections on European Cinema
Edited and introduced by Andrea Sabbadini

In Pursuit of Psychic Change: The Betty Joseph Workshop Edited by Edith
Hargreaves and Arturo Varchevker

*The Quiet Revolution in American Psychoanalysis: Selected Papers of Arnold M.
Cooper* Arnold M. Cooper. Edited and introduced by Elizabeth L.
Auchincloss

*Seeds of Illness and Seeds of Recovery: The Genesis of Suffering and the Role of
Psychoanalysis* Antonino Ferro

The Work of Psychic Figurability: Mental States Without Representation César
Botella and Sára Botella

*Key Ideas for a Contemporary Psychoanalysis: Misrecognition and Recognition of the
Unconscious* André Green

*The Telescoping of Generations: Listening to the Narcissistic Links Between
Generations* Haydée Faimberg

Glacial Times: A Journey Through the World of Madness Salomon Resnik

This Art of Psychoanalysis: Dreaming Undreamt Dreams and Interrupted Cries
Thomas H. Ogden

Psychoanalysis as Therapy and Storytelling Antonino Ferro

Psychoanalysis and Religion in the 21st Century: Competitors or Collaborators?
Edited by David M. Black

Recovery of the Lost Good Object Eric Brenman. Edited and introduced by
Gigliola Fornari Spoto

The Many Voices of Psychoanalysis Roger Kennedy

*Feeling the Words: Neuropsychoanalytic Understanding of Memory and the
Unconscious* Mauro Mancia

Projected Shadows: Psychoanalytic Reflections on the Representation of Loss in European Cinema Edited by Andrea Sabbadini

Encounters with Melanie Klein: Selected Papers of Elizabeth Spillius Elizabeth Spillius. Edited by Priscilla Roth and Richard Rusbridger

Constructions and the Analytic Field: History, Scenes and Destiny Domenico Chianese

Yesterday, Today and Tomorrow Hanna Segal. Edited by Nicola Abel-Hirsch

Psychoanalysis Comparable and Incomparable: The Evolution of a Method to Describe and Compare Psychoanalytic Approaches David Tuckett, Roberto Basile, Dana Birksted-Breen, Tomas Böhm, Paul Denis, Antonino Ferro, Helmut Hinz, Arne Jemstedt, Paola Mariotti and Johan Schubert

Time, Space and Phantasy Rosine Jozef Perelberg

Rediscovering Psychoanalysis: Thinking and Dreaming, Learning and Forgetting Thomas H. Ogden

Mind Works: Technique and Creativity in Psychoanalysis Antonino Ferro

Doubt, Conviction and the Analytic Process: Selected Papers of Michael Feldman Michael Feldman. Edited by Betty Joseph

Melanie Klein in Berlin: Her First Psychoanalysis of Children Claudia Frank. Edited by Elizabeth Spillius

The Psychotic Wavelength: A Psychoanalytic Perspective for Psychiatry Richard Lucas

Betweenity: A Discussion of the Concept of Borderline Judy Gammelgaard

The Intimate Room: Theory and Technique of the Analytic Field Giuseppe Civitarese

Bion Today Edited by Chris Mawson

Secret Passages: The Theory and Technique of Interpsychic Relations Stefano Bolognini

Intersubjective Processes and the Unconscious: An Integration of Freudian, Kleinian and Bionian Perspectives Lawrence Brown

TITLES IN THE NEW LIBRARY OF PSYCHOANALYSIS
TEACHING SERIES

Reading Freud: A Chronological Exploration of Freud's Writings Jean-Michel Quinodoz

Listening to Hanna Segal: Her Contribution to Psychoanalysis Jean-Michel Quinodoz

Reading French Psychoanalysis Edited by Dana Birksted-Breen, Sara Flanders and Alain Gibeault

Reading Winnicott Edited by Lesley Caldwell and Angela Joyce

THE NEW LIBRARY OF PSYCHOANALYSIS:
TEACHING SERIES

4

General Editor: Dana Birksted-Breen

Reading Winnicott

Edited by Lesley Caldwell and Angela Joyce

Routledge
Taylor & Francis Group

LONDON AND NEW YORK

First published 2011
by Routledge
27 Church Road, Hove, East Sussex, BN3 2FA

Simultaneously published in the USA and Canada
by Routledge
711 Third Avenue, New York NY 10017

Reprinted 2011

Routledge is an imprint of the Taylor & Francis Group, an Informa business

Typeset in Bembo and Helvetica by RefineCatch Limited, Bungay, Suffolk
Printed and bound in Great Britain by
TJ International Ltd, Padstow, Cornwall
Paperback cover design by Sandra Heath
Paperback cover photograph: courtesy of Topfoto

British Library Cataloguing in Publication Data
A catalogue record for this book is available from the British Library

Library of Congress Cataloging-in-Publication Data
Winnicott, D. W. (Donald Woods), 1896–1971.
[Selections. 2011]
Reading Winnicott / edited by Lesley Caldwell and Angela Joyce.
p. cm.
Includes bibliographical references.
1. Child psychology.   2. Child analysis.   I. Caldwell,
Lesley.   II. Joyce, Angela, 1948–.   III. Title.
BF721.W54 2011
155.4—dc22
2010036892

ISBN: 978-0-415-41594-1 (hbk)
ISBN: 978-0-415-41595-8 (pbk)

CONTENTS

ACKNOWLEDGEMENTS

The need for a reader that would introduce Winnicott to a wider audience in the universities and in fields where a psychoanalytic perspective is essential had been under discussion for some time. Since we accepted the original offer from Routledge several years have passed and we are grateful to Kate Hawes who has been remarkably patient in encouraging us to keep at it. We were given a decisive push by Dana Birksted-Breen who proposed we do it under the auspices of the New Library of Psychoanalysis Teaching Series. We are particularly grateful to Christopher Reeves for his contributions on the contexts of Winnicott's papers; to Bernard Barnett, David Riley, Helen Taylor Robinson, James Rose, Margaret Tonnesmann, Peter Shoenberg and Mandy O'Keeffe for reading and commenting on parts of the manuscript; and to other colleagues for sharing information that we just did not have: Andreas Giannakoulas for information on Masud Khan; Richard Carvalho, Helen Morgan, and Hester Solomon for information on the London Jung group; and Alain Vanier and Catherine Mathelin for detailed discussion of Lacan and for their own in-depth Winnicottian scholarship. We would like to thank Jan Abram for making available the initial on-line collection of Winnicott's works she compiled on behalf of the Winnicott Trust.

We would like to thank Matthew Caldwell for his generous and unfailing assistance with our computer problems and Mandy and Kieran Macdonald for their careful copy editing of the manuscript.

We are also indebted to all those Winnicottian and non-Winnicottian scholars whose work we have used and been enriched by.

It has been an enormous pleasure for us to work together and we have learned a great deal in the process. Deepening our own knowledge of Winnicott's work as we found ourselves striving to explain it to others, we have drawn on our respective areas of competence and the continuing support of colleagues at home and abroad. Our fellow Trustees, Judith Trowell, Barbie Antonis, Sheilagh Davies, Marianne Parsons, and earlier, Jennifer Johns and Helen Taylor Robinson, have encouraged us and provided an understanding environment for our work on this book and for all the work of the Winnicott Trust and its aims.

Our thanks for the forbearance and support of our agents, Steph Ebdon and Mark Paterson.

We thank Paterson Marsh Associates for permission to reproduce the following papers.

'The Observation of Infants in a Set Situation' (1941), 'Primitive Emotional Development' (1945), 'Hate in the Countertransference' (1947), 'Mind and its Relation to Psyche-Soma' (1949), 'Metapsychological and Clinical Aspects of Regression within the Psycho-Analytical Set-Up' (1954).

From *Through Paediatrics to Psycho-Analysis: Collected Papers* by D W Winnicott © The Winnicott Trust 1984. Reproduced here by kind permission of the Winnicott Trust.

'The Theory of the Parent-Infant Relationship' (1960), 'The Development of the Capacity for Concern' (1963), 'Communicating and Not Communicating Leading to a Study of Certain Opposites' (1963).

From *The Maturational Processes and the Facilitating Environment* by D W Winnicott © D W Winnicott 1965. Reproduced here by kind permission of the Winnicott Trust.

Fear of Breakdown (1963).

From *Psychoanalytic Explorations* edited by Clare Winnicott, Ray Shepherd and Madeleine Davis © The Winnicott Trust, 1989. Reproduced here by kind permission of the Winnicott Trust.

'A Clinical Study of the Effect of a Failure of the Average Expectable Environment on a Child's Mental Functioning' (1965). Reproduced here by kind permission of the *International Journal of Psychoanalysis*.

And by permission of Routledge: 'Playing: A Theoretical Statement' (1968), 'The Use of an Object and Relating through Identifications' (1968), 'Creativity and its Origins' (1971). Pages 38–52, 86–94, and 65–85 from *Playing and Reality* (Routledge 1991).

WINNICOTT CHRONOLOGY

	Biography	*Significant Publications*
1896	Donald Woods Winnicott born in Plymouth, Devon, England. Youngest child with two older sisters, the son of Elizabeth Martha Woods Winnicott and John Frederick Winnicott, a merchant who became mayor of the town	
1910	Goes to boarding school, The Leys School in Cambridge	
1914	Goes to Jesus College, Cambridge University, to read biology	
1917	Goes to St Bartholomew's Hospital to study medicine	
1923	Appointed children's physician at Paddington Green Children's Hospital and Queen Elizabeth's Hospital Marries Alice Taylor Starts analysis with James Strachey	
1925	Mother dies of cardiac disease	
1927	Starts psychoanalytic training at the Institute of Psychoanalysis, London supervised by Ella Freeman Sharpe and Nina Searl	
1931		Clinical Notes on Disorders of Childhood
1933	Finishes his 10-year analysis with James Strachey	

	Biography	Significant Publications
1934	Qualifies as adult psychoanalyst and becomes an associate member of the British Psychoanalytical Society (BPAS) Continues training as a child analyst under the supervision of Melanie Klein, Melitta Schmideberg (Klein's daughter) and Nina Searl	
1935	Qualifies as the first male child psychoanalyst at the British Society Melanie Klein asks him to analyze her son Eric Gives membership paper 'The Manic Defence' to the BPAS	The Manic Defence
1936	Starts second analysis with Joan Riviere Becomes full member of BPAS	Appetite and Emotional Disorder
1939	Freud dies in London	Aggression Letter to the *British Medical Journal*
1940s	Radio broadcasts on the BBC to 'the ordinary devoted mother'	Children and their Mothers
1941	Finishes analysis with Joan Riviere Appointed as psychiatric consultant to scheme for evacuated children in Oxfordshire Meets Clare Britton, social worker in charge of the scheme	The Observation of Infants in a Set Situation
1941–43	Named as one of five Kleinian training analysts and participates in the Controversial Discussions in the BPAS	
1944–48	Analyzes Marion Milner	
Mid 1940s	No longer regarded or regards self as a Kleinian	
1942		Why Children Play
1945		Getting to Know Your Baby Primitive Emotional Development
1946		What Do We Mean by a Normal Child?
1947		Hate in the Countertransference Residential Management as Treatment for Difficult Children

	Biography	Significant Publications
1948	Father dies Suffers his first coronary	Paediatrics and Psychiatry Children's Hostels in War and Peace Reparation in Respect of Mother's Organized Defence against Depression
1949	Leaves his first wife, Alice Suffers second coronary	The Ordinary Devoted Mother and Her Baby Mind and its Relation to the Psyche- Soma Birth Memories, Birth Trauma, and Anxiety
1949–55 & 1957	Analyzes Margaret Little	
1950	Suffers third coronary after a patient commits suicide Scientific secretary of BPAS	Some Thoughts on the Meaning of the Word Democracy Aggression in Relation to Emotional Development Growth and Development in Immaturity The Deprived Child and how he can be Compensated for Loss of Family Life
1951	Divorced from Alice Marries Clare Britton Training secretary of Institute of Psychoanalysis Masud Khan begins analysis with DWW	Transitional Objects and Transitional Phenomena The Foundation of Mental Health
1952	Suffers fourth coronary	Psychoses and Child Care Anxiety Associated with Insecurity
1952–53	President of Paediatric Council of the Royal Society of Medicine	
1953	Clare Winnicott starts analysis with	Symptom Tolerance in Paediatrics
1953–56	Vice-president of Paediatric Council of the Royal Society of Medicine	
1954	Fifth coronary April 7 entry date in Winnicott's clinical diary that Khan's analysis ends	Withdrawal and Regression The Depressive Position in Normal Emotional Development Metapsychological and Clinical Aspects of Regression within the Psycho- Analytical Set-Up
1955		Clinical Varieties of Transference

Biography	Significant Publications
1956	Primary Maternal Preoccupation
	The Antisocial Tendency
	Paediatrics and Childhood Neurosis
1956–59 President of BPAS for first time	
1957	The Child and the Family
	The Child and the Outside World
	On the Contribution of Direct Child
	Observation to Psychoanalysis
1958	Through Paediatrics to Psycho-Analysis
	The Capacity to be Alone
	Child Analysis in the Latency Period
	Psycho-Analysis and the Sense of Guilt
	The Family Affected by Depressive Ill-ness in One or Both Parents
	The Fate of the Transitional Object
1959–64	Classification: Is there a Psycho-Analytic Contribution to Psychiatric Classification?
1960 Melanie Klein dies	The Effect of Psychosis on Family Life
	The Theory of the Parent-Infant Relationship
	Ego Distortion in Terms of True and False Self
	String: A Technique of Communication
	Counter-Transference
	The Relationship of a Mother to her Baby at the Beginning
	Aggression, Guilt and Reparation
1961 Retires from Paddington Green Children's Hospital	Varieties of Psychotherapy
	The Effect of Psychotic Parents on the Emotional Development of the Child
1962 Lecture tour in USA	The Aims of Psycho-Analytical Treatment
	A Personal View of the Kleinian Contribution
	Ego Integration in Child Development
	Providing for the Child in Health and Crisis
1962–68 Analyzes Harry Guntrip 'on demand'	
1963 Retires from the NHS	The Development of the Capacity for Concern

Biography	Significant Publications
1963 Lecture tour in USA	Fear of Breakdown
	From Dependence towards
	Independence in the Development of
	the Individual
	Morals and Education
	Communicating and Not
	Communicating Leading to a Study of
	Certain Opposites
	Training for Child Psychiatry
	Psychotherapy of Character Disorders
	The Mentally Ill in your Caseload
	The Niffle
	Psychiatric Disorder in Terms of
	Infantile Maturational Processes
	Dependence in Infant-Care, in Child-
	Care, and in the Psycho-Analytic
	Setting
	Struggling Through the Doldrums
	The Value of Depression
1964	Psycho-Somatic Disorder
	The Concept of the False Self
	The Child, the Family and the Outside
	World
1964–68	The Squiggle Game
1965	The Family and Individual
	Development
	The Maturational Processes and the
	Facilitating Environment
	The Value of the Therapeutic
	Consultation
	A Clinical Study of the Effect of a
	Failure of the Average Expectable
	Environment on a Child's Mental
	Functioning
	The Psychology of Madness
1965–68 Second term as President of BPAS	
1966	The Absence and Presence of a Sense of
	Guilt Illustrated in Two Patients
	The Ordinary Devoted Mother
	The Child in the Family Group
	The Split-Off Male and Female
	Elements to be found in Men and
	Women

	Biography	Significant Publications
1967	Lecture tour in USA	The Location of Cultural Experience Mirror-Role of Mother and Family in Child Development The Concept of a Healthy Individual Delinquency as a Sign of Hope
1968	Lecture tour in USA Suffers serious coronary after giving 'Use of an Object' paper to the New York Psychoanalytic Society	Breast-Feeding as Communication Communication between Infant and Mother, and Mother and Infant, Compared and Contrasted The Use of an Object and Relating through Identifications *Sum* I am
	Awarded the James Spence Gold Medal for Paediatrics	
1969		The Use of an Object in the Context of *Moses and Monotheism* Mother's Madness Appearing in the Clinical Material as an Ego-Alien Factor
1970	Prepares to give keynote paper to the IPA biennial conference in Vienna in July	Dependence in Child Care On the Basis for Self in Body Residential Care as Therapy
1971	Dies of coronary in January	Playing and Reality Therapeutic Consultations in Child Psychiatry Dreaming, Fantasying, and Living: A Case-history describing a Primary Dissociation Playing: A Theoretical Statement Playing: Creative Activity and the Search for the Self Creativity and its Origins The Place Where We Live Interrelating Apart from Instinctual Drive and in Terms of Cross-Identifications Contemporary Concepts of Adolescent Development and their Implications for Higher Education

	Biography	Significant Publications
1977		The Piggle: An Account of the Psychoanalytic Treatment of a Little Girl
1982	The Squiggle Foundation established	
1984	Clare Winnicott dies Winnicott Trust founded	Deprivation and Delinquency
1986		Home is Where We Start From Holding and Interpretation: Fragment of an Analysis
1987		Babies and their Mothers The Spontaneous Gesture: selected Letters of D. W. Winnicott
1988		Human Nature
1989		Psychoanalytic Explorations
1993		Talking to Parents
1996		Thinking about Children

There is a complete bibliography of all Winnicott's published writings by Knud Hjulmand in J. Abram *The Language of Winnicott* (2nd edn.). London: Karnac Books, 2007.

PREFACE

Helen Taylor Robinson

Reading Winnicott is an important new book designed for advanced-level students and practitioners in clinical and academic trainings in psychoanalysis and related fields. It offers a scholarly reading of 14 key papers from the extensive body of writing on psychoanalytic theory and practice with children and adults by Donald Woods Winnicott (1896–1971). The two authors/editors each work broadly from within a Contemporary Freudian and Independent model of mind, and are very much in touch with European psychoanalysis and the international scene beyond. They have academic and clinical expertise over many years with infants, children, adolescents and adults. Furthermore, Dr Caldwell is the current Chair of the Winnicott Trust, and Ms Joyce a fellow Trustee and Editor. They inherited the project to create a Reader, originally put forward by Dr Jennifer Johns (then Chair and Editor), and myself (then fellow Trustee and Editor). This volume, produced under the auspices of the Winnicott Trust, is a fulfilment of the Trust's role with reference to Winnicott and his work. It finds a suitable home in the new Teaching imprint of the prestigious New Library of Psychoanalysis series.

André Green who values highly Winnicott's contributions to psycho-analysis from within the British tradition, nonetheless says in his Prolegomena to the book *Key Ideas for a Contemporary Psychoanalysis*, that 'It is difficult to situate Winnicott' whom he identifies as both a representative of the Independent Group in British psychoanalysis and 'a Kleinian dissident'. This new book on Winnicott is important, and I would add ambitious and innovative, because the two author/editors attempt to do exactly that – to situate Winnicott within and alongside the psychoanalytic ideas of yesterday and today.

In the closing paragraph of their General Introduction, Caldwell and Joyce write, referring to a British colleague's article:

Spurling wonders about what Winnicott represents now and what he repre-sented in the past; that is, he introduces a social and historical perspective about his character, theory, and practice, those of others, and the external relations, social networks, and specific modalities of developments in the

BPAS [British Psychoanalytical Society] over many decades. This invites both a psychoanalytic reading and an historical awareness, but contemporary psychoanalysis, like its earlier histories, often seems dominated by anxieties that are primarily defensive and addressed to splits internal to the psychoanalytic movement. His [Spurling's] article reveals the need for a scholarly history of Winnicott and the reception of his ideas in British psychoanalysis and psychotherapy in general, and as part of the history of the BPAS in particular.

In introducing the papers Dr Caldwell and Ms Joyce situate the work in the context of present and past psychoanalytic directions and developments, present and past history, present and past societal and other pressures, and present and past psychoanalytic figureheads in Britain and abroad. In one sense, this means recognizing Winnicott's debt to his colleagues over time, and the very real context in which his ideas grew from within a community of psychoanalytic thinkers. But Caldwell and Joyce also attempt to free Winnicott's work from some of the more restrictive anxieties and defensive splits that inevitably did, and still do, circle all psychoanalytic work, to give his individual originality and creativity its real weight. To provide such a scholarly overview requires much research to enable the reader to listen and take in what each of these historic papers continues to contribute. Re-investing in Winnicott through the scholarship and clinical acumen of two present-day psychoanalysts, reading him through the data and the interpretation their text affords (and of course it is 'their' reading, not 'the' reading of Winnicott that we are given) offers the reader the benefit of a serious and impressive contribution, not, in my view, attempted so wide-rangingly or so comprehensively before.

The format, where each paper offers an extended introductory reading, indicating other influences, together with Winnicott's growing personal interests and developing preoccupations, maintains the particular frame of Winnicott as a member of a group process – within psychoanalysis as a body of knowledge – and his own innovative individual contributions to it.

For a new audience the careful General Introduction offers the book's main scholarly thrust. The decision to focus on his **distinctiveness** in four main areas: The Relational Environment and the Place of Infantile Sexuality; Aggression and Destructiveness; Illusion and Transitional Phenomena; and the Theory and Practice of Psychoanalysis with Adults and Children, ensures that Winnicott is placed in dialogue with other important psychoanalytic creators and contributors such as Freud, Ferenczi, Klein, Balint, Fairbairn, Bowlby, Milner, Lacan, Jung.

In each area, it is the author/editors' fine discriminations between theories that may overlap or seem to be related that is of particular help to the reader: for example, Bion on the notion of containment, and Winnicott on the notion of holding, and the connections and differences between these terms; or, the different emphases of Klein and Winnicott on the nature of aggression in unconscious fantasy as destructiveness and acute anxiety followed by depressive concern, or aggression initially as muscle erotism, pre-ruth before the development of concern, and containing excitement and normal energy, a necessary evolutionary or developmental process.

But most of all, threading through the exploration of the four chosen areas it is Winnicott's emphasis on the meaning of dependence for the infant–mother relationship, his view, through long experience of the mother and baby couple, in health and ill health, of the inevitability of the unequal relationship that infancy is predicated upon, that takes his growing theory of environmental reality and its effect on internal reality further away from many fellow psychoanalytic thinkers. It is the infant, and later the human being, in all their various stages of inevitable helplessness that opens up for Winnicott such a wealth of visionary data and the psychoanalytic inference he bases on them. Thus infant studies, maternal health studies, observing and supporting the development of infants and their mothers are large growth research areas derived from Winnicott and, of course, Bowlby's work in this important field. As the author/editors demonstrate convincingly, it is the actual mother and baby couple and their internal concomitants that are his model, even as he studies psychosis, regression, aggression, and illusion and transitional objects. The latter, illusion, the capacity to form symbols through transitional objects, which enables psychic movement towards freedom and creativity within an acknowledged dependence or vulnerability is the major contribution that takes Winnicott into cultural and literary studies and the general theory of creativity and the arts.

The author/editors acknowledge that rereading Winnicott's familiar texts, the key papers that comprise the book, 'has offered us the opportunity for rethinking that [psychoanalytic] world and its concerns and the papers included in this collection demonstrate the continuing relevance of historical disputes for current debates about technique, training, and how psychoanalysis is understood'. Readers will judge from what follows, if the rereading, repositioning, and resituating of Winnicott and his psychoanalytic world then and now, will help them reread, reposition, resituate, and rethink their own psychoanalysis.

GENERAL INTRODUCTION

Lesley Caldwell and Angela Joyce

Donald Woods Winnicott was central to the establishment of British object relations theory, which, while remaining rooted in Freud, revolutionized modern psychoanalysis. He was unique among psychoanalysts in having trained in paediatrics and child psychiatry and he worked in the public health services throughout his career. The importance he attached to 'ordinary' living and his focus on experiencing life fully always informed his conceptual and clinical interests inside and outside the consulting room. Those who have found his approach challenging and sympathetic – Milner, Khan, Bollas, Green, Ogden, Wright, Farhi, Parsons, among others – have continued to emphasize a capacity for living, experiencing, and being aware as signs of successful analysis.

In this volume we present Winnicott's distinctiveness with reference to four areas: (1) the relational environment and the place of infantile sexuality; (2) aggression and destructiveness; (3) illusion and transitional phenomena; and (4) the theory and practice of psychoanalysis with adults and children. We begin with a brief account of his life and of his place in the history of psychoanalysis in relation to his predecessors, Freud and Ferenczi, and to his contemporary Melanie Klein. Comparisons are drawn with other British Psychoanalytical Society (BPAS) members, Michael Balint, Ronald Fairbairn, Marion Milner, and in specific chapter introductions, with Anna Freud and Wilfred Bion. Reference is also made to his relations with Jacques Lacan, and with Carl Jung.

The 14 papers presented here are one selection of possible papers from a writing career covering 50 years. All derive from ongoing clinical practice and a commitment to working in an extended arena, socially, medically, and culturally to make the insights from psychoanalysis more widely available. Any selection involves a reading and an interpretation and other papers would have traced other trajectories through the corpus of psychoanalytic theory and practice of the second half of the twentieth century. This selection aims to make Winnicott's key ideas available with some awareness of chronological development and also with the realization that an author's concerns may be there in potential from the start.

Biographical notes

Winnicott was born in 1896 in Plymouth, Devon, into a middle-class family, the youngest of three children and the only boy. His father was a merchant and twice mayor of the town. His mother seems to have been a shadowy, rather idealized figure (Kahr, 1996; Phillips, 1988; Rodman, 2003). Donald described himself as 'an only child with multiple mothers and with father extremely pre-occupied in my younger years with town as well as business matters' (quoted in Phillips, 1988: 23). As an adolescent he went to board at The Leys School, Cambridge and then to Cambridge University and, after a time as a 'surgeon probationer' in the last year of the war, to St Bartholomew's Medical College, London where he was influenced by his teacher, Thomas Horder, who placed great emphasis on listening carefully to the patient and taking as detailed a history as possible (Kanter, 2004: 260). Winnicott described psycho-analysis as an extension of this process (Rodman, 2003). He specialized in children's medicine, which did not distinguish then between paediatrics and child psychiatry. After qualification in 1920, he obtained posts at Paddington Green Children's Hospital and at Queen Elizabeth's in 1923, remaining at Paddington Green until his retirement in 1961.

In 1923, Winnicott began a 10-year psychoanalysis with James Strachey. Davis (1987: 493) said of this 'It is apparent that Strachey's deep knowledge of Freud's writing and first-hand experience of the classical technique were passed on to his patient', and Winnicott himself insisted on it. 'From my point of view any theories that I may have which are original are only valuable as a growth of ordinary psychoanalytic theory' (Rodman, 1987: 75). He began training in 1927, worked with Ella Freeman Sharpe and Nina Searl (King and Steiner, 1991: xxiv), and qualified in 1934. In 1935 he became the first man to qualify as a child analyst in the BPAS. Melanie Klein supervised his first child training case and he regarded her as 'a generous teacher, and I counted myself lucky' (1962c: 173). Melitta Schmideberg, Klein's daughter, and Nina Searl were his other 'controls' [supervisors of training cases] (King and Steiner, 1991: xxiv).

From 1936 to 1941 Winnicott had a second analysis with Joan Riviere that was marked by his increasing divergence from Kleinian thinking: 'Winnicott's unfolding need to think and write about the early environment led to his parting in the 1940s with Riviere, who apparently strongly disapproved of his preoccupation with the subject' (Davis, 1987: 496). Nonetheless in 1942 Winnicott was named one of five Kleinian training analysts (King and Steiner, 1991: xxiv). He participated in the Controversial Discussions but he 'was an individualist' (King and Steiner, 1991: xxiv) and by the early 1950s when he became Training Secretary of the Institute of Psychoanalysis, he was regarded as a member of the 'Middle Group'. However, he always remained appreciative of Klein's study of earliest infancy, regarding it as 'something of the soil in which I had become planted' (1962c: 171).

The evolution of British psychoanalytic thinking was decisively influenced by the Second World War. John Bowlby, Emmanuel Miller, and Winnicott had written to the *British Medical Journal* in December 1939 calling attention to the major psychological problems for young children separated from their families as a result of evacuation from the cities (Phillips, 1988) and Winnicott then became psychiatric consultant to the government scheme for the county of Oxfordshire which provided hostels for children who could not be placed with ordinary families. There, in 1941, he met Clare Britton, the social worker in charge of the service, who later trained as a psychoanalyst. They married in 1951; it was Winnicott's second marriage. His first in 1923 had been to Alice Taylor, a woman with a history of psychiatric illness, from whom he separated in 1949.

Winnicott was apparently a resource to staff: '[they could] think about what [they] did and discuss it with him as honestly [as they] could . . . these sessions with him were the highlight of the week and were invaluable learning experiences for us all including Winnicott' (Kanter, 2004: 17). This work provided further experience for thinking about children and, by extension, the patient in analysis, and contributed to his theory of the links between the environment and inner reality (Davis, 1987). In addition the partnership with Clare is deemed to have been a critically creative addition to his distinctive contribution to psychoanalysis (Kanter, 2004). It has been suggested that Clare Britton was the catalyst for his learning about the significance of the environment in psychic functioning and she continued to influence Winnicott's thinking throughout their marriage (personal communication Helen Taylor Robinson, April 2010).

Bowlby, a child psychiatrist and child psychoanalyst also supervised by Klein, had written of the effects of early separation on children seen by him in a London Child Guidance Clinic. The research showed a direct link between stealing and separation from the mother during infancy (Bowlby, 1944). Winnicott also addressed the effects of separation and loss on children's development, and it provided the basis for his theory of the antisocial tendency (Winnicott, Shepherd, and Davis, 1984). In his discussion of Bowlby and Winnicott, Reeves concludes that Bowlby regarded the 'environmental factors relating to the infant's upbringing as immediate causes and explanations of a child's later character, dispositions, behaviour. . . . For Winnicott they were neither immediate nor remote, but proximate causes' (Reeves, 2005a: 83). Winnicott (who opposed Bowlby's election to membership of the BPAS) objected to his 'impoverished concept of unconscious mental life' through 'his discarding of the concept of an internal world . . . [as] a crucible in which character, disposition, behaviour were moulded from the active, fluid convergence of different, often contrary, instinctual elements' (Reeves, 2005a: 83).

In 1941, Anna Freud established the Hampstead War Nurseries that provided a home for hundreds of children whose families were broken up by the Second World War. As a major source of observations of children's development they were also immensely valuable to her thinking (A. Freud, 1939–45/1973). All these experiences had a profound effect upon postwar psychoanalytic theory for Middle Group (later Independent) and B Group (Contemporary Freudian) members and attention to the impact of the external world in mental functioning became one distinguishing feature of non-Kleinian analysts.

Britton and Winnicott gave evidence to the Curtis Committee (1946), the statutory enquiry into the care of children separated from their parents, which led to the 1948 Children's Act in Great Britain and shaped postwar public policy (Reeves, 2005: 179). This interest in social affairs and in ordinary people was reflected in Winnicott's broadcasts to parents on the BBC in the 1940s and 1950s which were published in 1957 as *The Child and the Family* and *The Child and the Outside World*, then combined in 1964 as *the Child, The Family and the Outside World*. Winnicott was unique among British psychoanalysts in giving talks to non-analysts and contributing to non-psychoanalytic journals. He gave papers to professional societies concerned with paediatrics and child psychiatry, and was active in the British Psychological Society (BPS), where many psychoanalysts participated. He was chair of its medical section and gave several important papers there, among which were 'Mind and its Relation to Psyche-Soma' (1949) and 'The Depressive Position in Normal Emotional Development' (1954).

Although he seems to have felt distant from the training establishment of the BPAS and complained to Sylvia Payne in 1953 that he was 'seriously neglected as a teacher' (quoted in Rodman, 2003: 214), he was twice elected as its president, 1956–59 and 1965–68. His first major collection of psychoanalytic papers, gathered together with the assistance of his former analysand Masud Khan, was published as *Through Paediatrics to Psycho-Analysis* in 1958. Two further collections, *The Family and Individual Development* and *The Maturational Processes and the Facilitating Environment* were published in 1965.

He gave keynote papers at congresses of the International Psychoanalytical Association (IPA), and he was one of the European committee of the IPA delegated to investigate the setting up of a new group in Paris following the disputes with Lacan and his supporters. After the committee's deliberations on the situation of psychoanalysis in France, based on their meetings in Paris on 31 October and 1 November 1953, Winnicott, in a letter to Ruth Eissler (5/2/54) insisted on the urgency and gravity of the situation. He expressed dismay at the slowness of IPA procedures, and maintained the only questions and his primary concerns were whether the group around Lacan could offer a psychoanalytic training (he doubted it, given the number of personnel) and how damage to students could be minimized. The issue itself was finalized at the 1961 Edinburgh conference by which time all the personnel had changed.

Winnicott was known as 'an analyst's analyst, an analyst *of* analysts' (Gillespie, 1971: 528). Willoughby (2002: 61) says, 'Colleagues would turn to him when they were in difficulties although such requests could be burdensome as he intimated to Clifford Scott in December 1956 when he wrote, "The trouble is I get analysts throwing themselves on me when they feel they will let the side down by breaking down"'. In a book about his influence in France, Clancier and Kalmanovitch (1987: 105) wrote, 'Winnicott was in turn ignored, criticized, rejected, admired by his British colleagues, but in the end came to occupy what we regard as his true place that of a subtle, perceptive clinician and original researcher'.

Winnicott died in 1971 never having fully recovered from the last serious heart attack he suffered in New York in 1968. His widow, Clare Winnicott, established the Squiggle Foundation in 1982 to disseminate Winnicott's work among the caring professions and the Winnicott Trust to publish his many manuscripts and to administer his estate. A further 12 volumes of his writings have been published.

Theoretical links

Freud

Winnicott readily acknowledged that he took his ideas from everywhere and infrequently cited his references, but Freud was always there. With different emphases André Green (in Abram, 2000) and Dodi Goldman (1993) each insist on Winnicott's Freudianism as a taken for granted point of reference. Green offers a reading of the posthumous *Human Nature* (1988), a collection from the Winnicott Trust that gathers together lectures that were given at the University of London. While Green focuses on Winnicott's status as a thinker, Goldman describes Winnicott's own hesitations about such an appellation, especially in relation to Freud's metapsychology. 'It was a philosophy that made him deeply suspicious whenever metapsychological formulations were presented in a way that created the illusion of understanding when no such understanding really existed' (Goldman, 1993: 146). Commenting on a letter to Anna Freud (Rodman, 1987), Goldman offers a detailed comparison of Winnicott and Freud organized around the headings of 'Instincts, Relations and the Self' and 'Paths to Object Love'; his central, eminently convincing proposition is that Freud offered an enduring method, clinical psychoanalysis, to which Winnicott was completely committed. In Winnicott's espousal of that method and its originator, it was the speculative Freud to whom he responded, a 'Freud who recognized his own metapsychological constructions as "metaphors" (1900: 610), "fictions" (1911: 220fn) and "scientific fantasies" (1916–17)'. Goldman concludes, 'Winnicott admired tremendously Freud's ability to change his mind: it was always more important to him to "play" with Freud's ideas than to adhere to them' (1993: 147).

Drapeau (2002) also endorses the commitment to method and quotes Winnicott ' "I just feel that Freud gave us this method which we can use, and it doesn't matter what it leads us to. The point is, it does lead us to things; it's an objective way of looking at things and it's for people who can go to something without preconceived notions, which in a sense is science"' (Winnicott, 1967b, in Drapeau, 2002: 16).

Green agrees, concluding from *Human Nature* that Winnicott 'continued and completed Freud's work' and that he was 'an independent thinker' (2000: 70). He selects out Winnicott's attention to emotional development from the beginning as distinctive, and he reads it as distinctively British, importantly linking Winnicott with Bion (2000: 72). His summary of the similarities and differences between Freud and Winnicott includes the latter's close attention to psychosomatics: 'At first there is soma, then a psyche that in health gradually becomes anchored to the soma; sooner or later a third phenomenon appears which is called intellect or mind' (1988: 139, quoted in Abram, 2000: 75). Green makes the link between Freud's starting point in the body through the instincts and Winnicott's proposition that this *follows* from the integration of psyche and soma through time. The experience and toleration of the drives is predicated on early care in Winnicott and here he departs from Freud, though only as regards timing. Autoerotic satisfaction comes after the beginnings of mental activity in his model – a difference he maintains consistently in terms of developmental stages.

Ferenczi

While Freud is an assumed reference in Winnicott's work, the historical links with Sándor Ferenczi are striking but almost completely unreferenced. In identifying Ferenczi's extraordinary prescience in terms of the recognition of environmental provision, the study of ego development and the mother's adaptation to baby in 'Stages in the Development of the Sense of Reality', (1913), Tonnesmann (2002) links it with Winnicott's concern with 'the study of ego relatedness' (2002: 49) and the similarity between the infant's creating the breast when it is wanted, and Ferenczi's stage of hallucinatory magic omnipotence (2002: 50). Winnicott, like Ferenczi, stresses the importance of the mother's adaptation to the infant's need as the means of continuation of an illusion of omnipotence, and the mother's presentation of the breast at the right moment as proposing a creative hallucination for the baby. Martin-Cabrè (2001) identifies 'a striking resemblance' to Ferenczi in the importance of play in mediating the child's emotional needs with regard to the mother, in the concept of technical transparence and the notion of breakdown, and finally in the organization of the false self and the value of regression. (2001: 180). He too emphasizes Ferenczi's interest in the mother, claiming that in *Thalassa* regression, trauma and the mother are 'woven together throughout' (2001: 180).

Both Winnicott's and Ferenczi's awareness of the place of early traumata in the aetiology of later disturbance led to technical modifications in their work with difficult cases and their contributions to the understanding of psychosis. Martin-Cabrè regards Winnicott as the most faithful elaborator of Ferenczi's ideas, most significantly, the extension of the concept of trauma and especially the notions of relative trauma (1952a) deriving from not good-enough mothering, and that of the false self. He points to the disappearance of discussion about countertransference and regression for nearly three decades after Ferenczi, and it was Winnicott who returned to these topics (see Chapters 3 and 6, this volume).

Klein

The postwar divergence between Winnicott and Klein, that has had continuing implications for British psychoanalysis, 'grew from the affinity and mutual influence operating between them in Winnicott's Kleinian phase' (broadly described as up to 1951) (Aguayo, 2002). Aguayo proposes that 'Winnicott effected a disjunction from Klein's work through both his new mother infant interpersonal theory and his actual clinical practices' (2002: 1145). It was Winnicott's attention to the baby's need of the real mother and her centrality in his (the baby's) functioning and development that set him apart from Melanie Klein and her followers. His critique is based on what he sees Klein assuming and taking for granted. He gave her due recognition for opening up the whole area of infancy, but in his view she failed to see the conditions for earliest psychic growth, that is, the fundamental character of the infant's absolute dependence on the mother. Winnicott's growing interest in a theory of aggression that argues for its initial separateness from destructiveness (Chapter 7) would have consequences for what is interpreted in a session, a reduction in the analysis of aggression in the transference and the interpretation of the negative transference (2002: 1145). It also produced an interest in experimenting with the role of the analyst as mother. Aguayo links Winnicott's changing theory and his intense engagement with Klein as person and as theoretician from the 1930s onto shifts in analytic contacts and analytic debates on one side, and to Winnicott's own wartime experiences with evacuated children, his growing attention to the mother–child relation, and the mutual interrelation of his paediatric and analytic experience on the other.

'For Klein tragedy is a universal scenario inevitably encountered in the inner life of our species. Its implications cannot be evaded in the course of growth', Likierman (2007) announces in her article areas of compatibility and incompatibility between Winnicott and Klein. Like Green she identifies a common concern with 'early emotionality' that Freud overlooked, and a belief that the mother's presence was fundamental to the achievement of what Winnicott terms 'integration'. But Klein's account claims innate qualities of sadism and envy and a concern with the projective and introjective dimensions of the baby's inner world that fail to emphasize relationality as the distinguishing feature of healthy development. The very different assumptions about the person espoused by each theorist have ongoing implications for the conduct of an analysis and for its aims.

In an internet response to a paper by the American analyst Fred Busch and a rejoinder from the British analyst Betty Joseph, Charles Spezzano (2004) characterized their differences by describing Winnicott's theorizing on the unconscious as starting from excitement and Klein's from anxiety. He proposes that the Kleinian baby and patient are prey to destructive phantasies with accompanying anxiety and guilt which will be understood by and have their effects on the analyst who has to negotiate the transference relationship and its oscillation between the wish to make contact and the anxieties associated with that contact.

In his paper on 'Excitement in the Aetiology of Coronary Thrombosis' (1957a) Winnicott argued for understanding excitement as the precondition for instinctual experience. In his view, humans were constantly faced with the opportunity and danger of excitement, and, as the capacity to imagine develops, imagining scenes of excitement is the quintessential creative act' (D.W. Winnicott, C. Winnicott, Shepherd, and Davis, 1989: 37). Although Spezzano sets up a rather stark dualism in this description, one which overlooks the considerable agreement between Winnicott and Klein over an extended period and the attempts at dialogue between them when they did not agree, he also highlights the very different premises that can be attributed to their respective accounts of the bases of human life, and of the aims and the tasks of psychoanalysis.

Julia Kristeva takes a more nuanced view of the relation between these two British analysts in discussing Klein's posthumously published paper, 'On the Sense of Loneliness', which she sees as a response to Winnicott's 1957 paper, 'The Capacity to be Alone'. She says, 'We have here a good example of the back and forth exchange between Klein and Winnicott, an example that displays the originality of both analysts as well as their debt to each other. While Winnicott situates the capacity to be alone in a world of ecstasy we will see that Melanie never distanced herself from a tone of desolation that strikes at the very heart of the serenity she had gained (2001: 261, n.36).

In explaining why he was asked to write about Melanie Klein and Donald Winnicott together, John Padel, a member of the Independent Group, said, 'First they both wrote more than others – they presented more papers. Second both are looked on as founders of the object relations school of psychoanalysis. Third they were both charismatic personalities and attracted followers. . . . There is another reason for considering Klein and Winnicott together. They both performed on the same stage with reference to each other' (1991: 325).

It is clear that the dialogue between Klein and Winnicott was central to much of British psychoanalytic thinking in the post Second World War period and probably, continuingly important to both of them, although a detailed history of this relationship and its place in the evolving history of the Klein group has still to be undertaken.

Balint

Michael Balint, another major figure in the Middle Group, was always clear about his debt to Ferenczi in his interest in early infantile relations, sexuality, psychoanalytic technique, and, especially, regression, but these interests were also based in his own extensive clinical experience. They paralleled those of Winnicott while differing in certain basic respects. 'He (Balint) believed, as had Ferenczi, that the object relationship of the infant to its mother is primary, is a basic biological and psychological given, and is present in the very earliest deepest and most primitive layers of the mind. Winnicott continued to accept Freud's view, whereas Klein soon followed Balint in his rejection of primary narcissism' (Stewart, 1996: 8).

In accounting for the first stage of life Winnicott allies it with primary narcissism whereas Balint sees the baby as object related from the start, and narcissism as a secondary result of failures of the 'bad object'. 'Balint offers an alternative theory of primary object love in which the partners are in a harmonious inter-penetrating mix-up' (Barnett, 2001: 185). In a letter following Balint's presentation of 'Primary Narcissism and Primary Love' to the BPAS in February 1960, Winnicott disputes Balint's account of Freud on narcissism and says how much he would like a chance to discuss the idea of 'primary love' (Rodman, 1987: 128). He adds, 'You and I are both interested in the early environmental provision. I think we agree about what happens when there is a failure . . . Where I find myself disagreeing is on the positive side . . . I personally wonder very much whether an infant is aware when the environment is satisfactory . . . but is affected when it fails. For this reason I am unable to use the word primary love here because I cannot see that there is a relationship. I become more definitely in disagreement with you when you use the word harmonious in description of the relationship which you call primary love. As soon as the word harmonious is used I feel I know that a highly complex and sophisticated defence organization is at work in the child who is no longer a newly born baby or a pre-natal infant' (in Rodman, 1987: 128).

Peter Dreyfus proposes that their theoretical differences about primary narcissism are linked to their differing accounts of aggression, with Winnicott seeing aggression as innate and Balint seeing it as 'secondary to inevitable frustration' (Dreyfus, 2001: 237). In so far as there has been much debate about the different emphases of Winnicott and Balint it has focused on Balint's neglect of the place of hate and destructiveness (Stewart, 1992). Stewart also identifies a strong biological bias. Both were interested in the treatment of regressed patients and critical about the place of interpretation in what they both regard as a preverbal state (Tonnesmann, 2007: 133) (see Chapter 6 in this volume).

Fairbairn

Winnicott's review with Masud Khan (1953) of Fairbairn's *Psychoanalytic Studies of the Personality* (1952) is the main source for Winnicott's views of Fairbairn, together with the letters to Harry Guntrip, who had sent him a paper at the suggestion of Fairbairn (with whom he had been in analysis). These mention Winnicott's belief that Fairbairn's work was not necessarily opposed to that of Freud (in Rodman, 1987: 75). Winnicott insists that his own work, and he assumes Fairbairn's, and indeed Guntrip's, represents 'a growth of ordinary Freudian psycho-analytic theory', and in the follow-up letter he again encourages Guntrip to make up his own mind about Freud and about Klein and the introjection of the bad object. Winnicott says, 'It seems to me that it is impossible to jump from the recognition of the introjection of bad objects to the idea that the original introjection is of the bad rather than the good object' (1987: 78). In the 1953 review he had also insisted that Fairbairn does not replace Freud (1987: 413). Harry Guntrip went on to see Winnicott and later to write an account of his two analyses highlighting the different approaches of each of his analysts (Guntrip, 1975; republished 1996).

Milner

Winnicott and Marion Milner seem to have been in a continuing dialogue from the 1940s when Milner was in analysis with Winnicott, and in his 1951 critical notice of *On Not Being Able to Paint*, which Milner wrote under the pseudonym Joanna Field, Winnicott (1989: 390) identifies 'illusion and spontaneity as aspects of the subjective role of experiencing' that are found in both the intimate satisfactions and intensities offered by art, and also in un-remarkable aspects of living. He endorses Milner's arguments for going beyond the familiar psychoanalytic accounts of the arts as 'wishfulfilling escapes' to their bases in illusion 'as the essential basis for true objectivity' (p. 391) and emphasises her attention to the role of spontaneity in creative activity (p. 392). Milner's interest in the positive aspects of symbolism and the value and neces-sity of illusion inform a clinical practice which always stressed the potential freedom to explore offered by and within the boundaries of the session.

Her near contemporaneous paper, 'Aspects of Symbolism in Compre-hension of the Not-Self' (1952) echoed 'Transitional Objects and Transitional Phenomena' (Chapter 5), though Winnicott played down the importance of the strictly symbolic aspect of such objects relative to their actuality. The inner significance of 'transitional objects' represents 'the intermediate area of experience, between inner and outer worlds'. Both placed the origins of creativity in a period that precedes the individual's perceived need for reparation, a more fundamental experience belonging to an earlier stage of emotional development. In this period maternal care and empathy facilitate the conditions for the development of ego organization, and the establishment of a self made possible only through the guarantee of a continuity of being derived from the mother/baby couple. Winnicott was strongly influenced too by Milner's extended account (published in 1969) of the analysis and eventual recovery of the patient 'Susan', in whose treatment he had been much involved.

Lacan

Winnicott's 'Mirror-role of Mother and Family in Child Development' (1967b) begins with both an implicit and an explicit engagement with Lacan: 'In individual emotional development the precursor of the mirror is the mother's face. I wish to refer to the normal aspect of this and also to its psychopathology. Jacques Lacan's paper "le stade du miroir" (1949) has certainly influenced me. He refers to the use of the mirror in each individual's ego development. However, Lacan does not think of the mirror in terms of the mother's face in the way that I wish to do here' (1971a: 111).

Lacan's 'The Mirror Stage as Formative of the Function of the I' (1949a, 1949b) is an important statement on the ego and its constitution in a misrecognition, and one that also gives some attention to that constitution through sociality. The paper and the varying accounts of its history and context mention its precursors in his own doctoral thesis, 'On Paranoia and its Relation to Personality' (1932) and his reading of Wallon (1932) and Charlotte and Pichon (1934), all theorists whose work addresses the child's development. When read together with 'Aggressivity in Psychoanalysis' (Lacan, 1948), it provides a resonance with Winnicott whose concern with similar themes was also in process of evolution from the thirties. The rest of Lacan's title, 'as Revealed in Psychoanalytic Experience', adds a further shared theme; a concern with the practice of psychoanalysis, the evidence available from the consulting room, and the links between psychoanalytic practice and its theoretical assumptions.

'This act [that is, of recognizing him/herself in the mirror] . . . immediately rebounds in the case of the child in a series of gestures in which he experiences in play the relation between the movements assumed in the image and the reflected environment, and between this virtual complex and the reality it reduplicates – the child's own body, and the persons and things, around him' (Lacan, 1949b: 1).

Lacan's reference to 'play', perhaps incidental, is important, not merely because analytically it is a notion centrally associated with Winnicott, but because for him the capacity to play, which Lacan in a sense takes for granted, depends upon a set of prior conditions precisely established by the very phenomena Winnicott writes about in 'The Mirror-role of Mother and Family in Child Development' (1967b) and in 'Transitional Objects and Transitional Phenomena' (1953/1971; Chapter 5, this volume).

Lacan's emphasis on the mistaken primary identification with a (false) totality both other to, alienated from, and the inverse of, the reality of the infant body and the world of which it forms part, insists on what Muller and Richardson (1982: 31) call 'a primitive distortion in the ego's experience of reality that then accounts for the misrecognitions that characterise the ego in all its structures'. The English analyst, Martin James (1960) describes Winnicott's own interest in 'the results of a distortion in development in the preverbal period'. It might be possible to think of this fundamental misapprehension identified by Lacan in conjunction with Winnicott's account of the place of illusion generally, and the illusion of omnipotence in particular; that is, the conditions which must be fulfilled if the baby is to arrive at a sufficient stage of differentiation from the other/mother and integration of the self to be capable of recognizing and being occupied or enchanted by his/her own image.

In various published sources there is mention, with little or no detail, of an ongoing correspondence between Winnicott and Lacan, that dates from about 1953–54. The IPA archives yield nothing of any personal exchange, and the letters mentioned in secondary sources are supposedly among those given by Clare Winnicott to the American analyst, Bob Rodman in the 1980s. In Rodman's published selection, *The Spontaneous Gesture* (1987), only one letter to Lacan, dated 11 February 1960, appears. Lacan's reply (5 August 1960), appeared in French in *Ornicar?* in 1985 and, translated by Mehlman, was published in English in *October* in 1987. Their existence rather than their content is pertinent because they display an openness and a willingness to be in touch, despite fundamental differences. Although there were clearly connections between the two over the years, and passing mentions in written work, it would seem safer to accept Roudinesco's (1990: 490) characterization of their relationship as 'strained'. More sustained references are sparse, and when they do appear, they do not amount to any serious engagement with the other's ideas or theories.

Jung and the London Jungians

The medical section of the British Psychological Society provided a regular forum for discussion among psychoanalysts and Jungians from the 1940s to the 1970s. Winnicott, Rickman, Clifford Scott, and Bion all attended regularly, and the founder of the Society of Analytical Psychology (SAP) Michael Fordham was a member and chair. Fordham and Winnicott became friends and there were overlaps between them, although Fordham held to the Jungian view that the infant was a whole from the start. Where Winnicott's model begins from the state of unintegration, Fordham begins from the archetypal experience of the infant from an original integrate (Astor, 1990). The idea of the self as original, primary at birth then dividing in parts as the relation to the world develops is Fordham's, a process he called 'deintegration', linked with ego development. Deintegration and reintegration are the dynamic processes of the establishment of the self (Astor, 1990) but there seems to be an echo of Winnicott's idea of the true self in play here too. Astor describes Fordham's model as 'built up around experience', perhaps an influence on Winnicott's own concern with the value of the patient's experience as central to the psychoanalytic enterprise. The relation of ego and self and what each incorporates was an important point of discussion and Winnicott describes the 'jolt' he had when Fordham pointed out he was using the words as if they were synonyms (Winnicott, 1964, quoted in Maffei, 2001: 199).

In 1964 Winnicott had reviewed Jung's *Memories, Dreams, Reflections* and was struck by how Jung's capacity for imagination by-passed the destructive element in the self; he attributed this to Jung's self-healing from the early trauma of his mother's unavailability (1989: 484). This insight produced a series of reflections in the following years on the origins of creativity and imagination, and its links with destructiveness. Gordon (2001: 172) considers Winnicott and Jung to offer very similar views on creativity and its value, but she also emphasizes a less well-known concern of Jung's, that of the impact of the body on living creatively. That is, Gordon identifies in Jung an awareness of psyche-soma and its links with the sense of self. She proposes that Michael Fordham's term 'the original self' links with Jung's psychoid state, '(an early unitary state from which matter and psyche are then differentiated' (p171)), Fordham and Winnicott were both child analysts, and the London Jungians, especially in the Fordham years, focused on infant development. Their hypotheses about the early life of the human infant reveal similar preoccupations though Fordham was critical of Winnicott's emphasis on transitional phenomena for development (Astor, 1990).

What Gordon describes as Fordham's 'original self' refers to the existence of an early and primary and original state of wholeness, a self which de-integrates and integrates in the course of growth and development (Gordon, 2001: 169). His emphasis on the gradual development of an awareness of inner and outer and self and other echoes Winnicott's account of the infant's arriving at unit status and the doing that grows out of first being, 'In Winnicott's terms, the "doing" of deintegration is contained by the being of the breast' (Carvalho, 1992).

Winnicott's 1960 paper, 'Counter-Transference', derives from a symposium on the topic (Casement, 1995) a further indication of the productive exchanges of earlier years. There, Winnicott states he does not know the meaning of terms like 'transpersonal unconscious, archetype, counter-sexual component of the psyche, anima' (1960b: 159) and accepts that his own psychoanalytic terms may be equally foreign to Fordham. He argues that a discussion of countertransference can best be approached by clarifying the meaning and importance of 'transference' as the basis for any discussion (1960b: 158).

Four key areas in Winnicott's work

1. *The relational environment and the place of infantile sexuality*

Winnicott's interest in the relational environment in its extended meaning as providing the conditions for being, combines Freudian psychoanalysis with a consistent research and clinical interest in mothers and babies, and draws parallels between early development and the practices of the consulting room. He said, in 1962, 'When I came to treat children by psycho-analysis I was able to confirm the origin of psychoneurosis in the Oedipus complex, and yet I knew that troubles started earlier' (Winnicott, 1965a: 172).

His account of the infant–mother couple argues for the emergence of human subjectivity from a situation of initial non-differentiation for the baby. The baby comes to assume what he calls 'unit status' through the care of the 'ordinary devoted mother', who first enables the baby to 'create' her out of need, then has to be recognized as having her own separate existence. Initially she provides an environment where, for the baby, 'omnipotence is nearly a fact of experience' (Winnicott, 1971a: 13). The 'good-enough mother' 'holds' the baby over time and through her capacity to identify with his particularity, she adapts her responses allowing him to establish his own 'going-on-being', his own idiom.

The simple observation that there is no such thing as a baby, which Winnicott made in the early 1940s, emphasizes that separateness and differentiation, the foundations of healthy development, come about through ordinary infant care, and that physiological processes are the bases for psychological processes. The baby emerges as a differentiated individual with an awareness of separateness. S/he is possessed of the capacities, both physical and psychological, to engage with the world and the developmental tasks on which future health and living will depend. The father as a separate whole object facilitates the developing infant's 'own integration when just becoming at times a unit' (1989: 243). Before this the father's role is a protective one for the mother-baby unit or a mother substitute directly for the baby. While the mother's separateness is only gradually recognized, Winnicott claims that the baby always experiences the father as separate.

'His [Winnicott's] interest begins in the area where, for good scientific reasons, scrupulous writers like Anna Freud, Mahler, and Spitz have left off, fearing, for lack of observations that they could be merely speculating' (James,

1962a: 69). It is this willingness to speculate that has produced a convincing theory of the baby's development from being without self-consciousness or awareness of otherness, to an awareness of self and other.

Winnicott's version of primary narcissism, the 'illusion of omnipotence', differs from Freud in its dependence on the relational environment. He proposes that the infant first experiences the external world through an act of 'primary creativity', the infant believing he/she creates all that is experienced, the absence of which disrupts the basis for being. That absence derives from the mother's incapacity to foster sufficiently the conditions of this illusion in the earliest weeks and months of life, puncturing the possibility of the infant's necessary omnipotence. The usual psychoanalytic account of omnipotence as a defence belongs to a later stage, but the *illusion of omnipotence*, first sustained and then given up through the mother's graduated failures, is fundamental in its structuring and developmental function of the infant's inner world in relation to reality (De Silvestris, 2001: 60).

The Winnicottian baby is born with a potential for creative living that is enabled by maternal care. Her holding function (Chapter 8, this volume) involves physical holding, handling and the 'psychical elaboration' of her baby's experiences; it depends upon her capacity to identify projectively with her infant's states. If she experiences her own states as those of her infant, the baby will not feel seen. This is linked with impingement and the development of the false self (Winnicott, 1960a). 'The Mirror-role of Mother and Family in the Child's Development' (in 1971a) dates from 1967, but mirroring and the mother's face as mirror recur throughout Winnicott's work, notably in 'Ego Integration in Child Development' (1962b) where he tackles the terms 'ego' and 'self', stating that, 'the ego offers itself for study long before the word self has any relevance'.

'What', asks Winnicott, 'does the infant see when he or she looks at the mother's face? I am suggesting that ordinarily, what the baby sees is himself or herself. In other words the mother is looking at the baby and what she looks like is related to what she sees there' (1971a: 112). If this looking is interrupted or does not take the ordinary course, the baby sees not a mirror, but the mother's actual face; in Winnicott's words, 'perception takes the place of apperception', that is the baby perceives the actual mother rather than a primitive realization of his own previous experience. Developmentally, according to Winnicott, this interferes with the beginnings of a significant exchange with the world, the two-way process in which 'self enrichment alternates with the discovery of meaning in the world of seen things' (p. 112). An impingement results in the baby seeing the mother's separateness too soon; it forces an awareness of otherness that interrupts the illusion of omnipotence ordinarily fostered by the environment.

Holding is often used interchangeably with Bion's notion of containment but they derive from differing views of the infant's capacities and the function of the mother's mind. For Bion the mother's 'containing function' is to receive the infant's unbearable projective identifications and make them manageable, returning them to the infant who in turn introjects both them and the mother's containing function. Over time this becomes a structure in the baby's mind. The Bionian baby has some sense of an 'other' into whom projections may be put, but for Winnicott processes of projection and introjection and the development of the drives follow the establishment of the early infant–mother setup. Projections at the beginning derive from the inner world of the mother, a process which can be seen as precarious and risky. Ogden gives an account of these differences between Winnicott and Bion as observations about human functioning, within a perspective of the relational environment. He sees Winnicott's 'holding' and Bion's 'container-contained' 'as two vantage points from which to view an emotional experience' where holding is 'an ontological concept concerned with being and its relationship to time' and containing 'is centrally concerned with the processing (dreaming) of thoughts derived from lived emotional experience' (2005: 93).

The idea of the true and false self is regarded as an important aspect of Winnicott's theory. His 1960 paper, 'Ego Distortion in Terms of True and False Self' (1960a) locates this in the early relational environment. Winnicott links the distinction between them with 'Freud's division of the self into a part that is central and powered by the instincts (what Freud called sexuality), and a part that is turned outwards and is related to the world' (Winnicott, 1960a: 140). In health the 'false self' manages the impingements of external reality without loss of the true self, but in pathology the false self reveals a mental structure originating from an overwhelming impingement which halted any ongoing elaboration of the true self. Clinically, there may be a feeling of falseness in the personality, recognizable by the failure to individuate and the tendency to live a life of compliance. Internally, the person exists in alienation, the true self protected, but frozen, cut off, and inaccessible to the patient herself, so that the life of the self which springs from a primary creativity, the life worth living, is impossible. As a potential for aliveness, the true self requires interaction with the human world. Bollas, one of the analysts whose work has most developed that of Winnicott, says of it, 'As gestural expressions and intersubjective claims are never free of the other's interpretation, its evolution depends upon the mother's and father's facilitations . . . The life of the true self is to be found in the person's experiencing of the world' (1989: 9). Winnicott emphasizes the individual as essentially an isolate 'who could personalise and know self only through the other' (xiv, Khan 'Introduction' to *Through Paediatrics to Psycho-Analysis* added 1975) but who also has the desire not to communicate (Chapter 9, this volume).

Infantile sexuality

Despite his statement in *Human Nature* that 'Any theory that bypasses the importance of instinct and the significance of childhood sexuality is unhelpful'

(Winnicott, 1988), the impact of sexual difference and its organization of human individuality, the place of the drives and the dominance of sexuality so central to the Freudian schema, are not usually understood as forming an integral part of Winnicott's concerns. His account of human development, however, privileges the body and its handling in the acquisition of all the capacities of being human, and makes maternal care and the body fundamental to the development of mental functioning.

Infantile sexuality is certainly significant but only after the move from unintegration to integration has been effected, and the baby comes to a realization of a world outside itself and the limits imposed by that world on the preceding world of unlimited fantasy. Winnicott stresses, not loss and depression in the face of progressive disillusion, but the advantages of a realization that what can be imagined has its limits. He proposes that although what might be at stake in the idea that a baby's need *is* met, and how the baby may register such a moment in fantasy relates to the baby's desire, that desire has different components. He acknowledges the strength of a baby's wishes but sees the tasks confronting the infant in sustaining his or her instinctual experiences as secondary to negotiating the existence of a self that can take on that negotiation. This amounts to a divergence about the origins and the form of human individuality and difficulty, but, rather than a rejection of the Freudian schema, it may be seen as a revision based upon the evidence of close continuing observation, combined with a willingness to speculate convincingly about what is observed.

Both 'Primitive Emotional Development' (1945) and 'The Observation of Infants in a Set Situation' (1941) argue for an analytic and paediatric interest in the interrelation of body, mind, and psyche by hypothesizing about the probable psychological referents that accompany or produce minute shifts in physiological arousal in the infant. Winnicott's extensive interest in the somatic indicators of psychical states, and his elaboration of how the infant becomes a human being is an intensive study of the *conditions without which* the drives can never be accommodated sufficiently for the subject to begin to live a normal life (with all of the abnormal, psychoanalytically speaking, which that entails).

These concerns produced a form of theorizing predominantly interested in the implication for later health of early infantile states and they place Winnicott, and the originality of his attempts to describe the formation of the self, in a solidly English tradition of psychoanalytic work and thought. Eric Rayner's (1991) account of the Independent Group identifies the appeal of a particular way of going about things for the group of which Winnicott was a leading member, an appeal that formed part of a more general English approach where the impact of internal configurations on early development and a comprehensive turn to object relations displaced Freud's account of sexuality and the drives as the basis of human subjectivity. In this respect Winnicott's concerns echo those of the London Jungians who also emphasize experience and the self.

2. *Aggression and destructiveness*

Winnicott's evolving ideas about aggression and destructiveness offer a radically different psychoanalytic theory of their relationship to the recognition of reality. He postulates 'primary aggression' as synonymous with bodily activity and muscle erotism – a source of energy connected with the 'primitive love impulse' and the life force, not initially with destructiveness or anger: 'Sometimes aggression means spontaneity'. While locating the source of aggression in the body and motility he also insisted that 'all experience is both physical and non-physical' (1950, in 1958a: 205), and that its psychical representations and meanings are significant. How aggression comes to have destructive intent is a matter of the development of the self, and as a part function it requires integration before it can become purposive, conscious, and with the intention to hurt. It will be mobilized to express hate only later. For the infant the 'hitting' may facilitate the awareness of the existence of a world that is not co-terminus with himself. It links with how the infant connects with external reality, the movement from the infant towards the environment and/or vice versa.

The infant's earliest relation to the mother is in Winnicott's words, ruth-less, or, more accurately, 'pre-ruth', where 'ruth' (concern) relates to intentionality and the integration of the potential meanings of bodily action in the developing infant's sense of self. To have the possibility of integration the baby must be able to express this pre-ruth self, to claim and exact his rights over the mother and to experience her corresponding desires. If all goes well and he later develops the capacity for concern (Chapter 7, this volume) he might look back and say 'I was ruthless then'. In failure the baby may hide or inhibit his ruthlessness, eagerness, greed and fail to bring together in his mind the 'two mothers', the environment mother who tends to the baby's ordinary needs, and the object mother whose task is to receive the full impact of the baby's pre-ruth claims. In good-enough development the baby integrates his aggressive and libidinal impulses and their fusion enables him to have a passionate feed with the active sucking and devouring which allows for id gratification and integration. Although there is always the possibility of reactive aggression, 'destruction only becomes an ego responsibility when there is enough ego integration and organisation sufficient for the existence of anger and therefore fear of talion' (1958a: 210).

In 'finding' rather than 'creating' the other, the infant's 'destruction' of the object in omnipotent fantasy and the object's survival in reality represent the separateness of external and inner reality. The object has 'been there all the time' (1971: 221), although for the infant it had no existence until it was found. The object was fully objective, but there was no subjective subject able to acknowledge this status. The subject (the baby) was objectively present and acting, but without an awareness of itself. Scarfone suggests that 'the reality of the object is the emotional experience occurring within the subject-object compound. That is, the experience embedded in the relating does not require the subject to be clearly differentiated from the object. The subject exists, one could say, but it does not yet know. The object also exists, but is not yet known' (Scarfone, 2005: 40).

Winnicott was interested in how the individual comes to use aggression with the intention to inflict hurt. Since the fusion of primary aggression and libido is never complete for a variety of reasons, including insufficient adaptation by the maternal environment, aggressive elements are available for sadistic, masochistic, and persecutory purposes. Winnicott emphasized that the infant needs not just a satisfying object but 'an external object' which provides limits to his actions/movement and represents the boundary of self and other. For Winnicott, the fantasy of destructiveness creates the differentiation necessary for individuation, but only if the mother 'survives' and continues to respond (Chapter 13, this volume).

3. *Illusion and transitional phenomena*

The familiarity of Winnicott's idea of the transitional object should not obscure the real advance represented by the concept of transitionality and the extent to which it revolutionizes the aims of psychoanalysis through the links with illusion and play. For Winnicott the appearance of the transitional object depends on a good-enough continuing relationship with the mother and the beginnings of a perception of self and other. It proposes the infant's imaginative inhabiting of an area intermediate between internal and external reality on whose developmental and symbolic implications the future capacity for living well depends. It is not the 'object', but the 'illusion', as 'a universal in the field of experience', that is important. Winnicott stresses the importance of the mother's adaptation to the infant's need as the means of continuation of an illusion of omnipotence, and the mother's presentation of the breast at the right moment as proposing a creative hallucination for the baby. This 'illusion' provides a protective insulation for the infant without isolating him (Hernandez and Giannakoulas, 2001) and it becomes 'the ontological foundation of the subject' (Usuelli Kluzer, 2001: 51).

The potential inscribed in the concept of transitional space, and its availability from infancy to adulthood as the arena of particular experiences of the relation between self and world, derives from Winnicott's preferred emphasis on the normality of transitional phenomena in the life of the infant. The infant lives the move from purely subjective to objective and the acquisition of symbolic functioning diachronically, but this existence in time, this going-on-being itself produces a space *between* one thing and another. A mental space *between* one thing and another has to be established; once established, it becomes the condition for creative living. 'The symbolizing process is another complex ego function inextricably interrelated to the development of memory, representation, boundary formation, reality testing, apperception, and synthetic function' (Barkin, 1978: 530). The transitional object is a stage in the acquisition of these faculties. Scarfone (2005) proposes that 'until separateness is recognized, there is no mental *space* since the mental space metaphor demands a complex new development involving transitional objects and phenomena linking external and internal spaces' (Winnicott, 1953). To inhabit the transitional area, and, later, to play, involves illusion and disillusion, aspects of the same process (De Silvestris, 2001) that form the necessary basis of the mother–child relation, of 'play' and, for Winnicott, the basis of what happens in the consulting room and what is understood by analysis.

In his discussion of symbolism, Rycroft (1956) points out that although Winnicott and Marion Milner introduce the word 'illusion' to reinstate the distinction between fantasy and reality in classical theory, in their model 'illusion' belongs to an earlier stage, 'defining the nature of the relationship between (the capacity for) illusion and (the perception of) external reality during the period of maximal reciprocity between the infant and its mother'. Winnicott is interested in how disturbances in this relationship lead to the later, pathological divorce between illusion and reality, the terrain of classic psychopathology. Ogden emphasizes the classical framework in *The Primitive Edge of Experience* (1989) where he writes, 'the development of the idea of misrecognition of one's internal state is in a sense synonymous with the development of psychoanalytic theory. One of the cornerstones upon which Freud constructed his theory of psychological meanings is the idea that one knows more than he thinks he knows' (1989: 197). The continuing realization of misrecognition that is central to classical psychoanalysis is not Winnicottian illusion, which Rycroft links with 'imagination' and 'fantasy' and which, following Coleridge, he identifies 'in certain capacities of the mind'. In the accounts of Winnicott and Milner, the capacity for illusion gives meaning to experience (Usuelli Kluzer, 2001).

Many of the patients who inform Winnicott's work lack the mental framework within which general enjoyment, sex, pleasure have any ongoing meaning. To state this is to point to a serious deprivation, where the issue of living as having a sexual and an alive component is resolutely ignored or evaded.

4. *Theory and practice of psychoanalysis with adults and children*

Winnicott refers frequently to the possible applications of his discoveries about early infantile processes to the psychoanalytic enterprise, in terms of the actual work to be done and as model for clinical practice, especially with the most severely disturbed patients. Winnicott's analogy between psychoanalysis and the mother–infant relationship emerges from his interest in emotional development and he saw failures at different times producing different types of disturbance. He makes a strong argument for what we *can* learn about the one from the other and how we can learn it, in the course of making a very tight link between them and their interrelation. It forms part of his whole approach to analysis. In '*The Aims of Psychoanalytical Treatment*' (1962a: 169) he states 'The essential thing is that I do base my work on diagnosis'. He distinguishes between 'standard analysis' and 'working as a psychoanalyst', the crucial issue being whether the patient has sufficient ego integration based on a good-enough beginning.

In a talk shortly before he died Winnicott said 'Psychoanalysis is not just a matter of interpreting the repressed unconscious; it is rather the provision of a professional setting for trust, in which such work may take place' (1986: 115). His concern with the setting is derived from the very basis for trust in the earliest relationship. His discussion of cure emphasizes the care, adaptation and reliability, and the significance of consistency. 'Many of them suffer from precisely this, that they have been subjected as part of the pattern of their lives to the unpredictable. We cannot afford to fit into this pattern' (1986: 115). In his concern that the practising analyst must be much more reliable than people in ordinary life, even-tempered, punctual, non-judgemental, he emphasizes the very personal demands placed upon the analyst, especially with disturbed patients. He regards care/cure as 'an extension of the concept of holding' (1986: 115) and together with 'father–mother care', the basis of personal growth and the maturational process.

He regards essential human interaction as the basis of patient–doctor care, with the emphasis on continuity of contact and reciprocity between the participants, not in any sense of false comparability or equivalence, but with an awareness of the interdependence, the joint dependencies of both. The relation of patient and doctor is about reliability meeting dependence, both essential terms in the two areas he made his life's work, paediatrics and psychoanalysis.

If the analytic situation is regarded as analogous to the mother–infant relationship this raises questions as to whether this is always or primarily the case, whether it is first and foremost to be understood in that way, and what place is ascribed to the father. Ogden's view (1988: 649) that the early relationship of central interest in the analytic setting is not that of mother and infant but that of internal-object–mother and the internal-object–infant, emphasizes how the infant comes to represent early experiences in his internal world. This is not necessarily at odds with Winnicott's view which proposes the re-presentation of those early experiences in an analytic setting paradigmatic of the former relationship.

In Winnicott's writings on patients who regress in treatment, the transference provides the way for a re-experiencing of environmental/maternal failure that belongs to a period when, to all intents and purposes, environment and infant are one and the same. In this account the patient needs to reach beyond the transference trauma to the state of affairs that preceded the original trauma. This past and future thing *has to become* a thing of the here and now.

Here, experiencing is the equivalent of remembering, of the lifting of repression of classical Freudian analysis. Winnicott observes that this is very time consuming and painful but it is not futile: what is futile is when there is an analysis of psychoneurosis when the problems relate to an earlier stage, the stage of the establishment of ego organization.

Winnicott did not write extensively about the psychoanalysis of neurotic patients, suggesting not only that this was not his primary concern, but that he agreed with the prevailing view of treatment of 'whole persons' who could relate to others and recognize their inner reality and its conflicts. His interest was in those conditions, depression, the antisocial tendency, psychotic and borderline phenomena whose origins lay before whole person functioning. His interest in depression and the antisocial tendency for instance led him to investigate situations where a good-enough beginning was then lost. Both conditions belong to the stage of weaning in normal development and both are linked to the child's growing awareness of destructiveness, linked to the primitive love impulse, where a failure at that level resulted in the loss of what had previously been available (C. Winnicott *et al.*, 1984). He observed a potential undoing of the earlier processes leading to instinct inhibition and then loss of capacity for guilt; instinctual sensual gratifications were possible but without affection. There would be general personal impoverishment (Winnicott, 1954a). In his view the child would need experiences of loving someone who could first accept the strength and potency of their aggressive primitive love and then receive their restitutive and reparative giving. The importance of being able to receive would often be expressed in play. Without this sequence of experiences the child 'wet blankets the whole inner world and functions at low level of vitality: the mood is depression' (1954a).

Although Winnicott placed Klein's concept of the depressive position on a par with Freud's Oedipus Complex, he was critical of what he regarded as the pathologizing of a normal and necessary developmental stage through the use of that term (see Chapter 7, this volume). He emphasized the value of depression (1954a) and saw it as a developmental achievement. Joffe and Sandler refer rather scathingly to this in their 1965 paper: 'We deplore the tendency among some analysts to elevate depression to the status of a virtue without regard to the distinction between the mastery of pain in an adaptive way, the depressive response, and melancholia' (1965: 413). Winnicott did distinguish between a depressive illness and a depressed mood (1954a) and pointed to the predicament of the child whose mother was depressed and who might compensate by adopting a false brightness (Winnicott, 1948a). He saw depression as a state or a mood containing the seeds of its own recovery with time. In contrast, depression as an illness was associated with depersonalization, hopelessness and futility, and the development of a false self, all features of failures before the establishment of unit status. Technique with patients at this level would be linked to the adaptations of psychoanalysis which he termed 'management'.

The discussion of analytic technique and analytic work with patients whose problems originate in early mother–child interaction addresses both the ongoing implications of failure in these initial encounters, and the necessary changes in technique in their analyses. Martin-Cabrè (2001) cites Balint's observation that 'the historic event of the disagreement between Freud and Ferenczi had the effect of a trauma in the psychoanalytic world despite the fact that the dispute was limited to the problem of how to handle 'regressive patients that develop a very intense transference' (Balint, 1968: 152). Arguably, that trauma in the psychoanalytic world continues to have effects in debates about the technical demands placed upon the analyst in the treatment of severely regressed patients and the willingness to explore alternative approaches. Balint and Winnicott in the postwar period and Ferenczi in the 1920s took severely disturbed patients into analysis. Ferenczi observed that 'an abstinent analytic approach' did not work, and all three were aware of the danger of analysis repeating childhood traumas. Balint and Winnicott considerably refined the theoretical clinical and technical implications (Tonnesmann, 2007: 131) of this work, which has contributed enormously to the distinctiveness of the theory of technique within the Independent tradition in British psychoanalysis (Rayner, 1991; Stewart, 1992).

This work with severely regressed patients also grew from the debates about treating psychotics which, in the UK, were associated with Herbert Rosenfeld, and later with Hanna Segal and Wilfred Bion. Like many analysts practising in the 1940s and 1950s, Winnicott learned much from his analysis of psychotic and borderline patients and this work led to his revision of classical analytic practice in the analysis of *some* patients at *some* stages of their analyses. The debates could be quite heated: in January 1953 Winnicott wrote to Hanna Segal, following a discussion of a paper by Rosenfeld on treating schizophrenics, that she 'seemed to imply that there is no essential difference between the management needs of a psychotic and a neurotic patient. If you really mean this heaven help your psychotic patients and until you recover from this point of view I am afraid you will not make a very interesting contribution to the theory of psychosis' (Rodman, 1987: 47).

In '*Primitive Emotional Development*' (1945, see Chapter 2) Winnicott describes his primary interest in the child patient and the infant as requiring the study of psychosis in analysis. He had already begun to formulate his position that the clues to the psychopathology of psychosis are to be found in 'the early . . . development of the infant, before the infant knows himself (and therefore others) as the whole person that he is (and that they are)'. Tonnesmann, who considers this paper his first real challenge to Klein's account of early development, emphasizes these references to psychotic patients and infant states. 'During the war Winnicott had analyzed several young adult/adolescent psychotic patients who were under Clifford Scott at the Maudsley in south London. When Scott emigrated to Canada, Shenley a psychiatric hospital in north London, became a source of patients through his friendship with Hayward, who had set up a mother baby unit on the first floor of his unit (probably under the instructions of the Regional board). Winnicott used these rooms for his patients when he was away and a link with the London hospital operated in the same way. Winnicott thought that "the trouble with hospitalization was that patients were thrown out at the point they needed it most"' (Tonnesmann, personal communication, June 2006). This contributed to his practice in the consulting room with certain patients.

In *Impasse and Interpretation*, Rosenfeld (1987: 281–311) describes the variety of attempts to treat psychotics and their links with Freud's assessment of their non-analyzability. He differentiates two general approaches, schematically characterized as the approach of the Kleinians – Rosenfeld, Bion, and Segal – and the approach of a dispersed group of others including the Europeans – Federn (1905 on), Waelder (1925), Pierce Clark (1933) – and the Americans – Bullard, Sullivan, Fromm Reichmann, Jacobson, and Searles. He sees Winnicott's approach as directly in line with that of Pierce Clark and Fromm Reichmann's early experiments and recommendations (1987: 306) and as relating specifically to the importance of regression to dependence in the treatment. He describes this as a change from the 1940s to the late 1950s. 'Winnicott described that he was able to analyse psychotic patients at first without any change of analytic technique, and this means that he analysed the psychotic phenomena in the positive and negative transference situations. When he changed his views and felt that psychosis was a kind of deficiency disease he simultaneously changed his technique and stressed that the analyst would have to make up for the failure of the early environment' (1987: 288). Winnicott himself produces something similar: 'At about this time I was also gradually lured into the treatment of the more psychotic type of adult patient and I found that I could learn much about the psychopathology of early infancy from adults who were deeply regressed in the course of psychoanalytic treatment; much of which couldn't be learned by direct observation of infants, nor from the analyses even of children of two and a half years. This psychoanalytic work with adults of a psychotic type proved extremely exacting and time-absorbing and by no means always obviously successful. In one case which ended tragically, I gave 2,500 hours of my professional life, without hope of remuneration. Nevertheless, this work taught me more than any other kind' (1988: 50).

It is often this work that has provoked alarm and dismissal of Winnicott, but it derives from his account of early development and the origins of severe disturbance, and his experiences in the consulting room. 'In the more psychotic phenomena we are examining it is a breakdown of the . . . unit self that is indicated. The ego organises defences against breakdown of the ego-organisation, and it is the ego-organisation that is threatened. But the ego cannot organise against environmental failure in so far as dependence is a living fact.' (p. 201).

The link between Ferenczi and Winnicott is also to be discerned in the responses of the psychoanalytic community to their respective practices with severely disturbed patients and the wish to distance them from psychoanalytic orthodoxy. In the case of Ferenczi this was almost immediate and it led to his views going underground for decades. In the case of Winnicott concerns over modifications which he himself publicized were there from the 1950s but have gained ground in the wake of research into his links with Masud Khan (Hopkins, 2006; Willoughby, 2002). Winnicott's relations with Masud Khan, whom he analyzed, have become a focus following an article in the *London Review of Books* by the economist Wynne Godley, where he describes his analysis with Khan, to whom he had been referred by Winnicott in 1959 (2001). Khan himself claimed to have been in analysis with Winnicott for 15 years, a claim endorsed, largely unquestioningly, by recent writers (Hopkins, 2006) and the basis of accusations against Winnicott regarding boundary violations. Roger Willoughby's earlier account however (2002; 2004) is sceptical, noting that since Khan himself has been an unreliable witness on other matters, his claims here too should be treated with some scepticism, a position that appears to be supported by preliminary research undertaken by Jan Abram in the Winnicott archives at the Wellcome Institute in London (personal communication, May 2007).

It was not only in the treatment of psychotic and borderline patients that Winnicott's views on the psychoanalytic process changed. He increasingly suggests that interpretations can break up the evolution of the transference from the patient's growing trust in the analyst's technique and the setting; that deep change can be prevented by the analyst's need to interpret; that the patient's achievement in making his/her own interpretation is joyful for both patient and analyst; that only the patient knows the answers; and that the analyst's interpretations must be linked to the patient's ability to place the analyst outside the area of subjective phenomena, that is, to *use* the analyst. For Winnicott, not all patients are able to do this; developmentally they have not arrived at this stage and it may require considerable analytic time before a patient can operate at the level of whole persons assumed by classical psychoanalysis. In *Playing and Reality* (1971a), he famously wrote 'Psychotherapy takes place in the overlap of two areas of playing, that of the patient and that of the therapist. Psychotherapy has to do with two people playing together. The corollary of this is that where playing is not possible then the work done by the therapist is directed towards bringing the patient from a state of not being able to play into a state of being able to play' (1971a: 37).

In his article, 'Some Images of the Analyst's Participation in the Analytic Process', David Sedgwick (1997) quotes a remark of Winnicott's that gives some sense of his priorities 'I guess that the well behaving professional analyst is easier to come by than the analyst who (while behaving well) retains the vulnerability that belongs to a flexible defence organisation (Winnicott, 1960: 160)'.

Winnicott's definitive views on psychoanalysis shifted from the classical aim of making conscious the unconscious to psychoanalysis as facilitating emotional and psychical awareness and growth. This is reflected in the place accorded the analysand in the evolving clinical process and it is fundamentally dependent upon the state of mind of the analyst. In 'The *Aims of Psycho-analytical* Treatment' he says: 'In doing psycho-analysis I aim at: Keeping alive; Keeping well; Keeping awake; I aim at being myself and behaving myself. Having begun an analysis I expect to continue with it, to survive it, and to end it. I enjoy myself doing analysis and I always look forward to the end of each analysis. Analysis for analysis' sake has no meaning for me. I do analysis because that is what the patient needs to have done and to have done with' (1962a: 165).

Work with children

Winnicott's work with children comprised paediatrics, child psychiatry, child psychotherapy, and child analysis. Their different approaches, frameworks and assumptions all contributed to his developing understanding of children's health and pathology, and to the technical decisions about intervention in different therapeutic contexts. 'In my practice I have treated thousands of children of this age group by child psychiatry. I have (as a trained analyst) given individual psychotherapy to some hundreds. Also I have had a certain number of children of this age group for psychoanalysis, more than twelve and less than twenty. The borders are so vague that I would be unable to be exact' (1965: 115). Although his psychoanalytic training and identity were determining in this work, and although he did not practise as a paediatrician (but did as a child psychiatrist) after 1945 (Winnicott, Brazelton, Greenspan, and Spock, 2002), his medical training and background in paediatrics never lost its influence. Psychosomatic integrity in development was integral to his view of health and illness (Chapter 4, this volume).

With the establishment of the child guidance movement in the 1930s most 'applied' psychoanalytic work for children happened in child guidance clinics and Winnicott's clinic at Paddington Green Children's Hospital was one such setting. His special position there, before and after the establishment of the National Health Service in 1948, was hugely influential in the trajectory of his work with children since it gave him unique access to a vast range of childhood disorders usually unavailable in private practice. He is said to have written up 60,000 consultations seen in this clinic (Kanter, 2004).

His psychoanalytic work with children developed in the period of the conflicts between the great pioneers of child psychoanalysis, Melanie Klein and Anna Freud. Clare Winnicott described his reading Klein's 'Narrative of a Child Analysis' (1961) right through, and then a second time: 'It really caught his imagination and he used it of course and developed it differently from Mrs Klein or used it differently, but he certainly always acknowledged and felt he owed a great deal to her for that and to her for the supervision of his own thesis' (Kanter, 2004: 262). Despite being drawn to Klein's thinking (Phillips, 1988: 44) his views were remarkably similar to Anna Freud's, who saw the task of child analysis as being to restore the child to the path of 'normal development' (1965). Winnicott was not a close colleague of Freud's but certainly knew her work and respected it. He supported Klein in disagreeing about Freud's 'preparatory period' in child analysis and agreeing that 'child analysis was exactly like adult analysis' (1962, quoted in Phillips, 1988: 45) but there were parallels with Anna Freud. They were both keenly aware of how disturbances in the relational environment for very young children were potentially disruptive of their whole emotional and social development and they both attached importance to the child's actual parents and the circumstances in which they lived (Phillips, 1988).

The vast majority of references to his work with children are of child psychiatry cases, for instance, 'Symptom Tolerance in Paediatrics' (1953, published in 1958a)) and therapeutic consultations, a whole volume of which was published as *Therapeutic Consultations in Child Psychiatry* (1971b). 'It was from his work with children and with psychotics that he forged his ideas' (Geissman and Geissman, 1998: 233).

In his comparison of Winnicott and Bowlby, Reeves (2005a: 77) highlights their contrasting views in the 1930s about what constitutes a psychoanalytic treatment: 'For [Winnicott] five-times-a-week child analysis was sacrosanct'. But there is no complete account of a conventional five-times-per-week analytic treatment. The nearest is *The Piggle*, a posthumously published account of an intermittent treatment of a young girl (1977). Winnicott's later flexibility evolved at least in part as a result of his experiences with evacuated children. In a talk entitled *Varieties of Psychotherapy* given to MIASMA in 1961 (The Mental Illness Association Social and Medical Aspects in Cambridge) (C. Winnicott *et al.*, 1984: 232) he declared, 'My special interest here is in the way in which a trained analyst can do something other than analysis and do it usefully . . . Often these other treatments can look better than the treatments that I personally feel have a more profound effect i.e. psychoanalysis'. In 1965 he wrote in his introduction to what was later published as *The Piggle* (1977: 3), 'On the other hand it should not be thought that a compromise is valuable; either the child should have analysis on the basis of the daily session or else should be seen on demand'.

'The Piggle' (1977), a 2-½-year-old girl whose parents had consulted Winnicott when she became very anxious following the birth of her sister when she was 21 months old, was a case where he did something akin to psychoanalysis intermittently, 'on demand'. The work was presented at a meeting in London prior to the IPA Congress in Rome (1969) and Winnicott was publicly supervised by Ishak Ramzy of Kansas. In Ramzy's introduction to the published work he reminisces about that event (1977: xv): 'One issue in the subsequent discussion centred on the subject of whether the type of treatment

Winnicott described and called "psychoanalysis on demand" with its infrequent and irregular sessions was analysis or psychotherapy. Winnicott replied by directing attention to what he did with the transference and the unconscious, not to the formal arrangements of the analytic situation, or the frequency or regularity of the analytic sessions.' That is, Winnicott emphasizes the internal analytic setting maintained by the analyst that is available to the patient regardless of the external circumstances.

The Piggle gives a very clear idea of Winnicott's clinical sensibility: he enters the child's world in her play, takes in her way of being, facilitates her gaining meaning out of the play by first allowing that 'the game is played and enjoyed' (1977: 180). 'As a matter of principle, the analyst always allows the enjoyment to become established before the content of the play is used for interpretation' (p. 180). The method and style of work here reflects his general concern for how he can facilitate any patient's elaboration of the 'true self'. Lanyado observes (2006a: 205) that Winnicott's accounts of his work with children are 'in a manner which seems to say "Here is something, an idea to play with and if you find it interesting, we can play with it together"'. In that he sees play as 'work' his playing always had serious purpose (Chapter 12 this volume) which made him judicious in his use of interpretation and attentive to the provision of an appropriate setting. Play and interpretation were part and parcel of the clinical work, but interpretation should not pre-empt or disrupt the child's enjoyment in playing. Towards the end of his life he became much more circumspect about giving interpretations in all his work and in *Therapeutic Consultations* he said 'Dogmatic interpretation leaves the child with only two alternatives, an acceptance of what I have said as propaganda or a rejection of the interpretation and of me and the whole set up' (1971b: 10).

Play is part of Winnicott's overall psychoanalytic approach so, as a technique in work with children, it is rather different from its place in Melanie Klein's work, which he saw as 'concerned almost entirely with the use of play' (Winnicott, 1971b: 46). He appreciated the way her work opened up the inner phantasy world of the child, but for him playing and the capacity for play were indicative of basic health, and 'in his later work he would replace [Klein's] capacity to know by the capacity to play as a criterion for health' (Phillips, 1988: 47). For Winnicott play is intrinsically worthwhile and 'is itself a therapy' (Winnicott, 1971b: 58). He thought that excessive instinctual arousal made playing impossible, and like much of the English school he subsumed sexuality to object relating and to the development of the self, but in the work with children, and *The Piggle* is no exception, there is a consistent recourse to infantile sexuality and children's sexual fantasies and anxieties as the basis for childhood difficulty (Giannakoulas, 2005).

Winnicott was alert to the presence of health and he thought that the healthy part of the child was coming to work: 'It is from the description of the psychoanalytic work, however, that the reader can see the essential health in this child's personality, a quality that was always evident to the analyst even when clinically and at home the child was really ill. The treatment had a momentum of its own that was evident from its inception, and no doubt enhanced by the parents' and the patient's confidence in the analyst. The descriptions of the work done show that, from the beginning, [The Piggle] came to do work, and that each time when she came for treatment she brought a problem she was able to display' (1977: 3).

Winnicott is sensitive to the child's relations with her parents and, rather than seeing them as his competitors, he includes them and recognizes their potential therapeutic capacity in the changing needs of their children. He comments in the introduction to *The Piggle*: 'It is possible for the [psycho-analytic] treatment of a child actually to interfere with a very valuable thing which is the ability of the child's home to tolerate and to cope with the child's clinical states that indicate emotional strain and temporary holdups in emotional development, or even the fact of development itself' (p. 3).

There are extensive examples of the 'little that need be done' for children (Winnicott, 1962a). The 'therapeutic consultation' was both an intervention in itself for a specific purpose (to unhitch a developmental interruption in a brief intervention when psychoanalytic treatment is not possible) and a con-densation of psychoanalysis by working with the knowledge of unconscious processes that reveal themselves in the therapeutic encounter. It is not an expedient intervention on the grounds of scarce resources but, in the words of an eminent child psychotherapist, 'on the contrary I feel that brief work or timely consultations can be the best way forward for many children and families who come to us for help' (Lanyado, 2006: 204). The therapeutic consultation assumes that the child 'who comes with hope' will communicate what she/he needs to, if a receptive person is found to listen. The published volume, *Therapeutic Consultations in Child Psychiatry* (1971b) also demonstrated Winnicott's use of the 'squiggle technique' which he evolved specifically for making contact with children in the consultation setting. In the collection Winnicott is clear that if the therapeutic consultation does not resolve the presenting problem in the child, then psychoanalysis should be the treatment of choice. At other times he is more circumspect about what might work, especially with children whose developmental process may have already have been greatly disrupted, as in some cases of the antisocial tendency (Winnicott, 1956, 'The Antisocial Tendency', in C. Winnicott *et al.*, 1984), whose origins he located between the levels of psychosis and neurosis. Where psychosis derived from early impingements in the relational environment produced fundamental flaws in the structure of the ego, neurosis assumed good-enough development that produced an adequate internal mental structure (defined classically as a functioning ego and superego) and an inner life that could sustain a degree of internal conflict and personal responsibility. The developmental stage associated with the antisocial tendency is linked with the young child's experience of separation and loss from the primary parental figures, principally but not exclusively the mother, and Winnicott considers it to require a different kind of clinical work. Although his second child training case was of this kind, he argues that the antisocial tendency patient is suitable only for analysis near the beginning of its onset, before secondary gain, such as delinquency, has become a complicating factor (Winnicott, 1956, in C. Winnicott *et al.*, 1984). For more chronically disturbed antisocial children he recommended residential treatment where the therapeutic environment 'holds the failure situation' and the staff share the management of the difficulties that are acted out. In a lecture given to the Association of Workers for Maladjusted Children (C. Winnicott *et al.*, 1984) in January 1971, he gave due recognition to the work pioneered during the war by gifted individuals such as David Wills.

Conclusion

In *Reading Winnicott* we have given an outline of a major way of thinking and working psychoanalytically and drawn attention to the historical roots of some contemporary psychoanalytic pre-occupations, our own and those of the psychoanalytic community in Britain and abroad in which we work. The theoretical and clinical ideas which clinicians use are always produced within a psychoanalytic culture embedded in a certain intellectual and socio-historical context. Rereading these familiar texts has offered us the opportunity for rethinking that world and its concerns and the papers included in this collection demonstrate the continuing relevance of historical disputes for current debates about technique, training, and how psychoanalysis is understood.

The history of psychoanalysis has involved considerable creativity and innovation but it has also seen the stifling of debate and the denial or dismissal of difference. Ambrosiano (2008) links the contemporary situation with the dynamics of the earliest meetings of the Viennese group, and their externalization of conflicts and loyalties through processes of scapegoating and disillusionment, Ferenczi and Jung being the most obvious cases. She argues that these ways of handling conflict continue to shape our history. They may relate, among other things, to the widespread anxieties of a profession whose work is centrally involved with the unconscious and its intractability to conscious, rational aims. Nonetheless, such occurrences are profoundly anti-psychoanalytic. In recent years a similar trend may be discerned around Winnicott, which has had disastrous results for open discussion among colleagues. It has impeded the ongoing evaluation of his work and its links with others, the assessment of his clinical decisions about analytic parameters with certain patients, and, especially, any historical awareness of the differences between common analytic ways of working in the past (long sessions, going on holiday with patients, the analysis of one's own children, for instance) and ways of working now.

In an article documenting his own changing interest in Winnicott, Spurling (2003) describes his engagement and gradual disengagement from man and theory. In the course of this he raises a more general set of issues about the components of the clinical approach each of us comes to identify as our own. The main focus is the analyst and what a commitment to authority figures or (importantly) to theories *as* authority figures, may involve. While Jung's abandonment of Freud's theory coincides with his disillusion with Freud the person, and Didier Anzieu observed of his analysis with Lacan, 'Lacan the person and Lacan's ideas are intermingled as indicating the fusion of theory and person' (2003: 33), Spurling says the classic accounts of a change in theoretical perspective tend to claim that the ideas in themselves are no longer adequate rather than addressing the author's disappearing transference to them (2003: 34). His own transference to Winnicott involved a combination of theoretical ideas and ideas about a person whom he did not know, that together produced a psychic investment extending beyond the ideas themselves to the much wider cathexes with which any theory is necessarily invested by its adherents. It is not that Spurling disputes the autonomy of theory or the importance of separating ideas and author, but he does insist that espousal of any idea or theory is part of other aspects of what constitutes the person.

Spurling wonders about what Winnicott represents now and what he represented in the past, that is, he introduces a social and historical perspective about his character, theory, and practice, those of others, and the external relations, social networks, and specific modalities of developments in the BPAS over many decades. This invites both a psychoanalytic reading and an historical awareness, but contemporary psychoanalysis, like its earlier histories, often seems dominated by anxieties that are primarily defensive and addressed to splits internal to the psychoanalytic movement. His article reveals the need for a scholarly history of Winnicott and the reception of his ideas in British psychoanalysis and psychotherapy in general, and as part of the history of the BPAS in particular.

1 THE OBSERVATION OF INFANTS IN A SET SITUATION (1941)

OTHER WRITINGS

The Set Situation paper was published 15 years after Winnicott's first publication in the *British Journal of Children's Diseases* in 1926 (Winnicott and Gibbs, 1926). The first book *Clinical Notes on Disorders of Childhood* (1931) was aimed mainly at children's doctors and already showed the application of psychoanalytic thinking to medicine. Melanie Klein had published *The Psycho-Analysis of Children* in 1932 before he was supervised by her for his child case. His membership paper for the BPAS, 'The Manic Defence' (1935), which remained unpublished until 1958, reflected his interest in her ideas and followed her own paper on 'A Contribution to the Psychogenesis of Manic-Depressive States' (1935). In 1936 Winnicott had read 'Appetite and Emotional Disorder' to the Medical Section of the British Psychological Society (BPS), a setting in which he would give significant papers throughout his career. In 1939, his first discussion of *Aggression* was given to teachers, establishing his ongoing commitment to the dissemination of psychoanalytic ideas beyond psychoanalysis itself.

A. Aichhorn had published *Wayward Youth* in 1925 which Winnicott refers to in 'The Antisocial Tendency' (1956, in C. Winnicott *et al.*, 1984). Klein had given a paper to the Medical Section of the BPS 'On Criminality' in 1934 in which she had remarked on the 'common tendency to overestimate the importance of unsatisfactory surroundings' in understanding delinquency. She further claimed that 'the best remedy against delinquency would be to analyse children who show signs of abnormality' (pp. 280–281) – a position with which Winnicott would eventually disagree. In 1940 John Bowlby published his paper 'The Influence of the Early Environment in the Development of Neurosis and Neurotic Character' (*IJPA*) and in 1944 his study on 'Forty-Four Juvenile Thieves' (*IJPA*) which would lead him to take up a radically different position from Klein's.

EDITORS' INTRODUCTION

This early paper of Winnicott's continues to attract historical debate (Aguayo, 2002; Reeves, 2006) among contemporary theorists for its attempt to establish the conditions for a scientific study of early infantile processes and the emotional foundations of infant mental health. It has been seen as containing the bases for much of Winnicott's later work (Davis, 1993; Reeves, 2006) but as also demonstrating a distinctively Kleinian approach (Likierman, 2007). It is a significant paper in the history of psychoanalysis because it is willing to conjecture about psychic processes on the basis of consistent empirical data and to hypothesize about the close links between the psyche and the physiological processes discernible in the infant. It was first given at a meeting of the BPAS in April 1941, with the title 'Observations on Asthma in an Infant and Its Relation to Anxiety' (Reeves, 2006: 292, n. 3). The paper was revised for later publication in the *IJPA*, and both Rodman (2003) and Reeves (2006) argue for Melanie Klein's close involvement in the final version. Without an original version, however, these readings, though convincing, remain part of wider speculative debates tracing Klein's influence. Although the child with asthma appears in the published paper, the brief is much wider, and the paper is centred on the accumulated data from Winnicott's paediatric practice and his development of a common consultative procedure for all mothers and babies attending his clinic at Paddington Green.

Winnicott was always convinced that children's symptoms − shyness, eczema, asthma, enuresis − are never exclusively physiological but always a response to conflicts; this is illustrated here in the two clinical vignettes, but it is there from his first book, *Clinical Notes on Disorders of Childhood* (1931); another statement of it appears in the paper, 'What Do We Mean by a Normal Child?' (1946), and a later paper, 'Symptom Tolerance in Paediatrics: A Case History' (1953).

The paper represents an evolution in psychoanalytic ways of thinking, and both Freud and Ferenczi are important predecessors for the ideas expressed. The development of first-generation thinkers emphasizes the essential relation of child and adult as the condition of the child's relation with himself or herself, and there are clear parallels with Freud's account of the *fort/da* game based on observations of his grandchild. But Winnicott describes a situation formally set up with a much younger baby as the basis for his own hypotheses about human infants. This involved putting a spatula on a table near the baby and observing the baby's reactions. Like Ferenczi, Winnicott sees the infant coming to assume the capacities of a human subject through the encounter first with others, and then with the self that emerges through those encounters and their internalization. Davis offers a reading of this paper as transitional between a medical and a psychoanalytic model (1993: 65) even as she locates the seeds of most of Winnicott's developed theories and concepts here.

The emphasis on a methodology based on invariant procedures, empirical observation, a large sample, and a replicable situation with consistent elements provides a link with later work. The concentration is on the normal situation and what constitute deviations from it across a deliberately loose age range, about 5 to 13 months, accounted for by known facts about infant development: at 5 months infants grasp an object, but it is not till 6 months that they drop it deliberately. The upper age limit refers to the baby's widening interest in the world around him: while the anxieties are still evident, the baby's positive interest encompasses too many things, and any information deriving from his interest in the spatula is less clear.

Every encounter with the spatula involves:

(a) *Consistent elements*
1. The setting and the mother, and what they show of family dynamics and the mother's approach to mothering.
2. The child, and what he does at different moments in the encounter.

(b) *A series of three stages*
1. The baby displays interest but restraint, what Winnicott calls 'the period of hesitation'. This is accompanied by physiological changes, and Winnicott hypothesizes about these bodily changes, which cannot be known exclusively by observation, from a psychoanalytic perspective.
2. The baby's desire for the spatula can first be observed physically, in changes in the mouth, the tongue, and the saliva, then the infant mouths it, engages in free bodily movement, and plays with it.
3. The process of losing interest: the baby may drop it, as if by mistake, then deliberately; he may get down on the floor with it or lose interest.

Winnicott makes a claim about the psychic processes in operation and about the physical links with emotional development, which represent a step forward on two related levels. He insists on the importance for normal development of all the stages. In 'Appetite and Emotional Disorder' (1936) he describes a child whose only response belongs to the throwing-away stage. Davis (1993) links this with the antisocial tendency and its importance in the work with evacuated children in the 1940s.

In his play, the baby shows a rudimentary awareness of the distinction between inside and outside but also seems to be enjoying a process that actually involves completion. In his extended discussion of the riddance stage, Reeves (2006) disputes the parallels between Freud's account of the *fort/da* game (1920) and the younger child's ultimate loss of interest in the object that previously fascinated him. He suggests that the baby's final loss of interest in the spatula in this last stage – 'the leaving behind is everything' (Reeves, 2006: 278) – is very different symbolically from Freud's attention to his grandchild's capacity to lose and retrieve the cotton reel repeatedly. He proposes that Winnicott's assimilation of his own account to Freud's owes much to Klein and her reading of Freud's example as support for her theory of early infantile states (2006: 281).

Winnicott does describe this phase in terms of a model of internalized objects, where the child gains reassurance about the fate of his internal mother and her attitude, but he argues that there is a complex relation between symptoms, anxiety, physiological processes, and unconscious states which demonstrates the baby's realization of the existence of a world outside himself. The mental conflicts produced by the desire for the spatula and a fear of retaliation or prohibition by another about that desire – that is, a fear of an anticipated external situation that appears to be present internally whether the actual mother is disapproving or not – can nonetheless be dispelled by the experience with the real mother. The expectation of disapproval may echo Klein's account (Likierman, 2007), but, even at this stage in the evolution of Winnicott's own thinking, the early primitive superego forms the basis for a rather different emphasis in the matter of infantile fantasies. Its corollary, the infant's assumption about the mother and her insides, can produce a concern for her that leads to a relation between whole persons. This emphasis on the baby's fantasies prioritizes the idea that the development of the baby's rudimentary sense of self and his relations with more than one person are dependent on the distinction between external and internal as given by the real relation with the baby's real mother or caregiver. Winnicott's insistence that infant behaviour cannot be accounted for except on the assumption that the infant entertains fantasies that are full of content, but not attached to word presentations, offers a different approach to fantasy.

These processes have been further elaborated by psychoanalytically informed developmental researchers who have given the names 'social referencing' (Emde, Klingman, Reich, and Wade, 1978), 'secondary intersubjectivity' (Trevarthen and Hubley, 1978), and 'the domain of intersubjective relatedness' (Stern, 1985) to the moment when the baby is said to make a quantum leap in acquiring a sense that the mother, and therefore the baby himself, has a 'mind' with potentially interesting mental contents. Interest in the mother's expression and its meaning to the baby replaces the prospect of persecution that Winnicott notes. The beginnings of the acquisition of a 'theory of mind' observed and described here are developed further in 'Primitive Emotional Development' (Chapter 2, this volume).

The symbolic aspects of the spatula and the important difference represented by saying the spatula stands for a breast, and/or that it stands for a penis – or rather, what the baby later knows as a penis – are both understood in this approach as a quality of the mother, that leads to a sense of people more generally, a taking in of the world of others. Winnicott emphasizes the spatial connections involved in the initial recognition of persons and their inter-relation, and behaviour is not reduced to symbolic equivalences, though that dimension is also present. Awareness of the existence of external reality is seen as offering a limit to what is possible in a fantasy world where, in the most primitive state, the object works according to magic: if it vanishes when not wanted, this can mean its annihilation, a terrifying situation to which Winnicott refers in relation to the link between not wanting and being satisfied. Importantly, fantasy is not what the individual creates to deal with frustration; this he calls 'fantasying', an activity that is intent on going nowhere. The distinction between fantasy and fantasying refers to the centrality of illusion in his account. This is further developed in the paper on transitional objects and transitional phenomena (Chapter 5, this volume) but its most sustained discussion is to be found in the paper, 'Dreaming, Fantasying and Living', Chapter 2 of *Playing and Reality* (1971d). There he links fantasying to a paralysis of action deriving from an early environmental failure to provide a sufficiently adequate going on being for the infant to manage instinctual demands in their internal and external manifestations.

The adult lacks a capacity for living creatively and for dreaming. 'Fantasying' here involves a lack of spontaneity, a paralysis of action. The idea of 'fantasying' highlights what is involved in the possibility of using both the mind and the body (and, importantly, their inter-relation) as a creative function.

The baby's encounter with the spatula as a whole experience in the controlled conditions of the set situation forms one basis for Winnicott's understanding of what happens in analysis and the importance of regularity and reliability as the condition for richness of experience. His link between spatula and interpretation as glittering objects, ways of approaching the patient's greed, anticipates his interest in play and his questioning of interpretation as the central factor of psychoanalytic treatment.

The Observation of Infants in a Set Situation[1]
(1941)

For about twenty years I have been watching infants in my clinic at the Paddington Green Children's Hospital, and in a large number of cases I have recorded in minute detail the way infants behave in a given situation which is easily staged within the ordinary clinic routine. I hope gradually to gather together and present the many matters of practical and theoretical interest that can be gleaned from such work, but in this paper I wish to confine myself to describing the set situation and indicating the extent to which it can be used as an instrument of research. Incidentally I cite the case of an infant of seven months who developed and emerged out of an attack of asthma while under observation, a matter of considerable interest in psychosomatics.

I want, as far as possible, to describe the setting of the observations, and what it is that has become so familiar to me: that which I call the 'Set Situation', the situation into which every baby comes who is brought to my clinic for consultation.

In my clinic, mothers and their children wait in the passage outside the fairly large room in which I work, and the exit of one mother and child is the signal for the entrance of another. A large room is chosen because so much can be seen and done in the time that it takes the mother and her child to reach me from the door at the opposite end of the room. By the time the mother has reached me I have made a contact with her and probably with the child by my facial expression, and I have had a chance to remember the case if it is not a new patient.

If it is an infant, I ask the mother to sit opposite me with the angle of the table coming between me and her. She sits down with the baby on her knee. As a routine, I place a right-angled shining tongue-depressor at the edge of the table and I invite the mother to place the child in such a way that, if the child should wish to handle the spatula, it is possible. Ordinarily, a mother will understand what I am about, and it is easy for me gradually to describe to her that there is to be a period of time in which she and I will contribute as little as possible to the situation, so that what happens can fairly be put down to the child's account. You can imagine that mothers show by their ability or relative inability to follow this suggestion something of what they are like at home; if they are anxious about infection, or have strong moral feelings against putting things to the mouth, if they are hasty or move impulsively, these characteristics will be shown up.

It is very valuable to know what the mother is like, but ordinarily she follows my suggestion. Here, therefore, is the child on mother's knee, with a new person (a man, as it happens) sitting opposite, and there is a shining spatula on the table. I may add that if visitors are present, I have to prepare them often more carefully than the mother, because they tend to want to smile and take active steps in relation to the baby – to make love to him, or at least to give the reassurance of friendliness. If a visitor cannot accept the discipline which the situation demands, there is no point in my proceeding with the observation, which immediately becomes unnecessarily complicated.

THE INFANT'S BEHAVIOUR

The baby is inevitably attracted by the shining, perhaps rocking, metal object. If other children are present, they know well enough that the baby longs to take the spatula. (Often they cannot bear to see the baby's hesitation when it is pronounced, and take the spatula and shove it into the baby's mouth. This is, however, hastening forward.) Here we have in front of us the baby, attracted by a very attractive object, and I will now describe what, in my opinion, is a normal sequence of events. I hold that any variation from this, which I call normal, is significant.

Stage 1. The baby puts his hand to the spatula, but at this moment discovers unexpectedly that the situation must be given thought. He is in a fix. Either with his hand resting on the spatula and his body quite still he looks at me and his mother with big eyes, and watches and waits, or, in certain cases, he withdraws interest completely and buries his face in the front of his mother's blouse. It is usually possible to manage the situation so that active reassurance is not given, and it is very interesting to watch the gradual and spontaneous return of the child's interest in the spatula.

Stage 2. All the time, in 'the period of hesitation' (as I call it), the baby holds his body still (but not rigid). Gradually he becomes brave enough to let his feelings develop, and then the picture changes quite quickly. The moment at which this first phase changes into the second is evident, for the child's acceptance of the reality of desire for the spatula is heralded by a change in the inside of the mouth, which becomes flabby, while the tongue looks thick and soft, and saliva flows copiously. Before long he puts the spatula into his mouth and is chewing it with his gums, or seems to be copying father smoking a pipe. The change in the baby's behaviour is a striking feature. Instead of expectancy and stillness there now develops self-confidence, and there is free bodily movement, the latter related to manipulation of the spatula.

I have frequently made the experiment of trying to get the spatula to the infant's mouth during the stage of hesitation. Whether the hesitation corresponds to my normal or differs from it in degree or quality, I find that it is impossible during this stage to get the spatula to the child's mouth apart from the exercise of brutal strength. In certain cases where the inhibition is acute any effort on my part that results in the spatula being moved towards the child produces screaming, mental distress, or actual colic.

The baby now seems to feel that the spatula is in his possession, perhaps in his power, certainly available for the purposes of self-expression. He bangs with it on the table or on a metal bowl which is nearby on the table, making as much noise as he can; or else he holds it to my mouth and to his mother's mouth, very pleased if we *pretend* to be fed by it. He definitely wishes us to *play* at being fed, and is upset if we should be so stupid as to take the thing into our mouths and spoil the game as a game.

At this point, I might mention that I have never seen any evidence of a baby being disappointed that the spatula is, in fact, neither food nor a container of food.

Stage 3. There is a third stage. In the third stage the baby first of all drops the spatula as if by mistake. If it is restored he is pleased, plays with it again, and drops it once more, but this time less by mistake. On its being restored again, he drops it on purpose, and thoroughly enjoys aggressively getting rid of it, and is especially pleased when it makes a ringing sound on contact with the floor.

The end of this third phase comes when the baby either wishes to get down on the floor with the spatula, where he starts mouthing it and playing with it again, or else when he is bored with it and reaches out to any other objects that lie at hand.

This is reliable as a description of the normal only between the ages of about five months and thirteen months. After the baby is thirteen months old, interest in objects has become so widened that if the spatula is ignored and the baby reaches out for the blotting-pad, I cannot be sure that there is a real inhibition in regard to the primary interest. In other words, the situation rapidly becomes complicated and approaches that of the ordinary analytic situation which develops in the analysis of a two-year-old child, with the disadvantage (relative to the analytic) that as the infant is too young to speak material presented is correspondingly difficult to understand. Before the age of thirteen months, however, in this 'set situation' the infant's lack of speech is no handicap.

After thirteen months the infant's *anxieties* are still liable to be reflected in the set situation. It is his *positive interest* that becomes too wide for the setting.

I find that therapeutic work can be done in this set situation although it is not my object in this paper to trace the therapeutic possibilities of this work. I give a case that I published in 1931, in which I committed myself to the belief that such work could be done. In the intervening years I have confirmed my opinion formed then.

> This was the case of a baby girl who had attended from six to eight months on account of feeding disturbance, presumably initiated by infective gastro-enteritis. The emotional development of the child was upset by this illness and the infant remained irritable, unsatisfied, and liable to be sick after food. All play ceased, and by nine months not only was the infant's relation to people entirely unsatisfactory, but also she began to have fits. At eleven months fits were frequent.
>
> At twelve months the baby was having major fits followed by sleepiness. At this stage I started seeing her every few days and giving her twenty minutes' personal attention, rather in the manner of what I now describe as the set situation, but with the infant on my own knee.
>
> At one consultation I had the child on my knee observing her. She made a furtive attempt to bite my knuckle. Three days later I had her again on my knee, and waited to see what she would do. She bit my knuckle three times so severely that the skin was nearly torn. She then played at throwing spatulas on the floor incessantly for fifteen minutes. All the time she cried as if really unhappy. Two days later I had her on my knee for half-an-hour. She had had four convulsions in the previous two days. At first she cried as usual. She again bit my knuckle very severely, this time without showing guilt feelings, and then she played the game of biting and throwing away spatulas. While on my knee she became able to enjoy play. After a time she began to finger her toes.

Later the mother came and said that since the last consultation the baby had been 'a different child'. She had not only had no fits, but had been sleeping well at night – happy all day, taking no bromide. Eleven days later the improvement had been maintained, without medicine; there had been no fits for fourteen days, and the mother asked to be discharged.

I visited the child one year later and found that since the last consultation she had had no symptom whatever. I found an entirely healthy, happy, intelligent and friendly child, fond of play, and free from the common anxieties.

The fluidity of the infant's personality and the fact that feelings and unconscious processes are so close to the early stages of babyhood make it possible for changes to be brought about in the course of a few interviews. This fluidity, however, must also mean that an infant who is normal at one year, or who at this age is favourably affected by treatment, is not by any means out of the wood. He is still liable to neurosis at a later stage and to becoming ill if exposed to bad environmental factors. However, it is a good prognostic sign if a child's first year goes well.

DEVIATIONS FROM THE NORMAL

I have said that any variation from that which I have come to regard as the norm of behaviour in the set situation is significant.

The chief and most interesting variation is in the initial hesitation, which may either be exaggerated or absent. One baby will apparently have no interest in the spatula, and will take a long time before becoming aware of his interest or before summoning courage to display it. On the other hand, another will grab it and put it to his mouth in the space of one second. In either case there is a departure from the normal. If inhibition is marked there will be more or less distress, and distress can be very acute indeed.

In another variation from the norm an infant grabs the spatula and immediately throws it on the floor, and repeats this as often as it is replaced by the observer.

There is almost certainly a correlation between these and other variations from the norm and the infant's relation to food and to people.

USE OF TECHNIQUE ILLUSTRATED BY A CASE

The set situation which I have described is an instrument which can be adapted by any observer to the observation of any infant that attends his clinic. Before discussing the theory of the infant's normal behaviour in this setting,

I will give one case as an illustration, the case of a baby with asthma. The behaviour of the asthma, which came and went on two occasions while the baby was under observation, would perhaps have seemed haphazard were it not for the fact that the baby was being observed as a routine, and were it not for the fact that the details of her behaviour could be compared with that of other children in the same setting. The asthma, instead of having an uncertain relation to the baby's feelings, could be seen, because of the technique employed, to be related to a certain kind of feeling and to a certain clearly defined stage in a familiar sequence of events.

Margaret, a seven-months-old girl, is brought to me by her mother because the night before the consultation she has been breathing wheezily all night. Otherwise she is a very happy child who sleeps well and takes food well. Her relations with both parents are good, especially with her father, a night worker, who sees a lot of her. She already says 'Dad-dad', but not 'Ma-ma'. When I ask: 'Whom does she go to when she is in trouble?' the mother says: 'She goes to her father; he can get her to sleep.' There is a sister sixteen months older who is healthy, and the two children play together and like each other, although the baby's birth did arouse some jealousy in the older child.

The mother explains that she herself developed asthma when she became pregnant with this one, when the other was only seven months old. She was herself bad until a month before the consultation, since when she has had no asthma. Her own mother was subject to asthma, she also began to have asthma at the time when she started to have children. The relation between Margaret and her mother is good, and she is feeding at the breast satisfactorily.

The symptom, asthma, does not come entirely unheralded. The mother reports that for three days Margaret has been stirring in her sleep, only sleeping ten minutes at a time, waking with screaming and trembling. For a month she has been putting her fists to her mouth and this has recently become somewhat compulsive and anxious. For three days she has had a slight cough, but the wheeziness only became definite the night before the consultation.

It is interesting to note the behaviour of the child in the set situation. These are my detailed notes taken at the time. 'I stood up a right-angled spatula on the table and the child was immediately interested, looked at it, looked at me and gave me a long regard with big eyes and sighs. For five minutes this continued, the child being unable to make up her mind to take the spatula. When at length she took it, she was at first unable to make up her mind to put it to her mouth, although she quite clearly wanted to do so. After a time she found she was able to take it, as if gradually getting reassured from our staying as we were. On her taking it to herself I noted the usual flow of saliva, and then followed several minutes of enjoyment of the mouth experience.' It will be noted that this behaviour corresponded to what I call the normal.

'In the second consultation Margaret reached out to take the spatula, but again hesitated, exactly as at the first visit, and again only gradually became able to mouth and to enjoy the spatula with confidence. She was more eager in her mouthing of it than she had been at the previous occasion, and made noises while chewing it. She soon dropped it deliberately and on its being returned played with it with excitement and noise, looking at mother and me, obviously pleased, and kicking out. She played about and then threw down the spatula, put it to her mouth again on its being restored to her, made wild movements with her hands, and then began to be interested in other objects that lay near at hand, which included a bowl. Eventually she dropped the bowl, and as she seemed to want to go down we put her on the floor with the bowl and the spatula, and she looked up at us very pleased with life, playing with her toes and with the spatula and the bowl, but not with the spatula and the bowl together. At the end she reached for the spatula and seemed as if she would bring them together, but she just pushed the spatula right away in the other direction from that of the bowl. When the spatula was brought back she eventually banged it on the bowl, making a lot of noise.'

(The main point in this case relevant to the present discussion is contained in the first part of the description, but I have given the whole case-note because of the great interest that each detail could have if the subject under discussion were extended. For instance, the child only gradually came to the placing of the two objects together. This is very interesting and is representative of her difficulty, as well as of her growing ability in regard to the management of two *people* at the same time. In order to make the present issue as clear as possible I am leaving discussion of these points for another occasion.)

In this description of the baby's behaviour in the set situation, I have not yet said when it was that she developed asthma. The baby sat on her mother's lap with the table between them and me. The mother held the child round the chest with her two hands, supporting her body. It was therefore very easy to see when at a certain point the child developed bronchial spasm. The mother's hands indicated the exaggerated movement of the chest, both the deep inspiration and the prolonged obstructed expiration were shown up, and the noisy expiration could be heard. The mother could see as well as I did when the baby had asthma. *The asthma occurred on both occasions over the period in which the child hesitated about taking the spatula.* She put her hand to the spatula and then, as she controlled her body, her hand and her environment, she developed asthma, which involves an involuntary control of expiration. At the moment when she came to feel confident about the spatula which was at her mouth, when saliva flowed, when stillness changed to the enjoyment of activity and when watching changed into self-confidence, at this moment the asthma ceased.

A fortnight later the child had had no asthma, except the two attacks in the two consultations.[2] Recently (that is, twenty-one months after the episode I have described), the child had had no asthma, although of course she is liable to it.[3]

Because of the method of observation, it is possible for me to make certain deductions from this case about the asthma attacks and their relation to the infant's feelings. My main deduction is that in this case there was a close enough association between bronchial spasm and anxiety to warrant the postulation of a relationship between the two. It is possible to see, because of the fact that the baby was being watched under known conditions, that for this child asthma was associated with the moment at which there is normally hesitation, and hesitation implies mental conflict. An impulse has been aroused. This impulse is temporarily controlled, and asthma coincides on two occasions with the period of control of the impulse. This observation, especially if confirmed by similar observations, would form a good basis for discussion of the emotional aspect of asthma, especially if taken in conjunction with observations made during the psycho-analytic treatment of asthma subjects.

DISCUSSION OF THEORY

The hesitation in the first place is clearly a sign of anxiety, although it appears normally.

As Freud (1926) said, 'anxiety is *about* something'. There are two things, therefore, to discuss: the things that happen in the body and mind in a state of anxiety, and the something that there is anxiety about.

If we ask ourselves why it is that the infant hesitates after the first impulsive gesture, we must agree, I think, that this is a super-ego manifestation. With regard to the origin of this, I have come to the conclusion that, generally speaking, the baby's normal hesitation cannot be explained by a reference to the parental attitude. But this does not mean that I neglect the possibility that he does so because he has learned to expect the mother to disapprove or even to be angry whenever he handles or mouths something. The parent's attitude *does* make a lot of difference in certain cases.

I have learned to pick out fairly quickly the mothers who have a rooted objection to the child's mouthing and handling objects, but on the whole I can say that the mothers who come to my clinic do not stop what they tend to regard as an ordinary infantile interest. Among these mothers are even some who bring their babies because they have noticed that the infants have *ceased* to grab things and put them to their mouths, recognizing this to be a symptom.

Further, at this tender age before the baby is, say, fourteen months old, there is a fluidity of character which allows a certain amount of the mother's tendency to prohibit such indulgence to be over-ridden. I say to the mother: 'He can do that here if he wants to, but don't actually encourage him to.' I have found that in so far as the children are not driven by anxiety they are able to adjust themselves to this modified environment.

But whether it is or is not the mother's attitude that is determining the baby's behaviour, I suggest that the hesitation means that the infant *expects* to produce an angry and perhaps revengeful mother by his indulgence. In order that a baby shall feel threatened, even by a truly and obviously angry mother, he must have in his mind the notion of an angry mother. As Freud (1926) says: 'On the other hand, the external (objective) danger must have managed to become internalized if it is to be significant for the ego.'

If the mother has been really angry and if the child has real reason to expect her to be angry in the consultation when he grabs the spatula, we are led to the infant's apprehensive fantasies, just as in the ordinary case where the child hesitates in spite of the fact that the mother is quite tolerant of such behaviour and even expects it. The 'something' which the anxiety is about is in the infant's mind, an idea of potential evil or strictness, and into the novel situation anything that is in the infant's mind may be projected. When there has been no experience of prohibition, the hesitation implies conflict, or the existence in the baby's mind of a *fantasy* corresponding to the other baby's *memory* of his really strict mother. In either case, as a consequence, he has first to curb his interest and desire, and he only becomes able to find his desire again in so far as his testing of the environment affords satisfactory results. I supply the setting for such a test.

It can be deduced, then, that the 'something' that the anxiety is about is of tremendous importance to the infant. To understand more about the 'something' it will be necessary to draw on the knowledge gained from the analysis of children between two and four years old. I mention this age because it has been found by Melanie Klein, and I think by all who have analysed two year-olds, that there is something in the experience of such analyses which cannot be got from the analyses of even three-and-a-half- and four-year-old children, and certainly not from the analyses of children in the latency period. One of the characteristics of a child at the age of two is that the primary oral fantasies, and the anxieties and defences belonging to them, are clearly discernible along-side secondary and highly elaborated mental processes.

The idea that infants have fantasies is not acceptable to everyone, but probably all of us who have analysed children at two years have found it necessary to postulate that an infant, even an infant of seven months like the asthma baby whose case I have already quoted, has fantasies. These are not yet attached to word-presentations, but they are full of content and rich in emotion, and it can be said that they provide the foundation on which all later fantasy life is built.

These fantasies of the infant are concerned not only with external environment, but also with the fate and interrelationship of the people and bits of people that are being fantastically taken into him – at first along with his ingestion of food and subsequently as an independent procedure – and that build up the inner reality. A child feels that things inside are good or bad, just as outside things are good or bad. The qualities of good and bad depend on the relative acceptability of aim in the taking-in process. This in turn depends on the strength of the destructive impulses relative to the love impulses, and on the individual child's capacity to tolerate anxieties derived from destructive tendencies. Also, and connected with both of these, the nature of the child's defences has to be taken into account, including the degree of development of his capacity for making reparation. These things could be summed up by saying that the child's ability to keep alive what he loves and to retain his belief in his own love has an important bearing on how good or bad the things inside him and outside him feel to him to be; and this is to some extent true even of the infant of only a few months. Further, as Melanie Klein has shown, there is a constant interchange and testing between inner and outer reality; the inner reality is always being built up and enriched by instinctual experience in relation to external objects and by contributions from external objects (in so far as such contributions can be perceived); and the outer world is constantly being perceived and the individual's relationship to it being enriched because of the existence in him of a lively inner world.

The insight and conviction gained through the analysis of young children can be applied backwards to the first year of life, just as Freud applied what he found in adults to the understanding of children, and to the understanding not only of the particular patient as a child, but of children in general.

It is illuminating to observe infants directly, and it is necessary for us to do so. In many respects, however, the analysis of two-year-old children tells us much more about the infant than we can ever get from direct observation of infants. This is not surprising; the uniqueness of psycho–analysis as an instrument of research, as we know, lies in its capacity to discover the *unconscious* part of the mind and link it up with the conscious part and thus give us something like a full understanding of the individual who is in analysis. This is true even of the infant and the young child, though direct observation can tell us a great deal if we actually know how to look and what to look for. The proper procedure is obviously to get all we can both from observation and from analysis, and to let each help the other.

I now wish to say something about the physiology of anxiety. Is it not holding up the development of descriptive psychology that it is seldom, if ever, pointed out that the physiology of anxiety cannot be described in simple terms, for the reason that it is different in different cases and at different times? The teaching is that anxiety may be characterized by pallor and sweating and vomiting and diarrhoea and tachycardia. I was interested to find in my clinic, however, that there are really several alternative manifestations of anxiety, whatever organ or function is under consideration. An anxious child during physical examination in a heart clinic may have a heart that is thumping, or at times almost standing still, or the heart may be racing away, or just ticking over. To understand what is happening when we watch these symptoms I think we have to know something about the child's feelings and fantasies, and therefore about the amount of excitement and rage that is admixed, as well as the defences against these.

Diarrhoea, as is well known, is not always just a matter of physiology. Analytic experience with children and adults shows that it is often a process accompanying an unconscious fear of definite things, things inside that will harm the individual if kept inside. The individual may know he fears impulses, but this, though true, is only part of the story, because it is also true that he unconsciously fears specific bad things which exist somewhere for him. 'Somewhere' means either outside himself or inside himself – ordinarily, both outside and inside himself. These fantasies may, of course, in certain cases and, to some extent, be conscious, and they give colour to the hypochondriac's descriptions of his pains and sensations.

★   ★   ★

If we are examining the hesitation of an infant in my set situation, we may say that the mental processes underlying the hesitation are similar to the ones that underlie diarrhoea, though opposite in their effect. I have taken diarrhoea, but I might have taken any other physiological process which can be exaggerated or inhibited in accordance with the unconscious fantasy that happens to affect the particular function or organ. In the same way, in consideration of the hesitation of the infant in the set situation, it can be said that even if the baby's behaviour is a manifestation of fear, there is still room for the description of the same hesitation in terms of unconscious fantasy. What we see is the result of the fact that the infant's impulse to reach out and take is subjected to control even to the extent of temporary denial of the impulse. To go further and to describe what is in the infant's mind cannot be a matter of direct observation, but, as I have said, this does not mean that there is nothing in the infant's mind corresponding to the unconscious fantasy which through psycho-analysis we can prove to exist in the mind of an older child or of an adult who hesitates in a similar situation.

In my special case, given to illustrate the application of the technique, control includes that of the bronchial tubes. It would be interesting to discuss the relative importance of the control of the bronchus as an organ (the displacement of control, say, of the bladder) and control of expiration or of the breath that would have been expelled if not controlled. The breathing out might have been felt by the baby to be dangerous if linked to a dangerous idea – for instance, an idea of reaching *in* to take. To the infant, so closely in touch with his mother's body and the contents of the breast, which he actually takes, the idea of reaching in to the breast is by no means remote, and fear of reaching in to the inside of mother's body could easily be associated in the baby's mind with not breathing.[4]

It will be seen that the notion of a dangerous breath or of a dangerous breathing or of a dangerous breathing organ leads us once more to the infant's fantasies.

I am claiming that it could not have been purely by chance that the infant gained and lost asthma so clearly in relation to the control of an impulse on two separate occasions, and that it is therefore very much to the point if I examine every detail of the observations.

Leaving the special case of the asthma infant and returning to the normal hesitation of a baby in taking the spatula, we see that the danger exists in the infant's mind and can only be explained on the supposition that he has fantasies or something corresponding to them.

★   ★   ★

Now, what does the spatula stand for? The answer to this is complex because the spatula stands for different things.

That the spatula can stand for a breast is certain. It is easy to say that the spatula stands for a penis, but this is a very different thing from saying it stands for a breast, because the baby who is always familiar with either a breast or a bottle has very seldom indeed any real knowledge based on experience of an adult penis. In the vast majority of cases a penis must be the infant's fantasy of what a man might have. In other words, we have said no more by calling it a penis than that the infant may have a fantasy that there is something like a breast and yet different because it is associated more with father than with mother. The child is thought to draw on his or her own genital sensations and on the results of self-exploration in the construction of fantasy.

However, I think the truth is that what the baby later knows to be a penis, he earlier senses as a quality of mother, such as liveliness, punctuality at feed times, reliability and so on, or else as a thing in her breast equated with its sticking out or its filling up, or in her body equated with her erect posture, or a hundred other things about her that are not essentially herself. It is as if, when a baby goes for the breast and drinks milk, in fantasy he puts his hand in, or dives into, or tears his way into his mother's body, according to the strength of the impulse and its ferocity, and takes from her breast whatever is good there. In the unconscious this object of the reaching impulse is assimilated to what is later known as penis.

Besides standing for breast and penis, the spatula also stands for people, observation having clearly shown that the four-to-five-months infant may be able to take in persons as a whole, through the eyes, sensing the person's mood, approval or disapproval, or distinguishing between one person and another.[5]

I would point out that in the explanation of the period of hesitation by reference to actual experience of mother's disapproval, an assumption is being made that this infant is normal or developed enough to take in persons as a whole. This is by no means always true, and some infants who seem to show an interest in and a fear of the spatula nevertheless are unable to form an idea of a whole person.

Everyday observation shows that babies from an age certainly less than the age-group we are discussing (five to thirteen months) ordinarily not only recognize people, but also behave differently towards different people.

★   ★   ★

In the set situation the infant who is under observation gives me important clues to the state of his emotional development. He may only see in the spatula a thing that he takes or leaves, and which he does not connect with a human being. This means that he has not developed the capacity, or he has lost it, for building up the whole person behind the part object. Or he may show that he sees me or mother behind the spatula, and behave as if this were part of me (or of mother). In this case, if he takes the spatula, it is as if he took his mother's breast. Or, finally, he may see mother and me and think of the spatula as something to do with the relation between mother and myself. In so far as this is the case, in taking or leaving the spatula he makes a difference to the relationship of two people standing for father and mother.

There are intermediate stages. For instance, some infants obviously prefer to think of the spatula as related to the bowl, and they repeatedly take it out of the bowl and replace it with evident interest and pleasure and perhaps excitement. They seem to find an interest in two objects simultaneously more natural than an interest in the spatula as a thing that can be taken from me, fed to mother, or banged on to the table.

Only the actual observations can do justice to the richness of variation that a number of infants introduce into the simple setting which can so easily be provided.

The infant, if he has the capacity to do so, finds himself dealing with two persons at once, mother and myself. This requires a degree of emotional development higher than the recognition of one whole person, and it is true indeed that many neurotics never succeed in managing a relation to two people at once. It has been pointed out that the neurotic adult is often capable of a good relation with one parent at a time, but gets into difficulties in his relationship with both together. This step in the infant's development, by which he becomes able to manage his relationship to two people who are important to him (which fundamentally means to both his parents), at one and the same time, is a very important one, and until it is negotiated he cannot proceed to take his place satisfactorily in the family or in a social group. According to my observations this important step is first taken within the first year of life.

Before he is one year old the infant may feel that he is depriving others of things that are good or even essential because of the greed roused by his love. This feeling corresponds to his fear, which may easily be confirmed by experience, that when he is deprived of the breast or bottle and of his mother's love and attention, someone else enjoys more of her company. Actually this may be father, or a new baby. Jealousy and envy, essentially oral in their first associations, increase greed but also stimulate genital desires and fantasies, thus contributing to an extension of libidinal desires and of love, as well as of hatred. All these feelings accompany the infant's first steps in establishing a relation to both parents – steps which are also the initial stages of his Oedipus situation, the direct and the inverted one. The conflict between love and hatred and the ensuing guilt and fear of losing what is loved, first experienced in relation to the mother only, is carried further into the infant's relation to both parents and very soon to brothers and sisters as well. Fear and guilt stirred by the infant's destructive impulses and fantasies (to which experiences of frustration and unhappiness contribute) are responsible for the idea that if he desires his mother's breast too much he deprives father and other children of it, and if he desires some part of his father's body which corresponds to mother's breast, he deprives mother and others of it. Here lies one of the difficulties in the establishment of a happy relation between a child and both parents. I cannot deal with the complicated matter of the interplay of the child's greed and the different ways he has of controlling this greed or of counteracting its results by restoring and reconstructing, but it can readily be seen that these things become complicated where the child's relationship is to two persons instead of to mother alone.

It will be remembered that in my case-note of the infant with asthma, I referred to the relation between the child's growing ability to bring the spatula and the bowl together at the end of her game, and the mixtures of wishes and fears in regard to the management of a relation to two people at once.

Now this situation, in which the infant hesitates as to whether he can or cannot satisfy his greed without rousing anger and dissatisfaction in at least one of the two parents, is illustrated in the set situation of my observations in a way that is plain for all to see. In so far as the baby is normal, one of the main problems before him is the management of two people at once. In this set situation I seem sometimes to be the witness of the first success in this direction. At other times I see reflected in the infant's behaviour the successes and failures he is having in his attempts to become able to have a relation to two people at once at home. Sometimes I witness the onset of a phase of difficulties over this, as well as a spontaneous recovery.[6]

It is as if the two parents allow the infant gratification of desires about which he has conflicting feelings, tolerating his expression of his feelings about themselves. In my presence he cannot always make use of my consideration of his interests, or he can only gradually become able to do so.

The experience of daring to want and to take the spatula and to make it his own without in fact altering the stability of the immediate environment acts as a kind of object-lesson which has therapeutic value for the infant. At the age which we are considering and all through childhood such an experience is not merely temporarily reassuring: the cumulative effect of happy experiences and of a stable and friendly atmosphere round a child is to build up his confidence in people in the external world, and his general feeling of security. The child's belief in the good things and relationships inside himself is also strengthened. Such little steps in the solution of the central problems come in the everyday life of the infant and young child, and every time the problem is solved something is added to the child's general stability, and the foundation of emotional development is strengthened. It will not be surprising, then, if I claim that in the course of making my observations I also bring about some changes in the direction of health.

Whole Experiences

What there is of therapeutics in this work lies, I think, in the fact that the *full course of an experience is allowed*. From this one can draw some conclusions about one of the things that go to make a good environment for the infant. In the intuitive management of an infant a mother naturally allows the full course of the various experiences, keeping this up until the infant is old enough to understand her point of view. She hates to break into such experiences as feeding or sleeping or defaecating. In my observations I artificially give the baby the right to complete an experience which is of particular value to him as an object-lesson.

In psycho-analysis proper there is something similar to this. The analyst lets the patient set the pace and he does the next best thing to letting the patient decide when to come and go, in that he fixes the time and the length of the session, and sticks to the time that he has fixed. Psycho-analysis differs from this work with infants in that the analyst is always groping, seeking his way among the mass of material offered and trying to find out what, at the moment, is the shape and form of the thing which he has to offer to the patient, that which he calls the interpretation. Sometimes the analyst will find it of value to look behind all the multitude of details and to see how far the analysis he is conducting could be thought of in the same terms as those in which one can think of the relatively simple set situation which I have described. Each interpretation is a glittering object which excites the patient's greed.

NOTE ON THE THIRD STAGE

I have rather artificially divided the observations into three stages. Most of my discussion has concerned the first stage and the hesitation in it which denotes conflict. The second stage also presents much that is of interest. Here the infant feels that he has the spatula in his possession and that he can now bend it to his will or use it as an extension of his personality.[7] In this paper I am not developing this theme. In the third phase the infant practises ridding himself of the spatula, and I wish to make a comment on the meaning of this.

In this the third phase he becomes brave enough to throw the spatula down and to enjoy ridding himself of it, and I wish to show how this seems to me to relate to the game which Freud (1920) described, in which the boy mastered his feelings about his mother's departure. For many years I watched infants in this setting without seeing, or without recognizing, the importance of the third stage. There was a practical value for me in my discovery of the importance of this stage, because whereas the infant who is dismissed in the second stage is upset at the loss of the spatula, once the third stage has been reached the infant can be taken away and can leave the spatula behind him without being made to cry.

Although I have always known Freud's description of the game with the cotton-reel and have always been stimulated by it to make detailed observations on infant play, it is only in more recent years that I have seen the intimate connection between my third phase and Freud's remarks.

It now seems to me that my observations could be looked at as an extension backwards of this particular observation of Freud's. I think the cotton-reel, standing for the child's mother, is thrown away to indicate a getting rid of the mother because the reel in his possession had represented the mother *in his possession*. Having become familiar with the full sequence of incorporation, retention, and riddance, I now see the throwing-away of the cotton-reel as a part of a game, the rest being implied, or played at an earlier stage. In other words, when the mother goes away, this is not only a loss for him of the externally real mother but also a test of the child's relation to his *inside* mother. This inside mother to a large extent reflects his own feelings, and may be loving or terrifying, or changing rapidly from one attitude to the other. When he finds he can master his relation to his inside mother, including his aggressive riddance of her (Freud brings this out clearly), he can allow the disappearance of his *external* mother, and not too greatly fear her return.

In particular I have come to understand in recent years (applying Melanie Klein's work) the part played in the mind even of the infant by the fear of the loss of the mother or of both parents as valuable internal possessions. When the mother leaves the child he feels that he has lost not only an actual person, but also her counterpart in his mind, for the mother in the external world and the one in the internal world are still very closely bound up with each other in the infant's mind, and are more or less interdependent. The loss of the internal mother, who has acquired for the infant the significance of an inner source of love and protection and of life itself, greatly strengthens the threat of loss of the actual mother. Furthermore, the infant who throws away the spatula (and I think the same applies to the boy with the cotton-reel) does not only get rid of an external and internal mother who has stirred his aggression and who is being expelled, and yet can be brought back; in my opinion he also externalizes an internal mother whose loss is feared, so as to demonstrate to himself that this internal mother, now represented through the toy on the floor, has not vanished from his inner world, has not been destroyed by the act of incorporation, is still friendly and willing to be played with. And by all this the child revises his relations with things and people both inside and outside himself.

Thus one of the deepest meanings of the third phase in the set situation is that in it the child gains reassurance about the fate of his internal mother and about her attitude; a depressed mood which accompanies anxiety about the internal mother is relieved, and happiness is regained. These conclusions could, of course, never be arrived at through observation only, but neither could Freud's profound explanation of the game with the cotton-reel have been arrived at without knowledge gained through analysis proper. In the play-analyses of young children we can see that the destructive tendencies, which endanger the people that the child loves in external reality, and in his inner world, lead to fear, guilt, and sorrow. Something is missing until the child feels that by his activities in play he has made reparation and revived the people whose loss he fears.

SUMMARY

In this paper I have tried to describe a way by which infants can be observed objectively, a way based on the objective observation of patients in analysis and at the same time related closely to an ordinary home situation. I have described a set situation, and have given what I consider to be a normal (by which I mean healthy) sequence of events in this set situation. In this sequence there are many points at which anxiety may become manifest or implied, and to one of these, which I have called the moment of hesitation, I have drawn special attention by giving a case of a seven-months-old baby girl who developed asthma twice at this stage. I have shown that the hesitation indicates anxiety, and the existence of a super-ego in the infant's mind, and I have suggested that infant behaviour cannot be accounted for except on the assumption that there are infant fantasies.

Other set situations could easily be devised which would bring out other infantile interests and illustrate other infantile anxieties. The setting which I describe seems to me to have the special value that any physician can use it, so that my observations can be confirmed or modified, and it also provides a practical method by which some of the principles of psychology can be demonstrated clinically, and without causing harm to patients.

Notes

1. Based on a paper read before the British Psycho-Analytical Society, 23 April 1941, and published the same year in the *International Journal of Psychoanalysis* 22 (1941).
2. But the mother had re-developed it.

3. The mother again rather made a point that she, however, had been having asthma, as if she felt she had to have it unless the baby had it.
4. At the sight of something particularly wonderful we sometimes say, 'It takes my breath away'. This and similar sayings, which include the idea of modification of the physiology of breathing, have to be explained in any theory of asthma that is to command respect.
5. As Freud showed, the cotton-reel stood for the mother of the eighteen-months-old boy.
6. I have watched from start to finish a fortnight's illness in a nine-months-old infant girl. Accompanying earache, and secondary to it, was a psychological disturbance characterized not only by a lack of appetite but also by a complete cessation of handling and mouthing of objects at home. In the set situation the child had only to see the spatula to develop acute distress. She pushed it away as if frightened of it. For some days in the set situation there seemed to be acute pain as if indicating acute colic instead of what is normally hesitation, and it would have been unkind to have kept the child for long at a time in this painful situation. The earache soon cleared up, but it was a fortnight before the infant's interest in objects became normal again. The last stage of the recovery came dramatically when the child was with me. She had become able to catch hold of the spatula and to make furtive attempts to mouth it. Suddenly she braved it, fully accepted it with her mouth and dribbled saliva. Her secondary psychological illness was over and it was reported to me that on getting home she was found to be handling and mouthing objects as she had done before her illness started.
7. See Chapter 5. [*In Through Paediatrics to Psycho-Analysis.*]

Developing ideas: inner reality different from external reality and fantasy; manic defence to deal with mother's inner reality; observation of consistent elements; period of hesitation, riddance (throwing away stage); spatula game; play

2 PRIMITIVE EMOTIONAL DEVELOPMENT (1945)

OTHER WRITINGS

Winnicott published many articles during the war, several in the periodical, *New Era in Home and School*, and all reflecting his activities as psychiatric consultant to the evacuated children's scheme in Oxfordshire. He also published letters and papers in *The Lancet* and the *British Medical Journal* on physical treatments such as pre-frontal leucotomy, and on electric shock treatment to which he was opposed. In 1939 he began broadcasting to parents on the BBC about their young children and about the difficulties associated with the return of evacuated children after the war.

During the war the BPAS was engaged in the 'controversial discussions' (1941–45) which produced several significant contributions: Susan Isaacs's 'The Nature and Function of Phantasy' (1943), papers by Paula Heimann and Isaacs on regression (1943), and Melanie Klein's 'The Emotional Life and Ego-Development of the Infant with Special Reference to the Depressive Position' (1944). In 1942 several meetings explored different approaches to psychoanalytic technique (King and Steiner, 1991). Winnicott was to take an increasingly differentiated position from his former Kleinian colleagues on all these subjects. 'Primitive Emotional Development' marked his radical shift away from Kleinian thinking, although much of his later work can be read in part as an ongoing dialogue with her.

EDITORS' INTRODUCTION

This paper is a major elaboration of Winnicott's own account of early development, and the first serious challenge to Klein. Khan discusses it as the further development of an argument already present in 'The Manic Defence', a paper given in 1935 but unpublished until 1958 (Khan, 1987: xiv). The position described there, outlining the relation of inner reality, outer reality, and fantasy, was already an implicit challenge to the ways of conceptualizing the person then current in British psychoanalysis, because the comparison made is that between external reality and inner reality, not between external reality and fantasy, which is regarded as only a *part* of the individual's efforts to deal with inner reality. A 1957 footnote further emphasizes the distinction between psychic reality and inner reality, and in claiming that the former has no specific location Khan (1987: xiv) points to an implicit interest in the notion of transitional space, introduced in 'Transitional Objects and Transitional Phenomena' (Chapter 5, this volume) and developed in *Playing and Reality*. Both this footnote and Khan's commentary anticipate Winnicott's gathering together of his thoughts in 'The Location of Cultural Experience' (1967a). Fantasy *precedes* reality in his model; it is not created to deal with life's frustration (Isaacs, 1952) but with its separateness. Davis (1987) describes the delivery of this paper to the BPAS as the most significant event for the Society of the immediate postwar period, a position endorsed by Ogden (2001). Its content was influenced by Balint's paper on 'Early Developmental States of the Ego: Primary Object Love' (1939). Winnicott, like Balint, treats mother and baby in some respects as a psychic unit, but he emphasizes its paradoxical nature. Merell Middlemore's 1941 book *The Nursing Couple*, which he had reviewed in 1942, is somewhat similar in inspiration and outlook. She emphasized the womb-like 'emotional environment' in which the earliest psychological development of the infant takes place, and the importance of this shared 'internal environment' became increasingly central.

Winnicott addresses the beginnings of inner reality through processes of integration, personalization, and realization, and asks what constitutes the foundations of the primary relation to external reality. He proposes that successful early emotional development depends upon the negotiation of the overlap of two experiences of being alive, that of the mother, and that of the baby. For the baby those two worlds are initially one, and the mother's role first enables such an illusion, and then handles the inevitable process of disillusion in the course of her provision of ordinary care. In 'Primitive Emotional Development' the place where the infant's experience of its earliest relations with external reality comes together is not a place, in the sense of a location, but an experience, the act of feeling something, a sense of coming together from an experience of living in bits and pieces (unintegration). It is the mother's experience that provides the continuity of being necessary to enable the baby to become part of an experience lived together. To experience something with another demands, and is the condition of, a separate mother and baby. The early emotional development that Winnicott is here concerned with occurs before the baby knows himself as a whole person (and therefore others as whole people), and 'illusion' is central to how this is achieved. Failures in this arena are the clues to the psychopathology of psychosis. The move from primary unintegration to integration, and delay or failure in this process, predispose to later disintegration as a regressive return. Winnicott proposes that the personality is gathered together internally (integration) through the interaction of two different arenas: by ordinary infant care (externally), and by instinctual experiences (internally). Adaptation to reality assumes integration, but to be aware of reality first involves the individual's relation to objects in the self-created world of fantasy dependent on illusion. Only then can an ongoing exchange between fantasy and reality be appreciated and enjoyed accompanied by an awareness of external reality. The world, its joys and its frustrations, have to be brought to the baby in understandable form; this is the task of ordinary mothering. Winnicott emphasizes that the acceptance of reality brings advantages: subjective reality alone is too much, because there can be no limits to fantasy or to the consequences of love and hate. Such an internal constellation produces transference difficulties, failures in the capacity to be enriched by fantasy, and terror at the unlimited magical power of those fantasies.

The word 'illusion' is usually linked with delusion and the misapprehension of the external world, as in Freud's paper, 'The Future of an Illusion' (1927), but Winnicott has something quite different in mind. A positive account of illusion is central to his account, and such an account depends upon his positing of a state of primitive ruthlessness in the baby, who initially pursues his desires untrammelled by concern for the mother. 'Illusion' describes an infant's experience of the earliest relations with external reality, through the mother's and baby's living an experience together. But this experience cannot happen for the baby from the beginning, since the mother is the environment and a separate self does not exist. The process of illusion, in its Winnicottian usage, hypothesizes an excited baby who desires a breast entertaining the fantasy that when it is there he has produced it himself. The mother's consistent presentation of the breast as the baby begins to require it enables the repetition to create an expectation of a next time, and the hallucination, enriched by the actual details of smell, touch, and feel, builds up a capacity to conjure imaginatively what is there. The mother first provides the illusion that the baby has created what he seeks, and then, in necessarily disillusioning the baby gradually, enables a growing recognition of the external world, and of the mother and the baby himself as parts of it.

Referring to Winnicott's account here, Flarsheim says (1978: 508), 'Illusion in this sense is necessary for emotionally meaningful contact with the outside world and therefore becomes a precondition for ego development, integration and maturation'. The concept of illusion becomes fundamental for psychoanalytic theory and practice. The baby's illusion and the mother's fostering of it constitute the condition for the differentiation of subject and object, and the child's awareness of me and non-me, and of internal and external worlds. Ogden (2001: 301) claims that through this emphasis, Winnicott alters the foundations of human psychology and transforms psychoanalysis, as theory and as therapeutic practice, into the facilitation of the patient's being alive.

In his preamble Winnicott discusses analysis with reference to the differing expectations of different kinds of patient towards the analyst. Patients entertain fantasies about their analysts from the basis of their own psychic organization. An analysis may be conducted on the basis of a patient's whole relations and fantasies about other whole persons, but analytic work has become increasingly concerned with the analysis of the patient's fantasies of his/her own inner organization. This involves the analyst in very different countertransference phenomena, for instance, the patient's expectation of the analyst as a depressed mother he or she has to attend to, or the analyst as doing analytic work to repair his (the analyst's) own depression. For those patients seeking help for problems dating from early emotional development, the simultaneity of love and hate in the analyst, and its embodiment in the actual conditions of the setting, will be important.

The paper contains another of Winnicott's continuing references to what the analysis of psychotic patients reveals of infant states. 'Primarily interested in the child patient, and the infant, I decided that I must study psychosis in analysis' (p. 58). In the transference, unintegration appears as what was once natural in early development, which leads him to claim that the depersonalization phenomena of psychosis have infantile origins. Winnicott is familiar with disintegration as a common psychiatric diagnosis, but here he is concerned with the attempt to understand it as a return to a state (unintegration) initially experienced inadequately, so that any reappearance of it implies dread and unthinkable anxiety. Edward Glover's 1943 paper, 'On the Early Development of Mind' introduced the idea of healthy psychic development in the infant as the progressive agglomeration of 'ego nuclei' and their ultimate integration into an intact ego; conversely, psychic ill-health consisted in the non-integration or 'dissociation' of such structures. The brief section on dissociation, derived from Glover (1943), sees its origins in a primary unintegration, and offers some evocative thoughts about what can and cannot be taken for granted in the infant's reaching an awareness of self and other, and its related implications for patient and analyst.

Primitive Emotional Development[1]
(1945)

It will be clear at once from my title that I have chosen a very wide subject. All I can attempt to do is to make a preliminary personal statement, as if writing the introductory chapter to a book.

I shall not first give an historical survey and show the development of my ideas from the theories of others, because my mind does not work that way. What happens is that I gather this and that, here and there, settle down to clinical experience, form my own theories and then, last of all, interest myself in looking to see where I stole what. Perhaps this is as good a method as any.

About primitive emotional development there is a great deal that is not known or properly understood, at least by me, and it could well be argued that this discussion ought to be postponed five or ten years. Against this there is the fact that misunderstandings constantly recur in the Society's scientific meetings, and perhaps we shall find we do know enough already to prevent some of these misunderstandings by a discussion of these primitive emotional states.

Primarily interested in the child patient, and the infant, I decided that I must study psychosis in analysis. I have had about a dozen psychotic adult patients, and half of these have been rather extensively analysed. This happened in the war, and I might say that I hardly noticed the blitz, being all the time engaged in analysis of psychotic patients who are notoriously and maddeningly oblivious of bombs, earthquakes, and floods.

As a result of this work I have a great deal to communicate and to bring into alignment with current theories, and perhaps this paper may be taken as a beginning.

By listening to what I have to say, and criticizing, you help me to take my next step, which is the study of the sources of my ideas, both in clinical work and in the published writings of analysts. It has in fact been extremely difficult to keep clinical material out of this paper, which I wished nevertheless to keep short so that there might be plenty of time for discussion.

★   ★   ★

First I must prepare the way. Let me try to describe different types of psycho-analysis. It is possible to do the analysis of a suitable patient taking into account almost exclusively that person's personal relation to people, along with the conscious and unconscious fantasies that enrich and complicate these relationships between whole persons. This is the original type of psycho-analysis. In the last two decades we have been shown how to develop our interest in fantasy, and how the patient's own fantasy about his inner organization and its origin in instinctual experience is important as such.[2] We have been shown further that in certain cases it is this, the patient's fantasy about his inner organization, that is vitally important, so that the analysis of depression and the defences against depression cannot be done on the basis only of consideration of the patient's relations to real people and his fantasies about them. This new emphasis on the patient's fantasy of himself opened up the wide field of analysis of hypochondria in which the patient's fantasy about his inner world includes the fantasy that this is localized inside his own body. It became possible for us to relate, in analysis, the qualitative changes in the individual's inner world to his instinctual experiences. The quality of these instinctual experiences accounted for the good and bad nature of what is inside, as well as for its existence.

This work was a natural progression in psycho-analysis; it involved new understanding but not new technique. It quickly led to the study and analysis of still more primitive relationships, and it is these that I wish to discuss in this paper. The existence of these more primitive types of object relationship has never been in doubt.

I have said that no modification in Freud's technique was needed for the extension of analysis to cope with depression and hypochondria. It is also true, according to my experience, that the same technique can take us to still more primitive elements, provided of course that we take into consideration the changes in the transference situation inherent in such work.

I mean by this that a patient needing analysis of ambivalence in external relationships has a fantasy of his analyst and the analyst's work that is different from that of one who is depressed. In the former case the analyst's work is thought of as done out of love for the patient, hate being deflected on to hateful things. The depressed patient requires of his analyst the understanding that the analyst's work is to some extent his effort to cope with his own (the analyst's) depression, or shall I say guilt and grief resultant from the destructive elements in his own (the analyst's) love. To progress further along these lines, the patient who is asking for help in regard to his primitive, pre-depressive relationship to objects needs his analyst to be able to see the analyst's un-displaced and co-incident love and hate of him. In such cases the end of the hour, the end of the analysis, the rules and regulations, these all come in as important expressions of hate, just as the good interpretations are expressions of love, and symbolical of good food and care. This theme could be developed extensively and usefully.

★   ★   ★

Before embarking directly on a description of primitive emotional development I should also like to make it clear that the analysis of these primitive relationships cannot be undertaken except as an extension of the analysis of depression. It is certain that these primitive types of relationship, so far as they appear in children and adults, may come as a flight from the difficulties arising out of the next stages, after the classical conception of regression. It is right for a student analyst to learn first to cope with ambivalence in external relationships and with simple repression and then to progress to the analysis of the patient's fantasy about the inside and outside of his personality, and the whole range of his defences against depression, including the origins of the persecutory elements. These latter things the analyst can surely find in any analysis, but it would be useless or harmful for him to cope with principally depressive relationships unless he was fully prepared to analyse straightforward ambivalence. It is likewise true that it is useless and even dangerous to analyse the primitive pre-depressive relationships, and to interpret them as they appear in the transference, unless the analyst is fully prepared to cope with the depressive position, the defences against depression, and the persecutory ideas which appear for interpretation as the patient progresses.

★   ★   ★

I have more preparatory remarks to make. It has often been noted that, at five to six months, a change occurs in infants which makes it more easy than before for us to refer to their emotional development in the terms that apply to human beings generally. Anna Freud makes rather a special point of this and implies that in her view the tiny infant is concerned more with certain care-aspects than with specific people. Bowlby recently expressed the view that infants before six months are not particular, so that separation from their mother does not affect them in the same way as it does after six months. I myself have previously stated that infants reach something at six months, so that whereas many infants of five months grasp an object and put it to the mouth, it is not till six months that the average infant starts to follow this up by deliberately dropping the object as part of his play with it.

In specifying five to six months we need not try to be too accurate. If a baby of three or even two months or even less should reach the stage of development that it is convenient in general description to place at five months, no harm will be done.

In my opinion the stage we are describing, and I think one may accept this description, is a very important one. To some extent it is an affair of physical development, for the infant at five months becomes skilled to the extent that he grasps an object he sees, and can soon get it to his mouth. He could not have done this earlier. (Of course he may have wanted to. There is no exact parallel between skill and wish, and we know that many physical advances, such as the ability to walk, are often held up till emotional development releases physical attainment. Whatever the physical side of the matter, there is also the emotional.) We can say that at this stage a baby becomes able in his play to show that he can understand he has an inside, and that things come from outside. He shows he knows that he is enriched by what he incorporates (physically and psychically). Further, he shows that he knows he can get rid of something when he has got from it what he wants from it. All this represents a tremendous advance. It is at first only reached from time to time, and every detail of this advance can be lost as a regression because of anxiety.

The corollary of this is that now the infant assumes that his mother also has an inside, one which may be rich or poor, good or bad, ordered or muddled. He is therefore starting to be concerned with the mother and her sanity and her moods. In the case of many infants there is a relationship as between whole persons at six months. Now, when a human being feels he is a person related to people, he has already travelled a long way in primitive development.

Our task is to examine what goes on in the infant's feelings and personality before this stage which we recognize at five to six months, but which may be reached later or earlier.

There is also this question: how early do important things happen? For instance, does the unborn child have to be considered? And if so, at what age after conception does psychology come in? I would answer that if there is an important stage at five to six months there is also an important stage round about birth. My reason for saying this is the great differences that can be noticed if the baby is premature or post-mature. I suggest that at the end of nine months' gestation an infant becomes ripe for emotional development, and that if an infant is post-mature he has reached this stage in the womb, and one is therefore forced to consider his feelings before and during birth. On the other hand a premature infant is not experiencing much that is vital till he has reached the age at which he should have been born, that is to say some weeks after birth. At any rate this forms a basis for discussion.

Another question is: psychologically speaking, does anything *matter* before five to six months? I know that the view is quite sincerely held in some quarters that the answer is 'No'. This view must be given its due, but it is not mine.

The main object of this paper is to present the thesis that the early emotional development of the infant, before the infant knows himself (and therefore others) as the whole person that he is (and that they are), is vitally important: indeed that here are the clues to the psychopathology of psychosis.

EARLY DEVELOPMENTAL PROCESSES

There are three processes which seem to me to start very early: (1) integration, (2) personalization, and (3), following these, the appreciation of time and space and other properties of reality – in short, realization.

A great deal that we tend to take for granted had a beginning and a condition out of which it developed. For instance, many analyses sail through to completion without time being ever in dispute. But a boy of nine who loved to play with Ann, aged two, was acutely interested in the expected new baby. He said: 'When the new baby's born will he be born before Ann?' For him time-sense is very shaky. Again, a psychotic patient could not adopt any routine because if she did she had no idea on a Tuesday whether it was last week, or this week, or next week.

The localization of self in one's own body is often assumed, yet a psychotic patient in analysis came to recognize that as a baby she thought her twin at the other end of the pram was herself. She even felt surprised when her twin was picked up and yet she remained where she was. Her sense of self and other-than-self was undeveloped.

Another psychotic patient discovered in analysis that most of the time she lived in her head, behind her eyes. She could only see out of her eyes as out of windows and so was not aware of what her feet were doing, and in consequence she tended to fall into pits and to trip over things. She had no 'eyes in her feet'. Her personality was not felt to be localized in her body, which was like a complex engine that she had to drive with conscious care and skill. Another patient, at times, lived in a box 20 yards up, only connected with her body by a slender thread. In our practices examples of these failures in primitive development occur daily, and by them we may be reminded of the importance of such processes as integration, personalization, and realization.

It may be assumed that at the theoretical start the personality is unintegrated, and that in regressive disintegration there is a primary state to which regression leads. We postulate a primary unintegration.

Disintegration of personality is a well-known psychiatric condition, and its psychopathology is highly complex. Examination of these phenomena in analysis, however, shows that the primary unintegrated state provides a basis for disintegration, and that delay or failure in respect of primary integration predisposes to disintegration as a regression, or as a result of failure in other types of defence.

Integration starts right away at the beginning of life, but in our work we can never take it for granted. We have to account for it and watch its fluctuations.

An example of unintegration phenomena is provided by the very common experience of the patient who proceeds to give every detail of the week-end and feels contented at the end if everything has been said, though the analyst feels that no analytic work has been done. Sometimes we must interpret this as the patient's need to be known in all his bits and pieces by one person, the analyst. To be known means to feel integrated at least in the person of the analyst. This is the ordinary stuff of infant life, and an infant who has had no one person to gather his bits together starts with a handicap in his own self-integrating task, and perhaps he cannot succeed, or at any rate cannot maintain integration with confidence

The tendency to integrate is helped by two sets of experience: the technique of infant care whereby an infant is kept warm, handled and bathed and rocked and named, and also the acute instinctual experiences which tend to gather the personality together from within. Many infants are well on the way toward integration during certain periods of the first twenty-four hours of life. In others the process is delayed, or setbacks occur, because of early inhibition of greedy attack. There are long stretches of time in a normal infant's life in which a baby does not mind whether he is many bits or one whole being, or whether he lives in his mother's face or in his own body, provided that from time to time he comes together and feels something. Later I will try to explain why disintegration is frightening, whereas unintegration is not.

In regard to environment, bits of nursing technique and faces seen and sounds heard and smells smelt are only gradually pieced together into one being to be called mother. In the transference situation in analysis of psychotics we get the clearest proof that the psychotic state of unintegration had a natural place at a primitive stage of the emotional development of the individual.

It is sometimes assumed that in health the individual is always integrated, as well as living in his own body, and able to feel that the world is real. There is, however, much sanity that has a symptomatic quality, being charged with fear or denial of madness, fear or denial of the innate capacity of every human being to become unintegrated, depersonalized, and to feel that the world is unreal. Sufficient lack of sleep produces these conditions in anyone.[3]

Equally important with integration is the development of the feeling that one's person is in one's body. Again it is instinctual experience and the repeated quiet experiences of body-care that gradually build up what may be called satisfactory personalization. And as with disintegration so also the depersonalization phenomena of psychosis relate to early personalization delays.

Depersonalization is a common thing in adults and in children, it is often hidden for instance in what is called deep sleep and in prostration attacks with corpse-like pallor: 'She's miles away', people say, and they are right.

A problem related to that of personalization is that of the imaginary companions of childhood. These are not simple fantasy constructions. Study of the future of these imaginary companions (in analysis) shows that they are sometimes other selves of a highly primitive type. I cannot here formulate a clear statement of what I mean, and it would be out of place for me to explain this detail at length now. I would say, however, that this very primitive and magical creation of imaginary companions is easily used as a defence, as it magically by-passes all the anxieties associated with incorporation, digestion, retention, and expulsion.

DISSOCIATION

Out of the problem of unintegration comes another, that of dissociation. Dissociation can usefully be studied in its initial or natural forms. According to my view there grows out of unintegration a series of what are then called dissociations, which arise owing to integration being incomplete or partial. For example, there are the quiet and the excited states. I think an infant cannot be said to be aware at the start that while feeling this and that in his cot or enjoying the skin stimulations of bathing, he is the same as himself screaming for immediate satisfaction, possessed by an urge to get at and destroy something unless satisfied by milk. This means that he does not know at first that the mother he is building up through his quiet experiences is the same as the power behind the breasts that he has in his mind to destroy.

Also I think there is not necessarily an integration between a child asleep and a child awake. This integration comes in the course of time. Once dreams are remembered and even conveyed somehow to a third person, the dissociation is broken down a little; but some people never clearly remember their dreams, and children depend very much on adults for getting to know their dreams. It is normal for small children to have anxiety dreams and terrors. At these times children need someone to help them to remember what they dreamed. It is a valuable experience whenever a dream is both dreamed *and* remembered, precisely because of the breakdown of dissociation that this represents. However complex such a dissociation may be in child or adult, the fact remains that it can start in the natural alternation of the sleeping and awake states, dating from birth.

In fact the waking life of an infant can be perhaps described as a gradually developing dissociation from the sleeping state.

Artistic creation gradually takes the place of dreams or supplements them, and is vitally important for the welfare of the individual and therefore for mankind.

Dissociation is an extremely widespread defence mechanism and leads to surprising results. For instance urban life is a dissociation, a serious one for civilization. Also war and peace. The extremes in mental illness are well known. In childhood dissociation appears for instance in such common conditions as somnambulism, incontinence of faeces, in some forms of squinting, etc. It is very easy to miss dissociation when assessing a personality.

REALITY ADAPTATION

Let us now assume integration. If we do, we reach another enormous subject, the primary relation to external reality. In ordinary analyses we can and do take for granted this step in emotional development, which is highly complex and which, when it is made, represents a big advance in emotional development, yet is never finally made and settled. Many cases that we consider unsuitable for analysis are unsuitable indeed if we cannot deal with the transference difficulties that belong to an essential lack of true relation to external reality. If we allow analysis of psychotics, we find that in some analyses this essential lack of true relation to external reality is almost the whole thing.

I will try to describe in the simplest possible terms this phenomenon as I see it. In terms of baby and mother's breast (I am not claiming that the breast is essential as a vehicle of mother-love) the baby has instinctual urges and predatory ideas. The mother has a breast and the power to produce milk, and the idea that she would like to be attacked by a hungry baby. These two phenomena do not come into relation with each other till the mother and child *live an experience together*. The mother being mature and physically able has to be the one with tolerance and understanding, so that it is she who produces a situation that may with luck result in the first tie the infant makes with an external object, an object that is external to the self from the infant's point of view.

I think of the process as if two lines came from opposite directions, liable to come near each other. If they overlap there is a moment of *illusion* – a bit of experience which the infant can take as *either* his hallucination *or* a thing belonging to external reality.

In other language, the infant comes to the breast when excited, and ready to hallucinate something fit to be attacked. At that moment the actual nipple appears and he is able to feel it was that nipple that he hallucinated. So his ideas are enriched by actual details of sight, feel, smell, and next time this material is used in the hallucination. In this way he starts to build up a capacity to conjure up what is actually available. The mother has to go on giving the infant this type of experience. The process is immensely simplified if the infant is cared for by one person and one technique. It seems as if an infant is really designed to be cared for from birth by his own mother, or failing that by an adopted mother, and not by several nurses.

It is especially at the start that mothers are vitally important, and indeed it is a mother's job to protect her infant from complications that cannot yet be understood by the infant, and to go on steadily providing the simplified bit of the world which the infant, through her, comes to know. Only on such a foundation can objectivity or a scientific attitude be built. All failure in objectivity at whatever date relates to failure in this stage of primitive emotional development. Only on a basis of monotony can a mother profitably add richness.

One thing that follows the acceptance of external reality is the advantage to be gained from it. We often hear of the very real frustrations imposed by external reality, but less often hear of the relief and satisfaction it affords. Real milk is satisfying as compared with imaginary milk, but this is not the point. The point is that in fantasy things work by magic: there are no brakes on fantasy, and love and hate cause alarming effects. External reality has brakes on it, and can be studied and known, and, in fact, fantasy is only tolerable at full blast when objective reality is appreciated well. The subjective has tremendous value but is so alarming and magical that it cannot be enjoyed except as a parallel to the objective.

It will be seen that fantasy is not something the individual creates to deal with external reality's frustrations. This is only true of fantasying. Fantasy is more primary than reality, and the enrichment of fantasy with the world's riches depends on the experience of illusion.

It is interesting to examine the individual's relation to the objects in the self-created world of fantasy. In fact there are all grades of development and sophistication in this self-created world according to the amount of illusion that has been experienced, and so according to how much the self-created world has been unable or able to use perceived external world objects as material. This obviously needs a much more lengthy statement in another setting.

In the most primitive state, which may be retained in illness, and to which regression may occur, the object behaves according to magical laws, i.e. it exists when desired, it approaches when approached, it hurts when hurt. Lastly it vanishes when not wanted.

This last is most terrifying and is the only true annihilation. To not want, as a result of satisfaction, is to annihilate the object. This is one reason why infants are not always happy and contented after a satisfactory feed. One patient of mine carried this fear right on to adult life and only grew up from it in analysis, a man who had had an extremely good early experience with his mother and in his home.[4] His chief fear was of satisfaction.

I realize that this is only the bare outline of the vast problem of the initial steps in the development of a relation to external reality, and the relation of fantasy to reality. Soon we must add ideas of incorporation. But at the start a simple *contact* with external or shared reality has to be made, by the infant's hallucinating and the world's presenting, with moments of illusion for the infant in which the two are taken by him to be identical, which they never in fact are.

For this illusion to be produced in the baby's mind a human being has to be taking the trouble all the time to bring the world to the baby in understandable form, and in a limited way, suitable to the baby's needs. For this reason a baby cannot exist alone, psychologically or physically, and really needs one person to care for him at first.

The subject of illusion is a very wide one that needs study; it will be found to provide the clue to a child's interest in bubbles and clouds and rainbows and all mysterious phenomena, and also to his interest in fluff, which is most difficult to explain in terms of instinct direct. Somewhere here, too, is the interest in breath, which never decides whether it comes primarily from within or without, and which provides a basis for the conception of spirit, soul, anima.

PRIMITIVE RUTHLESSNESS (STAGE OF PRE-CONCERN)

We are now in a position to look at the earliest kind of relationship between a baby and his mother.

If one assumes that the individual is becoming integrated and personalized and has made a good start in his realization, there is still a long way for him to go before he is related as a whole person to a whole mother, and concerned about the effect of his own thoughts and actions on her.

We have to postulate an early ruthless object relationship. This may again be a theoretical phase only, and certainly no one can be ruthless after the concern stage except in a dissociated state. But ruthless dissociation states are common in early childhood, and emerge in certain types of delinquency, and madness, and must be available in health. The normal child enjoys a ruthless relation to his mother, mostly showing in play, and he needs his mother because only she can be expected to tolerate his ruthless relation to her even in play, because this really hurts her and wears her out. Without this play with her he can only hide a ruthless self and give it life in a state of dissociation.[5]

I can bring in here the great fear of disintegration as opposed to the simple acceptance of primary unintegration. Once the individual has reached the stage of concern he cannot be oblivious to the result of his impulses, or to the action of bits of self such as biting mouth, stabbing eyes, piercing yells, sucking throat, etc., etc. Disintegration means abandonment to impulses, uncontrolled because acting on their own; and, further, this conjures up the idea of similarly uncontrolled (because dissociated) impulses directed towards himself.[6]

PRIMITIVE RETALIATION

To go back half a stage: it is usual, I think, to postulate a still more primitive object relationship in which the object acts in a retaliatory way. This is prior to a true relation to external reality. In this case the object, or the environment, is as much part of the self as the instinct is which conjures it up.[7] In introversion of early origin and therefore of primitive quality the individual lives in this environment which is himself, and a very poor life it is. There is no growth because there is no enrichment from external reality.

★　★　★

To illustrate the application of these ideas I add a note on thumb-sucking (including fist- and finger-sucking). This can be observed from birth onwards, and therefore can be presumed to have a meaning which develops from the primitive to sophistication, and it is important both as a normal activity and as a symptom of emotional disturbance.

We are familiar with the aspect of thumb-sucking covered by the term auto-erotic. The mouth is an erotogenic zone, specially organized in infancy, and the thumb-sucking child enjoys pleasure. He also has pleasurable ideas.

Hate is also expressed when the child damages his fingers by too vigorous or continuous sucking, and in any case he soon adds nail-biting to cope with this part of his feelings. He is also liable to damage his mouth. But it is not certain that all the damage that may be done to a finger or mouth in this way is part of hate. It seems that there is in it the element that something must suffer if the infant is to have pleasure: the object of primitive love suffers by being loved, apart from being hated.

We can see in finger-sucking, and in nail-biting especially, a turning-in of love and hate, for reasons such as the need to preserve the external object of interest. Also we see a turning-in to self, in face of frustration in love of an external object.

The subject is not exhausted by this kind of statement and deserves further study.

I suppose anyone would agree that thumb-sucking is done for consolation, not just pleasure; the fist or finger is there instead of the breast or mother, or someone. For instance, a baby of about four months reacted to the loss of his mother by a tendency to put his fist right down his throat, so that he would have died had he not been physically prevented from acting this way.

Whereas thumb-sucking is normal and universal, spreading out into the use of the dummy, and indeed to various activities of normal adults, it is also true that thumb-sucking persists in schizoid personalities, and in such cases is extremely compulsive. In one patient of mine it changed at 10 years into a compulsion to be always reading.

These phenomena cannot be explained except on the basis that the act is an attempt to localize the object (breast, etc.), to hold it half-way between in and out. This is either a defence against loss of object in the external world or in the inside of the body, that is to say, against loss of control over the object.

I have no doubt that normal thumb-sucking has this function too.

The auto-erotic element is not always clearly of paramount importance and certainly the use of dummy and fist soon becomes a clear defence against insecurity feelings and other anxieties of a primitive kind.

Finally, every fist-sucking provides a useful dramatization of the primitive object relationship in which the object is as much the individual as is the desire for an object, because it is created out of the desire, or is hallucinated, and at the beginning is independent of co-operation from external reality.

Some babies put a finger in the mouth while sucking the breast, thus (in a way) holding on to self-created reality while using external reality.

SUMMARY

An attempt has been made to formulate the primitive emotional processes which are normal in early infancy, and which appear regressively in the psychoses.

Notes

1. Read before the British Psycho-Analytical Society, 28 November 1945. *International Journal of Psychoanalysis* 26 (1945).
2. Chiefly through the work of Melanie Klein.
3. Through artistic expression we can hope to keep in touch with our primitive selves whence the most intense feelings and even fearfully acute sensations derive, and we are poor indeed if we are only sane.
4. I will just mention another reason why an infant is not satisfied with satisfaction. He feels fobbed off. He intended, one might say, to make a cannibalistic attack and he has been put off by an opiate, the feed. At best he can postpone the attack.
5. There is in mythology a ruthless figure – Lilith – whose origin could be usefully studied.
6. Crocodiles not only shed tears when they do not feel sad – pre-concern tears; they also readily stand for the ruthless primitive self.
7. This is important because of our relationship to Jung's analytical psychology. We try to reduce everything to instinct, and the analytical psychologists reduce everything to this part of the primitive self which looks like environment but which arises out of instinct (archetypes). We ought to modify our view to embrace both ideas, and to see (if it is

true) that in the earliest theoretical primitive state the self has its own environment, self-created, which is as much the self as the instincts that produce it. This is a theme which requires development.

> **Developing ideas:** primary unintegration, integration, disintegration, personalization; realization; primary creativity; illusion; illusion of omnipotence; impingement; precocious ego development, compliance and the care-taker self; 'no such thing as a baby'; annihilation anxiety; primitive ruthlessness (stage of pre-concern); poor if only sane

3 HATE IN THE COUNTERTRANSFERENCE (1947/1949)

OTHER WRITINGS

The early postwar years saw Winnicott continuing to publish in both main-stream psychoanalytic journals and for a wider readership, and continuing his broadcasts on the BBC. His writings demonstrate the influence of his wartime experience, and this, together with his work with borderline patients and psychotics as 'research cases', encouraged a renewed interest in counter-transference phenomena. Michael and Alice Balint had published their paper 'On Transference and Counter-Transference' in the *IJPA* in 1939. It addressed the subject of the analyst's affective response and introduced the idea that countertransference was as often as not pathological but useful. Winnicott's paper followed and later others in the Independent tradition, notably Pearl King's 1978 paper 'Affective Responses of the Analyst to the Patient's Communication' (*IJPA*). Joseph Sandler, in the Contemporary Freudian tradition, published 'Countertransference and Role Responsiveness' in 1975 (*International Review of Psycho-Analysis*). These are increasingly differentiated from the tendency to use the concept of projective identification as the explanation for countertransference phenomena.

Several leading Kleinians published papers on their work with psychotic patients, following Klein's 'Notes on Some Schizoid Mechanisms' (1946): Herbert Rosenfeld (1947, 1950, 1954), and his books *Psychotic States* (1965) and *Impasse and Interpretation* (1987); Hanna Segal (1950, 1956); Wilfred Bion – several papers, later published together in *Second Thoughts* (1967). In the Contemporary Freudian tradition Thomas Freeman is best known for his work with psychotics (1962a, 1962b, 1965, 1973, 1988). In the USA many psychoanalysts including Harold Searles worked at Chestnut Lodge near Washington DC where treatment of psychotic patients was carried out within the tradition of classical psychoanalysis but incorporating ideas from Harry Stack Sullivan which stressed the contribution of early trauma in the psychogenesis of severe psychosis. Harold Searles's *Collected Papers on Schizophrenia and Related Subjects* (1963) was largely based on his work there. Despite much work with these 'research' cases there is now wide-spread recognition that understanding psychosis cannot be confined to a

EDITORS' INTRODUCTION

This paper was first given at a scientific meeting of the BPAS in February 1947 and published in the *IJPA* in 1949, but it does not seem to have occasioned much debate at the time. Although Ferenczi and the Hungarian school more generally had been concerned with the analyst's emotional responses to the patient from the 1920s onward (Ferenczi, 1933; Balint and Balint, 1939), a wider concern with countertransference phenomena only developed after Paula Heimann's paper, 'On Counter-Transference', was given at the congress of the IPA in 1949 (published 1950). At that time the analyst's countertransference, following Freud's remarks in the papers on technique (1910, 1915), was still primarily regarded as an impediment to the analytic work, an expression of insufficiently analyzed aspects of the analyst. From 1949 on, countertransference was referred to in a rather different way (Little, 1951; Reich, 1951), and Winnicott's paper may be regarded as anticipating this interest. Like the work of Ferenczi and his colleagues, Winnicott's approach grows out of the difficulties of work with psychotic patients, and this paper's significance lies in his conceptualization of the countertransference as a useful tool in understanding the patient, a shift usually associated with Paula Heimann (1950) and Heinrich Racker (1953).

The paper is specifically focused on work with patients for whom analysis was not originally intended, for whom, unlike neurotics, an integrated psychic structure, and therefore a good-enough early environment, could not be taken for granted. There was growing interest in these 'research cases', and the particular difficulties they raised in the treatment setting. These patients evoke a transference situation that may require something different from the psychoanalysis of neurotic patients, something Winnicott calls 'management'. His view that psychotic disturbance arises from 'environmental failure' in early development remains a consistent aspect of his theory, derived from his medical and psychoanalytic practice. The paper also reflects his experience as a psychiatrist consulting to hostels for disturbed evacuated children during the war, and he draws on one example of a child who came to live with the Winnicotts after the war. Psychotics and antisocial patients arouse intense affects, particularly hatred, in those who treat them, and classical psychoanalytic technique is confronted with a severe challenge in meeting these patients' different needs. It includes the task faced by the analyst in dealing with the intensity of negative feeling aroused by and originating in the patient. This theme of the different tasks and demands made upon the analyst by patients with different kinds of psychopathology recurs throughout Winnicott's work.

It is of particular interest that the psychotic patient's 'coincident love–hate state' is likely to produce the conviction that the analyst too, lives in such a state, and that any demonstration of love or concern will therefore be followed by hate and murder.

The analyst's task in maintaining his or her 'objectivity' concerns the attempt to understand the experience of the full force of the affect aroused by the patient. These concepts attempt to capture phenomena that are not 'real' or 'objective,' but phantasy elements that derive from the unconscious (Etchegoyen, 1990), and whose elucidation is central to the analytic process. The analyst's capacity not to be swayed by the intensity of his or her own affective responses, and to effect a split in the ego that enables internal work to bear, and to continue to think about the experience is the condition of further analytic work. Describing the challenge to the analyst to maintain an analytic attitude and not to retaliate in the face of intense provocation when treating severely disturbed patients, Winnicott likens it to the mother's task in tolerating her hatred for her baby without expressing it, 'without paying the child out'. The American psychoanalyst and psychiatrist Harold Searles contributed substantially to work in this area, and, without referencing this paper, he writes cogently of the predicament of the young therapist working with schizophrenic patients: 'A feeling of scorn on his part toward such behaviour is a humanly necessary self-protection against the inferiority feelings and the sense of chronic, impotent rage which patients, during this phase of the therapy, tend to kindle in one' (1962). He also warns of the attendant risk of 'adoration' or mutual idealization of therapist and patient to defend against the intensity of the scorn.

A central issue in the paper is the integration of love and hate in early development. In this further development of his theory of aggression, Winnicott insists on a stage before this integration when the infant cannot be said to have the intention to hurt, cannot be said to hate. It is only as the baby becomes integrated as a whole person that hate comes to have meaning. The analyst of neurotic patients can take these phenomena for granted, and hatred remains latent as a component of the countertransference. For the patient who has not had this good-enough beginning, the demand on the analyst may well be to be 'the first . . . to supply . . . [these] environmental essentials' (p. 77), and how this is to be done provides the challenge to classical technique and the aims of analytic treatment.

Winnicott's discussion of hatred in the infant leads him to consider hatred in the mother as a central aspect of her subjectivity for the infant, which she has first to allow and bear before the infant can come to recognize his or her own hate. The eighteen reasons a mother hates her baby may be shocking, but it is also a relief to have the everyday experience of motherhood acknowledged: mothering and psychoanalytic treatment have nothing to do with sentimentality. The mother has to face the full otherness of her baby while providing, for the baby, the experience of not knowing that so much is being provided. This has clinical significance for the psychotic and/or maximally dependent patient. The patient is not to know what the analyst has to bear until such time as he can know, and for some analysts, not even then. While Paula Heimann (1950) is clear that such a countertransference interpretation should never be made, Margaret Little (a patient of Winnicott's) maintains that letting the patient know what they have demanded of the analyst may be an aim (1951). Winnicott himself made it contingent on whether the patient has enough primary good experience to be used analytically. Although babies, or psychotic or antisocial persons, need the 'other' (mother/analyst) to know of their hatred before they themselves can risk hating, or knowing about it, this is different technically from actually telling them (Klauber, 1986).

In a later paper, 'Countertransference', Winnicott again considers the kinds of patients who exert pressure 'to completely alter the therapist's attitude' (Winnicott, 1960b: 162). There, he is more circumspect about whether psychoanalysis can treat these patients: 'They are better dealt with in other ways, though psychoanalysis can sometimes be usefully added' (1960b: 163).

Hate in the Countertransference[1]
(1947)

In this paper I wish to examine one aspect of the whole subject of ambivalence, namely, hate in the countertransference. I believe that the task of the analyst (call him a research analyst) who undertakes the analysis of a psychotic is seriously weighted by this phenomenon, and that analysis of psychotics becomes impossible unless the analyst's own hate is extremely well sorted-out and conscious. This is tantamount to saying that an analyst needs to be himself analysed, but it also asserts that the analysis of a psychotic is irksome as compared with that of a neurotic, and inherently so.

Apart from psycho-analytic treatment, the management of a psychotic is bound to be irksome. From time to time I have made acutely critical remarks about the modern trends in psychiatry, with the too easy electric shocks and the too drastic leucotomies. (Winnicott, 1947, 1949[a].) Because of these criticisms that I have expressed I would like to be foremost in recognition of the extreme difficulty inherent in the task of the psychiatrist, and of the mental nurse in particular. Insane patients must always be a heavy emotional burden on those who care for them. One can forgive those engaged in this work if they do awful things. This does not mean, however, that we have to accept whatever is done by psychiatrists and neuro-surgeons as sound according to principles of science.

Therefore although what follows is about psycho-analysis, it really has value to the psychiatrist, even to one whose work does not in any way take him into the analytic type of relationship to patients.

To help the general psychiatrist the psycho-analyst must not only study for him the primitive stages of the emotional development of the ill individual, but also must study the nature of the emotional burden which the psychiatrist bears in doing his work. What we as analysts call the countertransference needs to be understood by the psychiatrist too. However much he loves his patients he cannot avoid hating them and fearing them, and the better he knows this the less will hate and fear be the motives determining what he does to his patients.

★ ★ ★

One could classify countertransference phenomena thus:

1. Abnormality in countertransference feelings, and set relationships and identifications that are under repression in the analyst. The comment on this is that the analyst needs more analysis, and we believe this is less of an issue among psycho-analysts than among psychotherapists in general.
2. The identifications and tendencies belonging to an analyst's personal experiences and personal development which provide the positive setting for his analytic work and make his work different in quality from that of any other analyst.
3. From these two I distinguish the truly objective countertransference, or if this is difficult, the analyst's love and hate in reaction to the actual personality and behaviour of the patient, based on objective observation.

I suggest that if an analyst is to analyse psychotics or antisocials he must be able to be so thoroughly aware of the countertransference that he can sort out and study his *objective* reactions to the patient. These will include hate. Counter-transference phenomena will at times be the important things in the analysis.

I wish to suggest that the patient can only appreciate in the analyst what he himself is capable of feeling. In the matter of motive: the *obsessional* will tend to be thinking of the analyst as doing his work in a futile obsessional way. A *hypo-manic* patient who is incapable of being depressed, except in a severe mood swing, and in whose emotional development the depressive position has not been securely won, who cannot feel guilt in a deep way, or a sense of concern or responsibility, is unable to see the analyst's work as an attempt on the part of the analyst to make reparation in respect of his own (the analyst's) guilt feelings. A *neurotic* patient tends to see the analyst as ambivalent towards the patient, and to expect the analyst to show a splitting of love and hate; this patient, when in luck, gets the love, because someone else is getting the analyst's hate. Would it not follow that if a *psychotic* is in a 'coincident love-hate' state of feeling he experiences a deep conviction that the analyst is also only capable of the same crude and dangerous state of coincident love-hate relationship? Should the analyst show love, he will surely at the same moment kill the patient.

This coincidence of love and hate is something that characteristically recurs in the analysis of psychotics, giving rise to problems of management which can easily take the analyst beyond his resources. This coincidence of love and hate to which I am referring is something distinct from the aggressive component complicating the primitive love impulse, and implies that in the history of the patient there was an environmental failure at the time of the first object-finding instinctual impulses.

If the analyst is going to have crude feelings imputed to him he is best forewarned and so forearmed, for he must tolerate being placed in that position. Above all he must not deny hate that really exists in himself. Hate *that is justified* in the present setting has to be sorted out and kept in storage and available for eventual interpretation.

If we are to become able to be the analysts of psychotic patients we must have reached down to very primitive things in ourselves, and this is but another example of the fact that the answer to many obscure problems of psycho-analytic practice lies in further analysis of the analyst. (Psycho-analytic research is perhaps always to some extent an attempt on the part of an analyst to carry the work of his own analysis further than the point to which his own analyst could get him.)

A main task of the analyst of any patient is to maintain objectivity in regard to all that the patient brings, and a special case of this is the analyst's need to be able to hate the patient objectively.

Are there not many situations in our ordinary analytic work in which the analyst's hate is justified? A patient of mine, a very bad obsessional, was almost loathsome to me for some years. I felt bad about this until the analysis turned a corner and the patient became lovable, and then I realized that his unlikeable-ness had been an active symptom, unconsciously determined. It was indeed a wonderful day for me (much later on) when I could actually tell the patient that I and his friends had felt repelled by him, but that he had been too ill for us to let him know. This was also an important day for him, a tremendous advance in his adjustment to reality.

In the ordinary analysis the analyst has no difficulty with the management of his own hate. This hate remains latent. The main thing, of course, is that through his own analysis he has become free from vast reservoirs of unconscious hate belonging to the past and to inner conflicts. There are other reasons why hate remains unexpressed and even unfelt as such:

> Analysis is my chosen job, the way I feel I will best deal with my own guilt, the way I can express myself in a constructive way.
> I get paid, or I am in training to gain a place in society by psychoanalytic work.
> I am discovering things.

I get immediate rewards through identification with the patient, who is
making progress, and I can see still greater rewards some way ahead,
after the end of the treatment.

Moreover, as an analyst I have ways of expressing hate. Hate is expressed by
the existence of the end of the 'hour'.

I think this is true even when there is no difficulty whatever, and when
the patient is pleased to go. In many analyses these things can be taken for
granted, so that they are scarcely mentioned, and the analytic work is done
through verbal interpretation of the patient's emerging unconscious transference. The analyst takes over the role of one or other of the helpful
figures of the patient's childhood. He cashes in on the success of those
who did the dirty work when the patient was an infant.

These things are part of the description of ordinary psycho-analytic work,
which is mostly concerned with patients whose symptoms have a neurotic
quality.

In the analysis of psychotics, however, quite a different type and degree of
strain is taken by the analyst, and it is precisely this different strain that I am
trying to describe.

Recently for a period of a few days I found I was doing bad work. I made
mistakes in respect of each one of my patients. The difficulty was in myself and
it was partly personal but chiefly associated with a climax that I had reached in
my relation to one particular psychotic (research) patient. The difficulty
cleared up when I had what is sometimes called a 'healing' dream. (Incidentally
I would add that during my analysis and in the years since the end of my
analysis I have had a long series of these healing dreams which, although in
many cases unpleasant, have each one of them marked my arrival at a new stage
in emotional development.)

On this particular occasion I was aware of the meaning of the dream as I
woke or even before I woke. The dream had two phases. In the first I was in
the 'gods' in a theatre and looking down on the people a long way below
in the stalls. I felt severe anxiety as if I might lose a limb. This was associated
with the feeling I have had at the top of the Eiffel Tower that if I put my hand
over the edge it would fall off on to the ground below. This would be ordinary
castration anxiety.

In the next phase of the dream I was aware that the people in the stalls were
watching a play and I was now related through them to what was going on the
stage. A new kind of anxiety now developed. What I knew was that I had no
right side of my body at all. This was not a castration dream. It was a sense of
not having that part of the body.

As I woke I was aware of having understood at a very deep level what was
my difficulty at that particular time. The first part of the dream represented the
ordinary anxieties that might develop in respect of unconscious fantasies of my

neurotic patients. I would be in danger of losing my hand or my fingers if these patients should become interested in them. With this kind of anxiety I was familiar, and it was comparatively tolerable.

The second part of the dream, however, referred to my relation to the psychotic patient. This patient was requiring of me that I should have no relation to her body at all, not even an imaginative one; there was no body that she recognized as hers and if she existed at all she could only feel herself to be a mind. Any reference to her body produced paranoid anxieties, because to claim that she had a body was to persecute her. What she needed of me was that I should have only a mind speaking to her mind. At the culmination of my difficulties on the evening before the dream I had become irritated and had said that what she was needing of me was little better than hair-splitting. This had had a disastrous effect and it took many weeks for the analysis to recover from my lapse. The essential thing, however, was that I should understand my own anxiety and this was represented in the dream by the absence of the right side of my body when I tried to get into relation to the play that the people in the stalls were watching. This right side of my body was the side related to this particular patient and was therefore affected by her need to deny absolutely even an imaginative relationship of our bodies. This denial was producing in me this psychotic type of anxiety, much less tolerable than ordinary castration anxiety. Whatever other interpretations might be made in respect of this dream the result of my having dreamed it and remembered it was that I was able to take up this analysis again and even to heal the harm done to it by my irritability which had its origin in a reactive anxiety of a quality that was appropriate to my contact with a patient with no body.

The analyst must be prepared to bear strain without expecting the patient to know anything about what he is doing, perhaps over a long period of time. To do this he must be easily aware of his own fear and hate. He is in the position of the mother of an infant unborn or newly born. Eventually, he ought to be able to tell his patient what he has been through on the patient's behalf, but an analysis may never get as far as this. There may be too little good experience in the patient's past to work on. What if there be no satisfactory relationship of early infancy for the analyst to exploit in the transference?

There is a vast difference between those patients who have had satisfactory early experiences which can be discovered in the transference, and those whose very early experiences have been so deficient or distorted that the analyst has to be the first in the patient's life to supply certain environmental essentials. In the treatment of a patient of the latter kind all sorts of things in analytic technique become vitally important, things that can be taken for granted in the treatment of patients of the former type.

I asked a colleague whether he does analysis in the dark, and he said: 'Why, no! Surely our job is to provide an ordinary environment: and the dark would be extraordinary.' He was surprised at my question. He was orientated towards analysis of neurotics. But this provision and maintenance of an ordinary environment can be in itself a vitally important thing in the analysis of a psychotic, in fact it can be, at times, even more important than the verbal interpretations which also have to be given. For the neurotic the couch and warmth and comfort can be *symbolical* of the mother's love; for the psychotic it would be more true to say that these things *are* the analyst's physical expression of love. The couch *is* the analyst's lap or womb, and the warmth *is* the live warmth of the analyst's body. And so on.

There is, I hope, a progression in my statement of my subject. The analyst's hate is ordinarily latent and is easily kept so. In analysis of psychotics the analyst is under greater strain to keep his hate latent, and he can only do this by being thoroughly aware of it. I want to add that in certain stages of certain analyses the analyst's hate is actually sought by the patient, and what is then needed is hate that is objective. If the patient seeks objective or justified hate he must be able to reach it, else he cannot feel he can reach objective love.

It is perhaps relevant here to cite the case of the child of the broken home, or the child without parents. Such a child spends his time unconsciously looking for his parents. It is notoriously inadequate to take such a child into one's home and to love him. What happens is that after a while a child so adopted gains hope, and then he starts to test out the environment he has found, and to seek proof of his guardians' ability to hate objectively. It seems that he can believe in being loved only after reaching being hated.

During the second World War a boy of nine came to a hostel for evacuated children, sent from London not because of bombs but because of truancy. I hoped to give him some treatment during his stay in the hostel, but his symptom won and he ran away as he had always done from everywhere since the age of six when he first ran away from home. However, I had established contact with him in one interview in which I could see and interpret through a drawing of his that in running away he was unconsciously saving the inside of his home and preserving his mother from assault, as well as trying to get away from his own inner world, which was full of persecutors.

I was not very surprised when he turned up in the police station very near my home. This was one of the few police stations that did not know him intimately. My wife very generously took him in and kept him for three months, three months of hell. He was the most lovable and most maddening of children, often stark staring mad. But fortunately we knew what to expect. We dealt with the first phase by giving him complete freedom and a shilling whenever he went out. He had only to ring up and we fetched him from whatever police station had taken charge of him.

Soon the expected change-over occurred, the truancy symptom turned round, and the boy started dramatizing the assault on the inside. It was really a whole-time job for the two of us together, and when I was out the worst episodes took place.

Interpretation had to be made at any minute of day or night, and often the only solution in a crisis was to make the correct interpretation, as if the boy were in analysis. It was the correct interpretation that he valued above everything.

The important thing for the purpose of this paper is the way in which the evolution of the boy's personality engendered hate in me, and what I did about it.

Did I hit him? The answer is no, I never hit. But I should have had to have done so if I had not known all about my hate and if I had not let him know about it too. At crises I would take him by bodily strength, without anger or blame, and put him outside the front door, whatever the weather or the time of day or night. There was a special bell he could ring, and he knew that if he rang it he would be readmitted and no word said about the past. He used this bell as soon as he had recovered from his maniacal attack.

The important thing is that each time, just as I put him outside the door, I told him something; I said that what had happened had made me hate him. This was easy because it was so true.

I think these words were important from the point of view of his progress, but they were mainly important in enabling me to tolerate the situation without letting out, without losing my temper and without every now and again murdering him.

This boy's full story cannot be told here. He went to an Approved School. His deeply rooted relation to us has remained one of the few stable things in his life. This episode from ordinary life can be used to illustrate the general topic of hate justified in the present; this is to be distinguished from hate that is only justified in another setting but which is tapped by some action of a patient.

Out of all the complexity of the problem of hate and its roots I want to rescue one thing, because I believe it has an importance for the analyst of psychotic patients. I suggest that the mother hates the baby before the baby hates the mother, and before the baby can know his mother hates him.

Before developing this theme I want to refer to Freud. In *Instincts and their Vicissitudes* (1915), where he says so much that is original and illuminating about hate, Freud says: 'We might at a pinch say of an instinct that it "loves" the objects after which it strives for purposes of satisfaction, but to say that it "hates" an object strikes us as odd, so we become aware that the attitudes of love and hate cannot be said to characterize the relation of instincts to their objects, but are reserved for the relations of the ego as a whole to objects. . . .' This I feel is true and important. Does this not mean that the personality must be integrated before an infant can be said to hate? However early integration may be achieved – perhaps integration occurs earliest at the height of excitement or rage – there is a theoretical earlier stage in which whatever the infant does that hurts is not done in hate. I have used the term 'ruthless love' in describing this stage. Is this acceptable? As the infant becomes able to feel to be a whole person, so does the word hate develop meaning as a description of a certain group of his feelings.

The mother, however, hates her infant from the word go. I believe Freud thought it possible that a mother may in certain circumstances have only love for her boy baby; but we may doubt this. We know about a mother's love and we appreciate its reality and power. Let me give some of the reasons why a mother hates her baby, even a boy:

The baby is not her own (mental) conception.

The baby is not the one of childhood play, father's child, brother's child, etc.

The baby is not magically produced.

The baby is a danger to her body in pregnancy and at birth.

The baby is an interference with her private life, a challenge to preoccupation.

To a greater or lesser extent a mother feels that her own mother demands a baby, so that her baby is produced to placate her mother.

The baby hurts her nipples even by suckling, which is at first a chewing activity.

He is ruthless, treats her as scum, an unpaid servant, a slave.

She has to love him, excretions and all, at any rate at the beginning, till he has doubts about himself.

He tries to hurt her, periodically bites her, all in love.

He shows disillusionment about her.

His excited love is cupboard love, so that having got what he wants he throws her away like orange peel.

The baby at first must dominate, he must be protected from coincidences, life must unfold at the baby's rate and all this needs his mother's continuous and detailed study.

For instance, she must not be anxious when holding him, etc.

At first he does not know at all what she does or what she sacrifices for him. Especially he cannot allow for her hate.

He is suspicious, refuses her good food, and makes her doubt herself, but eats well with his aunt.

After an awful morning with him she goes out, and he smiles at a stranger, who says: 'Isn't he sweet?'

If she fails him at the start she knows he will pay her out for ever.

He excites her but frustrates – she mustn't eat him or trade in sex with him.

I think that in the analysis of psychotics, and in the ultimate stages of the analysis, even of a normal person, the analyst must find himself in a position comparable to that of the mother of a new-born baby. When deeply regressed the patient cannot identify with the analyst or appreciate his point of view any more than the foetus or newly born infant can sympathize with the mother.

A mother has to be able to tolerate hating her baby without doing anything about it. She cannot express it to him. If, for fear of what she may do, she cannot hate appropriately when hurt by her child she must fall back on masochism, and I think it is this that gives rise to the false theory of a natural masochism in women. The most remarkable thing about a mother is her ability to be hurt so much by her baby and to hate so much without paying the child out, and her ability to wait for rewards that may or may not come at a later date. Perhaps she is helped by some of the nursery rhymes she sings, which her baby enjoys but fortunately does not understand?

> *Rockabye Baby, on the tree top,*
> *When the wind blows the cradle will rock,*
> *When the bough breaks the cradle will fall,*
> *Down will come baby, cradle and all.*

I think of a mother (or father) playing with a small infant; the infant enjoying the play and not knowing that the parent is expressing hate in the words, perhaps in terms of birth symbolism. This is not a sentimental rhyme. Sentimentality is useless for parents, as it contains a denial of hate, and sentimentality in a mother is no good at all from the infant's point of view.

It seems to me doubtful whether a human child as he develops is capable of tolerating the full extent of his own hate in a sentimental environment. He needs hate to hate.

If this is true, a psychotic patient in analysis cannot be expected to tolerate his hate of the analyst unless the analyst can hate him.

If all this is accepted there remains for discussion the question of the interpretation of the analyst's hate to the patient. This is obviously a matter fraught with danger, and it needs the most careful timing. But I believe an analysis is incomplete if even towards the end it has not been possible for the analyst to tell the patient what he, the analyst, did unbeknown for the patient whilst he was ill, in the early stages. Until this interpretation is made the patient is kept to some extent in the position of infant – one who cannot understand what he owes to his mother.

An analyst has to display all the patience and tolerance and reliability of a mother devoted to her infant; has to recognize the patient's wishes as needs; has to put aside other interests in order to be available and to be punctual and objective; and has to seem to want to give what is really only given because of the patient's needs.

There may be a long initial period in which the analyst's point of view cannot be appreciated (even unconsciously) by the patient. Acknowledgement cannot be expected because, at the primitive root of the patient that is being looked for, there is no capacity for identification with the analyst; and certainly the patient cannot see that the analyst's hate is often engendered by the very things the patient does in his crude way of loving.

In the analysis (research analysis) or in ordinary management of the more psychotic type of patient, a great strain is put on the analyst (psychiatrist, mental nurse) and it is important to study the ways in which anxiety of psychotic quality and also hate are produced in those who work with severely ill psychiatric patients. Only in this way can there be any hope of the avoidance of therapy that is adapted to the needs of the therapist rather than to the needs of the patient.

Note

1. Based on a paper read to the British Psycho-Analytical Society on 5 February 1947. *International Journal of Psychoanalysis* 30 (1949).

Developing ideas: analyst's affective response to analysand; impact of very disturbed patients; different trajectories of hate and aggression; place of mother's hatred in infantile development

4 MIND AND ITS RELATION TO THE PSYCHE-SOMA (1949)

OTHER WRITINGS

The BBC talks were gathered together in pamphlet form as 'Getting to Know Your Baby' (1945a) and Winnicott published 'Residential Management as Treatment for Difficult Children' (Winnicott and Britton, 1947) and 'Children's Hostels in War and Peace' (1948c). He took over teaching child development at the Institute of Education from Susan Isaacs in 1947 having first lectured there at her invitation in 1936. In 1948 he addressed the Medical Section of the BPS from the chair in his paper 'Paediatrics and Psychiatry' (1948b), where he argues for the importance of doctors understanding early emotional development in its context of the relationship with maternal care. His unique integration of psychoanalysis with his medical and psychiatric practice (and his struggles with his own health) produced writings about the body: in development, in aggression (1950), as a source of anxiety (1949, this paper) and the place of the bodily relationship of the baby with the mother in the emergence of mind, an emphasis hinted at in 'Thinking and the Unconscious' (1945b). In France the Paris school of psychosomatics including Pierre Marty, Michel de M'Uzan, Christian David and Michel Fain published their findings from the early 1950s (Aisenstein, 2006). Winnicott was to refer to their work in his evolving theory of aggression and its links with motility (1954a).

EDITORS' INTRODUCTION

This paper draws on the central early developmental achievement of personalization described in 'Primitive Emotional Development' (1945) (Chapter 2, this volume). Published in 1949, it elaborates the environmental conditions necessary for the infant's integration of psyche and soma, with the mind as a specialized part of this overall organization. It also considers those conditions that lead to the mind as an unintegrated phenomenon, reflecting splitting, dissociation, and fragmentation. The trajectories from these elements led Winnicott in other directions, psychosomatic illness and the study of precocious ego development perhaps being the most significant.

Does the mind exist as an entity in itself? This question, posed by Ernest Jones (1946) and answered in the negative, is here re-examined by Winnicott to develop his own theory of the mind and its origins in the psychosomatic matrix created by the mother with her infant. The movement from dependence to independence physically is accompanied by a psychical parallel: the infant, in attaining the ordinary milestones of human development, develops a way of understanding them and symbolizing them to himself. Bodily achievements provide the basis for dimensions of internality, consciousness and unconsciousness. This account of psyche–soma makes the mind–body relation fundamental to a developmental approach that links the one-person model with a psychology of interdependence with an external caregiver, the mother. The mother implements and sustains the infant's earliest development through her adaptation to his bodily needs (handling) and through her imaginative elaboration of her infant's states (holding). Adam Phillips (1988: 93) describes as utopian this account of 'going on being', uninterrupted by impingement, which is fundamental to healthy living that Winnicott sees as the infant's initial experience.

In the achievement of healthy development, soma, psyche and mind are regarded as three components living in harmony, the 'psyche indwelling in the soma', the mind an integrated part of the psyche, all equally vital parts of 'unit status', the basis for the development of the self. In contrast perhaps to Phillips's view, the mind (equating to such ego capacities as thinking and intelligence) as a distinct part of the psyche, emerges from the mother's paradoxically necessary failing responses, and from the need to deal with external reality and its limitations. In the 'good-enough' environment the infant adjusts to these deficiencies through mental activity. That mind has its most important root in the need for a perfect environment originates in Freud (1911), for whom the absence of the breast promotes the infant's hallucinatory experience of satisfaction, the precursor of thought, leading ultimately to the recognition of the reality principle. Bion develops this theme in a related but different way (1962). For him, how the baby deals with the absent breast, that is, the experience of frustration, depends on the capacity for tolerance of that frustration. Facing reality in this sense leads to the development of a thinking mind. While Bion accords the mother's reverie a significant role in this process and his theory of the 'container-contained' has been a revolutionary development in Kleinian theory, his emphasis is on the infant's innate capacity for tolerance of frustration.

In contrast, for Winnicott the cornerstone of whether 'failure' leads to the development of mind as a healthy entity is the mother's sensitivity to her infant's states, only allowing frustration in a gradual way contingent with the baby's maturing capacities. If or when the infant has to deal with environmental (maternal) failure beyond his capacities, he is faced with a completely different situation, one where he has to adapt to impingements. There are several possibilities in which one or other of these entities is excluded and not integrated, resulting in distorted development: (a) over-activity in mental functioning, where psyche–soma is in opposition to mind and 'thinking' results in a precociously self-sufficient child; (b) a 'without mind' state, where the self affects stupidity; (c) a 'without psyche' self, where the imagination is curtailed; (d) a 'false self' acting as a carapace to protect the hidden true self (Winnicott, 1960a). Winnicott explores the processes of dissociation between psyche and soma that can give rise to mind as a split-off phenomenon, or to illness manifested in the body. These processes constitute the 'true illness' manifest both in the phenomenology of the illness and in the common split environmental responses to the patient (Winnicott et al., 1989).

Echoing Freud, Winnicott wrote about the need for the doctor treating psychosomatic disorders to be able 'to ride two horses, one foot on each of two saddles, both reins in deft hands', to connect what was sundered through the dissociation of psyche and soma. While often considered a psychoanalyst not particularly interested in the sexual, Winnicott is very concerned with how the individual experiences his or her body and whether that body is felt to be owned, real, and lived in. In *Clinical Notes on Disorders of Childhood* (1931) and subsequent papers he was already exploring the child's emotional experience of his body: overwhelming anxiety as central in some cases of convulsions (Winnicott, 1931: 157–71); conscious and unconscious fantasies about the insides of the body as important in treating a child with vomiting and diarrhoea (Winnicott, 1936: 33–51); the anxiety-laden moment of hesitation before the spatula is grasped (see Chapter 1, this volume).

Various clinicians and practitioners interested in psychosomatic medicine recognize Winnicott's seminal work in this area. Joyce (2009) examines the impact of traumatized maternal states of mind on a young infant and demonstrates how a young baby's apparent epilepsy constituted dissociated states that defended her against the impact of her mother. Shoenberg (2001, 2007), following Winnicott's recognition of the consequences for failure of integration of psyche–soma and mind, describes the psychosomatic patient who feels threatened by emotions (the psyche) which are then registered as physical symptoms. He distinguishes between the schizoid patient, where the link between the psyche and soma might appear to be almost missing, and the psychosomatic patient, where the bodily symptom 'provides a sort of linkage in which the emotions are not registered at a mental level' (2007: 45). According to Shoenberg, Joyce McDougall (1980) is close to Winnicott in her conceptualization of psychosomatic patients as needing their body illness to preserve their psychic survival, while the schizoid patient is more prone to depersonalization. In a similar vein, Aisenstein (2006: 677), from the French school of psychosomatics, describes being confronted with patients who treat their bodies 'like a foreign land' which becomes the site of enactments that may be explosive. She sees this as an indication of the lack of that integration of psyche and soma that Winnicott saw as forming the basis of the true self.

In his thesis on premature ego development (1960), Martin James develops a description of the mind as a split-off entity, contending that early patterning arising out of the failures of the maternal environment may lead to psycho-somatic illness. He observes the precocious motor movements of an infant, who, because her mother was unable to feed her for the first three months was underfed and left hungry. She gave the impression of a much older baby which, in his view, reflected her being 'forced to tolerate delay [. . .] Premature ego development would imply that the infant, during the phase of primary narcissism, took over functions from the mother in actuality, or started as though to do so. This would not be phase-adequate behaviour under three months' (James, 1960: 289). Khan extends James's hypothesis to include Winnicott's concept of the false self. He proposes that 'in certain children, given a certain proclivity and endowment for premature ego development in response to traumata, there can be a precocious structuralisation of the developmental process by acute dissociation and splitting, leading to a false-self' (Khan, 1971: 246). He describes a rigid structuring of internalized primary objects and fantasies and negativity toward all new experience, which alienate such children not only from others but themselves too. They live attached and dependent, but unreceptive and unrelating.

In his last paper on these matters, 'Basis for Self in Body' (1970a), Winnicott summarizes his thinking about the integration of psyche, mind, and soma. He sees 'personalization' as an achievement in health, of integration and the self living in the body, created out of 'the mother's constantly introducing and re-introducing the baby's body and psyche to each other' (Winnicott, 1970a: 271). It is the positive form of depersonalization, the loss of contact with the body and body functioning seen in the treatment of borderline and schizoid patients. When available to the child (always in the context of a relationship of trust), personalization can temporarily be given up or abandoned, as in the 'restful undoing of integrative processes' (Winnicott, 1970a: 261) but he regards the forward development of integration as too frightening if there is no sense of a possible return to 'total dependence'. The self that comes to reside in the body has a shape in internal psychic reality that can be 'modified by the mother's and father's expectations and by external life'. In health these modifications can be accepted because they do not undermine the sense of personalization and self-realization that was established through good-enough early development.

Mind and its Relation to the Psyche-Soma[1]
(1949)

> To ascertain what exactly comprises the irreducible mental elements, particularly those of a dynamic nature, constitutes in my opinion one of our most fascinating final aims. These elements would necessarily have a somatic and probably a neurological equivalent, and in that way we should by scientific method have closely narrowed the age-old gap between mind and body. I venture to predict that then the antithesis which has baffled all the philosophers will be found to be based on an illusion. In other words, *I do not think that the mind really exists as an entity* – possibly a startling thing for a psychologist to say [my italics]. When we talk of the mind influencing the body or the body influencing the mind we are merely using a convenient shorthand for a more cumbrous phrase . . .
>
> (Jones, 1946)

This quotation by Scott (1949) stimulated me to try to sort out my own ideas on this vast and difficult subject. The body scheme with its temporal and spatial aspects provides a valuable statement of the individual's diagram of himself, and in it I believe there is no obvious place for the mind. Yet in clinical practice we do meet with the mind as an entity localized somewhere by the patient; a further study of the paradox that 'mind does not really exist as an entity' is therefore necessary.

MIND AS A FUNCTION OF PSYCHE-SOMA

To study the concept of mind one must always be studying an individual, a total individual, and including the development of that individual from the very beginning of psychosomatic existence. If one accepts this discipline then one can study the mind of an individual as it specializes out from the psyche part of the psyche-soma.

The mind does not exist as an entity in the individual's scheme of things provided the individual psyche-soma or body scheme has come satisfactorily through the very early developmental stages; mind is then no more than a special case of the functioning of the psyche-soma.

In the study of a developing individual the mind will often be found to be developing *a false entity*, and *a false localization*. A study of these abnormal tendencies must precede the more direct examination of the mind-specialization of the healthy or normal psyche.

We are quite used to seeing the two words mental and physical opposed and would not quarrel with their being opposed in daily conversation. It is quite another matter, however, if the concepts are opposed in scientific discussion.

The use of these two words physical and mental in describing disease leads us into trouble immediately. The psychosomatic disorders, half-way between the mental and the physical, are in a rather precarious position. Research into psychosomatics is being held up, to some extent, by the muddle to which I am referring (MacAlpine, 1952). Also, neuro-surgeons are doing things to the normal or healthy brain in an attempt to alter or even improve mental states. These 'physical' therapists are completely at sea in their theory; curiously enough they seem to be leaving out the importance of the physical body, of which the brain is an integral part.

Let us attempt, therefore, to think of the developing individual, starting at the beginning. Here is a body, and the psyche and the soma are not to be distinguished except according to the direction from which one is looking. One can look at the developing body or at the developing psyche. I suppose the word psyche here means the *imaginative elaboration of somatic parts, feelings, and functions*, that is, of physical aliveness. We know that this imaginative elaboration is dependent on the existence and the healthy functioning of the brain, especially certain parts of it. The psyche is not, however, felt by the individual to be localized in the brain, or indeed to be localized anywhere.

Gradually the psyche and the soma aspects of the growing person become involved in a process of mutual interrelation. This interrelating of the psyche with the soma constitutes an early phase of individual development [see Chapter 2, this volume]. At a later stage the live body, with its limits, and with an inside and an outside, is *felt by the individual* to form the core for the imaginative self. The development to this stage is extremely complex, and although this development may possibly be fairly complete by the time a baby has been born a few days, there is a vast opportunity for distortion of the natural course of development in these respects. Moreover, whatever applies to very early stages also applies to some extent to all stages, even to the stage that we call adult maturity.

THEORY OF MIND

On the basis of these preliminary considerations I find myself putting forward a theory of mind. This theory is based on work with analytic patients who have needed to regress to an extremely early level of development in the transference. In this paper I shall only give one piece of illustrative clinical material, but the theory can, I believe, be found to be valuable in our daily analytic work.

Let us assume that health in the early development of the individual entails *continuity of being*. The early psyche-soma proceeds along a certain line of development provided its *continuity of being is not disturbed*; in other words, for the healthy development of the early psyche-soma there is a need for a *perfect* environment. At first the need is absolute.

The perfect environment is one which *actively adapts* to the needs of the newly formed psyche-soma, that which we as observers know to be the infant at the start. A bad environment is bad because by failure to adapt it becomes an *impingement* to which the psyche-soma (i.e. the infant) must *react*. This reacting disturbs the continuity of the going-on-being of the new individual. In its beginnings the good (psychological) environment is a physical one, with the child in the womb or being held and generally tended; only in the course of time does the environment develop a new characteristic which necessitates a new descriptive term, such as emotional or psychological or social. Out of this emerges the ordinary good mother with her ability to make active adaptation to her infant's needs arising out of her devotion, made possible by her narcissism, her imagination, and her memories, which enable her to know through identification what are her baby's needs.

The need for a good environment, which is absolute at first, rapidly becomes relative. *The ordinary good mother is good enough.* If she is *good enough* the infant becomes able to allow for her deficiencies by mental activity. This applies to meeting not only instinctual impulses but also all the most primitive types of ego need, even including the need for negative care or an alive neglect. The mental activity of the infant turns a *good-enough* environment into a perfect environment, that is to say, turns relative failure of adaptation into adaptive success. What releases the mother from her need to be near-perfect is the infant's understanding. In the ordinary course of events the mother tries not to introduce complications beyond those which the infant can understand and allow for; in particular she tries to insulate her baby from coincidences and from other phenomena that must be beyond the infant's ability to comprehend. In a general way she keeps the world of the infant as simple as possible.

The mind, then, has as one of its roots a variable functioning of the psyche-soma, one concerned with the threat to continuity of being that follows any failure of (active) environmental adaptation. It follows that mind-development is very much influenced by factors not specifically personal to the individual, including chance events.

In infant care it is vitally important that mothers, at first physically, and soon also imaginatively, can start off by supplying this active adaptation, but also it is a characteristic maternal function to provide *graduated failure of adaptation*, according to the growing ability of the individual infant to allow for relative failure by mental activity, or by understanding. Thus there appears in the infant a tolerance in respect of both ego need and instinctual tension.

It could perhaps be shown that mothers are released slowly by infants who eventually are found to have a low I.Q. On the other hand, an infant with an exceptionally good brain, eventually giving a high I.Q., releases the mother earlier.

According to this theory then, in the development of every individual, the mind has a root, perhaps its most important root, in the need of the individual, at the core of the self, for a perfect environment. In this connection, I might refer to my view of psychosis as an environmental deficiency disease (see Winnicott, 1952[a]). There are certain developments of this theory which seem to me to be important. Certain kinds of failure on the part of the mother, especially erratic behaviour, produce over-activity of the mental functioning. Here, in the overgrowth of the mental function reactive to erratic mothering, we see that there can develop an opposition between the mind and the psyche-soma, since in reaction to this abnormal environmental state the thinking of the individual begins to take over and organize the caring for the psyche-soma, whereas in health it is the function of the environment to do this. In health the mind does not usurp the environment's function, but makes possible an understanding and eventually a making use of its relative failure.

The gradual process whereby the individual becomes able to care for the self belongs to later stages in individual emotional development, stages that must be reached in due course, at the pace that is set by natural developmental forces.

To go a stage further, one might ask what happens if the strain that is put on mental functioning organized in defence against a tantalizing early environment is greater and greater? One would expect confusional states, and (in the extreme) mental defect of the kind that is not dependent on brain–tissue deficiency. As a more common result of the lesser degrees of tantalizing infant care in the earliest stages we find *mental functioning becoming a thing in itself*, practically replacing the good mother and making her unnecessary. Clinically, this can go along with dependence on the actual mother and a false personal growth on a compliance basis. This is a most uncomfortable state of affairs, especially because the psyche of the individual gets 'seduced' away into this mind from the intimate relationship which the psyche originally had with the soma. The result is a mind-psyche, which is pathological.

A person who is developing in this way displays a distorted pattern affecting all later stages of development. For instance, one can observe a tendency for easy identification with the environmental aspect of all relationships that involve dependence, and a difficulty in identification with the dependent individual. Clinically one may see such a person develop into one who is a *marvellously good mother to others* for a limited period; in fact a person who has developed along these lines may have almost magical *healing properties* because of an extreme capacity to make active adaptation to primitive needs. The falsity of these patterns for expression of the personality, however, becomes evident in practice. Breakdown threatens or occurs, because what the individual is all the time needing is *to find someone else* who will make real this 'good environment' concept, so that the individual may return to the dependent psyche-soma which forms the only place to live from. In this case, 'without mind' becomes a desired state.

There cannot of course be a direct partnership between the mind-psyche and the body of the individual. But the mind-psyche is localized by the individual, and is placed either inside the head or outside it in some special relation to the head, and this provides an important source for headache as a symptom.

The question has to be asked why the head should be the place inside which the mind tends to become localized by the individual, and I do not know the answer. I feel that an important point is the individual's need to localize the mind because it is an enemy, that is to say, for control of it. A schizoid patient tells me that the head is the place to put the mind because, *as the head cannot be seen by oneself*, it does not obviously exist as part of oneself. Another point is that the head has special experiences during the birth process, but in order to make full use of this latter fact I must go on to consider another type of mental functioning which can be specially activated during the birth process. This is associated with the word 'memorizing'.

As I have said, the continuity of being of the developing psyche-soma (internal and external relationships) is disturbed by reactions to environmental impingements, in other words by the results of failures of the environment to make active adaptation. By my theory a rapidly increasing amount of reaction to impingement disturbing continuity of psyche-soma becomes expected and allowed for according to mental capacity. Impingements demanding *excessive* reactions (according to the next part of my theory) cannot be allowed for. All that can happen apart from confusion is that the reactions can be *catalogued*.[2] Typically at birth there is apt to be an excessive disturbance of continuity because of reactions to impingements, and the mental activity which I am describing at the moment is that which is concerned with exact memorizing during the birth process. In my psycho-analytic work I sometimes meet with regressions fully under control and yet going back to prenatal life. Patients regressed in an ordered way go over the birth process again and again, and I have been astonished by the convincing proof that I have had that an infant during the birth process not only memorizes every reaction disturbing the continuity of being, but also appears to memorize these in the correct order. I have not used hypnosis, but I am aware of the comparable discoveries, less convincing to me, that are achieved through use of hypnosis. Mental functioning of the type that I am describing, which might be called memorizing or cataloguing, can be extremely active and accurate at the time of a baby's birth. I shall illustrate this by details from a case, but first I want to make clear my point that *this type of mental functioning is an encumbrance to the psyche-soma*, or to the individual human being's continuity of being which constitutes the self. The individual may be able to make use of it to relive the birth process in play or in a carefully controlled analysis. But this cataloguing type of mental functioning acts like a foreign body if it is associated with environmental adaptive failure that is beyond understanding or prediction.

No doubt in health it may happen that the environmental factors are held fixed by this method until the individual is able to make them his own after having experienced libidinous and especially aggressive drives, which can be projected. In this way, and it is essentially a false way, the individual gets to feel responsible for the bad environment for which in fact he was not responsible and which he could (if he knew) justly blame on the world because it disturbed the continuity of his innate developmental processes before the psyche–soma had become sufficiently well organized to hate or to love. Instead of hating these environmental failures the individual became disorganized by them because the process existed prior to hating.

CLINICAL ILLUSTRATION

The following fragment of a case history is given to illustrate my thesis. Out of several years' intensive work it is notoriously difficult to choose a detail; nevertheless, I include this fragment in order to show that what I am putting forward is very much a part of daily practice with patients.

A woman[3] who is now 47 years old had made what seemed to others but not to herself to be a good relationship to the world and had always been able to earn her own living. She had achieved a good education and was generally liked; in fact I think she was never actively disliked. She herself, however, felt completely dissatisfied, as if always aiming to find herself and never succeeding. Suicidal ideas were certainly not absent but they were kept at bay by her belief which dated from childhood that she would ultimately solve her problem and find herself. She had had a so-called 'classical' analysis for several years but somehow the core of her illness had been unchanged. With me it soon became apparent that this patient must make a very severe regression or else give up the struggle. I therefore followed the regressive tendency, letting it take the patient wherever it led; eventually the regression reached the limit of the patient's need, and since then there has been a natural progression with the true self instead of a false self in action.

For the purpose of this paper I choose for description one thing out of an enormous amount of material. In the patient's previous analysis there had been incidents in which the patient had thrown herself off the couch in an hysterical way. These episodes had been interpreted along ordinary lines for hysterical phenomena of this kind. In the deeper regression of this new analysis light was thrown on the meaning of these falls. In the course of the two years of analysis with me the patient has repeatedly regressed to an early stage which was certainly prenatal. The birth process had to be relived, and eventually I recognized how this patient's unconscious need to relive the birth process underlay what had previously been an hysterical falling off the couch.

A great deal could be said about all this, but the important thing from my point of view here is that evidently every detail of the birth experience had been retained, and not only that, but the details had been retained in the exact sequence of the original experience. A dozen or more times the birth process was relived and each time the reaction to one of the major external features of the original birth process was singled out for re-experiencing.

Incidentally, these relivings illustrated one of the main functions of acting out; by acting out the patient informed herself of the bit of psychic reality which was difficult to get at the moment, but of which the patient so acutely needed to become aware. I will enumerate some of the acting-out patterns, but unfortunately I cannot give the sequence which nevertheless I am quite sure was significant.

The breathing changes to be gone over in most elaborate detail.

The constrictions passing down the body to be relived and so remembered.

The birth from the fantasy inside of the belly of the mother, who was a depressive, unrelaxed person.

The changeover from not feeding to feeding from the breast, and then from the bottle.

The same with the addition that the patient had sucked her thumb in the womb and on coming out had to have the fist in relation to the breast or bottle, thus making continuity between object relationships within and without.

The severe experience of pressure on the head, and also the extreme of awfulness of the release of pressure on the head; during which phase, unless her head were held, she could not have endured the re-enactment. There is much which is not yet understood in this analysis about the bladder functions affected by the birth process.

The changeover from pressure all round (which belongs to the intra-uterine state) to pressure from underneath (which belongs to the extrauterine state). Pressure if not excessive means love. After birth therefore she was loved on the under side only, and unless turned round periodically became confused.

Here I must leave out perhaps a dozen other factors of comparable significance.

Gradually the re-enactment reached the worst part. When we were nearly there, there was the anxiety of having the head crushed. This was first got under control by the patient's identification with the crushing mechanism. This was a dangerous phase because if acted out outside the transference situation it meant suicide. In this acting–out phase the patient existed in the crushing boulders or whatever might present, and the gratification came to her then from *destruction* of the head (including mind and false psyche) which had lost significance for the patient as part of the self.

Ultimately the patient had to accept annihilation. We had already had many indications of a period of blackout or unconsciousness, and con-vulsive movements made it likely that there was at some time in infancy a minor fit. It appears that in the actual experience there was a loss of consciousness which could not be assimilated to the patient's self until accepted as a death. When this had become real the word death became wrong and the patient began to substitute 'a giving-in', and eventually the appropriate word was 'a not-knowing'.

In a full description of the case I should want to continue along these lines for some time, but development of this and other themes must be made in future publications. Acceptance of not-knowing produced tremendous relief. 'Knowing' became transformed into 'the analyst knows', that is to say, 'behaves reliably in active adaptation to the patient's needs'. The patient's whole life had been built up around mental functioning which had become falsely the place (in the head) from which she lived, and her life which had rightly seemed to her false had been developed out of this mental functioning.

Perhaps this clinical example illustrates what I mean when I say that I got from this analysis a feeling that the cataloguing of reactions to environmental impingements belonging to the time around about birth had been exact and complete; in fact I felt that the only alternative to the success of this cataloguing was absolute failure, hopeless confusion and mental defect.

But the case illustrates my theme in detail as well as generally.

I quote again from Scott (1949):

> Similarly when a patient in analysis loses his mind in the sense that he loses the illusion of needing a psychic apparatus which is separate from all that which he has called his body, his world, etc., etc., this loss is equivalent to the gain of all that conscious access to and control of the connections between the superficies and the depths, the boundaries and solidity of his Body Scheme – its memories, its perceptions, its images, etc., etc., which he had given up at an earlier period in his life when the duality soma psyche began.
>
> Not infrequently in a patient whose first complaint is of fear of 'losing his mind' – the desire to lose such a belief and obtain a better one soon becomes apparent.

At this point of not-knowing in this analysis there appeared the memory of a bird that was seen as 'quite still except for the movements of the belly which indicated breathing'. In other words, the patient had reached, at 47 years, the state in which physiological functioning in general constitutes living. The psychical elaboration of this could follow. This psychical elaboration of physiological functioning is quite different from the intellectual work which so easily becomes artificially a thing in itself and falsely a place where the psyche can lodge.

Naturally only a glimpse of this patient can be given, and even if one chooses a small part, only a bit of this part can be described. I would like, however, to pursue a little the matter of the gap in consciousness. I need not describe the gap as it appeared in more 'forward' terms, the bottom of a pit, for instance, in which in the dark were all sorts of dead and dying bodies. Just now 1 am concerned only with the most primitive of the ways in which the gap was found, by the patient, by the reliving processes belonging to the transference situation. The gap in continuity, which throughout the patient's life had been actively denied, now became something urgently sought. We found a need to have the head broken into, and violent head-banging appeared as part of an attempt to produce a blackout. At times there was an urgent need for the destruction of the mental processes located by the patient in the head. A series of defences against full recognition of the desire to reach the gap in continuity of consciousness had to be dealt with before there could be acceptance of the not-knowing state. It happened that on the day on which this work reached its climax the patient stopped writing her diary.[4] This diary had been kept throughout the analysis, and it would be possible to reconstruct the whole of her analysis up to this time from it. There is little that the patient could perceive that has not been at least indicated in this diary. The meaning of the diary now became clear – it was a projection of her mental apparatus, and not a picture of the true self, which, in fact, had never lived till, at the bottom of the regression, there came a new chance for the true self to start.

The results of this bit of work led to a temporary phase in which there was no mind and no mental functioning. There had to be a temporary phase in which the breathing of her body was all. In this way the patient became able to accept the not-knowing condition because I was holding her and keeping a continuity by my own breathing, while she let go, gave in, knew nothing; it could not be any good, however, if I held her and maintained my own continuity of life if she were dead. What made my part operative was that I could see and hear her belly moving as she breathed (like the bird) and therefore I knew that she was alive.

Now for the first time she was able to have a psyche, an entity of her own, a body that breathes and in addition the beginning of fantasy belonging to the breathing and other physiological functions.

We as observers know, of course, that the mental functioning which enables the psyche to be there enriching the soma is dependent on the intact brain. But we do not place the psyche anywhere, not even in the brain on which it depends. For this patient, regressed in this way, these things were at last not important. I suppose she would now be prepared to locate the psyche wherever the soma is alive.

This patient has made considerable progress since this paper was read. Now in 1953 we are able to look back on the period of the stage I have chosen for description, and to see it in perspective. I do not need to modify what I have written. Except for the violent complication of the birth process body-memories, there has been no major disturbance of the patient's regression to a certain very early stage and subsequent forward movement towards a new existence as a real individual who feels real.

MIND LOCALIZED IN THE HEAD

I now leave my illustration and return to the subject of the localizing of the mind in the head. I have said that the imaginative elaboration of body parts and functions is not localized. There may, however, be localizations which are quite logical in the sense that they belong to the way in which the body functions. For instance, the body takes in and gives out substances. An inner world of personal imaginative experience therefore comes into the scheme of things, and shared reality is on the whole thought of as outside the personality. Although babies cannot draw pictures, I think that they are capable (except through lack of skill) of depicting themselves by a circle at certain moments in their first months. Perhaps if all is going well, they can achieve this soon after birth; at any rate we have good evidence that at six months a baby is at times using the circle or sphere as a diagram of the self. It is at this point that Scott's body scheme is so illuminating and especially his reminder that we are referring to time as well as to space. In the body scheme as I understand it there seems to me to be no place for the mind, and this is not a criticism of the body scheme as a diagram; it is a comment on the falsity of the concept of the mind as a localized phenomenon.

In trying to think out why the head is the place where either the mind is localized, or else outside which it is localized, I cannot help thinking of the way in which the head of the human baby is affected during birth, the time at which the mind is furiously active cataloguing reactions to a specific environmental persecution.

Cerebral functioning tends to be localized by people in the head in popular thought, and one of the consequences of this deserves special study. Until quite recently surgeons could be persuaded to open the skulls of mentally defective infants to make possible further development of their brains which were supposed to be constricted by the bones of the skull. I suppose the early trephining of the skull was for relief of *mind* disorders, i.e. for cure of persons whose mental functioning was their enemy and who had falsely localized their mental functioning in their heads. At the present time the curious thing is that once again in medical scientific thought the brain has got equated with the mind, which is felt by a certain kind of ill person to be an enemy, and a thing in the skull. The surgeon who does a leucotomy would *at first* seem to be doing what the patient asks for, that is, to be relieving the patient of mind activity, the mind having become the enemy of the psyche-soma. Nevertheless, we can see that the surgeon is caught up in the mental patient's false localization of the mind in the head, with its sequel, the equating of mind and brain. When he has done his work he has failed in the second half of his job. The patient wants to be relieved of the *mind activity* which has become a threat to the psyche-soma, but the patient next needs the full-functioning brain tissue *in order to be able to have psyche-soma existence*. By the operation of leucotomy with its irreversible brain changes the surgeon has made this impossible. The procedure has been of no use except through what the operation means to the patient. But the imaginative elaboration of somatic experience, the psyche, and for those who use the term, the soul, depend on the intact brain, as we know. We do not expect the *unconscious* of anyone to know such things, but we feel the neuro-surgeon ought to be *to some extent* affected by intellectual considerations.

In these terms we can see that one of the aims of *psychosomatic illness* is to draw the psyche from the mind back to the original intimate association with the soma. It is not sufficient to analyse the hypochondria of the psychosomatic patient, although this is an essential part of the treatment. One has also to be able to see the *positive value of the somatic disturbance* in its work of counteracting a 'seduction' of the psyche into the mind. Similarly, the aim of physiotherapists and the relaxationists can be understood in these terms. They do not have to know what they are doing to be successful psychotherapists. In one example of the application of these principles, if one tries to teach a pregnant woman how to do all the right things one not only makes her anxious, but one feeds the tendency of the psyche to lodge in the mental processes. *Per contra*, the relaxation methods at their best enable the mother to become body-conscious, and (if she is not a mental case) these methods help her to a continuity of being, and enable her to live as a psyche-soma. This is essential if she is to experience child-birth and the first stages of mothering in a natural way.

SUMMARY

1. The true self, a continuity of being, is in health based on psyche-soma growth.
2. Mental activity is a special case of the functioning of the psyche-soma.
3. Intact brain functioning is the basis for psyche-being as well as for mental activity.
4. There is no localization of a mind self, and there is no thing that can be called mind.
5. Two distinct bases for normal mental functioning can already be given, viz.: (*a*) conversion of good-enough environment into perfect (adapted) environment, enabling minimum of reaction to impingement, and maximum of natural (continuous) self-development; and (*b*) cataloguing of impingements (birth trauma, etc.) for assimilation at later stages of development.
6. It is to be noted that psyche-soma growth is universal and its complexities are inherent, whereas mental development is somewhat dependent on variable factors such as the quality of early environmental factors, the chance phenomena of birth and of management immediately after birth, etc.

7. It is logical to oppose psyche and soma and therefore to oppose the emotional development and the bodily development of an individual. It is not logical, however, to oppose the mental and the physical as these are not of the same stuff. Mental phenomena are complications of variable importance in psyche–soma continuity of being, in that which adds up to the individual's 'self'.

Notes

1. A paper read before the Medical Section of the British Psychological Society, 14 December, 1949, and revised October 1953. *British Journal of Medical Psychology* 27 (1954).
2. Cf. Freud's theory of obsessional neurosis (1909[a]).
3. Case referred to again in another paper (see Chapter 6 [in Through Paediatrics to Psycho-Analysis]).
4. The diary was resumed at a later date, for a time, with a looser function, and a more positive aim including the idea of one day using her experiences profitably.

Developing ideas: special function of the mind as distinct from psyche; unit status; psyche–indwelling-in-soma; ordinary devoted, good-enough mother; the 'graduated failure' of the good-enough mother; absolute dependence; continuity of being

5 TRANSITIONAL OBJECTS AND TRANSITIONAL PHENOMENA (1951; 1971)

OTHER WRITINGS

Winnicott's writings continued to tackle his interest in inner reality and the external world and their inter-relation in healthy living. 'Growth and Development in Immaturity' (1950a), 'The Deprived Child and how he can be Compensated for Loss of Family Life' (1950b; given to the Nursery School Association), and 'The Foundation of Mental Health' (1951) published in the *BMJ*, drew on his work on the emergence of independence from dependence, and this fundamental paper made use of illusion in proposing attention to potential space and its constitution.

M. Sechehaye, whom Winnicott references, had published *Symbolic Realization* in 1951 and Marion Milner, an analysand and later a close colleague of Winnicott's, gave the first written critique of Ernest Jones's theory of symbolization in her paper 'The Role of Illusion in Symbol Formation' in 1952 (see 1987a). Her idiom was close to Winnicott's, but according to Rayner they came to their ideas 'almost independently, only later seeing how close they were' (Rayner, 1991: 52). Despite thinking, like Hanna Segal (1957), that symbolization is a normal process, Milner and Winnicott's interest in illusion and primary creativity led them to different conclusions and 'illusion' was to become a significant interest within the Independent tradition. Later figures such as Charles Rycroft (1955, 1968) and John Klauber (1987) would take up Winnicott and Milner's interests in this relation between phantasy and reality, and its value in health. A recent Kleinian comment upon Winnicott's concept of transitional space, interprets it as a pathological retreat from the work of distinguishing 'fact from fantasy', and akin to Riesenberg-Malcolm's 'as-if' patient, rather than seeing it as the necessary pre-condition for the life of the imagination and inner reality (Britton, 1998).

EDITORS' INTRODUCTION

The area of transitional objects and phenomena is the one for which Winnicott is best known, and it is often claimed as his most significant contribution (Modell, 1985; Rycroft, 1972; Turner, 2002). It was introduced in a paper given to the BPAS in May 1951, published first in the *IJPA* in 1953, and republished in a slightly revised version as the first chapter of *Playing and Reality* (1971a). The original version had been intended for inclusion in a Festschrift for Klein (Rodman, 2003: 164–166) and would appear to have undergone considerable revision for its 1953 publication. The later version, republished here, contains some small revisions and the inclusion of clinical material. Both versions propose an intermediate area between external and internal as fundamental to human development, and the subsequent extension of this infantile stage, loosely ascribed to 4 to 12 months, to the arenas of art, culture, and religion.

Winnicott describes *Playing and Reality* itself as the redevelopment of the original paper and his conviction that 'cultural experience has not found its true place in the theory used by analysts in their work and their thinking' (Winnicott, 1971a: xi). But, in the paper, he is primarily concerned with infantile development, the baby, and the implications for the analytic setting.

He links the transitional object's appearance and its being invested with importance to the relation with the mother, the beginnings of a perception of self and other, and the separation this entails. An interest in a transitional object is part of a good-enough continuing relationship with the mother, and, as such, it indicates the infant's imaginative inhabiting of an area intermediate between internal and external reality and its developmental and symbolic implications. The prior internalization of the mother makes the baby's interest in an object beyond itself and her both feasible and necessary. The transitional object's existence, or rather, its healthy existence, is thus dependent upon the relation with the mother. Winnicott prefers the term 'transitional' to 'intermediate' because it connotes more strongly the idea of movement, and a set of *processes* located in the infant. It is not the externality of the actual object, for instance, a teddy bear, but the internal processes that must be in place to arrive at the capacity to use it that are significant.

The first version (1953) refers to a paper by Wulff, which is concerned with the pathological uses of external objects. Wulff approaches 'fetish objects' in terms of 'the psychopathology of fetishism', the ordinary theory of the sexual perversions (Wulff, 1946; see Winnicott, 1987: 241), and the *delusion* of a maternal phallus; an extensive literature discusses this theme further (Greenacre, 1969; Grolnick and Barkin, 1978). For Winnicott, however, the universality of illusion allows this as normal and non-pathological: 'We can allow the transitional object to be potentially a maternal phallus but originally the breast, that is to say, the thing created by the infant and at the same time provided by the environment' (1987: 241). It is not the 'object', but the 'illusion', as 'a universal in the field of experience', that is important. This insight can be used to understand fetishism, addiction, and thieving (Winnicott, 1987: 242). Variations in what is used and what it may mean, the relation between an internal object and an external object, the healthy and pathological uses of these objects, can all provide important clinical information, since they are organized around the different mental involvement and mental space that the child brings to the chosen object. Other research on the transitional object has been concerned with classification and the information it can provide on development, both normal and abnormal (Gaddini, 1970; Stevenson, 1954). Although Winnicott insists that the transitional object's importance lies in its normality as a developmental gain, the clinical examples added to the later version discuss cases of psychopathology.

Both versions insist on the intermediate area of experiencing and its characteristics, and describe how a baby becomes able to participate in it. The potential ascribed to the concept of transitional space, and its availability from infancy to adulthood as an arena of particular experiences of the relation between self and world, derives from Winnicott's preferred emphasis on the normality of transitional phenomena in the life of the infant, and the centrality of time that accompanies the move from purely subjective to objective and the acquisition of symbolic functioning.

It is the space that exists *between* the one thing and the other which conveys a sense of the something more that happens for the infant in the time frame lived between 'inability' and 'growing ability' to recognize and accept reality (p. 104). The shift from the baby's use of his own thumb to his use of something beyond himself has temporal and spatial dimensions, and both are important in the growing moves towards an incipient capacity for symbolization. The special qualities of the relationship with the object are given by what the infant may want, and may be inferred as wanting, the parents' acceptance of the child's control of this possession, and its ultimate fate as unimportant. Winnicott agrees that a transitional object is also symbolic of something else, for instance, the relation with the mother, but its actuality, its real existence, is the most important thing.

Alvarez assumes that the transitional object's existence is developmentally located between Segal's idea of symbolic equation and the true symbol, and suggests that its clinical relevance cannot be overestimated. 'The child in the intermediate or transitional stage has a mixed experience of an object which is partly his very own and partly not, but he also has an experience of himself as someone who is partly an owner and partly not' (Alvarez, 1996: 379). Deri (1978: 50) prefers to regard it as a protosymbol (in the sense of vehicles which present meanings rather than represent them), a self-created image that leads to the absent need/love object, and whose aim is connectedness. How this is enabled by the real mother influences the future dimensions of symbolization and creativity in the child. She adds, 'though still not a symbol representing mother, if environmental circumstances remain conducive, the object should lead to the successful use of symbolic means to bridge over to the desired but physically absent object. They can enhance the qualities of the external world and enable its continuing use' (Deri, 1978: 59). As Barkin (1978: 530) describes it, 'The symbolizing process is another complex ego function inextricably interrelated to the development of memory, representation, boundary formation, reality testing, apperception, and synthetic function'. The transitional object is a stage in the acquisition of these faculties. It embodies the link between motility and aggressive reaching out, and an awareness of the environment as separate and objective. The mental space that exists *between* one thing and another has to be established, since, for Winnicott, there is no space at the start between thumb and mouth for the baby. The space that has opened up between mouth and transitional object, the first not-me possession (both parts, 'not-me' and 'possession', are of relevance) becomes the condition for creative living. Something more happens for the infant in the time frame lived between 'inability' and 'growing ability to recognize and accept reality' (Winnicott, 1987: 230), and that something more is represented in a configured space that is both mental and physical, involving a subjective reality and an objective reality. Ken Wright argues for 'transitional experience as the experience of remaining related to the mother when she is not there' and the transitional object as plugging the hole created by the mother's absence' (disillusion) (1991: 77). The baby uses sensory elements that replace the mother (softness, malleability) so her absence is not experienced. Wright links this process with primary creativity rather than reparation.

To arrive at a capacity to inhabit the transitional area, and, later, to play, involves those processes of illusion and disillusion that form the basis of the mother–child relation. 'Illusion refers to an expanded perception, in which primary and secondary process both take part, whereas primary process alone refers to inner reality and secondary process concerns the effects on the psychic apparatus of the perception of external reality' (Flarsheim, 1978: 509). Play occurs in this transitional space, and 'play' and, even more, 'playing' are to be understood as extending the scope of what happens in the consulting room and the very basis of analytic work.

This paper encapsulates Winnicott's insistence that neither the one-person model of the infant nor the two-person model which is dependent upon the awareness of another and its implications for psychic life contain all the factors that are basic to human development. Read in conjunction with the rest of the papers in *Playing and Reality*, the two versions of this paper offer insight into developments in his thinking about the nature of the person and the nature of the analytic encounter through the later use of play and paradox, and they reveal his consistent interest in the nature of experience.

Transitional Objects and Transitional Phenomena
(1971)

In this chapter I give the original hypothesis as formulated in 1951, and I then follow this up with two clinical examples.

I. ORIGINAL HYPOTHESIS[1]

It is well known that infants as soon as they are born tend to use fist, fingers, thumbs in stimulation of the oral erotogenic zone, in satisfaction of the instincts at that zone, and also in quiet union. It is also well known that after a few months infants of either sex become fond of playing with dolls, and that most mothers allow their infants some special object and expect them to become, as it were, addicted to such objects.

There is a relationship between these two sets of phenomena that are separated by a time interval, and a study of the development from the earlier into the later can be profitable, and can make use of important clinical material that has been somewhat neglected.

THE FIRST POSSESSION

Those who happen to be in close touch with mothers' interests and problems will be already aware of the very rich patterns ordinarily displayed by babies in their use of the first 'not-me' possession. These patterns, being displayed, can be subjected to direct observation.

There is a wide variation to be found in a sequence of events that starts with the newborn infant's fist-in-mouth activities, and leads eventually on to an attachment to a teddy, a doll or soft toy, or to a hard toy.

It is clear that something is important here other than oral excitement and satisfaction, although this may be the basis of everything else. Many other important things can be studied, and they include:

1. The nature of the object.
2. The infant's capacity to recognize the object as 'not-me'.
3. The place of the object – outside, inside, at the border.
4. The infant's capacity to create, think up, devise, originate, produce an object.
5. The initiation of an affectionate type of object-relationship.

I have introduced the terms 'transitional objects' and 'transitional phenomena' for designation of the intermediate area of experience, between the thumb and the teddy bear, between the oral erotism and the true object-relationship, between primary creative activity and projection of what has already been introjected, between primary unawareness of indebtedness and the acknowledgement of indebtedness ('Say: "ta"').

By this definition an infant's babbling and the way in which an older child goes over a repertory of songs and tunes while preparing for sleep come within the intermediate area as transitional phenomena, along with the use made of objects that are not part of the infant's body yet are not fully recognized as belonging to external reality.

Inadequacy of Usual Statement of Human Nature

It is generally acknowledged that a statement of human nature in terms of interpersonal relationships is not good enough even when the imaginative elaboration of function and the whole of fantasy both conscious and unconscious, including the repressed unconscious, are allowed for. There is another way of describing persons that comes out of the researches of the past two decades. Of every individual who has reached to the stage of being a unit with a limiting membrane and an outside and an inside, it can be said that there is an *inner reality* to that individual, an inner world that can be rich or poor and can be at peace or in a state of war. This helps, but is it enough?

My claim is that if there is a need for this double statement, there is also need for a triple one: the third part of the life of a human being, a part that we cannot ignore, is an intermediate area of *experiencing*, to which inner reality and external life both contribute. It is an area that is not challenged, because no claim is made on its behalf except that it shall exist as a resting-place for the individual engaged in the perpetual human task of keeping inner and outer reality separate yet interrelated.

It is usual to refer to 'reality-testing', and to make a clear distinction between apperception and perception. I am here staking a claim for an intermediate state between a baby's inability and his growing ability to recognize and accept reality. I am therefore studying the substance of *illusion*, that which is allowed to the infant, and which in adult life is inherent in art and religion, and yet becomes the hallmark of madness when an adult puts too powerful a claim on the credulity of others, forcing them to acknowledge a sharing of illusion that is not their own. We can share a respect for *illusory experience*, and if we wish we may collect together and form a group on the basis of the similarity of our illusory experiences. This is a natural root of grouping among human beings.

I hope it will be understood that I am not referring exactly to the little child's teddy bear or to the infant's first use of the fist (thumb, fingers). I am not specifically studying the first object of object-relationships. I am concerned with the first possession, and with the intermediate area between the subjective and that which is objectively perceived.

Development of a Personal Pattern

There is plenty of reference in psychoanalytic literature to the progress from 'hand to mouth' to 'hand to genital', but perhaps less to further progress to the handling of truly 'not-me' objects. Sooner or later in an infant's development there comes a tendency on the part of the infant to weave other-than-me objects into the personal pattern. To some extent these objects stand for the breast, but it is not especially this point that is under discussion.

In the case of some infants the thumb is placed in the mouth while fingers are made to caress the face by pronation and supination movements of the forearm. The mouth is then active in relation to the thumb, but not in relation to the fingers. The fingers caressing the upper lip, or some other part, may be or may become more important than the thumb engaging the mouth. Moreover, this caressing activity may be found alone, without the more direct thumb–mouth union.

In common experience one of the following occurs, complicating an auto-erotic experience such as thumb-sucking:

(i)   with the other hand the baby takes an external object, say a part of a sheet or blanket, into the mouth along with the fingers; or

(ii)   somehow or other the bit of cloth is held and sucked, or not actually sucked; the objects used naturally include napkins and (later) hand-kerchiefs, and this depends on what is readily and reliably available; or

(iii) the baby starts from early months to pluck wool and to collect it and to use it for the caressing part of the activity; less commonly, the wool is swallowed, even causing trouble; or

(iv)   mouthing occurs, accompanied by sounds of 'mum-mum', babbling, anal noises, the first musical notes, and so on.

One may suppose that thinking, or fantasying, gets linked up with these functional experiences.

All these things I am calling *transitional phenomena*. Also, out of all this (if we study any one infant) there may emerge some thing or some phenomenon – perhaps a bundle of wool or the corner of a blanket or eiderdown, or a word or tune, or a mannerism – that becomes vitally important to the infant for use at the time of going to sleep, and is a defence against anxiety, especially anxiety of depressive type. Perhaps some soft object or other type of object has been found and used by the infant, and this then becomes what I am calling a *transitional object*. This object goes on being important. The parents get to know its value and carry it round when travelling. The mother lets it get dirty and even smelly, knowing that by washing it she introduces a break in continuity in the infant's experience, a break that may destroy the meaning and value of the object to the infant.

I suggest that the pattern of transitional phenomena begins to show at about four to six to eight to twelve months. Purposely I leave room for wide variations.

Patterns set in infancy may persist into childhood, so that the original soft object continues to be absolutely necessary at bed-time or at time of loneliness or when a depressed mood threatens. In health, however, there is a gradual extension of range of interest, and eventually the extended range is maintained, even when depressive anxiety is near. A need for a specific object or a behaviour pattern that started at a very early date may reappear at a later age when deprivation threatens.

This first possession is used in conjunction with special techniques derived from very early infancy, which can include or exist apart from the more direct auto-erotic activities. Gradually in the life of an infant teddies and dolls and hard toys are acquired. Boys to some extent tend to go over to use hard objects, whereas girls tend to proceed right ahead to the acquisition of a family. It is important to note, however, that *there is no noticeable difference between boy and girl in their use of the original 'not-me' possession*, which I am calling the transitional object.

As the infant starts to use organized sounds ('mum', 'ta', 'da') there may appear a 'word' for the transitional object. The name given by the infant to these earliest objects is often significant, and it usually has a word used by the adults partly incorporated in it. For instance, 'baa' may be the name, and the 'b' may have come from the adult's use of the word 'baby' or 'bear'.

I should mention that sometimes there is no transitional object except the mother herself. Or an infant may be so disturbed in emotional development that the transition state cannot be enjoyed, or the sequence of objects used is broken. The sequence may nevertheless be maintained in a hidden way.

Summary of Special Qualities in the Relationship

1. The infant assumes rights over the object, and we agree to this assumption. Nevertheless, some abrogation of omnipotence is a feature from the start.
2. The object is affectionately cuddled as well as excitedly loved and mutilated.
3. It must never change, unless changed by the infant.
4. It must survive instinctual loving, and also hating and, if it be a feature, pure aggression.
5. Yet it must seem to the infant to give warmth, or to move, or to have texture, or to do something that seems to show it has vitality or reality of its own.
6. It comes from without from our point of view, but not so from the point of view of the baby. Neither does it come from within; it is not a hallucination.

7. Its fate is to be gradually allowed to be decathected, so that in the course of years it becomes not so much forgotten as relegated to limbo. By this I mean that in health the transitional object does not 'go inside' nor does the feeling about it necessarily undergo repression. It is not forgotten and it is not mourned. It loses meaning, and this is because the transitional phenomena have become diffused, have become spread out over the whole intermediate territory between 'inner psychic reality' and 'the external world as perceived by two persons in common', that is to say, over the whole cultural field.

At this point my subject widens out into that of play, and of artistic creativity and appreciation, and of religious feeling, and of dreaming, and also of fetishism, lying and stealing, the origin and loss of affectionate feeling, drug addiction, the talisman of obsessional rituals, etc.

Relationship of the Transitional Object to Symbolism

It is true that the piece of blanket (or whatever it is) is symbolical of some part-object, such as the breast. Nevertheless, the point of it is not its symbolic value so much as its actuality. Its not being the breast (or the mother), although real, is as important as the fact that it stands for the breast (or mother).

When symbolism is employed the infant is already clearly distinguishing between fantasy and fact, between inner objects and external objects, between primary creativity and perception. But the term transitional object, according to my suggestion, gives room for the process of becoming able to accept difference and similarity. I think there is use for a term for the root of symbolism in time, a term that describes the infant's journey from the purely subjective to objectivity; and it seems to me that the transitional object (piece of blanket, etc.) is what we see of this journey of progress towards experiencing.

It would be possible to understand the transitional object while not fully understanding the nature of symbolism. It seems that symbolism can be properly studied only in the process of the growth of an individual and that it has at the very best a variable meaning. For instance, if we consider the wafer of the Blessed Sacrament, which is symbolic of the body of Christ, I think I am right in saying that for the Roman Catholic community it *is* the body, and for the Protestant community it is a *substitute*, a reminder, and is essentially not, in fact, actually the body itself. Yet in both cases it is a symbol.

CLINICAL DESCRIPTION OF A TRANSITIONAL OBJECT

For anyone in touch with parents and children, there is an infinite quantity and variety of illustrative clinical material. The following illustrations are given merely to remind readers of similar material in their own experiences.

Two Brothers: Contrast in Early Use of Possessions

Distortion in use of transitional object. X, now a healthy man, has had to fight his way towards maturity. The mother 'learned how to be a mother' in her management of X when he was an infant and she was able to avoid certain mistakes with the other children because of what she learned with him. There were also external reasons why she was anxious at the time of her rather lonely management of X when he was born. She took her job as a mother very seriously and she breast-fed X for seven months. She feels that in his case this was too long and he was very difficult to wean. He never sucked his thumb or his fingers and when she weaned him 'he had nothing to fall back on'. He had never had the bottle or a dummy or any other form of feeding. He had a very strong and early *attachment to her herself*, as a person, and it was her actual person that he needed.

From twelve months he adopted a rabbit which he would cuddle, and his affectionate regard for the rabbit eventually transferred to real rabbits. This particular rabbit lasted till he was five or six years old. It could be described as a *comforter*, but it never had the true quality of a transitional object. It was never, as a true transitional object would have been, more important than the mother, an almost inseparable part of the infant. In the case of this particular boy the kinds of anxiety that were brought to a head by the weaning at seven months later produced asthma, and only gradually did he conquer this. It was important for him that he found employment far away from the home town. His attachment to his mother is still very powerful, although he comes within the wide definition of the term normal, or healthy. This man has not married.

★　　★　　★

Typical use of transitional object. X's younger brother, Y, has developed in quite a straightforward way throughout. He now has three healthy children of his own. He was fed at the breast for four months and then weaned without difficulty. Y sucked his thumb in the early weeks and this again 'made weaning easier for him than for his older brother'. Soon after weaning at five to six months he adopted the end of the blanket where the stitching finished. He was pleased if a little bit of the wool stuck out at the corner and with this he would tickle his nose. This very early became his 'Baa'; he invented this word for it himself as soon as he could use organized sounds. From the time when he was about a year old he was able to substitute for the end of the blanket a soft green jersey with a red tie. This was not a 'comforter' as in the case of the depressive older brother, but a 'soother'. It was a sedative which always worked. This is a typical example of what I am calling a *transitional object*. When Y was a little boy it was always certain that if anyone gave him his 'Baa' he would immediately suck it and lose anxiety, and in fact he would go to sleep within a few minutes if the time for sleep were at all near. The thumb-sucking continued at the same time, lasting until he was three or four years old, and he remembers thumb-sucking and a hard place on one thumb which resulted from it. He is now interested (as a father) in the thumb-sucking of his children and their use of 'Baas'.

The story of seven ordinary children in this family brings out the following points, arranged for comparison in the table below:

		Thumb	Transitional Object		Type of Child
X	Boy	0	Mother	Rabbit (comforter)	Mother-fixated
Y	Boy	+	'Baa'	Jersey (soother)	Free
					Late maturity
Twins	Girl	0	Dummy	Donkey (friend)	Latent
	Boy	0	'Ee'	Ee (protective)	psychopathic
	Girl	0	'Baa'	Blanket (reassurance)	Developing well
Children of Y	Girl	+	Thumb	Thumb (satisfaction)	Developing well
	Boy	+	'Mimis'	Objects (sorting)[1]	Developing well

[1] Added note: This was not clear, but I have left it as it was. D.W.W., 1971.

Value in History-taking

In consultation with a parent it is often valuable to get information about the early techniques and possessions of all the children of the family. This starts the mother off on a comparison of her children one with another, and enables her to remember and compare their characteristics at an early age.

The Child's Contribution

Information can often be obtained from a child in regard to transitional objects. For instance:

Angus (eleven years nine months) told me that his brother 'has tons of teddies and things' and 'before that he had little bears', and he followed this up with a talk about his own history. He said he never had teddies. There was a bell rope that hung down, a tag end of which he would go on hitting, and so go off to sleep. Probably in the end it fell, and that was the end of it. There was, however, something else. He was very shy about this. It was a purple rabbit with red eyes. 'I wasn't fond of it. I used to throw it around. Jeremy has it now, I gave it to him. I gave it to Jeremy because it was naughty. It *would* fall off the chest of drawers. *It still visits me. I like it to visit me.*' He surprised himself when he drew the purple rabbit.

It will be noted that this eleven-year-old boy with the ordinary good reality-sense of his age spoke as if lacking in reality-sense when describing the transitional object's qualities and activities. When I saw the mother later she expressed surprise that Angus remembered the purple rabbit. She easily recognized it from the coloured drawing.

Ready Availability of Examples

I deliberately refrain from giving more case-material here, particularly as I wish to avoid giving the impression that what I am reporting is rare. In practically every case-history there is something to be found that is interesting in the transitional phenomena, or in their absence.

THEORETICAL STUDY

There are certain comments that can be made on the basis of accepted psychoanalytic theory:

1. The transitional object stands for the breast, or the object of the first relationship.
2. The transitional object antedates established reality-testing.
3. In relation to the transitional object the infant passes from (magical) omnipotent control to control by manipulation (involving muscle erotism and coordination pleasure).
4. The transitional object may eventually develop into a fetish object and so persist as a characteristic of the adult sexual life. (See Wulff's (1946) development of the theme.)
5. The transitional object may, because of anal erotic organization, stand for faeces (but it is not for this reason that it may become smelly and remain unwashed).

Relationship to Internal Object (Klein)

It is interesting to compare the transitional object concept with Melanie Klein's (1934) concept of the internal object. The transitional object is *not an internal object* (which is a mental concept) – it is a possession. Yet it is not (for the infant) an external object either.

The following complex statement has to be made. The infant can employ a transitional object when the internal object is alive and real and good enough (not too persecutory). But this internal object depends for its qualities on the existence and aliveness and behaviour of the external object. Failure of the latter in some essential function indirectly leads to deadness or to a persecutory quality of the internal object.[2] After a persistence of inadequacy of the external object the internal object fails to have meaning to the infant, and then, and then only, does the transitional object become meaningless too. The transitional object may therefore stand for the 'external' breast, but *indirectly*, through standing for an 'internal' breast.

The transitional object is never under magical control like the internal object, nor is it outside control as the real mother is.

Illusion-Disillusionment

In order to prepare the ground for my own positive contribution to this subject I must put into words some of the things that I think are taken too easily for granted in many psychoanalytic writings on infantile emotional development, although they may be understood in practice.

There is no possibility whatever for an infant to proceed from the pleasure principle to the reality principle or towards and beyond primary identification (see Freud, 1923), unless there is a good-enough mother. The good-enough 'mother' (not necessarily the infant's own mother) is one who makes active adaptation to the infant's needs, an active adaptation that gradually lessens, according to the infant's growing ability to account for failure of adaptation and to tolerate the results of frustration. Naturally, the infant's own mother is more likely to be good enough than some other person, since this active adaptation demands an easy and unresented preoccupation with the one infant; in fact, success in infant care depends on the fact of devotion, not on cleverness or intellectual enlightenment.

The good-enough mother, as I have stated, starts off with an almost complete adaptation to her infant's needs, and as time proceeds she adapts less and less completely, gradually, according to the infant's growing ability to deal with her failure.

The infant's means of dealing with this maternal failure include the following:

1. The infant's experience, often repeated, that there is a time-limit to frustration. At first, naturally, this time-limit must be short.
2. Growing sense of process.
3. The beginnings of mental activity.
4. Employment of auto-erotic satisfactions.
5. Remembering, reliving, fantasying, dreaming; the integrating of past, present, and future.

If all goes well the infant can actually come to gain from the experience of frustration, since incomplete adaptation to need makes objects real, that is to say hated as well as loved. The consequence of this is that *if all goes well* the infant can be disturbed by a close adaptation to need that is continued too long, not allowed its natural decrease, since exact adaptation resembles magic and the object that behaves perfectly becomes no better than a hallucination. Nevertheless, *at the start* adaptation needs to be almost exact, and unless this is so it is not possible for the infant to begin to develop a capacity to experience a relationship to external reality, or even to form a conception of external reality.

Illusion and the Value of Illusion

The mother, at the beginning, by an almost 100 per cent adaptation affords the infant the opportunity for the *illusion* that her breast is part of the infant. It is, as it were, under the baby's magical control. The same can be said in terms of infant care in general, in the quiet times between excitements. Omnipotence is nearly a fact of experience. The mother's eventual task is gradually to dis-illusion the infant, but she has no hope of success unless at first she has been able to give sufficient opportunity for illusion.

In another language, the breast is created by the infant over and over again out of the infant's capacity to love or (one can say) out of need. A subjective phenomenon develops in the baby, which we call the mother's breast.[3] The mother places the actual breast just there where the infant is ready to create, and at the right moment.

From birth, therefore, the human being is concerned with the problem of the relationship between what is objectively perceived and what is subjectively conceived of, and in the solution of this problem there is no health for the human being who has not been started off well enough by the mother. *The intermediate area to which I am referring is the area that is allowed to the infant between primary creativity and objective perception based on reality-testing.* The transitional phenomena represent the early stages of the use of illusion, without which there is no meaning for the human being in the idea of a relationship with an object that is perceived by others as external to that being.

The idea illustrated in *Figure 1* is this: that at some theoretical point early in the development of every human individual an infant in a certain setting provided by the mother is capable of conceiving of the idea of something that would meet the growing need that arises out of instinctual tension. The infant cannot be said to know at first what is to be created. At this point in time the mother presents herself. In the ordinary way she gives her breast and her potential feeding urge. The mother's adaptation to the infant's needs, when good enough, gives the infant the *illusion* that there is an external reality that corresponds to the infant's own capacity to create. In other words, there is an overlap between what the mother supplies and what the child might conceive of. To the observer, the child perceives what the mother actually presents, but this is not the whole truth. The infant perceives the breast only in so far as a breast could be created just there and then. There is no interchange between the mother and the infant. Psychologically the infant takes from a breast that is part of the infant, and the mother gives milk to an infant that is part of herself. In psychology, the idea of interchange is based on an illusion in the psychologist.

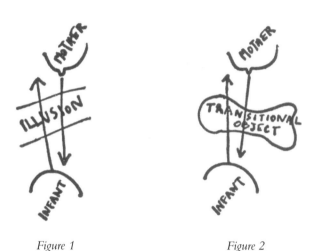

Figure 1   Figure 2

In *Figure 2* a shape is given to the area of illusion, to illustrate what I consider to be the main function of the transitional object and of transitional phenomena. The transitional object and the transitional phenomena start each human being off with what will always be important for them, i.e. a neutral area of experience which will not be challenged. *Of the transitional object it can be said that it is a matter of agreement between us and the baby that we will never ask the question: 'Did you conceive of this or was it presented to you from without?' The important point is that no decision on this point is expected. The question is not to be formulated.*

This problem, which undoubtedly concerns the human infant in a hidden way at the beginning, gradually becomes an obvious problem on account of the fact that the mother's main task (next to providing opportunity for illusion) is disillusionment. This is preliminary to the task of weaning, and it also continues as one of the tasks of parents and educators. In other words, this matter of *illusion* is one that belongs inherently to human beings and that no individual finally solves for himself or herself, although a *theoretical* understanding of it may provide a *theoretical* solution. If things go well, in this gradual disillusionment process, the stage is set for the frustrations that we gather together under the word weaning; but it should be remembered that when we talk about the phenomena (which Klein (1940) has specifically illuminated in her concept of the depressive position) that cluster round weaning we are assuming the underlying process, the process by which opportunity for illusion and gradual disillusionment is provided. If illusion-disillusionment has gone astray the infant cannot get to so normal a thing as weaning, nor to a reaction to weaning, and it is then absurd to refer to weaning at all. The mere termination of breast-feeding is not a weaning.

We can see the tremendous significance of weaning in the case of the normal child. When we witness the complex reaction that is set going in a certain child by the weaning process, we know that this is able to take place in that child because the illusion-disillusionment process is being carried through so well that we can ignore it while discussing actual weaning.

Development of the Theory of Illusion-Disillusionment

It is assumed here that the task of reality-acceptance is never completed, that no human being is free from the strain of relating inner and outer reality, and that relief from this strain is provided by an intermediate area of experience (cf. Riviere, 1936) which is not challenged (arts, religion, etc.). This intermediate area is in direct continuity with the play area of the small child who is 'lost' in play.

In infancy this intermediate area is necessary for the initiation of a relationship between the child and the world, and is made possible by good-enough mothering at the early critical phase. Essential to all this is continuity (in time) of the external emotional environment and of particular elements in the physical environment such as the transitional object or objects.

The transitional phenomena are allowable to the infant because of the parents' intuitive recognition of the strain inherent in objective perception, and we do not challenge the infant in regard to subjectivity or objectivity just here where there is the transitional object.

Should an adult make claims on us for our acceptance of the objectivity of his subjective phenomena we discern or diagnose madness. If, however, the adult can manage to enjoy the personal intermediate area without making claims, then we can acknowledge our own corresponding intermediate areas, and are pleased to find a degree of overlapping, that is to say common experience between members of a group in art or religion or philosophy.

SUMMARY

Attention is drawn to the rich field for observation provided by the earliest experiences of the healthy infant as expressed principally in the relationship to the first possession.

This first possession is related backwards in time to auto-erotic phenomena and fist- and thumb-sucking, and also forwards to the first soft animal or doll and to hard toys. It is related both to the external object (mother's breast) and to internal objects (magically introjected breast), but is distinct from each.

Transitional objects and transitional phenomena belong to the realm of illusion which is at the basis of initiation of experience. This early stage in development is made possible by the mother's special capacity for making adaptation to the needs of her infant, thus allowing the infant the illusion that what the infant creates really exists.

This intermediate area of experience, unchallenged in respect of its belonging to inner or external (shared) reality, constitutes the greater part of the infant's experience, and throughout life is retained in the intense experiencing that belongs to the arts and to religion and to imaginative living, and to creative scientific work.

An infant's transitional object ordinarily becomes gradually decathected, especially as cultural interests develop.

What emerges from these considerations is the further idea that paradox accepted can have positive value. The resolution of paradox leads to a defence organization which in the adult one can encounter as true and false self organization (Winnicott, 1960[a]).

II. AN APPLICATION OF THE THEORY

It is not the object, of course, that is transitional. The object represents the infant's transition from a state of being merged with the mother to a state of being in relation to the mother as something outside and separate. This is often referred to as the point at which the child grows up out of a narcissistic type of object-relating, but I have refrained from using this language because I am not sure that it is what I mean; also, it leaves out the idea of dependence, which is so essential at the earliest stages before the child has become sure that anything can exist that is not part of the child.

PSYCHOPATHOLOGY MANIFESTED IN THE AREA OF TRANSITIONAL PHENOMENA

I have laid great stress on the normality of transitional phenomena. Nevertheless, there is a psychopathology to be discerned in the course of the clinical examination of cases. As an example of the child's management of separation and loss I draw attention to the way in which separation can affect transitional phenomena.

As is well known, when the mother or some other person on whom the infant depends is absent, there is no immediate change owing to the fact that the infant has a memory or mental image of the mother, or what we call an internal representation of her, which remains alive for a certain length of time. If the mother is away over a period of time which is beyond a certain limit measured in minutes, hours, or days, then the memory or the internal representation fades. As this takes effect, the transitional phenomena become gradually meaningless and the infant is unable to experience them. We may watch the object becoming decathected. Just before loss we can sometimes see the exaggeration of the use of a transitional object as part of *denial* that there is a threat of its becoming meaningless. To illustrate this aspect of denial I shall give a short clinical example of a boy's use of string.

String[4]

A boy aged seven years was brought to the Psychology Department of the Paddington Green Children's Hospital by his mother and father in March 1955. The other two members of the family also came: a girl aged ten, attending an ESN school, and a rather normal small girl aged four. The case was referred by the family doctor because of a series of symptoms indicating a character disorder in the boy. An intelligence test gave the boy an IQ of 108. (For the purposes of this description all details that are not immediately relevant to the main theme of this chapter are omitted.)

I first saw the parents in a long interview in which they gave a clear picture of the boy's development and of the distortions in his development. They left out one important detail, however, which emerged in an interview with the boy.

It was not difficult to see that the mother was a depressive person, and she reported that she had been hospitalized on account of depression. From the parents' account I was able to note that the mother cared for the boy until the sister was born when he was three years three months. This was the first separation of importance, the next being at three years eleven months, when the mother had an operation. When the boy was four years nine months the mother went into a mental hospital for two months, and during this time he was well cared for by the mother's sister. By this time everyone looking after this boy agreed that he was difficult, although showing very good features. He was liable to change suddenly and to frighten people by saying, for instance, that he would cut his mother's sister into little pieces. He developed many curious symptoms, such as a compulsion to lick things and people; he made compulsive throat noises; often he refused to pass a motion and then made a mess. He was obviously anxious about his elder sister's mental defect, but the distortion of his development appears to have started before this factor became significant.

After this interview with the parents I saw the boy in a personal interview. There were present two psychiatric social workers and two visitors. The boy did not immediately give an abnormal impression and he quickly entered into a squiggle game with me. (In this squiggle game I make some kind of an impulsive line-drawing and invite the child whom I am interviewing to turn it into something, and then he makes a squiggle for me to turn into something in my turn.)

The squiggle game in this particular case led to a curious result. The boy's laziness immediately became evident, and also nearly everything I did was translated by him into something associated with string. Among his ten drawings there appeared the following:

> lasso
> whip
> crop
> a yo-yo string
> a string in a knot
> another crop
> another whip.

After this interview with the boy I had a second one with the parents, and asked them about the boy's preoccupation with string. They said that they were glad that I had brought up this subject, but they had not mentioned it because they were not sure of its significance. They said that the boy had become obsessed with everything to do with string, and in fact whenever they went into a room they were liable to find that he had joined together chairs and tables; and they might find a cushion, for instance, with a string joining it to the fireplace. They said that the boy's preoccupation with string was gradually developing a new feature, one that had worried them instead of causing them ordinary concern. He had recently tied a string round his sister's neck (the sister whose birth provided the first separation of this boy from his mother).

In this particular kind of interview I knew I had limited opportunity for action: it would not be possible to see these parents or the boy more frequently than once in six months, since the family lived in the country. I therefore took action in the following way. I explained to the mother that this boy was dealing with a fear of separation, attempting to deny separation by his use of string, as one would deny separation from a friend by using the telephone. She was sceptical, but I told her that should she come round to finding some sense in what I was saying I should like her to open up the matter with the boy at some convenient time, letting him know what I had said, and then developing the theme of separation according to the boy's response.

I heard no more from these people until they came to see me about six months later. The mother did not report to me what she had done, but I asked her and she was able to tell me what had taken place soon after the visit to me. She had felt that what I had said was silly, but one evening she had opened the subject with the boy and found him to be eager to talk about his relation to her and his fear of a lack of contact with her. She went over all the separations she could think of with him with his help, and she soon became convinced that what I had said was right, because of his responses. Moreover, from the moment that she had this conversation with him the string play ceased. There was no more joining of objects in the old way. She had had many other conversations with the boy about his feeling of separateness from her, and she made the very significant comment that she felt the most important separation to have been his loss of her when she was seriously depressed; it was not just her going away, she said, but her lack of contact with him because of her complete preoccupation with other matters.

At a later interview the mother told me that a year after she had had her first talk with the boy there was a return to playing with string and to joining together objects in the house. She was in fact due to go into hospital for an operation, and she said to him: 'I can see from your playing with string that you are worried about my going away, but this time I shall only be away a few days, and I am having an operation which is not serious.' After this conversation the new phase of playing with string ceased.

I have kept in touch with this family and have helped with various details in the boy's schooling and other matters. Recently, four years after the original interview, the father reported a new phase of string pre-occupation, associated with a fresh depression in the mother. This phase lasted two months; it cleared up when the whole family went on holiday, and when at the same time there was an improvement in the home situation (the father having found work after a period of unemployment). Associated with this was an improvement in the mother's state. The father gave one further interesting detail relevant to the subject under discussion. During this recent phase the boy had acted out something with rope which the father felt to be significant, because it showed how intimately all these things were connected with the mother's morbid anxiety. He came home one day and found the boy hanging upside down on a rope.

He was quite limp and acting very well as if dead. The father realized that he must take no notice, and he hung around the garden doing odd jobs for half an hour, after which the boy got bored and stopped the game. This was a big test of the father's lack of anxiety. On the following day, however, the boy did the same thing from a tree which could easily be seen from the kitchen window. The mother rushed out severely shocked and certain that he had hanged himself.

The following additional detail might be of value in the understanding of the case. Although this boy, who is now eleven, is developing along 'tough-guy' lines, he is very self-conscious and easily goes red in the neck. He has a number of teddy bears which to him are children. No one dares to say that they are toys. He is loyal to them, expends a great deal of affection over them, and makes trousers for them, which involves careful sewing. His father says that he seems to get a sense of security from his family, which he mothers in this way. If visitors come he quickly puts them all into his sister's bed, because no one outside the family must know that he has this family. Along with this is a reluctance to defaecate, or a tendency to save up his faeces. It is not difficult to guess, therefore, that he has a maternal identification based on his own insecurity in relation to his mother, and that this could develop into homosexuality. In the same way the preoccupation with string could develop into a perversion.

Comment

The following comment seems to be appropriate.

★   ★   ★

1. String can be looked upon as an extension of all other techniques of communication. String joins, just as it also helps in the wrapping up of objects and in the holding of unintegrated material. In this respect string has a symbolic meaning for everyone; an exaggeration of the use of string can easily belong to the beginnings of a sense of insecurity or the idea of a lack of communication. In this particular case it is possible to detect abnormality creeping into the boy's use of string, and it is important to find a way of stating the change which might lead to its use becoming perverted.

It would seem possible to arrive at such a statement if one takes into consideration the fact that the function of the string is changing from communication into a *denial of separation*. As a denial of separation string becomes a thing in itself, something that has dangerous properties and must needs be mastered. In this case the mother seems to have been able to deal with the boy's use of string just before it was too late, when the use of it still contained hope. When hope is absent and string represents a denial of separation, then a much more complex state of affairs has arisen − one that becomes difficult to cure, because of the secondary gains that arise out of the skill that develops whenever an object has to be handled in order to be mastered.

This case therefore is of special interest if it makes possible the observation of the development of a perversion.

★　　★　　★

2. It is also possible to see from this material the use that can be made of parents. When parents can be used they can work with great economy, especially if the fact is kept in mind that there will never be enough psycho-therapists to treat all those who are in need of treatment. Here was a good family that had been through a difficult time because of the father's unemployment; that had been able to take full responsibility for a backward girl in spite of the tremendous drawbacks, socially and within the family, that this entails; and that had survived the bad phases in the mother's depressive illness, including one phase of hospitalization. There must be a great deal of strength in such a family, and it was on the basis of this assumption that the decision was made to invite these parents to undertake the therapy of their own child. In doing this they learned a great deal themselves, but they did need to be informed about what they were doing. They also needed their success to be appreciated and the whole process to be verbalized. The fact that they have seen their boy through an illness has given the parents confidence with regard to their ability to manage other difficulties that arise from time to time.

Added Note 1969

In the decade since this report was written I have come to see that this boy could not be cured of his illness. The tie-up with the mother's depressive illness remained, so that he could not be kept from running back to his home. Away, he could have had personal treatment, but at home personal treatment was impracticable. At home he retained the pattern that was already set at the time of the first interview.

In adolescence this boy developed new addictions, especially to drugs, and he could not leave home in order to receive education. All attempts to get him placed away from his mother failed because he regularly escaped and ran back home.

He became an unsatisfactory adolescent, lying around and apparently wasting his time and his intellectual potential (as noted above, he had an IQ of 108).

The question is: would an investigator making a study of this case of drug addiction pay proper respect to the psychopathology manifested in the area of transitional phenomena?

III. CLINICAL MATERIAL: ASPECTS OF FANTASY

In the later part of this book I shall explore some of the ideas that occur to me while I am engaged in clinical work and where I feel that the theory I have formed for my own benefit in regard to transitional phenomena affects what I see and hear and what I do.

Here I shall give in detail some clinical material from an adult patient to show how the sense of loss itself can become a way of integrating one's self-experience.

The material is of one session of a woman patient's analysis, and I give it because it collects together various examples of the great variety that characterizes the vast area between objectivity and subjectivity.

> This patient, who has several children, and who has a high intelligence which she uses in her work, comes to treatment because of a wide range of symptomatology which is usually collected together under the word 'schizoid'. It is probable that those who have dealings with her do not recognize how ill she feels, and certainly she is usually liked and is felt to have value.
>
> This particular session started with a dream which could be described as depressive. It contained straightforward and revealing transference material with the analyst as an avaricious dominating woman. This leaves way for her hankering after a former analyst who is very much a male figure for her. This is dream, and as dream could be used as material for interpretation. The patient was pleased that she was dreaming more. Along with this she was able to describe certain enrichments in her actual living in the world.
>
> Every now and again she is overtaken by what might be called *fantasying*. She is going on a train journey; there is an accident. How will the children know what has happened to her? How indeed will her analyst know? She might be screaming, but her mother would not hear. From this she went on to talk about her most awful experience in which she left a cat for a little while and she heard afterwards that the cat had been crying for several hours. This is 'altogether too awful' and joins up with the very many separations she experienced throughout her childhood, separations that went beyond her capacity to allow for, and were therefore traumatic, necessitating the organization of new sets of defences.
>
> Much of the material in this analysis has to do with coming to the negative side of relationships; that is to say, with the gradual failure that has to be experienced by the child when the parents are not available. The patient is extremely sensitive to all this in regard to her own children and ascribes much of the difficulty that she has with her first child to the fact that she left this child for three days to go for a holiday with her husband when she had started a new pregnancy; that is to say, when the child was

nearly two. She was told that the child had cried for four hours without stopping, and when she came home it was no use for quite a long time for her to try to re-establish rapport.

We were dealing with the fact that animals and small children cannot be told what is happening. The cat could not understand. Also, a baby under two years cannot be properly informed about a new baby that is expected, although 'by twenty months or so' it becomes increasingly possible to explain this in words that a baby can understand.

When no understanding can be given, then when the mother is away to have a new baby she is dead from the point of view of the child. This is what dead means.

It is a matter of days or hours or minutes. Before the limit is reached the mother is still alive; after this limit has been overstepped she is dead. In between is a precious moment of anger, but this is quickly lost, or perhaps never experienced, always potential and carrying fear of violence.

From here we come to the two extremes, so different from each other: the death of the mother when she is present, and her death when she is not able to reappear and therefore to come alive again. This has to do with the time just before the child has built up the ability to bring people alive in the inner psychic reality apart from the reassurance of seeing, feeling, smelling.

It can be said that this patient's childhood had been one big exercise exactly in this area. She was evacuated because of the war when she was about eleven; she completely forgot her childhood and her parents, but all the time she steadily maintained the right not to call those who were caring for her 'uncle' and 'auntie', which was the usual technique. She managed *never to call them anything* the whole of those years, and this was the negative of remembering her mother and father. It will be understood that the pattern for all this was set up in her early childhood.

From this my patient reached the position, which again comes into the transference, that the only real thing is the gap; that is to say, the death or the absence or the amnesia. In the course of the session she had a specific amnesia and this bothered her, and it turned out that the important communication for me to get was that there could be a blotting out, and that this blank could be the only fact and the only thing that was real. The amnesia is real, whereas what is forgotten has lost its reality.

In connection with this the patient remembered that there is a rug available in the consulting-room which she once put around herself and once used for a regressive episode during an analytic session. At present she is not going over to fetch this rug or using it. The reason is that the rug that is not there (because she does not go for it) is more real than the rug that the analyst might bring, as he certainly had the idea to do. Consideration of this brings her up against the absence of the rug, or perhaps it would be better to say against the unreality of the rug in its symbolic meaning.

From here there was a development in terms of the idea of symbols. The last of her former analysts 'will always be more important to me than my present analyst'. She added: 'You may do me more good, but I like him better. This will be true when I have completely forgotten him. The negative of him is more real than the positive of you.' These may not be exactly her words but it is what she was conveying to me in clear language of her own, and it was what she needed me to understand.

The subject of nostalgia comes into the picture: it belongs to the precarious hold that a person may have on the inner representation of a lost object. This subject reappears in the case-report that follows (1971[d]).

The patient then talked about her imagination and the limits of what she believed to be real. She started by saying: 'I didn't really believe that there was an angel standing by my bed; on the other hand, I used to have an eagle chained to my wrist.' This certainly did feel real to her and the accent was on the words 'chained to my wrist'. She also had a white horse which was as real as possible and she 'would ride it everywhere and hitch it to a tree and all that sort of thing'. She would like really to own a white horse now so as to be able to deal with the reality of this white horse experience and make it real in another way. As she spoke I felt how easily these ideas could be labelled hallucinatory except in the context of her age at the time and her exceptional experiences in regard to repeated loss of otherwise good parents. She exclaimed: 'I suppose I want something that never goes away.' We formulated this by saying that the real thing is the thing that is not there. The chain is a denial of the eagle's absence, which is the positive element.

From here we got on to the symbols that fade. She claimed that she had had some success in making her symbols real for a long time in spite of the separations. We both came to something here at the same time, which is that her very fine intellect has been exploited, but at cost. She read from very early, and read a great deal; she has done a great deal of thinking from the earliest times and she has always used her intellect to keep things going and she has enjoyed this; but she was relieved (I thought) when I told her that with this use of the intellect there is all the time a fear of mental defect. From this she quickly reached over to her interest in autistic children and her intimate tie-up with a friend's schizophrenia, a condition that illustrates the idea of mental defect in spite of good intellect. She has felt tremendously guilty about having a great pride in her good intellect, which has always been a rather obvious feature. It was difficult for her to think that perhaps her friend may have had a good intellectual potential although in his case it would be necessary to say that he had slipped over into the obverse, which is mental retardation through mental illness.

She described various techniques for dealing with separation; for instance: a paper spider and pulling the legs off for every day that her mother was away. Then she also had flashes, as she called them, and she would suddenly see, for instance, her dog Toby, a toy: 'Oh there's Toby.' There is a picture in the family album of herself with Toby, a toy, that she has forgotten except in the flashes. This led on to a terrible incident in which her mother had said to her: 'But we "heard" you cry all the time we were away.' They were four miles apart. She was two years old at the time and she thought: 'Could it possibly be that my mother told me a lie?' She was not able to cope with this at the time and she tried to deny what she really knew to be true, that her mother had in fact lied. It was difficult to believe in her mother in this guise because everyone said: 'Your mother is so marvellous.'

From this it seemed possible for us to reach to an idea which was rather new from my point of view. Here was the picture of a child and the child had transitional objects, and there were transitional phenomena that were evident, and all of these were symbolical of something and were real for the child; but gradually, or perhaps frequently for a little while, she had to *doubt the reality of the thing that they were symbolizing.* That is to say, if they were symbolical of her mother's devotion and reliability they remained real in themselves but what they stood for was not real. The mother's devotion and reliability were unreal.

This seemed to be near the sort of thing that has haunted her all her life, losing animals, losing her own children, so that she formulated the sentence: 'All I have got is what I have not got.' There is a desperate attempt here to turn the negative into a last-ditch defence against the end of everything. The negative is the only positive. When she got to this point she said to her analyst: 'And what will you do about it?' I was silent and she said; 'Oh, I see.' I thought perhaps that she was resenting my masterly inactivity. I said: 'I am silent because I don't know what to say.' She quickly said that this was all right. Really she was glad about the silence, and she would have preferred it if I had said nothing at all. Perhaps as a silent analyst I might have been joined up with the former analyst that she knows she will always be looking for. She will always expect him to come back and say 'Well done!' or something. This will be long after she has forgotten what he looks like. I was thinking that her meaning was: when he has become sunk in the general pool of subjectivity and joined up with what she thought she found when she had a mother and before she began to notice her mother's deficiencies as a mother, that is to say, her absences.

Conclusion

In this session we had roamed over the whole field between subjectivity and objectivity, and we ended up with a bit of a game. She was going on a railway journey to her holiday house and she said: 'Well I think you had better come with me, perhaps half-way.' She was talking about the way in which it matters to her very much indeed that she is leaving me. This was only for a week, but there was a rehearsal here for the summer holiday. It was also saying that after a little while, when she has got away from me, it will not matter any longer. So, at a half-way station, I get out and 'come back in the hot train', and she derided my maternal identification aspects by adding: 'And it will be very tiring, and there will be a lot of children and babies, and they will climb all over you, and they will probably be sick all over you, and serve you right.'

(It will be understood that there was no idea of my *really* accompanying her.)

Just before she went she said: 'Do you know I believe when I went away at the time of evacuation [in the war] I could say that *I went to see if my parents were there*. I seem to have believed I would find them there.' (This implied that they were certainly not to be found at home.) And the implication was that she took a year or two to find the answer. The answer was that they were not there, and that *that* was reality. She had already said to me about the rug that she did not use: 'You know, don't you, that the rug might be very comfortable, but reality is more important than comfort and *no rug* can therefore be more important than *a rug*.'

This clinical fragment illustrates the value of keeping in mind the distinctions that exist between phenomena in terms of their position in the area between external or shared reality and the true dream.

Notes

1. Published in the *International Journal of Psycho-Analysis*. Vol. 34, Part 2 (1953); and in D. W. Winnicott, *Collected Papers: Through Paediatrics to Psycho-Analysis* (1958[a]), London: Tavistock Publications.
2. Text modified here, though based on the original statement.
3. I include the whole technique of mothering. When it is said that the first object is the breast, the word 'breast' is used, I believe, to stand for the technique of mothering as well as for the actual flesh. It is not impossible for a mother to be a good-enough mother (in my way of putting it) with a bottle for the actual feeding.
4. Published in *Child Psychology and Psychiatry*, Vol. 1 (1960[c]); and in Winnicott, *The Maturational Processes and the Facilitating Environment* (1965[a]), London: Hogarth Press and the Institute of Psycho-Analysis.

Developing ideas: transitional object/phenomena; the baby's first possession; potential/transitional space; illusion and paradox; disillusionment

6 METAPSYCHOLOGICAL AND CLINICAL ASPECTS OF REGRESSION WITHIN THE PSYCHO-ANALYTICAL SET-UP (1954)

OTHER WRITINGS

Winnicott's growing understanding of the aetiology of serious mental illness further developed the themes begun in 'Hate in the Countertransference', and presented in 'Psychoses and Child Care' (1952a) and 'Anxiety Associated with Insecurity' (1952b). He located a sense of 'being' within the 'environment–individual set-up', that is, the mother–infant relationship. The 1953 paper, 'Symptom Tolerance in Paediatrics: A Case History' to the Royal Society of Medicine referred to the importance of the father in development.

From 1951 Winnicott wrote prolifically and his work increasingly constituted a critique of Kleinian ideas. In a letter to the Kleinian analyst, Roger Money-Kyrle, he clarified his use of the term 'good-enough mother' (Rodman, 1987: 38–43). He elaborated the implications of his 'research cases' for psycho-analytic practice and in 1954 he presented 'Withdrawal and Regression' to the Seventeenth Conference of Psychoanalysts of the Romance Languages in Paris.

Michael Balint had begun publishing papers following a similar interest in the place of regression in psychoanalysis and culminating in *Thrills and Regressions* (1959). Significant psychoanalytic contributions were made in the late 1940s and early 1950s. The group around Klein published papers which were concerned with extending their understanding of psychoanalysis in the fest-schrift collection *New Directions in Psychoanalysis* (Klein, Heimann, and Money-Kyrle, 1955) which also included a paper by Marion Milner; papers on politics (Money-Kyrle, 1951) and on industrial relations (Jaques, 1951). Pearl King, who was supervised by Winnicott for a child case, and who was to become a significant contributor to the Independent tradition, gave her first paper at the BPAS the 'Experiences of Success and Failure as Essential to the Process of Development' in 1953 (King, 1953/2005). In the USA, Erik Erikson published *Childhood and Society* (1950) which incorporated social anthropology with psychoanalysis.

EDITORS' INTRODUCTION

This paper gains from being read together with 'Withdrawal and Regression', Winnicott's other main paper on the topic (Winnicott, 1954b). Both describe a situation that may happen in certain analyses, what he calls 'a regression to dependence'. In this situation he argues for an adaptation of classical technique and a prioritization of the importance of the setting in preference to the normal interpreting tools of analytic work. In certain cases of severe psychopathology this regression to dependence becomes a feature of the analysis. Both states are different from more transient states of regression that analysts recognize in their more intact patients.

The concept of regression has a long history in psychoanalysis but its definition remains imprecise; it includes the id regression to previous stages of libidinal development, with their corresponding fantasies and wishes, and the idea of fixation points in psychosexual development suggested by Freud. In these approaches, involving a kind of temporal retreat, the regression is almost always considered as defensive. Either the patient returns mentally to the freezing and encapsulation of an earlier situation as an escape from a more conflicted present, or there is a return from later difficulties to a 'good' pregenital situation that contains the memory of a good encounter with the environment. In both cases it is regarded as a defence against conflict.

For Winnicott, Freud's work seems to confirm the early maternal environment taken for granted and represented in the setting he created for the work of analysis. In his own approach to regression, the reliability of that setting assumes greater importance than any other factor and may involve modifications of normal analytic practice that have long been the focus for debate.

Regression has always been a notion that is taken for granted yet tends to the imprecise and vague. It is mostly used to suggest the arrival of something in the analytic work, an affect, a state of mind that is 'earlier' or 'more primitive', 'the reversal of higher forms of organisation to lower developmentally earlier ones whether of libido-development, ego functioning or object relating' (Tonnesmann, 1993: 9). From some contemporary perspectives, its utility and necessity are questionable (Spurling, 2008; Tyson and Tyson, 1993); so it is important to approach Winnicott's accounts with two differing historical contexts in mind, that of the period in which they were written, and their reception now. At the time they constituted a research in progress which produced advances in the understanding of a wider clinical case base and 'Fragment of an Analysis', originally written in 1955 (published as Winnicott with Khan, 1986) provides verbatim reports of sessions to illustrate the meaning of a 'regression to independence' (Abram, 2007). Winnicott was influenced by Balint, who in 1952, had postulated the need of a 'new beginning' for patients whose problems derived from early failures: analysis had to recapture the individual's primitive need to be loved for his or her own sake. Tonnesmann (1993: 9), for example, links the idea of regression as 'a function of value which may operate in the service of ultimate progression signifying hope, as Winnicott said', with the object relations theories of Balint, Fairbairn and Winnicott. More recently, a questioning of historical construction in treatment (O'Shaughnessy, 2008), and anxieties about orthodoxy and unorthodoxy among senior psychoanalysts (Segal, 2006) have resulted in a more critical reception.

Regression cannot be a matter of simple reversal, since progress, as an evolutionary activity with a biological basis involving the integration of psyche–soma, personality and mind (intellect) leading to character formation and socialization, cannot simply be reversed. For those patients able to regress in analysis in the way Winnicott discusses, a certain level of ego organization is required. There is a threat of chaos, but there is also a false-self structure in place that has been produced by an early failure of adaptation. With such a mental organization the capacity to regress to dependence can be attempted. The idea of the false self and the need to dismantle it to allow a true self to emerge become central. The provision of specialized adaptation in the clinical situation to meet the need for regression to the state of original failure may then result in a new forward emotional development.

Without a relatively structured mental organization, a therapeutic regression in this sense cannot occur, so the considerations Winnicott raised do not indicate regression and the difficulties of its management for all cases of severe psychopathology. The sustained appearance of regression to dependence in a treatment relates to patients who present with difficulties at the stage before the establishment of the personality; its appearance in the analysis has parallels with the area of primitive emotional development in the life of the baby, which, to be handled appropriately, involves sufficient environmental adaptation to meet that infant's needs. With this parallel in mind, and an assumption about the patient and the patient's psychopathology based on the experience of the transference and the consulting room, Winnicott argues for different treatment priorities: the consistency and reliability of the setting and, within it, the analyst, together with the abandonment, for a time, of any interpretative approach. Patients who exhibit problems at this level, what Balint (1968) would call 'the basic fault', are likely to require more emphasis on what Winnicott calls 'management' and a much more literal and less symbolic invocation of the setting as a whole. This view of development and psychopathology requires a form of analytic intervention that emphasizes the patient's dependency upon the analyst, something which is experienced as a great risk by the patient. It also demands much of the analyst if the false self is to be given up and a movement towards an emergence of the true self take place.

Winnicott locates psychosis, futility, unreality, and the false-self personality in early environmental failure. With certain patients only, the emphasis is on changes in technique in the idea of regression to dependence. In the process of analysis the setting reproduces early mothering and invites regression, seen here as an organized return to early dependency and the success of primary narcissism. The aim would be the emergence of the true self which, without the organization of the false self to protect it from experience, puts realness in the place of futility by surrendering to the total ego.

Individual growth, involving the unfreezing of the original situation of failure, and subsequently anger about that original failure, can then happen. All this implies 'good-enough adaptation', as in the early mother–infant situation, and it is this that can lead to development of ego integration, psyche–soma integration and relatedness to objects.

Regression in this sense implies a situation of need, which, if not met, results in futility and despair. It puts heavy demands upon the analyst, who has to make certain judgements since, for this type of regressed patient, for whom time registers a different meaning, the existence of a third cannot be conceived of, and the normal analytic tools are not available. One kind of analysis does not preclude the other. The key question is when to work with the change of emphasis.

Winnicott's clinical practice and its departures from classical technique with patients of this kind have periodically been raised as constituting boundary violations and unacceptable practice. The areas identified include longer sessions, management outside the session, and physical contact. These discussions on regression invite consideration of the links, or potential links, between theory and clinical technique, an area of concern from at least Ferenczi onward and one frequently raised in discussion of different patient populations and their requirements.

Winnicott's way of working with disturbed, more borderline patients and the related ideas about the benefits of clinical regression encounter those same practices that are held up as instances of boundary violations and unacceptable breaks in the analytic frame. They were part of a search for alternative ways of working that respond to the clinical needs of particular patients and, perhaps, on occasion, to a somewhat idealized version of the receptive mother attuned to her baby, where the analyst becomes the person who knows and has to hold the patient. On both counts – the attuned mother and the apparently direct re-creation of the mother–infant couple rather than its symbolic actualization (Tyson and Tyson, 1993: 228) – Winnicott's approach has been much questioned. Tonnesmann, however, is quite clear that 'the analytic management of regressed patients, such as Balint and Winnicott practised, fostered the analytic process. Here the so-called analytic management did not consist of the analyst's pre-conceived judgement of the patient's needs to be actively introduced into the analytic session. Instead, they were spontaneous responses to the patient's pre-verbal communications and regressed needs as they were perceived at any one moment during the session' (Tonnesmann, 1993: 10). For her, they remained true to Freud's original understanding of analysis: 'the analyst always responds to the patient's communication; he never initiates communications in his own right' (Tonnesmann, 1993: 10). These are ongoing debates about what happens and what can happen in an analysis and how it can be explained and demonstrated.

Metapsychological and Clinical Aspects of Regression within the Psycho-Analytical Set-Up[1]
(1954)

The study of the place of regression in analytic work is one of the tasks Freud left us to carry out, and I think it is a subject for which this Society is ready. I base this idea on the fact that material relevant to the subject occurs frequently in papers read before the Society. Usually attention is not specifically drawn to this aspect of our work, or else it is referred to casually under the guise of the intuitive or 'art' aspect of psycho-analytic practice.

The subject of regression is one that has been forced on my attention by certain cases during the past dozen years of my clinical work. It is, of course, too vast for full presentation here and now. I shall choose therefore those aspects that seem to me to introduce the discussion in a fruitful way.

Analysis is not only a technical exercise. It is something that we become able to do when we have reached a stage in acquiring a basic technique. What we become able to do enables us to co-operate with the patient in following the *process*, that which in each patient has its own pace and which follows its own course; all the important features of this process derive from the patient and not from ourselves as analysts.

Let us therefore clearly keep before our minds the difference between technique and the carrying through of a treatment. It is possible to carry through a treatment with limited technique, and it is possible with highly developed technique to fail to carry through a treatment.

Let us also bear in mind that by the legitimate method of careful choice of case we may and usually do avoid meeting aspects of human nature that must take us beyond our technical equipment.

Choice of case implies classification. For my present purpose I group cases according to the technical equipment they require of the analyst. I divide cases into the following three categories. *First* there are those patients who operate as whole persons and whose difficulties are in the realm of interpersonal relationships. The technique for the treatment of these patients belongs to psychoanalysis as it developed in the hands of Freud at the beginning of the century.

Then *secondly* there come the patients in whom the wholeness of the personality only just begins to be something that can be taken for granted; in fact one can say that analysis has to do with the first events that belong to and inherently and immediately follow not only the achievement of wholeness but also the coming together of love and hate and the dawning recognition of dependence. This is the analysis of the stage of concern, or of what has come to be known as the 'depressive position'. These patients require the analysis of mood. The technique for this work is not different from that needed by patients in the first category; nevertheless some new management problems do arise on account of the increased range of clinical material tackled. Important from our point of view here is the idea of the *survival of the analyst* as a dynamic factor.

In the *third* grouping I place all those patients whose analyses must deal with the early stages of emotional development before and up to the establishment of the personality as an entity, before the achievement of space-time unit status. The personal structure is not yet securely founded. In regard to this third grouping, the accent is more surely on management, and sometimes over long periods with these patients ordinary analytic work has to be in abeyance, management being the whole thing.

To recapitulate in terms of environment, one can say that in the first group-ing we are dealing with patients who develop difficulties in the ordinary course of their home life, assuming a home life in the pre-latency period, and assuming satisfactory development at the earlier infantile stages. In the second category, the analysis of the depressive position, we are dealing with the mother–child relationship especially around the time that weaning becomes a meaningful term. The mother holds a situation in time. In the third category there comes primitive emotional development, that which needs the mother actually holding the infant.

Into the last of these three categories falls one of my patients who has perhaps taught me most about regression. On another occasion I may be able to give a full account of this treatment, but at present I must do little more than point out that I have had the experience of allowing a regression absolutely full sway, and of watching the result.

Briefly, I have had a patient (a woman now in middle age) who had had an ordinary good analysis before coming to me but who obviously still needed help. This case had originally presented itself as one in the first category of my classification, but although the diagnosis of psychosis would never have been made by a psychiatrist, an analytical diagnosis needed to be made that took into account a very early development of a false self. For treatment to be effectual, there had to be a regression in search of the true self. Fortunately in this case I was able to manage the whole regression myself, that is to say, without the help of an institution. I decided at the start that the regression must be allowed its head, and no attempt, except once near the beginning, was made to interfere with the regressive process which followed its own course. (The one occasion was an interpretation I made, arising out of the material, of oral erotism and sadism in the transference. This was correct but about six years too early because I did not yet fully believe in the regression. For my own sake I had to test the effect of one ordinary interpretation. When the right time came for this interpretation it had become unnecessary.) It was a matter of about three or four years before the depth of the regression was reached, following which there started up a progress in emotional development. There has been no new regression. There has been an absence of chaos, though chaos has always threatened.

I have therefore had a unique experience even for an analyst. I cannot help being different from what I was before this analysis started. Non-analysts would not know the tremendous amount that this kind of experience of *one* patient can teach, but amongst analysts I can expect it to be fully understood that this one experience that I have had has tested psycho-analysis in a special way, and has taught me a great deal.

The treatment and management of this case has called on everything that I possess as a human being, as a psycho-analyst, and as a paediatrician. I have had to make personal growth in the course of this treatment which was painful and which I would gladly have avoided. In particular I have had to learn to examine my own technique whenever difficulties arose, and it has always turned out in the dozen or so resistance phases that the cause was in a countertransference phenomenon which necessitated further self-analysis in the analyst. It is not my aim in this paper to give a description of this case, since one must choose whether to be clinical or theoretical in one's approach, and I have chosen to be theoretical. Nevertheless I have this case all the time in mind.[2]

The main thing is that in this case, as in many others that have led up to it in my practice, I have needed to re-examine my technique, even that adapted to the more usual case. Before I explain what I mean I must explain my use of the word regression.

For me, the word regression simply means the reverse of progress. This progress itself is the evolution of the individual, psyche-soma, personality, and mind with (eventually) character formation and socialization. Progress starts from a date certainly prior to birth. There is a biological drive behind progress.

It is one of the tenets of psycho-analysis that health implies continuity in regard to this evolutionary progress of the psyche and that health is maturity of emotional development appropriate to the age of the individual, maturity that is to say in regard to this evolutionary process.

On closer examination one observes immediately that *there cannot be a simple reversal of progress*. For this progress to be reversed there has to be in the individual an organization which enables regression to occur.

We see:

A failure of adaptation on the part of the environment that results in the development of a false self.

A belief in the possibility of a correction of the original failure represented by a latent capacity for regression which implies a complex ego organization.

Specialized environmental provision, followed by actual regression.

New forward emotional development, with complications that will be described later.

Incidentally I think it is not useful to use the word regression whenever infantile behaviour appears in a case history. The word regression has derived a popular meaning which we need not adopt. When we speak of regression in psycho-analysis we imply the existence of an ego organization and a threat of chaos. There is a great deal for study here in the way in which the individual stores up memories and ideas and potentialities. It is as if there is an expectation that favourable conditions may arise justifying regression and offering a new chance for forward development, that which was rendered impossible or difficult initially by environmental failure.

It will be seen that I am considering the idea of regression within a highly organized ego-defence mechanism, one which involves the existence of a false self. In the patient referred to above this false self gradually became a 'caretaker self', and only after some years could the caretaker self become handed over to the analyst, and the self surrender to the ego.

One has to include in one's theory of the development of a human being the idea that it is normal and healthy for the individual to be able to defend the self against specific environmental failure by a *freezing of the failure situation*. Along with this goes an unconscious assumption (which can become a conscious hope) that opportunity will occur at a later date for a renewed experience in which the failure situation will be able to be unfrozen and re-experienced, with the individual in a regressed state, in an environment that is making adequate adaptation. The theory is here being put forward of regression as part of a healing process, in fact, a normal phenomenon that can properly be studied in the healthy person. In the very ill person there is but little hope of new opportunity. In the extreme case the therapist would need to go to the patient and actively present good mothering, an experience that could not have been expected by the patient.

There are several ways in which the healthy individual deals with specific early environmental failures; but there is one of them that I am calling here the freezing of the failure situation. There must be a relation between this and the concept of the fixation point.

In psycho-analytic theory we often state that in the course of instinct development in the pregenital phases *unfavourable situations* can create fixation points in the emotional development of the individual. At a later stage, for instance at the stage of genital dominance, that is to say when the whole person is involved in interpersonal relationships (and when it is quite ordinarily Freudian to speak about the Oedipus complex and castration fears), anxiety may lead to a regression in terms of instinct quality to that operative at the fixation point, and the consequence is a reinforcement of the original failure situation. This theory has proved its value and is in daily use, and there is no need to abandon it while at the same time looking at it afresh.

> A simple example would be that of a boy whose infancy had been normal, who at the time of tonsillectomy was given an enema, first by his mother,

and then by a group of nurses who had to hold him down. He was then two. Following this he had bowel difficulty but at the age of nine (age at consultation) he appears clinically as a severe case of constipation. In the meantime there has been a serious interference with his emotional development in terms of genital fantasy. In this case there happens to be the complication that the boy has reacted to the giving of the enema as if it had been a revenge on the part of the mother on account of his homosexuality, and what went into repression was the homosexuality and along with it the anal-erotic potential. In the analysis of this boy one knows that there would be acting out to be dealt with, a repetition compulsion associated with the original trauma. One knows also that the changes in this boy would not follow a simple re-enactment of the trauma but would follow ordinary Oedipus complex interpretation in the transference neurosis.

I give this as an ordinary case illustrating a symptom which was a regression to a fixation point where a trauma was clearly present.

Analysts have found it necessary to postulate that more normally there are *good* pregenital situations to which the individual can return when in difficulties at a later stage. This is a health phenomenon. There has thus arisen the idea of two kinds of regression in respect of instinct development, the one being a going back to an early failure situation and the other to an early success situation.

I think that insufficient attention has been drawn to the difference between these two phenomena. In the case of the environmental failure situation what we see is evidence of *personal defences* organized by the individual and requiring analysis. In the case of the more normal early success situation what we see more obviously is the memory of *dependence*, and therefore we encounter an *environmental situation* rather than a personal defence organization. The personal organization is not so obvious because it has remained fluid, and less defensive. I should mention at this point that I am relying on an assumption which I have often made before and which is by no means always accepted, namely, that towards the theoretical beginning there is less and less of personal failure, eventually only failure of environmental adaptation.

We are concerned, therefore, not merely with regression to good and bad points in the instinct experiences of the individual, but also to good and bad points in the environmental adaptation to ego needs and id needs in the individual's history.

We can think in terms of genital and pregenital stages of the development of *instinct* quality, we can use the word regression simply as a reversal of progress, a voyage back from genital to phallic, phallic to excretory, excretory to ingestive. But however much we develop our thinking in this direction we have to admit that a great deal of clinical material cannot be fitted into the framework of this theory.

The alternative is to put the accent on ego development and on dependence, and in this case when we speak of regression we immediately speak of environmental adaptation in its successes and failures. One of the points that I am trying to make especially clear is that our thinking on this subject has been confused by an attempt to trace back the ego without ourselves evolving as we go an increasing interest in environment. We can build theories of *instinct* development and agree to leave out the environment, but there is no possibility of doing this in regard to formulation of *early ego* development. We must always remember, I suggest, that the end result of our thinking about ego development is primary narcissism. In primary narcissism the environment is holding the individual, and *at the same time* the individual knows of no environment and is at one with it.

If I had time I would point out the way in which an organized regression is sometimes confused with pathological withdrawal and defensive splittings of various kinds. These states are related to regression in the sense that they are defensive organizations. The organization that makes regression useful has this quality distinct from the other defence organizations in that it carries with it the hope of a new opportunity for an unfreezing of the frozen situation and a chance for the environment, that is to say, the present-day environment, to make adequate though belated adaptation.

From this is derived the fact, if it be a fact, that it is from psychosis that a patient can make spontaneous recovery, whereas psychoneurosis makes no spontaneous recovery and the psycho-analyst is truly needed. In other words, psychosis is closely related to health, in which innumerable environmental failure situations are frozen but are reached and unfrozen by the various healing phenomena of ordinary life, namely friendships, nursing during physical illness, poetry, etc., etc.

It seems to me that it is only lately in the literature that *regression to dependence* has taken its rightful place in clinical descriptions. The reason for this must be that it is only recently that we have felt strong enough in our understanding of individual psyche-soma and mental development to be able to allow ourselves to examine and allow for the part that environment plays.

★   ★   ★

I now want to go directly to Freud, and I want to make a somewhat artificial distinction between two aspects of Freud's work. We see Freud developing the psycho-analytic method out of the clinical situation in which it was logical to use hypnosis.

Let us look and see what Freud did in choosing his cases. We can say that out of the total psychiatric pool, which includes all the mad people in asylums as well as those outside, he took those cases which had been *adequately provided for in earliest infancy*, the psychoneurotics. It might not be possible to confirm this by a close examination of the early cases on which Freud did work, but of one thing we can be certain, and this is most important, that Freud's own early personal history was of such a kind that he came to the Oedipus or prelatency period in his life as a whole human being, ready to meet whole human beings, and ready to deal in interpersonal relationships. His own infancy experiences had been good enough, so that in his self-analysis he could take the mothering of the infant for granted.

Freud takes for granted the early mothering situation and my contention is that *it turned up in his provision of a setting for his work*, almost without his being aware of what he was doing. Freud was able to analyse himself as an independent and whole person, and he interested himself in the anxieties that belong to interpersonal relationships. Later of course he looked at infancy theoretically and postulated pregenital phases of instinct development, and he and others proceeded to work out details and to go further and further back in the history of the individual. This work on the pregenital phases could not come to full fruition because it was not based on the study of patients who needed to regress in the analytic situation.[3]

Now I wish to make clear in what way I artificially divide Freud's work into two parts. First, there is the technique of psycho-analysis as it has gradually developed, and which students learn. The material presented by the patient is to be *understood* and to be *interpreted*. And, second, there is the *setting* in which this work is carried through.

Let us now glance at Freud's clinical setting. I will enumerate some of the very obvious points in its description.

1. At a stated time daily, five or six times a week, Freud put himself at the service of the patient. (This time was arranged to suit the convenience of both the analyst and the patient.)
2. The analyst would be reliably there, on time, alive, breathing.
3. For the limited period of time prearranged (about an hour) the analyst would keep awake and become preoccupied with the patient.
4. The analyst expressed love by the positive interest taken, and hate in the strict start and finish and in the matter of fees. Love and hate were honestly expressed, that is to say not denied by the analyst.
5. The aim of the analysis would be to get into touch with the process of the patient, to understand the material presented, to communicate this understanding in words. Resistance implied suffering and could be allayed by interpretation.
6. The analyst's method was one of objective observation.
7. This work was to be done in a room, not a passage, a room that was quiet and not liable to sudden unpredictable sounds, yet not dead quiet and not free from ordinary house noises. This room would be lit properly, but not by a light staring in the face, and not by a variable light. The room would certainly not be dark and it would be comfortably warm. The patient would be lying on a couch, that is to say,

comfortable, if able to be comfortable, and probably a rug and some water would be available.

8. The analyst (as is well known) keeps moral judgment out of the relationship, has no wish to intrude with details of the analyst's personal life and ideas, and the analyst does not wish to take sides in the persecutory systems even when these appear in the form of real shared situations, local, political, etc. Naturally if there is a war or an earthquake or if the king dies the analyst is not unaware.

9. In the analytic situation the analyst is much more reliable than people are in ordinary life; on the whole punctual, free from temper tantrums, free from compulsive falling in love, etc.

10. There is a very clear distinction in the analysis between fact and fantasy, so that the analyst is not hurt by an aggressive dream.

11. An absence of the talion reaction can be counted on.

12. The analyst survives.

A good deal more could be said, but the whole thing adds up to the fact that the analyst *behaves* himself or herself, and behaves without too much cost simply because of being a relatively mature person. If Freud had not behaved well he could not have developed the psycho-analytic technique or the theory to which the use of his technique led him. This is true however clever he might at the same time have been. The main point is that almost any one detail can be found to be of extreme importance at a specific phase of an analysis involving some regression of the patient.

There is rich material here for study, and it will be noted that there is a very marked similarity between all these things and the ordinary task of parents, especially that of the mother with her infant or with the father playing a mother role, and in some respects with the task of the mother at the very beginning.

Let me add that for Freud there are three people, one of them excluded from the analytic room. If there are only two people involved then there has been a regression of the patient in the analytic setting, and the setting represents the mother with her technique, and the patient is an infant. There is a further state of regression in which there is only one present, namely the patient, and this is true even if in another sense, from the observer's angle, there are two.

My thesis up to this point can be stated thus:

> Psychotic illness is related to environmental failure at an early stage of the emotional development of the individual. The sense of futility and unreality belongs to the development of a false self which develops in protection of the true self.
>
> The setting of analysis reproduces the early and earliest mothering techniques. It invites regression by reason of its reliability.

The regression of a patient is an organized return to early dependence or double dependence. The patient and the setting merge into the original success situation of primary narcissism.

Progress from primary narcissism starts anew with the true self able to meet environmental failure situations without organization of the defences that involve a false self protecting the true self.

To this extent psychotic illness can only be relieved by specialized environmental provision interlocked with the patient's regression.

Progress from the new position, with the true self surrendered to the total ego, can now be studied in terms of the complex processes of individual growth.

In practice there is a sequence of events:

1. The provision of a setting that gives confidence.
2. Regression of the patient to dependence, with due sense of the risk involved.
3. The patient feeling a new sense of self, and the self hitherto hidden becoming surrendered to the total ego. A new progression of the individual processes which had stopped.
4. An unfreezing of an environmental failure situation.
5. From the new position of ego strength, anger related to the early environmental failure, felt in the present and expressed.
6. Return from regression to dependence, in orderly progress towards independence.
7. Instinctual needs and wishes becoming realizable with genuine vitality and vigour.

All this repeated again and again.

Here a comment must be made on the diagnosis of psychosis.

In consideration of a group of mad people there is a big distinction to be drawn between those whose defences are in a chaotic state, and those who have been able to organize an illness. It must surely be that when psycho-analysis comes to be applied to psychosis it will be more likely to succeed where there is a highly organized illness. My own personal horror of leucotomy and suspicion of E.C.T. derives from my view of psychotic illness as a defensive organization designed to protect the true self; and also, from my feeling that apparent health with a false self is of no value to the patient. Illness, with the true self well hidden away, however painful, is the only good state unless we can go back with the patient as therapists and displace the original environmental failure situation.

Another consideration follows naturally here. In a group of psychotic patients there will be those who are clinically regressed and those who are not. It is by no means true that the clinically regressed are the more ill. From the psycho-analyst's point of view it may be easier to tackle the case of a patient who has had a breakdown than to tackle a comparable case in a state of flight to sanity.

It takes a great deal of courage to have a breakdown, but it may be that the alternative is a *flight to sanity*, a condition comparable to the manic defence against depression. Fortunately in most of our cases the breakdowns can be caught within the analytic hours, or they are limited and localized so that the social milieu of the patient can absorb them or cope with them.

To clarify the issue I wish to make a few comparisons:

> The couch and the pillows are there for the patient's use. They will appear in ideas and dreams and then will stand for the analyst's body, breasts, arms, hands, etc., in an infinite variety of ways. In so far as the patient is regressed (for a moment or for an hour or over a long period of time) the couch *is* the analyst, the pillows *are* breasts, the analyst *is* the mother at a certain past era. In the extreme it is no longer true to say the couch stands for the analyst.
>
> It is proper to speak of the patient's *wishes*, the wish (for instance) to be quiet. With the regressed patient the word wish is incorrect; instead we use the word *need*. If a regressed patient *needs* quiet, then without it nothing can be done at all. If the need is not met the result is not anger, only a reproduction of the environmental failure situation which stopped the processes of self growth. The individual's capacity to 'wish' has become interfered with, and we witness the reappearance of the original cause of a sense of futility.
>
> The regressed patient is near to a reliving of dream and memory situations; an acting out of a dream may be the way the patient discovers what is urgent, and talking about what was acted out follows the action but cannot precede it.
>
> Or take the detail of being on time. The analyst is not one who keeps patients waiting. Patients dream about being kept waiting and all the other variations on the theme, and they can be angry when the analyst is late. This is all part of the way the material goes. But patients who regress are different about the initial moment. There come phases when everything hangs on the punctuality of the analyst. If the analyst is there ready waiting, all is well – if not, well then both analyst and patient may as well pack up and go home, since no work can be done. Or, if one considers the patient's own unpunctuality, a neurotic patient who is late may perhaps be in a state of negative transference. A depressive patient is more likely by being late to be giving the analyst a little respite, a little longer for other activities and interests (protection from aggression, greed).
>
> The psychotic (regressive) patient is probably late because there is not yet established any hope that the analyst will be on time. It is futile to be

on time. So much hangs on this detail that the risk cannot be taken, so the patient is late; therefore no work gets done.

Again, neurotic patients like to have the third person always *excluded*, and the hate roused by sight of other patients may disturb the work in unpredictable ways. Depressive patients may be glad to see other patients till they reach the primitive or greedy love, which engenders their guilt. Regressive patients either have no objection to there being other patients or else they cannot conceive of there being another patient. Another patient is none other than a new version of the self.

A patient curls up on the couch and rests the head on the hand and seems warm and contented. The rug is right over the head. The patient is alone. Of course we are used to all varieties of angry withdrawal, but the analyst has to be able to recognize this *regressive* withdrawal in which he is not being insulted but is being used in a very primitive and positive way.

Another point is that regression to dependence is part and parcel of the analysis of early infancy phenomena, and if the couch gets wetted, or if the patient soils, or dribbles, we know that this is inherent, not a complication. Interpretation is not what is needed, and indeed speech or even move-ment can ruin the process and can be excessively painful to the patient.

An important element in this theory is the postulate of the observing ego. Two patients very similar in their immediate clinical aspect may be very different in regard to the degree of organization of the observer ego. At one extreme the observing ego is almost able to identify with the analyst and there can be a recovery from the regression at the end of the analytic hour. At the other extreme there is very little observing ego, and the patient is unable to recover from the regression in the analytic hour, and must be nursed.

Acting out has to be tolerated in this sort of work, and with the acting out in the analytic hour the analyst will find it necessary to play a part, although usually in token form. There is nothing more surprising both to the patient and to the analyst than the revelations that occur in these moments of acting out. The actual acting out in the analysis is only the beginning, however, and there must always follow a putting into words of the new bit of understanding. There is a sequence here:

1. A statement of what happened in the acting out.
2. A statement of what was needed of the analyst. From this can be deduced:
3. What went wrong in the original environmental failure situation. This produces some relief, but there follows:
4. Anger belonging to the original environmental failure situation. This anger is being felt perhaps for the first time, and the analyst may now have to take part by being used in respect of his failures rather than of his successes. This is disconcerting unless it is understood. The

progress has been made through the analyst's very careful attempt at adaptation, and yet it is the *failure* that at this moment is singled out as important on account of its being a reproduction of the original failure or trauma. In favourable cases there follows at last:

5.   A new sense of self in the patient and a sense of the progress that means true growth. It is this last that must be the analyst's reward through his identification with his patient. Not always will a further stage arrive in which the patient is able to understand the strain which the analyst has undergone and is able to say thank-you with real meaning.

This strain on the analyst is considerable, especially if lack of understanding and unconscious negative countertransference complicate the picture. On the other hand, I can say that in this kind of treatment I have not felt bewildered, and this is to some extent a compensation. The strain can be quite simple.

In one vitally important hour near the beginning of such a treatment I remained and knew I must remain absolutely still, only breathing. This I found very difficult indeed, especially as I did not yet know the special significance of the silence to my patient. At the end the patient came round from the regressed state and said: 'Now I know you can do my analysis.'

The idea is sometimes put forward: of course everyone wants to regress; regression is a picnic; we must stop our patients from regression; or, Winnicott likes or invites his patients to regress.

Let me make some basic observations on the subject of organized regression to dependence.

This is always extremely painful for the patient:

(*a*)   at one extreme is the patient who is fairly normal; here pain is experienced almost all the time;

(*b*)   midway we find all degrees of painful recognition of the precariousness of dependence and of double dependence;

(*c*)   at the other extreme is the mental hospital case; here the patient presumably does not suffer at the time on account of dependence. Suffering results from sense of futility, unreality, etc.

This is not to deny that in a localized way extreme satisfaction can be derived from the regression experience. This satisfaction is not sensuous. It is due to the fact that regression reaches and provides a starting-place, what I would call a *place* from which to operate. The self is reached. The subject becomes in touch with the basic self-processes that constitute true development, and what happens from here is felt as real. The satisfaction belonging to this is so much more important than any sensuous element in the regression experience that the latter need not be more than mentioned.

There are no reasons why an analyst should *want* a patient to regress, except grossly pathological reasons. If an analyst likes patients to regress, this must eventually interfere with the management of the regressed situation. Further, psycho-analysis which involves clinical regression is very much more difficult all along than that in which no special adaptive environmental provision has to be made. In other words it would be pleasant if we were to be able to take for analysis only those patients whose mothers at the very start and also in the first months had been able to provide good-enough conditions. But this era of psycho-analysis is steadily drawing to a close.

But the question arises, what do analysts do when regression (even of minute quantity) turns up?

> Some crudely say: Now sit up! Pull your socks up! Come round! Talk! But this is not psycho-analysis.
> Some divide their work into two parts, though unfortunately they do not always fully acknowledge this:

> (a) they are strictly analytic (free association in words; interpretation in words; no reassurances);

and also

> (b) they act intuitively.
> Here comes the idea of psycho-analysis as an *art*.

> Some say: unanalysable, and throw up the sponge. A mental hospital takes over.

The idea of psycho-analysis as an art must gradually give way to a study of environmental adaptation relative to patients' regressions. But while the scientific study of environmental adaptation is undeveloped, then I suppose analysts must continue to be artists in their work. An analyst may be a good artist, but (as I have frequently asked): what patient wants to be someone else's poem or picture?

I know from experience that some will say: all this leads to a theory of development which ignores the early stages of the development of the individual, which ascribes early development to environmental factors. This is quite untrue.

In the early development of the human being the environment that behaves well enough (that makes good-enough active adaptation) *enables personal growth to take place*. The self processes then may continue active, in an unbroken line of living growth. If the environment behaves not well enough, then the individual is engaged in reactions to impingement, and the self processes are interrupted. If this state of affairs reaches a quantitative limit the core of the self begins to get protected; there is a hold-up, the self cannot make new progress unless and until the environment failure situation is corrected in the way I have described. With the true self protected there develops a false self built on a defence-compliance basis, the acceptance of reaction to impingement. The development of a false self is one of *the most successful defence organizations* designed for the protection of the true self's core, and its existence results in the sense of futility. I would like to repeat myself and to say that while the individual's operational centre is in the false self there is a sense of futility, and in practice we find the change to the feeling that life is worthwhile coming at the moment of shift of the operational centre from the false to the true self, even before full surrender of the self's core to the total ego.

From this one can formulate a fundamental principle of existence: that which proceeds from the true self feels real (later good) whatever its nature, however aggressive; that which happens in the individual as a reaction to environmental impingement feels unreal, futile (later bad), however sensually satisfactory.

Lastly, let us examine the concept of regression by putting up against it the concept of reassurance. This becomes necessary because of the fact that the adaptive technique that must meet a patient's regression is often classed (wrongly, I am sure) as reassurance.

We assume that reassurance is not part of the psycho-analytic technique. The patient comes into the analytic setting and goes out of it, and within that setting there is no more than interpretation, correct and penetrating and well-timed.

In teaching psycho-analysis we must continue to speak against reassurance. As we look a little more carefully, however, we see that this is too simple a language. It is not just a question of reassurance and no reassurance.

In fact, the whole matter needs examination. What is a reassurance? What could be more reassuring than to find oneself being well analysed, to be in a reliable setting with a mature person in charge, capable of making penetrating and accurate interpretation, and to find one's personal process respected? It is foolish to deny that reassurance is present in the classical analytic situation.

The whole set-up of psycho-analysis is one big reassurance, especially the reliable objectivity and behaviour of the analyst, and the transference interpretations constructively using instead of wastefully exploiting the moment's passion.

This matter of reassurance is much better discussed in terms of *counter-transference*. Reaction formations in the behaviour of the analyst are harmful not because they appear in the form of reassurances and denials but because they represent repressed unconscious elements in the analyst, and these mean limitation of the analyst's work.

What would be said of an analyst's *inability* to reassure? If an analyst were suicidal? *A belief in human nature and in the developmental process exists in the analyst* if work is to be done at all, and this is quickly sensed by the patient.

There is no value to be got from describing regression to dependence, with its concomitant environmental adaptation, in terms of reassurance, just as there is a very real point in considering harmful reassurance in terms of countertransference.

What, if anything, am I asking analysts to do about these matters in their practical work?

1. I am *not* asking them to take on psychotic patients.
2. Nothing I have said affects the principles of ordinary practice in so far as

   (*a*) the analyst is in the first decade of his analytic career;
   (*b*) the case is a true neurotic (not psychotic).

3. I do suggest that while analysts are waiting to be in a position, through their increasing personal experience, to tackle a case in which regression must occur, there is much they can do to prepare themselves. They can:

   (*a*) watch the operation of setting factors;
   (*b*) watch the minor examples of regression with natural termination that appear in the course of analytic sessions; and
   (*c*) watch and use the regressive episodes that occur in the patient's life outside analysis, episodes, I may say, which are usually wasted, much to the impoverishment of the analysis.

The main result of the ideas I am putting forward, if they are accepted, will be a more accurate, rich, and profitable use of the setting phenomena in ordinary analyses of non-psychotics, resulting, I believe, in a new approach to the understanding of psychosis, and its treatment by psycho-analysts doing psycho-analysis.

SUMMARY

Attention is drawn to the subject of regression as it occurs in the psycho-analytic setting. Case reports of successful psychological treatments of adults and children show that techniques that allow of regression are increasingly being used. It is the psycho-analyst, familiar with the technique required in treatment of psychoneurosis, who can best understand regression and the theoretical implication of the patient's expectations that belong to the need to regress.

Regression can be of any degree, localized and momentary, or total and involving a patient's whole life over a phase. The less severe regressions provide fruitful material for research.

Emerging from such study comes a fresh understanding of the 'true self' and the 'false self', and of the 'observing ego', and also of the ego organization which enables regression to be a healing mechanism, one that remains potential unless there be provided a new and reliable environmental adaptation which can be used by the patient in correction of the original adaptive failure.

Here the therapeutic work in analysis links up with that done by child care, by friendship, by enjoyment of poetry, and cultural pursuits generally. But psycho-analysis can allow and use the hate and anger belonging to the original failure, important effects which are liable to destroy the value of therapeusis brought about by non-analytic methods.

On recovery from regression the patient, with the self now more fully surrendered to the ego, needs ordinary analysis as designed for the management of the depressive position and of the Oedipus complex in interpersonal relationships. For this reason, if for no other, the student should acquire proficiency in the analysis of the carefully-chosen non-psychotic before proceeding to the study of regression. Preliminary work can be done by a study of the setting in classical psycho-analysis.

Notes

1. Paper read before the British Psycho-Analytical Society on 17 March 1954. *International Journal of Psychoanalysis* 36 (1955).
2. Case also referred to in Chapter 4, this volume.
3. You will observe that I am not saying that this theoretical work on pregenital instinct could not succeed on account of a lack in Freud of direct contact with infants, because I see no reason why Freud should not have had very good experience as an observer of the mother-infant situation within his own family and his work. Further I am reminded that Freud worked in a children's clinic and made detailed observation on infants when studying Little's disease. The point that I wish to make here is that fortunately for us Freud found his interest at the beginning not in the patient's need to regress in the analysis but in what happens in the analytic situation when regression is not necessary and when it is possible to take for granted the work done by the mother and by the early environmental adaptation in the individual patient's past history.

Developing ideas: regression to dependence; freezing of failure situation; survival of the analyst; psychosis related to environmental failure; the significance of the psychoanalytic setting; the flight into sanity; importance of father in development; the theoretical first feed; true and false self; change from pre-ruth to ruth in stage of concern; environment-individual set-up; survival of the mother; depression as a healing mechanism

7

THE THEORY OF THE PARENT-INFANT RELATIONSHIP (1960)

OTHER WRITINGS

The second half of the 1950s saw the continuation of Winnicott's immense productivity, his innovative thinking, and his commitment both to psychoanalysis itself and to its application to a far wider ambience than those patients reached in the consulting room.

'Clinical Varieties of Transference' was given as a paper at the IPA congress in Geneva in 1955 and published in the *IJPA* in 1956; the early mother–infant relationship was addressed in 'Primary Maternal Preoccupation' (1956b) and 'The Relationship of a Mother to her Baby at the Beginning' (1960d); the impact of the parents' psychopathology in 'The Family Affected by Depressive Illness in One or Both Parents' (1958e) and 'The Effect of Psychotic Parents on the Emotional Development of the Child' (1959; see 1961b), both given as talks to social workers. He read a series of exceptional papers at the BPAS: 'The Antisocial Tendency in Psychoanalysis' in 1956 (published 1958); 'Psycho-Analysis and the Sense of Guilt' in 1956 (1958c); 'The Capacity to be Alone' in 1957 (1958d); and 'Aggression, Guilt and Reparation' in 1960. 'The Fate of the Transitional Object' was presented at a meeting of the Association for Child Psychology and Psychiatry in Glasgow in 1958, and in that year he also wrote 'Child Analysis in the Latency Period' (1958b). 'Classification: is there a Psycho-Analytic Contribution to Psychiatric Classification?' followed in 1959, and in 1960 'Countertransference' was published in the British Journal of Medical Psychology.

During the 1950s several papers reflected the new interest in countertransference: Heimann (1950), Little (1951, 1957), Racker (1953), and Money-Kyrle (1956). Several publications either directly or indirectly linked to Winnicott's work also appeared: by his close colleague Martin James about the impact of impingement in early life (1960) and by John Bowlby on separation anxiety (1960). Bowlby would publish his three volumes on attachment separation and loss later in the 1960s and 1970s (1969, 1973, 1980). Close collaborators of Bowlby, James and Joyce Robertson made ground-breaking films about the impact of separation on young children ('John'; 'A Two Year Old Goes to Hospital', etc.) which had huge impact upon both thinking about early development and also public policy for example in relation to parents' access to their hospitalized children (Robertson, 1958).

Winnicot and Phyllis Greenacre's contribution to the panel, The Parent Infant Relationship, at the IPA Congress were published in 1960. Many of the responses including pieces by Anna Freud, Masud Khan, Angel Garma, Serge Lebovici, Daniel Lagache, Michael Balint and others were published subsequently (*IJPA* 1962).

This paper contains a fundamental Winnicottian concept 'holding'. He references only one source which is a paper written in 1954 by his wife Clare Winnicott. She had emphasized holding in her consideration of what social workers provide for their clients. Her contribution to the evolution of Donald's thinking is considered to be underrated (Kanter, 2004).

EDITORS' INTRODUCTION

This paper was published in the *IJPA* in advance of the 1961 congress of the IPA, held in Edinburgh where it was given in a panel to which the American psychoanalyst, Phyllis Greenacre, also contributed. The event was chaired by John Bowlby, whose book *Child Care and the Growth of Love*, originally published in 1953, had become an instant classic. Winnicott was critical of Bowlby's neglect of the child's 'inner world experience' of the effects of separation, but agreed with his attention to the infant's basic dependency on the mother for physical and psychological wellbeing and development. Winnicott stressed the 'environment' as both subjective and objective in thinking about a child's mental state; and Greenacre's presentation on the interaction of maturation and maternal care, complemented his focus on the maternal environment. He would draw these two aspects together in the title of his second collection of papers (*Maturational Processes*) 4 years later.

Winnicott had already challenged the orthodoxy of a one-person psychology approach in understanding human development: in a much-quoted remark at a BPAS meeting in the 1940s when he had claimed, ' "There is no such thing as an infant", meaning, of course, that whenever one finds an infant one finds maternal care, and without maternal care there would be no infant' (p. 168). 'On Transference' (1956a) also contains many of the ideas presented here but in this paper he insists that he is talking of infancy and not primarily psychoanalysis to avoid adding to the 'existing confusion about the relative importance of personal and environmental influences in the develop-ment of the individual' (p. 152). However it has profound implications for psychoanalysis, especially in the treatment of non-neurotic patients.

Winnicott describes the conditions of earliest development if the preverbal infant is to have the necessary experience of at-one-ness with the mother to emerge as a differentiated subject. He frequently refers to the success or failure of these early processes which become evident clinically in patients' functioning. He recognizes that, experientially, the infant and mother (or maternal care) 'cannot be disentangled', at the beginning, and yet to chart early development demands precisely this: the gradual emergence of the new human subject, infant, out of the infant–mother matrix. In a footnote, he himself wonders whether this elaboration of the remark referred to above was an unconscious reference to 'Formulations on the Two Principles of Mental Functioning', where Freud, in discussing the pleasure principle, states, 'The employment of a fiction like this is, however, justified when one considers [. . .] the infant – provided one includes with it the care it receives from its mother' (Freud, 1911: 220, quoted in this paper). Winnicott remarks that Freud recognizes this unity but both he and Klein take it for granted, and do not really consider the implications of full dependence.

Winnicott takes as his twin foci mother and infant, who cannot be differentiated but who, over time, will become so. He invokes classical psychoanalysis's framework of earliest infantile functioning – primary process, identification, autoerotism, and primary narcissism – but his own interest is in their 'living reality'. In the state of absolute dependency, the aspect of this early phase he privileges, it is the conditions for coming into 'being' that are central. They depend on the presence of the holding function of the mother, and it is only through her contribution that the baby's inherited potential can assume the continuity of 'going on being'. He had used this term in 'Primary Maternal Preoccupation' (Winnicott, 1956b: 303), where he elaborates the particular internal processes in the mother during the latter part of pregnancy and early post-natal life which facilitate her adaptation to her infant. The variations of this pre-subjective state in the infant depend on the confluence of each individual baby with each particular mother.

The tasks of the holding phase constitute a reprise of features Winnicott had already identified in the 1940s and 1950s: the achievement of structured integration so that disintegration is a possibility and unintegration a resource (Phillips, 1988); psychosomatic existence with a sense of boundary between inner and outer reality, the development of mind as distinct from psyche, and the dawning of thought and intelligence; the fusion of aggression with libido, and the emerging capacity for object relations based on a differentiated sense of 'I' and 'you'. All this, the detail of 'unit status', is predicated on the holding presence of maternal care.

Winnicott departs from classical psychoanalytic understanding of these early phenomena in maintaining that it is only through the integration of the primitive ego that id experiences can come to be significant in the baby's life. He turns on its head the classical view that the ego emerges from the id. Instead, he is concerned with how and if the integration of the id in the ego takes place. In health the id strengthens the ego; in ill health it can be 'totally external' to the ego, threatening the development of psychotic defences. But all this follows the inception, through a continuity of being, of the self and ego.

The section describing maternal care contains an exposition of his central concept of 'holding'. While he emphasizes the physicality of this feature of mothering, the baby being held in the mother's arms, taking account of and sustaining continuity between the moment-to-moment changes in his states of being, 'holding' is also a metaphor. The holding mother elaborates her baby's experiences in her psyche and mind, both conscious and unconscious aspects of her imagination and thinking. Its congruence with the baby's states depends on the mother's capacity for identification with the baby, what Winnicott refers to as 'projective identification', a rather different use of the concept from Melanie Klein's. Although he privileges the mother in these processes he does refer to their also being in the father, and the inclusive term 'parent' is used to describe the special state necessary for mothering as a function to be carried out in this early stage.

At this same congress Wilfred Bion presented 'A Psycho-Analytic Study of Thinking' (1962) in which he introduced the concept of the 'container-contained'. Winnicott's concept of 'holding' and Bion's 'containment' are often elided which leads to conceptual confusion as well as misunderstanding about their different clinical application. These concepts derive from different views of the very young infant's capacities and the function of the mother's psyche and mind in her relationship to him. For Bion, the mother's containing function enables her, in her reverie, to receive and make manageable the infant's unbearable projective identifications. Over time the baby re-introjects them and the mother's containment becomes a structure in the baby's mind. Bion's conceptualization was developed through his work with adult patients, not, as in the case of Winnicott through an extensive exposure to ordinary mothers and babies over many decades. For Winnicott this pre-supposes too much development, it means that the baby already has a sense of an 'other' and projective processes are possible. For him, the mother's function of 'holding' initially relates to the presumed situation at the beginning when, from the infant's point of view, the mother and baby are a unit, the infant–environment set-up.

The movement of the projections here, dependent upon the healthy inner world of the mother, is the opposite of the process described by Bion, although the actual processes in the mother's mind may not be so different: 'imaginative elaboration' (Winnicott) and 'reverie' (Bion) both imply psychic work on the part of the mother despite their different conceptualizations of how the mother comes to know what the baby is experiencing.

If the holding presence of the mother is impaired at this stage of absolute dependency, the baby is exposed to potentially devastating consequences. Winnicott describes the core self as fundamentally, necessarily isolated (see Chapter 9, this volume), and especially vulnerable if not protected from impingement. Winnicott alludes to the profound nature of anxiety, referred to here as 'annihilation' anxiety, felt as a rupture to 'being'. Bion's (1962) account refers to these primitive anxieties as 'nameless dread'. If this is a feature of the baby's earliest existence it is the source of primitive disturbance, of psychotic anxiety. Again Winnicott implicitly refutes the concept of the death instinct, and distinguishes 'annihilation' from 'death', in so far as knowledge of the latter is only possible when the baby has become a differentiated human being, and at a time when hate and sadism come to have meaning.

The mothering function initially protects the baby from the impingements of external reality, so that he does not yet have to attend to the 'relentless unalterable otherness of time' (Ogden, 2005: 94). Holding allows the baby the time to experience his own rhythms, physical and psychological, upon which his own subjectivity will develop. It sustains the going-on-being-ness of the illusion of omnipotence until it is given up as the sense of an 'I' emerges. As the mother's adaptation becomes contingent with that of her baby, a space opens up and the quality of her holding changes. Instead of her relying upon her identification with the baby to know what is needed, the baby now needs her to recognize his emerging capacity to give her clues or signals as to what he needs or wants. Winnicott's account of the mother's need to change her adaptation to her baby also indicates the potential psychopathology to which she can contribute in the holding phase. She can be both not good enough and too good. In the former case her baby is not protected from impingements and is exposed to the anxieties described above. If she is too good and pre-empts her baby's potential spontaneity, she can interrupt this process, interfering with the normal move towards separateness (Hopkins, 1996).

This paper also contains further reference to the processes involved in the illusion of omnipotence and implicitly to its relevance to psychoanalytic clinical practice. In health, all the baby's experiences are felt to emanate from themselves, and this is sustained and then appropriately subverted by the adaptive mother. In situations where babies have suffered impingements that expose them to primitive anxieties ('In infancy, however, good and bad things happen to the infant that are quite outside the infant's range', p. 152), the illusion is shattered and, with it, the sense of having created the world. One might say their incipient psychic reality is hijacked by the external world rather than being facilitated by it.

Winnicott is interested in that time in development when, in his view, what happens cannot be interpreted as a projection (psychic reality): it is the real relationship that the parent provides over which the infant has no control. When Winnicott describes the analyst being 'prepared to wait till the patient becomes able to present the environmental factors in terms that allow of their interpretation as projections' (p. 153) he is referring to the patient's regression to and recovery from the effects of a traumatic failure situation. Following this the patient can take responsibility for his own impulses rather than retreat behind a false-self solution to the original trauma. Classical psychoanalysis is more interested in the psychic reality of the patient than in whatever the real primary objects did or did not do.

Although Winnicott uses the language of the Freudian structural model he is closer to describing the development of the experiencing self than structure formation. His emphasis on being and experience suggests his interest in subjectivity and what it feels like to be the experiencing subject, rather than the functions of the ego per se. His account is closer to an existential/phenomenological one and when he refers to the 'central self' there is also a Jungian allusion.

The Theory of the Parent–Infant Relationship[1]
(1960)

The main point of this paper can perhaps best be brought out through a comparison of the study of infancy with the study of the psycho-analytic transference.[2] It cannot be too strongly emphasized that my statement is about infancy, and not primarily about psycho-analysis. The reason why this must be understood reaches to the root of the matter. If this paper does not contribute constructively, then it can only add to the existing confusion about the relative importance of personal and environmental influences in the development of the individual.

In psycho-analysis as we know it there is no trauma that is outside the individual's omnipotence. Everything eventually comes under ego-control, and thus becomes related to secondary processes. The patient is not helped if the analyst says: 'Your mother was not good enough' ... 'your father really seduced you' ... 'your aunt dropped you.' Changes come in an analysis when the traumatic factors enter the psycho-analytic material in the patient's own way, and within the patient's omnipotence. The interpretations that are alterative are those that can be made in terms of projection. The same applies to the benign factors, factors that led to satisfaction. Everything is interpreted in terms of the individual's love and ambivalence. The analyst is prepared to wait a long time to be in a position to do exactly this kind of work.

In infancy, however, good and bad things happen to the infant that are quite outside the infant's range. In fact infancy is the period in which the capacity for gathering external factors into the area of the infant's omnipotence is in process of formation. The ego-support of the maternal care enables the infant to live and develop in spite of his being not yet able to control, or to feel responsible for, what is good and bad in the environment.

The events of these earliest stages cannot be thought of as lost through what we know as the mechanisms of repression, and therefore analysts cannot expect to find them appearing as a result of work which lessens the forces of repression. It is possible that Freud was trying to allow for these phenomena when he used the term primary repression, but this is open to argument. What is fairly certain is that the matters under discussion here have had to be taken for granted in much of the psycho-analytic literature.[3]

Returning to psycho-analysis, I have said that the analyst is prepared to wait till the patient becomes able to present the environmental factors in terms that allow of their interpretation as projections. In the well-chosen case this result comes from the patient's capacity for confidence, which is rediscovered in the reliability of the analyst and the professional setting. Sometimes the analyst needs to wait a very long time; and in the case that is *badly* chosen for classical psycho-analysis it is likely that the reliability of the analyst is the most important factor (or more important than the interpretations) because the patient did not experience such reliability in the maternal care of infancy, and if the patient is to make use of such reliability he will need to find it for the first time in the analyst's behaviour. This would seem to be the basis for research into the problem of what a psycho-analyst can do in the treatment of schizophrenia and other psychoses.

In borderline cases the analyst does not always wait in vain; in the course of time the patient becomes able to make use of the psycho-analytic interpretations of the original traumata as projections. It may even happen that he is able to accept what is good in the environment as a projection of the simple and stable going-on-being elements that derive from his own inherited potential.

The paradox is that what is good and bad in the infant's environment is not in fact a projection, but in spite of this it is necessary, if the individual infant is to develop healthily, that everything shall seem to him to be a projection. Here we find omnipotence and the pleasure principle in operation, as they certainly are in earliest infancy; and to this observation we can add that the recognition of a true 'not-me' is a matter of the intellect; it belongs to extreme sophistication and to the maturity of the individual.

⋆   ⋆   ⋆

In the writings of Freud most of the formulations concerning infancy derive from a study of adults in analysis. There are some childhood observations ('Cotton reel' material (1920)), and there is the analysis of Little Hans (1909[b]). At first sight it would seem that a great deal of psycho-analytic theory is about early childhood and infancy, but in one sense Freud can be said to have neglected infancy as a state. This is brought out by a footnote in *Formulations on the Two Principles of Mental Functioning* (1911, p. 220) in which he shows that he knows he is taking for granted the very things that are under discussion in this paper. In the text he traces the development from the pleasure principle to the reality principle, following his usual course of reconstructing the infancy of his adult patients. The note runs as follows:

> It will rightly be objected that an organization which was a slave to the pleasure-principle and neglected the reality of the external world could

not maintain itself alive for the shortest time, so that it could not have come into existence at all. The employment of a fiction like this is, however, justified when one considers that the infant – provided one includes with it the care it receives from its mother – does almost realize a psychical system of this kind.

Here Freud paid full tribute to the function of maternal care, and it must be assumed that he left this subject alone only because he was not ready to discuss its implications. The note continues:

> It probably hallucinates the fulfilment of its internal needs; it betrays its unpleasure, when there is an increase of stimulus and an absence of satisfaction, by the motor discharge of screaming and beating about with its arms and legs, and it then experiences the satisfaction it has hallucinated. Later, as an older child, it learns to employ these manifestations of discharge intentionally as methods of expressing its feelings. Since the later care of children is modelled on the care of infants, the dominance of the pleasure principle can really come to an end only when a child has achieved complete psychical detachment from its parents.

The words: 'provided one includes with it the care it receives from its mother' have great importance in the context of this study. The infant and the maternal care together form a unit.[4] Certainly if one is to study the theory of the parent-infant relationship one must come to a decision about these matters, which concern the real meaning of the word dependence. It is not enough that it is acknowledged that the environment is important. If there is to be a discussion of the theory of the parent–infant relationship, then we are divided into two if there are some who do not allow that at the earliest stages the infant and the maternal care belong to each other and cannot be disentangled. These two things, the infant and the maternal care, disentangle and dissociate themselves in health; and health, which means so many things, to some extent means a disentanglement of maternal care from something which we then call the infant or the beginnings of a growing child. This idea is covered by Freud's words at the end of the footnote: 'the dominance of the pleasure principle can really come to an end only when a child has achieved complete psychical detachment from its parents'. (The middle part of this footnote will be discussed in a later section, where it will be suggested that Freud's words here are inadequate and misleading in certain respects, if taken to refer to the earliest stage.)

THE WORD 'INFANT'

In this paper the word infant will be taken to refer to the very young child. It is necessary to say this because in Freud's writings the word sometimes seems to include the child up to the age of the passing of the Oedipus complex. Actually the word infant implies 'not talking' (*infans*), and it is not un-useful to think of infancy as the phase prior to word presentation and the use of word symbols. The corollary is that it refers to a phase in which the infant depends on maternal care that is based on maternal empathy rather than on understanding of what is or could be verbally expressed.

This is essentially a period of ego development, and integration is the main feature of such development. The id-forces clamour for attention. At first they are external to the infant. In health the id becomes gathered into the service of the ego, and the ego masters the id, so that id-satisfactions become ego-strengtheners. This, however, is an achievement of healthy development and in infancy there are many variants dependent on relative failure of this achievement. In the ill-health of infancy achievements of this kind are minimally reached, or may be won and lost. In infantile psychosis (or schizophrenia) the id remains relatively or totally 'external' to the ego, and id-satisfactions remain physical, and have the effect of threatening the ego structure, that is, until defences of psychotic quality are organized.[5]

I am here supporting the view that the main reason why in infant development the infant usually becomes able to master, and the ego to include, the id, is the fact of the maternal care, the maternal ego implementing the infant ego and so making it powerful and stable. How this takes place will need to be examined, and also how the infant ego eventually becomes free of the mother's ego-support, so that the infant achieves mental detachment from the mother, that is, differentiation into a separate personal self.

In order to examine the parent-infant relationship it is necessary first to attempt a brief statement of the theory of infant emotional development.

HISTORICAL

In psycho-analytic theory as it grew up the early hypothesis concerned the id and the ego mechanisms of defence. It was understood that the id arrived on the scene very early indeed, and Freud's discovery and description of pre-genital sexuality, based on his observations of the regressive elements found in genital fantasy and in play and in dreams, are main features of clinical psychology.

Ego mechanisms of defence were gradually formulated.[6] These mechanisms were assumed to be organized in relation to anxiety which derived either from instinct tension or from object loss. This part of psycho-analytic theory pre-supposes a separateness of the self and a structuring of the ego, perhaps a personal body scheme. At the level of the main part of this paper this state of affairs cannot yet be assumed. The discussion centres round the establishment of precisely this state of affairs, namely the structuring of the ego which makes anxiety from instinct tension or object loss possible. Anxiety at this early stage is not castration anxiety or separation anxiety; it relates to quite other things, and is, in fact, anxiety about annihilation (cf. the aphanisis of Jones).

In psycho-analytic theory ego mechanisms of defence largely belong to the idea of a child that has an independence, a truly personal defence organization. On this borderline the researches of Klein add to Freudian theory by clarifying the interplay of primitive anxieties and defence mechanisms. This work of Klein concerns earliest infancy, and draws attention to the importance of aggressive and destructive impulses that are more deeply rooted than those that are reactive to frustration and related to hate and anger; also in Klein's work there is a dissection of early defences against primitive anxieties, anxieties that belong to the first stages of the mental organization (splitting, projection, and introjection).

What is described in Melanie Klein's work clearly belongs to the life of the infant in its earliest phases, and to the period of dependence with which this paper is concerned. Melanie Klein made it clear that she recognized that the environment was important at this period, and in various ways at all stages.[7] I suggest, however, that her work and that of her co-workers leaves open for further consideration the development of the theme of full dependence, that which appears in Freud's phrase: '. . . the infant, provided one includes with it the care it receives from its mother . . .' There is nothing in Klein's work that contradicts the idea of absolute dependence, but there seems to me to be no specific reference to a stage at which the infant exists only because of the maternal care, together with which it forms a unit.

What I am bringing forward for consideration here is the difference between the analyst's acceptance of the reality of dependence, and his working with it in the transference.[8]

It would seem that the study of ego-defences takes the investigator back to pregenital id-manifestations, whereas the study of ego psychology takes him back to dependence, to the maternal-care–infant unit.

One half of the theory of the parent-infant relationship concerns the infant, and is the theory of the infant's journey from absolute dependence, through relative dependence, to independence, and, in parallel, the infant's journey from the pleasure principle to the reality principle, and from autoerotism to object relationships. The other half of the theory of the parent-infant relationship concerns maternal care, that is to say the qualities and changes in the mother that meet the specific and developing needs of the infant towards whom she orientates.

A. THE INFANT

The key word in this part of the study is *dependence*. Human infants cannot start to *be* except under certain conditions. These conditions are studied below, but they are part of the psychology of the infant. Infants come into *being* differently according to whether the conditions are favourable or unfavourable. At the same time conditions do not determine the infant's potential. This is inherited, and it is legitimate to study this inherited potential of the individual as a separate issue, *provided always that it is accepted that the inherited potential of an infant cannot become an infant unless linked to maternal care.*

The inherited potential includes a tendency towards growth and development. All stages of emotional growth can be roughly dated. Presumably all developmental stages have a date in each individual child. Nevertheless, not only do these dates vary from child to child, but also, *even if they were known in advance* in the case of a given child, they could not be used in predicting the child's actual development because of the other factor, maternal care. If such dates could be used in prediction at all, it would be on the basis of assuming a maternal care that is adequate in the important respects. (This obviously does not mean adequate only in the physical sense; the meaning of adequacy and inadequacy in this context is discussed below.)

THE INHERITED POTENTIAL AND ITS FATE

It is necessary here to attempt to state briefly what happens to the inherited potential if this is to develop into an infant, and thereafter into a child, a child reaching towards independent existence. Because of the complexities of the subject such a statement must be made on the assumption of satisfactory maternal care, which means parental care. Satisfactory parental care can be classified roughly into three overlapping stages:

(*a*) Holding.
(*b*) Mother and infant living together. Here the father's function (of dealing with the environment for the mother) is not known to the infant.
(*c*) Father, mother, and infant, all three living together.

The term 'holding' is used here to denote not only the actual physical holding of the infant, but also the total environmental provision prior to the concept of *living with*. In other words, it refers to a three-dimensional or space relationship with time gradually added. This overlaps with, but is initiated prior to, instinctual experiences that in time would determine object relationships. It includes the management of experiences that are inherent in existence, such as the *completion* (and therefore the *non-completion*) of processes, processes which from the outside may seem to be purely physiological but which belong to infant psychology and take place in a complex psychological field, determined by the awareness and the empathy of the mother. (This concept of holding is further discussed below.)

The term 'living with' implies object relationships, and the emergence of the infant from the state of being merged with the mother, or his perception of objects as external to the self.

This study is especially concerned with the 'holding' stage of maternal care, and with the complex events in infants' psychological development that are related to this holding phase. It should be remembered, however, that a division of one phase from another is artificial, and merely a matter of convenience, adopted for the purpose of clearer definition.

Infant Development During the Holding Phase

In the light of this some characteristics of infant development during this phase can be enumerated. It is at this stage that

> primary process
> primary identification
> auto–erotism
> primary narcissism

are living realities.

In this phase the ego changes over from an unintegrated state to a structured integration, and so the infant becomes able to experience anxiety associated with disintegration. The word disintegration begins to have a meaning which it did not possess before ego integration became a fact. In healthy development at this stage the infant retains the capacity for re-experiencing unintegrated states, but this depends on the continuation of reliable maternal care or on the build-up in the infant of memories of maternal care beginning gradually to be perceived as such. The result of healthy progress in the infant's development during this stage is that he attains to what might be called 'unit status'. The infant becomes a person, an individual in his own right.

Associated with this attainment is the infant's psychosomatic existence, which begins to take on a personal pattern; I have referred to this as the psyche indwelling in the soma.[9] The basis for this indwelling is a linkage of motor and sensory and functional experiences with the infant's new state of being a person. As a further development there comes into existence what might be called a limiting membrane, which to some extent (in health) is equated with the surface of the skin, and has a position between the infant's 'me' and his 'not-me'. So the infant comes to have an inside and an outside, and a body-scheme. In this way meaning comes to the function of intake and output; moreover, it gradually becomes meaningful to postulate a personal or inner psychic reality for the infant.[10]

During the holding phase other processes are initiated; the most important is the dawn of intelligence and the beginning of a mind as something distinct from the psyche. From this follows the whole story of the secondary processes and of symbolic functioning, and of the organization of a personal psychic content, which forms a basis for dreaming and for living relationships.

At the same time there starts in the infant a joining up of two roots of impulsive behaviour. The term 'fusion' indicates the positive process whereby diffuse elements that belong to movement and to muscle erotism become (in health) fused with the orgiastic functioning of the erotogenic zones. This concept is more familiar as the reverse process of defusion, which is a complicated defence in which aggression becomes separated out from erotic experience after a period in which a degree of fusion has been achieved. All these developments belong to the environmental condition of *holding*, and without a good enough holding these stages cannot be attained, or once attained cannot become established.

A further development is in the capacity for object relationships. Here the infant changes from a relationship to a subjectively conceived object to a relationship to an object objectively perceived. This change is closely bound up with the infant's change from being merged with the mother to being separate from her, or to relating to her as separate and 'not-me'. This development is not specifically related to the holding, but is related to the phase of 'living with' . . .

Dependence

In the holding phase the infant is maximally dependent. One can classify dependence thus:

(i) *Absolute Dependence.* In this state the infant has no means of knowing about the maternal care, which is largely a matter of prophylaxis. He cannot gain control over what is well and what is badly done, but is only in a position to gain profit or to suffer disturbance.

(ii) *Relative Dependence.* Here the infant can become aware of the need for the details of maternal care, and can to a growing extent relate them to personal impulse, and then later, in a psycho-analytic treatment, can reproduce them in the transference.

(iii) *Towards Independence.* The infant develops means for doing without actual care. This is accomplished through the accumulation of memories of care, the projection of personal needs and the introjection of care details, with the development of confidence in the environment. Here must be added the element of intellectual understanding with its tremendous implications.

Isolation of the Individual

Another phenomenon that needs consideration at this phase is the hiding of the core of the personality. Let us examine the concept of a central or true self. The central self could be said to be the inherited potential which is experiencing a continuity of being, and acquiring in its own way and at its own speed a personal psychic reality and a personal body-scheme.[11] It seems necessary to allow for the concept of the isolation of this central self as a characteristic of health. Any threat to this isolation of the true self constitutes a major anxiety at this early stage, and defences of earliest infancy appear in relation to failures on the part of the mother (or in maternal care) to ward off impingements which might disturb this isolation.

Impingements may be met and dealt with by the ego organization, gathered into the infant's omnipotence and sensed as projections.[12] On the other hand they may get through this defence in spite of the ego-support which maternal care provides. Then the central core of the ego is affected, and this is the very nature of psychotic anxiety. In health the individual soon becomes invulnerable in this respect, and if external factors impinge there is merely a new degree and quality in the hiding of the central self. In this respect the best defence is the organization of a false self. Instinctual satisfactions and object relationships themselves constitute a threat to the individual's personal going-on-being. *Example:* a baby is feeding at the breast and obtains satisfaction. This fact by itself does not indicate whether he is having an ego-syntonic id experience or, on the contrary, is suffering the trauma of a seduction, a threat to personal ego continuity, a threat by an id experience which is not ego-syntonic, and with which the ego is not equipped to deal.

In health object relationships can be developed on the basis of a compromise, one which involves the individual in what later would be called cheating and dishonesty, whereas a direct relationship is possible only on the basis of regression to a state of being merged with the mother.

Annihilation[13]

Anxiety in these early stages of the parent-infant relationship relates to the threat of annihilation, and it is necessary to explain what is meant by this term.

In this place which is characterized by the essential existence of a holding environment, the 'inherited potential' is becoming itself a 'continuity of being'. The alternative to being is reacting, and reacting interrupts being and annihilates. Being and annihilation are the two alternatives. The holding environment therefore has as its main function the reduction to a minimum of impingements to which the infant must react with resultant annihilation of personal being. Under favourable conditions the infant establishes a continuity of existence and then begins to develop the sophistications which make it possible for impingements to be gathered into the area of omnipotence. At this stage the word death has no possible application, and this makes the term death instinct unacceptable in describing the root of destructiveness. Death has no meaning until the arrival of hate and of the concept of the whole human person. When a whole human person can be hated, death has meaning, and close on this follows that which can be called maiming; the whole hated and loved person is kept alive by being castrated or otherwise maimed instead of killed. These ideas belong to a phase later than that characterized by dependence on the holding environment.

Freud's Footnote Re-examined

At this point it is necessary to look again at Freud's statement quoted earlier. He writes: 'Probably it (the baby) hallucinates the fulfilment of its inner needs; it betrays its pain due to increase of stimulation and delay of satisfaction by the motor discharge of crying and struggling, and then experiences the hallucinated satisfaction.' The theory indicated in this part of the statement fails to cover the requirements of the earliest phase. Already by these words reference is being made to object relationships, and the validity of this part of Freud's statement depends on his taking for granted the earlier aspects of maternal care, those which are here described as belonging to the holding phase. On the other hand, this sentence of Freud fits exactly the requirements in the *next* phase, that which is characterized by a relationship between infant and mother in which object relationships and instinctual or erotogenic-zone satisfactions hold sway; that is, when development proceeds well.

B. THE ROLE OF THE MATERNAL CARE

I shall now attempt to describe some aspects of maternal care, and especially holding. In this paper the concept of holding is important, and a further development of the idea is necessary. The word is here used to introduce a full development of the theme contained in Freud's phrase '. . . when one considers that the infant – provided one includes with it the care it receives from its mother – does almost realize a psychical system of this kind'. I refer to the actual state of the infant-mother relationship at the beginning when the infant has not separated out a self from the maternal care on which there exists absolute dependence in a psychological sense.[14]

At this stage the infant needs and in fact usually gets an environmental provision which has certain characteristics:

It meets physiological needs. Here physiology and psychology have not yet become distinct, or are only in the process of doing so; and

It is reliable. But the environmental provision is not mechanically reliable. It is reliable in a way that implies the mother's empathy.

Holding:

Protects from physiological insult.

Takes account of the infant's skin sensitivity – touch, temperature, auditory sensitivity, visual sensitivity, sensitivity to falling (action of gravity) and of the infant's lack of knowledge of the existence of anything other than the self.

It includes the whole routine of care throughout the day and night, and it is not the same with any two infants because it is part of the infant, and no two infants are alike.

Also it follows the minute day-to-day changes belonging to the infant's growth and development, both physical and psychological.

It should be noted that mothers who have it in them to provide good-enough care can be enabled to do better by being cared for themselves in a way that acknowledges the essential nature of their task. Mothers who do not have it in them to provide good-enough care cannot be made good enough by mere instruction.

Holding includes especially the physical holding of the infant, which is a form of loving. It is perhaps the only way in which a mother can show the infant her love. There are those who can hold an infant and those who cannot; the latter quickly produce in the infant a sense of insecurity, and distressed crying.

All this leads right up to, includes, and co-exists with the establishment of the infant's first object relationships and his first experiences of instinctual gratification.[15]

It would be wrong to put the instinctual gratification (feeding etc.) or object relationships (relation to the breast) before the matter of ego organization (i.e. infant ego reinforced by maternal ego). The basis for instinctual satisfaction and for object relationships is the handling and the general management and the care of the infant, which is only too easily taken for granted when all goes well.

The mental health of the individual, in the sense of freedom from psychosis or liability to psychosis (schizophrenia), is laid down by this maternal care, which when it goes well is scarcely noticed, and is a continuation of the physiological provision that characterizes the prenatal state. This environmental provision is also a continuation of the tissue aliveness and the functional health which (for the infant) provides silent but vitally important ego-support. In this way schizophrenia or infantile psychosis or a liability to psychosis at a later date is related to a failure of environmental provision. This is not to say, however, that the ill-effects of such failure cannot be described in terms of ego distortion and of the defences against primitive anxieties, that is to say in terms of the individual. It will be seen, therefore, that the work of Klein on the splitting defence mechanisms and on projections and introjections and so on, is an attempt to state the effects of failure of environmental provision in terms of the individual. This work on primitive mechanisms gives the clue to only one part of the story, and a reconstruction of the environment and of its failures provides the other part. This other part cannot appear in the transference because of the patient's lack of knowledge of the maternal care, either in its good or in its failing aspects, as it existed in the original infantile setting.

Examination of One Detail of Maternal Care

I will give an example to illustrate subtlety in infant care. An infant is merged with the mother, and while this remains true the nearer the mother can come to an exact understanding of the infant's needs the better. A change, however, comes with the end of merging, and this end is not necessarily gradual. As soon as mother and infant are separate, from the infant's point of view, then it will be noted that the mother tends to change in her attitude. It is as if she now realizes that the infant no longer expects the condition in which there is an almost magical understanding of need. The mother seems to know that the infant has a new capacity, that of giving a signal so that she can be guided towards meeting the infant's needs. It could be said that if now she knows too well what the infant needs, this is magic and forms no basis for an object relationship. Here we get to Freud's words: 'It (the infant) probably hallucinates the fulfilment of its internal needs; it betrays its unpleasure, when there is an increase of stimulus and an absence of satisfaction, by the motor discharge of screaming and beating about with its arms and legs, and it then experiences the satisfaction it has hallucinated.' In other words, at the end of merging, when the child has become separate from the environment, an important feature is that the infant has to give a signal.[16] We find this subtlety appearing clearly in the transference in our analytic work. It is very important, except when the patient is regressed to earliest infancy and to a state of merging, that the analyst shall *not* know the answers except in so far as the patient gives the clues. The analyst gathers the clues and makes the interpretations, and it often happens that patients fail to give the clues, making certain thereby that the analyst can do nothing. This limitation of the analyst's power is important to the patient, just as the analyst's power is important, represented by the interpretation that is right and that is made at the right moment, and that is based on the clues and the unconscious co-operation of the patient who is supplying the material which builds up and justifies the interpretation. In this way the student analyst sometimes does better analysis than he will do in a few years' time when he knows more. When he has had several patients he begins to find it irksome to go as slowly as the patient is going, and he begins to make interpretations based not on material supplied on that particular day by the patient but on his own accumulated knowledge or his adherence for the time being to a particular group of ideas. This is of no use to the patient. The analyst may appear to be very clever, and the patient may express admiration, but in the end the correct interpretation is a trauma, which the patient has to reject, because it is not his. He complains that the analyst attempts to hypnotize him, that is to say, that the analyst is inviting a severe regression to dependence, pulling the patient back to a merging in with the analyst.

The same thing can be observed with the mothers of infants; mothers who have had several children begin to be so good at the technique of mothering that they do all the right things at the right moments, and then the infant who has begun to become separate from the mother has no means of gaining control of all the good things that are going on. The creative gesture, the cry, the protest, all the little signs that are supposed to produce what the mother does, all these things are missing, because the mother has already met the need just as if the infant were still merged with her and she with the infant. In this way the mother, by being a seemingly good mother, does something worse than castrate the infant. The latter is left with two alternatives: either being in a permanent state of regression and of being merged with the mother, or else staging a total rejection of the mother, even of the seemingly good mother.

We see therefore that in infancy and in the management of infants there is a very subtle distinction between the mother's understanding of her infant's need based on empathy, and her change over to an understanding based on something in the infant or small child that indicates need. This is particularly difficult for mothers because of the fact that children vacillate between one state and the other; one minute they are merged with their mothers and require empathy, while the next they are separate from her, and then if she knows their needs in advance she is dangerous, a witch. It is a very strange thing that mothers who are quite uninstructed adapt to these changes in their developing infants satisfactorily and without any knowledge of the theory. This detail is reproduced in psycho-analytic work with borderline cases, and in all cases at certain moments of great importance when dependence in transference is maximal.

It is axiomatic in these matters of maternal care of the holding variety that when things go well the infant has no means of knowing what is being properly provided and what is being prevented. On the other hand it is when things do not go well that the infant becomes aware, not of the failure of maternal care, but of the results, whatever they may be, of that failure; that is to say, the infant becomes aware of reacting to some impingement. As a result of success in maternal care there is built up in the infant a continuity of being which is the basis of ego-strength; whereas the result of each failure in maternal care is that the continuity of being is interrupted by reactions to the consequences of that failure, with resultant ego-weakening.[17] Such interruptions constitute annihilation, and are evidently associated with pain of psychotic quality and intensity. In the extreme case the infant exists only on the basis of a continuity of reactions to impingement and of recoveries from such reactions. This is in great contrast to the continuity of being which is my conception of ego-strength.

C. THE CHANGES IN THE MOTHER

It is important in this context to examine the changes that occur in women who are about to have a baby or who have just had one. These changes are at first almost physiological, and they start with the physical holding of the baby in the womb. Something would be missing, however, if a phrase such as 'maternal instinct' were used in description. The fact is that in health women change in their orientation to themselves and to the world, but however deeply rooted in physiology such changes may be, they can be distorted by mental ill-health in the woman. It is necessary to think of these changes in psychological terms and this in spite of the fact that there may be endocrinological factors which can be affected by medication.

No doubt the physiological changes sensitize the woman to the more subtle psychological changes that follow.

Soon after conception, or when conception is known to be possible, the woman begins to alter in her orientation, and to be concerned with the changes that are taking place within her. In various ways she is encouraged by her own body to be interested in herself.[18] The mother shifts some of her sense of self on to the baby that is growing within her. The important thing is that there comes into existence a state of affairs that merits description and the theory of which needs to be worked out.

The analyst who is meeting the needs of a patient who is reliving these very early stages in the transference undergoes similar changes of orientation; and the analyst, unlike the mother, needs to be aware of the sensitivity which develops in him or her in response to the patient's immaturity and dependence. This could be thought of as an extension of Freud's description of the analyst as being in a voluntary state of attentiveness.

A detailed description of the changes in orientation in a woman who is becoming or who has just become a mother would be out of place here, and I have made an attempt elsewhere to describe these changes in popular or non-technical language (Winnicott, 1949[b]).

There is a psycho-pathology of these changes in orientation, and the extremes of abnormality are the concern of those who study the psychology of puerperal insanity. No doubt there are many variations in quality which do not constitute abnormality. It is the degree of distortion that constitutes abnormality.

By and large mothers do in one way or another identify themselves with the baby that is growing within them, and in this way they achieve a very powerful sense of what the baby needs. This is a projective identification. This identification with the baby lasts for a certain length of time after parturition, and then gradually loses significance.

In the ordinary case the mother's special orientation to the infant carries over beyond the birth process. The mother who is not distorted in these matters is ready to let go of her identification with the infant as the infant needs to become separate. It is possible to provide good initial care, but to fail to complete the process through an inability to let it come to an end, so that the mother tends to remain merged with her infant and to delay the infant's separation from her. It is in any case a difficult thing for a mother to separate from her infant at the same speed at which the infant needs to become separate from her.[19]

The important thing, in my view, is that the mother through identification of herself with her infant knows what the infant feels like and so is able to provide almost exactly what the infant needs in the way of holding and in the provision of an environment generally. Without such an identification I consider that she is not able to provide what the infant needs at the beginning, which is *a live adaptation to the infant's needs*. The main thing is the physical holding, and this is the basis of all the more complex aspects of holding, and of environmental provision in general.

It is true that a mother may have a baby who is very different from herself so that she miscalculates. The baby may be quicker or slower than she is, and so on. In this way there may be times when what she feels the baby needs is not in fact correct. However, it seems to be usual that mothers who are not distorted by ill-health or by present-day environmental stress do tend on the whole to know accurately enough what their infants need, and further, they like to provide what is needed. This is the essence of maternal care.

With 'the care that it receives from its mother' each infant is able to have a personal existence, and so begins to build up what might be called *a continuity of being*. On the basis of this continuity of being the inherited potential gradually develops into an individual infant. If maternal care is not good enough then the infant does not really come into existence, since there is no continuity of being; instead the personality becomes built on the basis of reactions to environmental impingement.

All this has significance for the analyst. Indeed it is not from direct observation of infants so much as from the study of the transference in the analytic setting that it is possible to gain a clear view of what takes place in infancy itself. This work on infantile dependence derives from the study of the transference and counter-transference phenomena that belong to the psycho-analyst's involvement with the borderline case. In my opinion this involvement is a legitimate extension of psycho-analysis, the only real alteration being in the diagnosis of the illness of the patient, the aetiology of whose illness goes back behind the Oedipus complex, and involves a distortion at the time of absolute dependence.

Freud was able to discover infantile sexuality in a new way because he reconstructed it from his analytic work with psychoneurotic patients. In extending his work to cover the treatment of the borderline psychotic patient it is possible for us to reconstruct the dynamics of infancy and of infantile dependence, and the maternal care that meets this dependence.

SUMMARY

(i) An examination is made of infancy; this is not the same as an examination of primitive mental mechanisms.

(ii) The main feature of infancy is dependence; this is discussed in terms of the holding environment.

(iii) Any study of infancy must be divided into two parts:

(a) Infant development facilitated by good-enough maternal care;
(b) Infant development distorted by maternal care that is not good enough.

(iv) The infant ego can be said to be weak, but in fact it is strong because of the ego support of maternal care. Where maternal care fails the weakness of the infant ego becomes apparent.

(v) Processes in the mother (and in the father) bring about, in health, a special state in which the parent is orientated to the infant, and is thus in a position to meet the infant's dependence. There is a pathology of these processes.

(vi) Attention is drawn to the various ways in which these conditions inherent in what is here termed the holding[20] environment can or cannot appear in the transference if at a later date the infant should come into analysis.

Notes

1. This paper, together with one by Dr Phyllis Greenacre on the same theme, was the subject of a discussion at the 22nd International Psycho-Analytical Congress at Edinburgh, 1961. It was first published in the *International Journal of Psychoanalysis* 41: 585–95.
2. I have discussed this from a more detailed clinical angle in 'Primitive Emotional Development' [see Chapter 2, this volume].
3. I have reported (1954 [Chapter 6, this volume]) some aspects of this problem, as met with in the case of a female patient while she was in deep regression.
4. I once said: 'There is no such thing as an infant', meaning, of course, that whenever one finds an infant one finds maternal care, and without maternal care there would be no infant. (Discussion at a Scientific Meeting of the British Psycho-Analytical Society, *circa* 1940.) Was I influenced, without knowing it, by this footnote of Freud's?
5. I have tried to show the application of this hypothesis to an understanding of psychosis in my paper, 'Psychoses and Child Care' (Winnicott, 1952[a]).
6. Researches into defence mechanisms which followed Anna Freud's *The Ego and the Mechanisms of Defence* (1936) have from a different route arrived at a re-evaluation of the role of mothering in infant care and early infant development. Anna Freud (1953) has reassessed her views on the matter. Willi Hoffer (1955) also has made observations relating to this area of development. My emphasis in this paper, however, is on the importance of an understanding of the role of the early parental environment in infant development, and on the way this becomes of clinical significance for us in our handling of certain types of case with affective and character disorders.
7. I have given a detailed account of my understanding of Melanie Klein's work in this area in two papers (Winnicott, 1954[a] and 1958[c]). See Klein (1946, p. 297).
8. For a clinical example see my paper, 'Withdrawal and Regression' (1954[b]).
9. For an earlier statement by me on this issue see my paper, 'Mind and its Relation to the Psyche-Soma' [see Chapter 4, this volume].
10. Here the work on primitive fantasy, with whose richness and complexity we are familiar through the teachings of Melanie Klein, becomes applicable and appropriate.
11. In 'The Capacity to Be Alone' (1958[d]) I have tried to discuss another aspect of this developmental phase as we see it in adult health. Cf. Greenacre (1958).
12. I am using the term 'projections' here in its descriptive and dynamic and not in its full metapsychological sense. The function of primitive psychic mechanisms, such as introjection, projection, and splitting, falls beyond the scope of this paper.
13. I have described clinical varieties of this type of anxiety from a slightly different aspect in a previous paper (1949[c]).
14. Reminder: to be sure of separating this off from object relationships and instinct-gratification I must *artificially* confine my attention to the body needs of a general kind. A patient said to me: 'A good analytic hour in which the right interpretation is given at the right time *is* a good feed.'
15. For further discussion of this aspect of the developmental processes see my paper, 'Transitional Objects and Transitional Phenomena' [see Chapter 5, this volume].
16. Freud's later (1926) theory of anxiety as a signal to the ego.
17. In character cases it is this ego-weakening and the individual's various attempts to deal with it that presents itself for immediate attention, and yet only a true view of the aetiology can make possible a sorting out of the defence aspect of this presenting symptom from its origin in environmental failure. I have referred to one specific aspect of this in the diagnosis of the antisocial tendency as the basic problem behind the Delinquency Syndrome.

18. For a more detailed statement on this point see 'Primary Maternal Preoccupation' (1956[b]).
19. Case-material to illustrate one type of problem that is met with clinically and relates to this group of ideas is presented in an earlier paper (1948[a]).
20. Concept of 'holding' in case work: Cf. Winnicott, C. (1954).

Developing ideas: primary maternal preoccupation; ego relatedness; isolation of the individual; going-on-being; annihilation anxiety; capacity to be alone; subjective objects; the antisocial tendency; pre-ruth and ruthless love; ego orgasm; holding; clinical varieties of transference and psychiatric classification linked to stages of development; good-enough adaptation by the analyst; correct interpretation as trauma

8 THE DEVELOPMENT OF THE CAPACITY FOR CONCERN (1963)

OTHER WRITINGS

Winnicott retired from the National Health Service in 1963 and the next three papers date from that year. While representing only a tiny part of his output [Abram (2007) lists 70 papers on psychoanalysis and over a 100 on child development in the last decade of his life] these papers represent further advances in Winnicott's evolving theory. They are testimony to the breadth of his interest in human functioning and in the psychoanalytic process and they approach his fundamental concern with living and its meaning from his own emphasis on the achievement developmentally of the child's concern for the mother, his proposal of the human need both to communicate and not communicate, and his statements about the self. His critical review (1959b) of Klein's *Envy and Gratitude* especially disputed her account of primary envy in the baby's relationship to the mother and his disagreement with the Klein group over this major late contribution continued. Nonetheless, following her death in 1960, he gave an appreciative account of her contribution to candidates at the Los Angeles Psychoanalytic Society in October 1962 (1962c). After her death the group around Klein (Segal, Rosenfeld, Bion, Joseph) extended her ideas about intra and interpersonal processes and Wilfred Bion's work in particular interested Winnicott. After Bion had given his paper, 'A Theory of Thinking' to the BPAS in November 1961 (see 1967, pp. 110–119) in which he described the containing function of the mother in her reverie, Winnicott wrote 'I know that your statement does contain something new to me and vitally important'. Later, he berated John Wisdom in a letter for commenting on Bion's theories without relating them to his own ideas. Winnicott wrote 'It is important to me that Bion states (obscurely of course) what I have been trying to state for two and a half decades but against the terrific opposition of Melanie . . . Bion says . . . "What happens depends . . ." . . . Melanie Klein absolutely would not allow this and my relation to her was (though always warm and good) impaired by her adamant objection to "what happens depends. . . ." You should have mentioned this fact that Bion goes deeper than Melanie here, or finds a way of stating what Melanie would not allow. . . . I like Bion's treatment of this subject, and I can learn something from it. But if you (not he) are talking about it you ought to say:

EDITORS' INTRODUCTION

This paper was presented to The Topeka Psychoanalytic Society in October 1962, and first published in the *Bulletin of the Menninger Clinic*. It is the culmination of Winnicott's thinking on a significant range of issues: ambivalence, aggression, guilt, the origins of morality and the superego. He had rehearsed the conclusions he comes to here in several previous papers on aggression (1939), the depressive position (1954a), the sense of guilt (1958c), and morals and education (1963a). He disagrees with Klein's account in 'Our Adult World and Its Roots in Infancy' (1959) that the vicissitudes of infantile persecutory anxiety consequent on birth and the experience of an initial state of helplessness fundamentally determine the course of all subsequent development. Klein herself, in adding that love and understanding can mitigate early anxieties and 'lead to a certain unconscious oneness between mother and baby' so that 'the feeling of being understood underlies the most fundamental relation of life – the relation to the mother' (p. 248) may be read in part as responding to Winnicott's challenge to her account of the roots of aggression, and the related matter of analytic technique. The 'capacity for concern' is a reworking of Klein's thesis, and in it he changes her formulation (Greenberg and Mitchell, 1983). She had placed the infant's guilt about its destructive attacks and the reparative urge towards the mother at the centre of her theory of the depressive position (Klein, 1940). Winnicott, being interested in health and normal development, thought that 'depressive position' was 'a bad name' (1954a: 264), and he introduced the 'stage of concern' to reflect his own thinking; as Phillips puts it, 'something sounding remarkably like a psychiatric syndrome becomes a more ordinary recognisable feeling' (1988: 107).

The 'stage of concern' assumes that the infant has achieved 'unit status' as the outcome of the earlier stages of normal development and is in transition towards 'the capacity for interpersonal relationships which characterise the toddler stage in health and for whom the analysis of the infinite variations of triangular human relations is feasible' (Winnicott, 1954a: 262). He emphasized the time factor emerging as part of the mother's function, to 'hold [the] situation so that the infant has the chance to work through the consequences of instinctual experiences' (p. 263). He saw the development of the capacity for concern as belonging to the weaning age, being able to relate to the external world realistically. In the earlier paper (1954a) Winnicott had written about the mother in the infant's most primitive development combining two functions corresponding to his quiet and excited states. In the present paper the 'environment mother' and the 'object mother' have to come together in the baby's experience as a whole person. The infant's concern for the mother depends upon the transformations as these 'two mothers' come together. This is not predicated on the processes of splitting good and bad which Klein regards as a central feature of the infant's earliest functioning.

These transformations depend on the nature and fate of aggression in earliest development. His account equates aggression at the most primary level with movement. He places aggression as part of the life force and distinguishes it from hate and destructiveness, though these may be appropriated, mobilized, and used by the aggressive impulse through the course of experience. It is immensely important that the infant can express this aggression without inhibition and that he is 'not too quickly robbed of zest' as this leaves him with 'aggression undischarged' (1954a: 268). Aggression can further be seen in the 'destructive' aspects of loving as it becomes fused with the 'primitive love impulse' evident in the actions of sucking, biting, and chewing, physical processes which are elaborated in primitive phantasy in the psyche (see Chapter 4, this volume); and aggression and love are linked.

The environment mother 'holds' the infant over time and allows herself to be related to as the object of the baby's 'ruthless' devouring. As maturation proceeds in this facilitating environment a crisis is precipitated in the baby by the realization that these two mothers are the same: the one on whom the baby depends in quiet times is also the one who is the object of these ruthless attacks. 'By the same process he will connect himself as a desiring person with the more quiescent and comfortable person he is between feeds' (Phillips, 1988: 107). The transformation of the infant from being entirely 'needs'-focused towards the recognition of 'desire' and 'want' also suggests the experience of lack and the need for it to be integrated into the developing ego.

Winnicott emphasizes the role of the actual mother in holding this situation so that the guilt the baby feels can be transformed into concern. The mother's presence is essential to receive the baby's 'spontaneous gesture'. This is Winnicott's version of 'reparation'. He emphasizes the process, repeatedly held over time by the mother, so that a benign circle of recognition of the complications of instinctual experience ('the hole', 1954a: 270) may be perceived by the baby and 'sorted out'. This leads to reparation and restitution, the capacity to contribute, and the 'spontaneous gesture'. The language of the body, 'gesture', emphasizes the material reality as well as the psychic significance of an interpersonal and intrapsychic process. This is not just a transformation of quality in the affect experienced (from guilt to concern) but also the beginnings of a capacity in the baby's developing ego: a developmental stage but also an essential aspect of ego formation that contributes to further integration and particularly to the establishment of emotional object constancy. The capacity to hold in mind the image of the loved and hated object in its absence, that is, the capacity for ambivalence, is the hallmark of increasing maturation and independence (Davis and Wallbridge, 1981).

In Winnicott's thinking about the development of morality and of delinquency, the very existence or the fate of the capacity for concern is crucial. In the good-enough environment the baby's innate morality will emerge (1963a; 1966a) and Winnicott considered that the development of authenticity in the true self, meant that 'immorality for the infant is to comply at the expense of the personal way of life' (Winnicott, 1963a: 102).

He was impressed with Klein's reworking of the psychoanalytic theory of the superego, where she postulated a primitive superego – a radical departure from Freudian theory, where the superego is the outcome of the resolution of the Oedipus complex much later in the child's development. Klein was interested not so much in the external social and parental sources of the sense of guilt as in their personal intrapsychic origins. Winnicott saw an aspect of the parent's role as mitigating the ferocity of the early primitive superego for very young children.

If the environment is deficient or not good enough in providing the conditions necessary for the emergence of 'a capacity to stand feeling guilt in regard to destructive impulses and ideas, to stand being generally responsible for destructive ideas, because of having become confident in regard to reparative impulses and opportunities for contributing' (1963a: 103), then the child is in trouble. The outcome of this deficiency at this stage of development, which he regarded as deprivation, or loss of what had earlier been good enough, would probably be the 'antisocial tendency' or delinquency. He distinguished the kind of depression that is seen in psychiatric clinics from the reactions to failure in the capacity for concern, saying in his critique of Klein's concept the 'these phenomena belong to the era before that of the depressive position in the individual's development' (1954a: 272).

Phillips (1988) discusses the role of aggression and reparation or concern in Winnicott's developing theory of creativity. He points out that as early as 1948 Winnicott was critical of the Kleinian view which sees creativity deriving from reparation in the depressive position. But Winnicott was already placing its origins earlier, 'with the primitive love impulse, the wholehearted earliest instinctual experiences which included an aggressive ruthlessness' (Phillips, 1988: 112). Phillips quotes from 'Psycho-Analysis and the Sense of Guilt' where this view is quite explicit: 'The creative artist or thinker may in fact fail to understand or even may despise the feelings of concern that motivate a less creative person.' It is the artist's ruthlessness that 'does in fact achieve more than guilt-driven labour' (Winnicott, 1958c in Phillips, 1988). Phillips adds: 'Reparation could be a flight from inspiration' (1988: 113).

The Development of the Capacity for Concern[i]
(1963)

The origin of the capacity to be concerned presents a complex problem. Concern is an important feature in social life. Psycho-analysts usually seek origins in the emotional development of the individual. We want to know the aetiology of concern, and the place where concern appears in the child's development. We also are interested in the failure of the establishment of an individual's capacity for concern, and in the loss of concern that has to some extent been established.

The word 'concern' is used to cover in a positive way a phenomenon that is covered in a negative way by the word 'guilt'. A sense of guilt is anxiety linked with the concept of ambivalence, and implies a degree of integration in the individual ego that allows for the retention of good object-imago along with the idea of a destruction of it. Concern implies further integration, and further growth, and relates in a positive way to the individual's sense of responsibility, especially in respect of relationships into which the instinctual drives have entered.

Concern refers to the fact that the individual *cares*, or *minds*, and both feels and accepts responsibility. At the genital level in the statement of the theory of development, concern could be said to be the basis of the family, where both partners in intercourse – beyond their pleasure – take responsibility for the result. But in the total imaginative life of the individual, the subject of concern raises even wider issues, and a capacity for concern is at the back of all constructive play and work. It belongs to normal, healthy living, and deserves the attention of the psycho-analyst.

There is much reason to believe that concern – with its positive sense – emerges in the earlier emotional development of the child at a period before the period of the classical Oedipus complex, which involves a relationship between three persons, each felt to be a whole person by the child. But there is no need to be precise about timing, and indeed most of the processes that start up in early infancy are never fully established, and continue to be strengthened by the growth that continues in later childhood, and indeed in adult life, even in old age.

It is usual to describe the origin of the capacity for concern in terms of the infant-mother relationship, when already the infant is an established unit, and when the infant feels the mother, or mother-figure, to be a whole person. It is a development belonging essentially to the period of a two-body relationship.

In any statement of child-development, certain principles are taken for granted. Here I wish to say that the maturation processes form the basis of infant- and child-development, in psychology as in anatomy and physiology. Nevertheless, in emotional development it is clear that certain external conditions are necessary if maturation potentials are to become actual. That is, development depends on a good-enough environment, and the earlier we go back in our study of the baby, the more true it is that without good-enough mothering the early stages of development cannot take place.

A great deal has happened in the development of the baby before we begin to be able to refer to concern. The capacity to be concerned is a matter of health, a capacity which, once established, presupposes a complex ego-organization which cannot be thought of in any way but as an achievement, both an achievement of infant- and child-care and an achievement in terms of the internal growth-processes in the baby and child. I shall take for granted a good-enough environment in the early stages, in order to simplify the matter that I wish to examine. What I have to say, then, follows on complex maturational processes dependent for their becoming realized on good-enough infant- and child-care.

Of the many stages that have been described by Freud and the psychoanalysts who have followed him, I must single out one stage which has to involve the use of the word 'fusion'. This is the achievement of emotional development in which the baby experiences erotic and aggressive drives toward the same object at the same time. On the erotic side there is both satisfaction-seeking and object-seeking, and on the aggressive side, there is a complex of anger employing muscle erotism, and of hate, which involves the retention of a good object-imago for comparison. Also in the whole aggressive-destructive impulse is contained a primitive type of object relationship in which love involves destruction. Some of this is necessarily obscure, and I do not need to know all about the origin of aggression in order to follow my argument, because I am taking it for granted that the baby has become able to combine erotic and aggressive experience, and in relation to one object. Ambivalence has been reached.

By the time that this becomes a fact in the development of a child, the infant has become able to experience ambivalence in fantasy, as well as in body-function of which the fantasy is originally an elaboration. Also, the infant is beginning to relate himself to objects that are less and less subjective phenomena, and more and more objectively perceived 'not-me' elements. He has begun to establish a self, a unit that is both physically contained in the body's skin and that is psychologically integrated. The mother has now become – in the child's mind – a coherent image, and the term 'whole object' now becomes applicable. This state of affairs, precarious at first, could be nick-named the 'humpty-dumpty stage', the wall on which Humpty Dumpty is precariously perched being the mother who has ceased to offer her lap.

This development implies an ego that begins to be independent of the mother's auxiliary ego, and there can now be said to be an inside to the baby, and therefore an outside. The body-scheme has come into being and quickly develops complexity. From now on, the infant lives a psychosomatic life. The inner psychic reality which Freud taught us to respect now becomes a real thing to the infant, who now feels that personal richness resides within the self.

This personal richness develops out of the simultaneous love–hate experience which implies the achievement of ambivalence, the enrichment and refinement of which leads to the emergence of concern.

It is helpful to postulate the existence for the immature child of two mothers – shall I call them the object-mother and the environment-mother? I have no wish to invent names that become stuck and eventually develop a rigidity and an obstructive quality, but it seems possible to use these words 'object-mother' and 'environment-mother' in this context to describe the vast difference that there is for the infant between two aspects of infant-care, the mother as object, or owner of the part-object that may satisfy the infant's urgent needs, and the mother as the person who wards off the unpredictable and who actively provides care in handling and in general management. What the infant does at the height of id-tension and the use thus made of the object seems to me very different from the use the infant makes of the mother as part of the total environment.[ii]

In this language it is the environment-mother who receives all that can be called affection and sensuous co-existence; it is the object-mother who becomes the target for excited experience backed by crude instinct-tension. It is my thesis that concern turns up in the baby's life as a highly sophisticated experience in the coming-together in the infant's mind of the object-mother and the environment-mother. The environmental provision continues to be vitally important here, though the infant is beginning to be able to have that inner stability that belongs to the development of independence.

In favourable circumstances, when the baby has reached the necessary stage in personal development, there comes about a new fusion. For one thing, there is the full experience of, and fantasy of, object-relating based on instinct, the object being used without regard for consequences, used ruthlessly (if we use the term as a description of our view of what is going on). And alongside this is the more quiet relationship of the baby to the environment-mother. These two things come together. The result is complex, and it is this that I especially wish to describe.

The favourable circumstances necessary at this stage are these: that the mother should continue to be alive and available, available physically and available in the sense of not being preoccupied with something else. The object-mother has to be found to survive the instinct-driven episodes, which have now acquired the full force of fantasies of oral sadism and other results of fusion. Also, the environment-mother has a special function, which is to continue to be herself, to be empathic towards her infant, to be there to receive the spontaneous gesture, and to be pleased.

The fantasy that goes with full-blooded id-drives contains attack and destruction. It is not only that the baby imagines that he eats the object, but also that the baby wants to take possession of the contents of the object. If the object is not destroyed, it is because of its own survival capacity, not because of the baby's protection of the object. This is one side of the picture.

The other side of the picture has to do with the baby's relation to the environment-mother, and from this angle there may come so great a protection of the mother that the child becomes inhibited or turns away. Here is a positive element in the infant's experience of weaning and one reason why some infants wean themselves.

In favourable circumstances there builds up a technique for the solution of this complex form of ambivalence. The infant experiences anxiety, because if he consumes the mother he will lose her, but this anxiety becomes modified by the fact that the baby has a contribution to make to the environment-mother. There is a growing confidence that there will be opportunity for contributing-in, for giving to the environment-mother, a confidence which makes the infant able to hold the anxiety. The anxiety held in this way becomes altered in quality and becomes a sense of guilt.

Instinct-drives lead to ruthless usage of objects, and then to a guilt-sense which is held, and is allayed by the contribution to the environment-mother that the infant can make in the course of a few hours. Also, the opportunity for giving and for making reparation that the environment-mother offers by her reliable presence, enables the baby to become more and more bold in the experiencing of id-drives; in other words, frees the baby's instinctual life. In this way, the guilt is not felt, but it lies dormant, or potential, and appears (as sadness or a depressed mood) only if opportunity for reparation fails to turn up.

When confidence in this benign cycle and in the expectation of opportunity is established, the sense of guilt in relation to the id-drives becomes further modified, and we then need a more positive term, such as 'concern'. The infant is now becoming able to be concerned, to take responsibility for his own instinctual impulses and the functions that belong to them. This provides one of the fundamental constructive elements of play and work. But in the developmental process, it was the opportunity to contribute that enabled concern to be within the child's capacity.

A feature that may be noted, especially in respect of the concept of anxiety that is 'held', is that integration *in time* has become added to the more static integration of the earlier stages. Time is kept going by the mother, and this is one aspect of her auxiliary ego-functioning; but the infant comes to have a personal time-sense, one that lasts at first only over a short span. This is the same as the infant's capacity to keep alive the imago of the mother in the inner world which also contains the fragmentary benign and persecutory elements that arise out of the instinctual experiences. The length of the time-span over which a child can keep the imago alive in inner psychic reality depends partly on maturational processes and partly on the state of the inner defence organization.

I have sketched some aspects of the origins of concern in the early stages in which the mother's continued presence has a specific value for the infant, that is, if the instinctual life is to have freedom of expression. But this balance has to be achieved over and over again. Take the obvious case of the management of adolescence, or the equally obvious case of the psychiatric patient, for whom occupational therapy is often a start on the road towards a constructive relation to society. Or consider a doctor, and his needs. Deprive him of his work, and where is he? He needs his patients, and the opportunity to use his skills, as others do.

I shall not develop at length the theme of lack of development of concern, or of loss of this capacity for concern that has been almost, but not quite, established. Briefly, failure of the object-mother to survive or of the environment-mother to provide reliable opportunity for reparation leads to a loss of the capacity for concern, and to its replacement by crude anxieties and by crude defences, such as splitting, or disintegration. We often discuss separation-anxiety, but here I am trying to describe what happens between mothers and their babies and between parents and their children when there is *no* separation, and when external continuity of child-care is *not* broken. I am trying to account for things that happen when separation is avoided.

To illustrate my communication I shall give a few examples from clinical work. I do not want, however, to suggest that I am referring to anything rare. Almost any psycho-analysis would provide an example in the course of a week. And it must be remembered that in any clinical example taken from an analysis there is a host of mental mechanisms that the analyst needs to be able to understand which belong to later stages of the individual's development, and to the defences that are called psycho-neurotic. These can be ignored only when the patient is in a state of severe regression to dependence in the transference, and is, in effect, a baby in the care of a mother-figure.

Example I: First I cite the case of the boy of twelve whom I was asked to interview. He was a boy whose *forward* development led him to depression, which included a vast quantity of unconscious hate and aggression, and whose *backward* development, if I may use the phrase, led him to seeing faces, to experiences that were horrible because they represented dreams dreamed in the waking state, hallucinosis. There was good evidence of ego-strength in this boy, as witness his depressive moods. One way that this ego-strength showed in the interview was as follows:

> He drew a nightmare, with a huge horned male-creature threatening a tiny self, an 'ant'-self. I asked if he had ever dreamed of himself as the huge horned male, with the ant as someone else, his brother, for instance, at the time of the brother's infancy. He allowed this. When he did not reject my interpretation of his hatred of his brother, I gave him an opportunity to tell me of his reparative potential. This came quite naturally through his description of his father's job as a refrigeration mechanic. I asked him what he himself might want one day to be. He 'had no idea', and he was distressed. He then reported 'not a sad dream, but what a sad dream would be: his father dead'. He was near tears. In this phase of the interview there

was a long period of nothing much happening. At length the boy said, very shyly, that he would like to be a scientist.

Here, then, he had shown that he could think of himself as contributing. Though he may not have had the requisite ability, he had the idea. Incidentally, this pursuit would bring him right ahead of his father because, as he said, his father's job was not at all that of a scientist, it was 'just being a mechanic'.

I then felt the interview could end in its own time; I felt the boy could go away without being disturbed by what I had done. I had interpreted his potential destructiveness, but it was true that he had it in him to be constructive. His letting me know he had an aim in life enabled him to go, without feeling he had made me think he was only a hater and a destroyer. And yet, I had not reassured him.

Example II: A patient of mine doing psychotherapy started off a session by telling me that he had been to see one of his patients performing; that is to say, he had gone outside the role of a therapist dealing with the patient in the consulting room, and had seen this patient at work. The work of my patient's patient was highly skilled, and he was very successful in a particular job in which he used quick movements which in the therapeutic hour made no sense, but moved him around on the couch as if he were possessed. Although doubtful about having seen this man at work, my patient felt that probably it was a good thing. He then referred to his own activities in the holidays. He had a garden, and he very much enjoyed physical labour and all kinds of constructive activity, and he liked gadgets, which he really used.

I had been alerted to the importance of his constructive activities by his report of his having gone to see his patient at work. My patient returned to a theme which had been important in the recent analysis in which various kinds of engineering tools were important. On his way to the analytic session he often stopped and gazed at a machine tool in a shop window near my house. The tool had the most splendid teeth. This was my patient's way of getting at his oral aggression, the primitive love-impulse with all its ruthlessness and destructiveness. We could call it 'eating in the transference relationship'. The trend in his treatment was towards this ruthlessness and primitive loving, and the resistance against getting to the deep layers of it was tremendous. Here was a new integration and a concern about the survival of the analyst.

When this new material came up relating to primitive love and to the destruction of the analyst, *there had already been* some reference to constructive work. When I made the interpretation that the patient needed from me, about his destruction of me (eating), I could have reminded him of what he had said about construction. I could have said that just as he saw his patient performing, and the performance made sense of the jerky movements, so I might have seen him working in his garden, using gadgets in order to improve the property. He could cut through walls and trees, and it was all enjoyed tremendously. If such activity had come apart from a report of the constructive aim it would have been a senseless maniacal episode, a transference madness.

I would say that human beings cannot accept the destructive aim in their very early loving attempts. The idea of destruction of the object-mother in loving can be tolerated, however, if the individual who is getting towards it has evidence of a constructive aim already at hand, and of an environment-mother ready to accept.

Example III: A man patient came into my room and saw a tape-recorder. This gave him ideas, and he said as he lay down and as he gathered himself together for the work of the analytic hour, 'I would like to think that when I have finished treatment, what has happened here with me will be of value to the world in some way or other.' I said nothing, but I made a mental note that this remark *might* indicate that the patient was near to one of those bouts of destructiveness with which I had had to deal repeatedly in two years of his treatment. Before the end of the hour, the patient had truly reached a new awareness of his envy of me, an envy which was the outcome of his thinking I was a good analyst. He had the impulse to thank me for being good, and for being able to do what he needed me to do. We had had all this before, but he was now more than on previous occasions in touch with his destructive feelings towards what might be called a good object, his analyst.

When I linked these two things, he said that this felt right, but he added how awful it would have been if I had interpreted on the basis of his first remark. He meant, if I had taken up his wish to be of use and had told him that this indicated an unconscious wish to destroy. He had to reach to the destructive urge before I acknowledged the reparation, and he had to reach it in his own time and in his own way. No doubt it was his capacity to have an idea of ultimately contributing that was making it possible for him to get into more intimate contact with his destructiveness. But constructive effort is false and meaningless unless, as he said, one has first reached to the destruction.

Example IV: An adolescent girl was having treatment from a therapist who was also taking care of the girl at the same time in the therapist's home, along with her own children. This arrangement had advantages and disadvantages.

The girl had been severely ill, and at the time of the incident I shall recount she was emerging from a long period of regression to dependence and to an infantile state. She is no longer regressed in her relation to the home and the family, but is still in a very special state in the limited area of the treatment sessions which occur at a set time each day.

A time came when the girl expressed the deepest hate of the therapist (who is both caring for her and doing her treatment). All was well in the rest of the twenty-four hours, but in the treatment area the therapist was destroyed utterly, and repeatedly. It is difficult to convey the degree of the girl's hate of the therapist and, in fact, the annihilation of her. Here it was not a case of the therapist going out to see the patient at work, for the therapist had charge of the girl all the time, and there were two separate relationships going on between them simultaneously. In the day, all sorts of new things began to happen: the girl began to want to help clean the house, to polish the furniture, to be of use. This helping was absolutely new, and had never been a feature in this girl's personal pattern in her own home, even before she became acutely ill. And it happened silently (so to speak) alongside the utter destructiveness that the girl began to find in the primitive aspects of her loving, which she reached in her relation to the therapist in the therapy sessions.

You see the same idea repeating itself here. Naturally, the fact that the patient was becoming conscious of the destructiveness, made possible the constructive activity which appeared in the day. *But it is the other way round that I want to make plain here and now.* The constructive and creative experiences were making it possible for the child to get to the experience of her destructiveness. And thus, in the treatment, conditions were present that I have tried to describe. The capacity for concern is not only a maturational node, but it also depends for its existence on an emotional environment that has been good enough over a period of time.

SUMMARY

Concern, as the term has been used here, describes the link between the destructive elements in drive-relationships to objects, and the other positive aspects of relating. Concern is presumed to belong to a period prior to the classical Oedipus complex, which is a relationship between three whole persons. The capacity for concern belongs to the two-body relationship between the infant and the mother or mother-substitute.

In favourable circumstances, the mother by continuing to be alive and available is both the mother who receives all the fullness of the baby's id-drives, and also the mother who can be loved as a person and to whom reparation can be made. In this way, the anxiety about the id-drives and the fantasy of these drives becomes tolerable to the baby, who can then experience guilt, or can hold it in full expectation of an opportunity to make reparation for it. To this guilt that is held but not felt as such, we give the name 'concern'. In the initial stages of development, if there is no reliable mother-figure to receive the reparation-gesture, the guilt becomes intolerable, and concern cannot be felt. Failure of reparation leads to a losing of the capacity for concern, and to its replacement by primitive forms of guilt and anxiety.

Notes

[i] Presented to The Topeka Psychoanalytic Society, 12 October 1962, and first published in the *Bulletin of the Menninger Clinic* 27: 167–76.

[ii] This is a theme that has recently been developed in a book by Harold Searles (1960).

9 COMMUNICATING AND NOT COMMUNICATING LEADING TO A STUDY OF CERTAIN OPPOSITES (1963)

EDITORS' INTRODUCTION

This paper opens a discussion about communication by making a claim for the right not to communicate, and relates it to a personal realization. It is developed through the familiar territory of the preverbal forms of communication that are set up between mother and baby in any ordinary, good–enough nursing couple. It insists upon their fundamental importance for the more elaborate forms of communication that ensue in human contact with others and with the self, and it links this with what happens in any analysis.

Winnicott concentrates on the changing relations to the object that form the experiences of the baby and what they presage for health and development. The nature of the object, its location, and where and when an object can be placed mentally, beyond and outside the baby, represent necessary developmental steps, which, when achieved, mean that the object can be hated, refused, and repudiated. To arrive at this point, a shift in the way the object is perceived has to occur. This shift is fundamental for Winnicott's theory of communication, which depends upon the development of object relations. A significant part of the paper regards communicating with an object as central to the possibility of any communication with the self. In turn, this depends upon a theory of the emergence of a self through an awareness of the environment and its separateness. Implicit and explicit communication, the enjoyment of communicating, the necessity for non-communication, an exploration of different forms of communicating and not communicating, become the focus for what can be either the basis for normal healthy living or its opposite – an essentially false, compliant relationship with the external world. This produces an undeveloped internal relationship with fantasized subjective objects that may keep the person safe from an encounter with the world, at the cost of really being alive.

While Winnicott describes relationships first with the environment-mother and then with the object-mother, he is particularly concerned with the move from one to the other that emerges through the necessary unreliability of the actual real-life relationship. This unreliability produces the conditions for the emergence of the self, and Winnicott, speaking of the development of object-relating, makes the unsatisfied state its motor, thus echoing Freud's descriptions of lack of satisfaction as a foundation stone of development. It is not just a matter of whether communication is explicit in the early first relationship but whether, and to what extent, it makes sense to talk about communication at all, if communication involves two beings – for Winnicott has already outlined a model where, to all intents and purposes, the distance and separation required for communication to be necessary has not been established.

In his terms, however, the individual's possession of a non-communicating self and its existence alongside a different state, one which involves objects, arises from this period. What is at stake is how the infant emerges from a state of primary narcissism and the gradual separation of self and other. Different types of communication are central – the wish to communicate, and the equally important wish not to communicate – as they regard the species-specific qualities of humanness. Whether it is a matter of verbal or non-verbal communication, the issue is how the object is perceived, and how this becomes a possibility for the infant. The distinction is between a subjective object, where perception of the object is not present, and an object objectively per-ceived, which involves a sense of object as other. Elsewhere Winnicott (1962b) describes this distinction as allowing a discrepancy between what is observed and what is being experienced in the baby

For the objectively perceived object, Winnicott discusses a difference between 'a simple non-communicating', which he allies to being at rest, possibly just being, and 'a non-communicating that is active or reactive', and which can be considered in terms of health or pathology, and the false or compliant self. It derives from an originally presenting object that has 'failed,' and a 'self' that relates to what he again calls, 'a subjective object' adding, 'or to mere phenomena based on body experiences, these being scarcely influenced by an objectively perceived world' (p. 299). This argues significantly for a fundamental split in the self that belongs to health and to human subjectivity, but with profound consequences for ill health if that split develops in a way that is governed by compliance with an impinging environment.

So communicating and communication invite thought about the *ways* of communicating with the self and the obstacles to it. Winnicott emphasizes that the barriers to internal communication and non-communication have their origins in early environmental failures that also set in place external forms of communication that are false and empty.

The distinction between false and true self, and between subjective objects and an object objectively perceived, concepts that have been explored in earlier papers, will be added to in the posthumously published papers on mutuality (1969; Winnicott et al., 1989). They develop the vital importance of symbolic communication for healthy living and for psychoanalysis (see also the paper 'String: A Technique of Communication' from the same period, 1960c). The extremely personal introduction about the right not to communicate forms part of a continuing investigation of the person and the implications of such an investigation for the experience of an analysis.

An important addition to the general discussion of communicating is to be found in the implications for infants of being with a mother who herself has not arrived at the position of object-relating or of seeing her infant as objectively separate. The consequences for the infant who, in some way or other, has to come to operate in relations with the external world, may involve a series of defences that disallow a lively relation with his own subjective phenomena and the proliferation of feelings of absence, deadness, or non-aliveness (which Winnicott does not consider the same).

A core to the personality that corresponds to the true self of the split personality (p. 191) and that is permanently non-communicating has implications for theories of the person, health, ill-health and psychoanalysis.

In this piece Winnicott refers approvingly to Laing's work on self and other, pathological withdrawal and healthy self-communication, and the 'making patent of the latent self' (Laing, 1961: 117) and to Peter Lomas whose paper on 'Family Role and Identity Formation' had appeared in 1961. When it comes to the practice of psychoanalysis, there is a need to distinguish between non-communicating as health and those forms of communication that are pathological and amount to non-communication with real objects. In either case the analyst's task is different.

The statement that an important basis for ego development lies in the area of the individual's communicating with subjective phenomena, which alone gives the feeling of being real (p. 192), and Winnicott's quoting of Fordham's review of the Jungian concept of the self – 'the over-all fact remains that the primordial experience occurs in solitude' – all seem to imply a link between silent communication and primary narcissism.

Communicating and Not Communicating Leading to a Study of Certain Opposites[1]
(1963)

Every point of thought is the centre of an intellectual world

(Keats)

I have started with this observation of Keats because I know that my paper contains only one idea, a rather obvious idea at that, and I have used the opportunity for re-presenting my formulations of early stages in the emotional development of the human infant. First I shall describe object-relating and I only gradually get to the subject of communicating.

Starting from no fixed place I soon came, while preparing this paper for a foreign society, to staking a claim, to my surprise, to the right not to communicate. This was a protest from the core of me to the frightening fantasy of being infinitely exploited. In another language this would be the fantasy of being eaten or swallowed up. In the language of this paper it is *the fantasy of being found*. There is a considerable literature on the psychoanalytic patient's silences, but I shall not study or summarize this literature here and now. Also I am not attempting to deal comprehensively with the subject of communication, and in fact I shall allow myself considerable latitude in following my theme wherever it takes me. Eventually I shall allow a subsidiary theme, the study of opposites. First I find I need to restate some of my views on early object-relating.

OBJECT-RELATING

Looking directly at communication and the capacity to communicate one can see that this is closely bound up with relating to objects. Relating to objects is a complex phenomenon and the development of a capacity to relate to objects is by no means a matter simply of the maturational process. As always, *maturation* (in psychology) *requires and depends on the quality of the facilitating environment*. Where neither privation nor deprivation dominates the scene and where, therefore, the facilitating environment can be taken for granted in the theory of the earliest and most formative stages of human growth, there gradually develops in the individual a change in the nature of the object. The object *being at first a subjective phenomenon becomes an object objectively perceived*. This process takes time, and months and even years must pass before privations and deprivations can be accommodated by the individual without distortion of essential processes that are basic to object-relating.

At this early stage the facilitating environment is giving the infant the *experience of omnipotence*; by this I mean more than magical control, I mean the term to include the creative aspect of experience. Adaptation to the reality principle arises naturally out of the experience of omnipotence, within the area, that is, of a relationship to subjective objects.

Margaret Ribble (1943), who enters this field, misses, I think, one important thing, which is the mother's identification with her infant (what I call the temporary state of Primary Maternal Preoccupation). She writes:

> The human infant in the first year of life should not have to meet frustration or privation, for these factors immediately cause exaggerated tension and stimulate latent defense activities. If the effects of such experiences are not skillfully counteracted, behavior disorders may result. For the baby, the pleasure principle must predominate, and what we can safely do is to bring balance into his functions and make them easy. Only after a considerable

degree of maturity has been reached can we train an infant to adapt to what we as adults know as the reality principle.

She is referring to the matter of object-relating, or of id-satisfactions, but I think she could also subscribe to the more modern views on ego-relatedness.

The infant experiencing omnipotence under the aegis of the facilitating environment *creates and re-creates the object*, and the process gradually becomes built in, and gathers a memory backing.

Undoubtedly that which eventually becomes the intellect does affect the immature individual's capacity to make this very difficult transition from relating to subjective objects to relating to objects objectively perceived, and I have suggested that that which eventually gives results on intelligence testing does affect the individual's capacity to survive relative failures in the area of the adapting environment.

In health the infant creates what is in fact lying around waiting to be found. But in health *the object is created, not found*. This fascinating aspect of normal object-relating has been studied by me in various papers, including the one on 'Transitional Objects and Transitional Phenomena' [see Chapter 5, this volume]. A good object is no good to the infant unless created by the infant. Shall I say, created out of need? Yet the object must be found in order to be created. This has to be accepted as a paradox, and not solved by a restatement that, by its cleverness, seems to eliminate the paradox.

There is another point that has importance if one considers the location of the object. The change of the object from 'subjective' to 'objectively per-ceived' is jogged along less effectually by satisfactions than by dissatisfactions. The satisfaction to be derived from a feed has less value in this respect of the establishment of object-relating than when the object is, so to speak, in the way. Instinct-gratification gives the infant a personal experience and *does but little to the position of the object*; I have had a case in which satisfactions eliminated the object for an adult schizoid patient, so that he could not lie on the couch, this reproducing for him the situation of the infantile satisfactions that eliminated external reality or the externality of objects. I have put this in another way, saying that the infant feels 'fobbed off' by a satisfactory feed, and it can be found that a nursing mother's anxiety can be based on the fear that if the infant is not satisfied then the mother will be attacked and destroyed. After a feed the satisfied infant is not dangerous for a few hours, has lost object-cathexis.

Per contra, the infant's experienced aggression, that which belongs to muscle erotism, to movement, and to irresistible forces meeting immovable objects, this aggression, and the ideas bound up with it, lends itself to the process of placing the object, to placing the object separate from the self, in so far as the self has begun to emerge as an entity.

In the area of development that is prior to the achievement of fusion one must allow for the infant's behaviour that is reactive to failures of the facilitating environment, or of the environment-mother, and this may look like aggression; actually it is distress.

In health, when the infant achieves fusion, the frustrating aspect of object behaviour has value in educating the infant in respect of the existence of a not-me world. Adaptation failures have value *in so far as the infant can hate the object*, that is to say, can retain the idea of the object as potentially satisfying while recognizing its failure to behave satisfactorily. As I understand it, this is good psycho-analytic theory. What is often neglected in statements of this detail of theory is the immense development that takes place in the infant for fusion to be achieved, and for environmental failure therefore to play its positive part, enabling the infant to begin to know of a world that is repudiated. I deliberately do not say external.

There is an intermediate stage in healthy development in which the patient's most important experience in relation to the good or potentially satisfying object is the refusal of it. The refusal of it is part of the process of creating it. (This produces a truly formidable problem for the therapist in anorexia nervosa.)

Our patients teach us these things, and it is distressing to me that I must give these views as if they were my own. All analysts have this difficulty, and in a sense it is more difficult for an analyst to be original than for anyone else, because everything that we say truly has been taught us yesterday, apart from the fact that we listen to each other's papers and discuss matters privately. In our work, especially in working on the schizoid rather than the psycho-neurotic aspects of the personality, we do in fact wait, if we feel we know, until the patients tell us, and in doing so creatively make the interpretation we might have made; if we make the interpretation out of our own cleverness and experience then the patient must refuse it or destroy it. An anorexia patient is teaching me the substance of what I am saying now as I write it down.

THEORY OF COMMUNICATION

These matters, although I have stated them in terms of object-relating, do seem to affect the study of communication, because naturally there comes about a change in the purpose and in the means of communication *as the object changes over* from being subjective to being objectively perceived, in so far as the child gradually leaves the area of omnipotence as a living experience. In so far as the object is subjective, *so far is it unnecessary for communication with it to be explicit.* In so far as the object is objectively perceived, communication is either explicit or else dumb. Here then appear two *new* things, the individual's use and enjoyment of modes of communication, and the individual's non-communicating self, or the personal core of the self that is a true isolate.

A complication in this line of argument arises out of the fact that the infant develops two kinds of relationships at one and the same time – that to the environment-mother and that to the object, which becomes the object-mother. The environment-mother is human, and the object-mother is a thing, although it is also the mother or part of her.

Intercommunication between infant and environment-mother is undoubtedly subtle to a degree, and a study of this would involve us in a study of the mother as much as of the infant. I will only touch on this. Perhaps for the infant there is communication with the environment-mother, brought into evidence by the experience of her *unreliability*. The infant is shattered, and this may be taken by the mother as a communication if the mother can put herself in the infant's place, and if she can recognize the shattering in the infant's clinical state. When her *reliability* dominates the scene the infant could be said to communicate simply by going on being, and by going on developing according to personal processes of maturation, but this scarcely deserves the epithet communication.

Returning to object-relating: as the object becomes objectively perceived by the child so does it become meaningful for us to contrast communication with one of its opposites.

THE OBJECTIVELY PERCEIVED OBJECT

The objectively perceived object gradually becomes a person with part objects. Two opposites of communication are:

1. A simple not-communicating.
2. A not-communicating that is active or reactive.

It is easy to understand the first of these. Simple not-communicating is like resting. It is a state in its own right, and it passes over into communicating, and reappears as naturally. To study the second it is necessary to think in terms both of pathology and of health. I will take pathology first.

So far I have taken for granted the facilitating environment, nicely adjusted to need arising out of being and arising out of the processes of maturation. In the psycho-pathology that I need for my argument here the facilitation has failed in some respect and in some degree, and in the matter of object-relating the infant has developed a split. By one half of the split the infant relates to the presenting object, and for this purpose there develops what I have called a false or compliant self. By the other half of the split the infant relates to a subjective object, or to mere phenomena based on body experiences, these being scarcely influenced by an objectively perceived world. (Clinically do we not see this in autistic rocking movements, for instance; and in the abstract picture that is a cul-de-sac communication, and that has no general validity?)

In this way I am introducing the idea of a communication with subjective objects and at the same time the idea of an active non-communication with that which is objectively perceived by the infant. There seems to be no doubt that for all its futility from the observer's point of view, the cul-de-sac communication (communication with subjective objects) carries all the sense of real. *Per contra*, such communication with the world as occurs from the false self does not feel real; it is not a true communication because it does not involve the core of the self, that which could be called a true self.

Now, by studying the extreme case we reach the psychopathology of severe illness, infantile schizophrenia; what must be examined, however, is the pattern of all this in so far as it can be found in the more normal individual, the individual whose development was not distorted by gross failure of the facilitating environment, and in whom the maturational processes did have a chance.

It is easy to see that in the cases of slighter illness, in which there is some pathology and some health, there must be expected an active non-communication (clinical withdrawal) because of the fact that communication so easily becomes linked with some degree of false or compliant object-relating; silent or secret communication with subjective objects, carrying a sense of real, must periodically take over to restore balance.

I am postulating that in the healthy (mature, that is, in respect of the development of object-relating) person there is a need for something that corresponds to the state of the split person in whom one part of the split communicates silently with subjective objects. There is room for the idea that significant relating and communicating is silent.

Real health need not be described only in terms of the residues in healthy persons of what might have been illness-patterns. One should be able to make a positive statement of the healthy use of non-communication in the establishment of the feeling of real. It may be necessary in so doing to speak in terms of man's cultural life, which is the adult equivalent of the transitional phenomena of infancy and early childhood, and in which area communication is made without reference to the object's state of being either subjective or objectively perceived. It is my opinion that the psycho-analyst has no other language in which to refer to cultural phenomena. He can talk about the mental mechanisms of the artist but not about the experience of communication in art and religion unless he is willing to peddle in the intermediate area whose ancestor is the infant's transitional object.

In the artist of all kinds I think one can detect an inherent dilemma, which belongs to the co-existence of two trends, the urgent need to communicate and the still more urgent need not to be found. This might account for the fact that we cannot conceive of an artist's coming to the end of the task that occupies his whole nature.

In the early phases of emotional development in the human being, silent communicating concerns the subjective aspect of objects. This links, I suppose, with Freud's concept of psychic reality and of the unconscious that can never become conscious. I would add that there is a direct development, in health, from this silent communicating to the concept of inner experiences that Melanie Klein described so clearly. In the case descriptions of Melanie Klein certain aspects of a child's play, for instance, are shown to be 'inside' experiences; that is to say, there has been a wholesale projection of a constellation from the child's inner psychic reality so that the room and the table and the toys are subjective objects, and the child and the analyst are both there in this sample of the child's inner world. What is outside the room is outside the child. This is familiar ground in psycho-analysis, although various analysts describe it in various ways. It is related to the concept of the 'honeymoon period' at the beginning of an analysis, and to the special clarity of certain first hours. It is related to dependence in the transference. It also joins up with the work that I am doing myself on the full exploitation of first hours in the short treatments of children, especially antisocial children, for whom full-scale analysis is not available and not even always advisable.

But my object in this paper is not to become clinical but to get to a very early version of that which Melanie Klein referred to as 'internal'. At the beginning the word internal cannot be used in the Klein sense since the infant has not yet properly established an ego boundary and has not yet become master of the mental mechanisms of projection and introjection. At this early stage 'inner' only means personal, and personal in so far as the individual is a person with a self in process of becoming evolved. The facilitating environment, or the mother's ego-support to the infant's immature ego, these are still essential parts of the child as a viable creature.

In thinking of the psychology of mysticism, it is usual to concentrate on the understanding of the mystic's withdrawal into a personal inner world of sophisticated introjects. Perhaps not enough attention has been paid to the mystic's retreat to a position in which he can communicate secretly with subjective objects and phenomena, the loss of contact with the world of shared reality being counterbalanced by a gain in terms of feeling real.

> A woman patient dreamed: two women friends were customs officers at the place where the woman works. They were going through all the possessions of the patient and her colleagues with absurd care. She then drove a car, by accident, through a pane of glass.

There were details in the dream that showed that not only had these two women no right to be there doing this examining, but also they were making fools of themselves by their way of looking at everything. It became clear that the patient was mocking at these two women. They would not in fact get at the secret self. They stood for the mother who does not allow the child her secret. The patient said that in childhood (nine years) she had a stolen school book in which she collected poems and sayings, and she wrote in it 'My private book'. On the front page she wrote: 'What a man thinketh in his heart, so is he.' In fact her mother had asked her: 'Where did you get this saying from?'

This was bad because it meant that the mother must have read her book. It would have been all right if the mother had read the book but had said nothing.

Here is a picture of a child establishing a private self that is not communicating, and at the same time wanting to communicate and to be found. It is a sophisticated game of hide-and-seek in which *it is joy to be hidden but disaster not to be found.*

Another example that will not involve me in too deep or detailed a description comes from a diagnostic interview with a girl of seventeen. Her mother worries lest she become schizophrenic as this is a family trait, but at present it can be said that she is in the middle of all the doldrums and dilemmas that belong to adolescence.

Here is an extract from my report of the interview:

> X. then went on to talk about the glorious irresponsibility of childhood. She said: 'You see a cat and you are with it; it's a subject, not an object.'
>
> I said: 'It's as if you were living in a world of subjective objects.' And she said: 'That's a good way of putting it. That's why I write poetry. That's the sort of thing that's the foundation of poetry.'
>
> She added: 'Of course it's only an idle theory of mine, but that's how it seems and this explains why it's men who write poetry more than girls. With girls so much gets caught up in looking after children or having babies and then the imaginative life and the irresponsibility goes over to the children.'
>
> We then spoke about bridges to be kept open between the imaginative life and everyday existence. She kept a diary when she was 12 and again at 14, each time apparently for a period of seven months.
>
> She said: 'Now I only write down things that I feel in poems; in poetry something crystallizes out,' – and we compared this with autobiography which she feels belongs to a later age.
>
> She said: 'There is an affinity between old age and childhood.'
>
> When she needs to form a bridge with childhood imagination it has to be crystallized out in a poem. She would get bored to write an autobiography. She does not publish her poems or even show them to anybody because although she is fond of each poem for a little while she soon loses interest in it. She has always been able to write poems more easily than her friends because of a technical ability which she seems to have naturally. But she is not interested in the question: are the poems really good? or not? that is to say: would other people think them good?

I suggest that in health there is a core to the personality that corresponds to the true self of the split personality; I suggest that this core never communicates with the world of perceived objects, and that the individual person knows that it must never be communicated with or be influenced by external reality. This is my main point, the point of thought which is the centre of an intellectual world and of my paper. Although healthy persons communicate and enjoy communicating, the other fact is equally true, that *each individual is an isolate, permanently non-communicating, permanently unknown, in fact unfound.*

In life and living this hard fact is softened by the sharing that belongs to the whole range of cultural experience. At the centre of each person is an incommunicado element, and this is sacred and most worthy of preservation. Ignoring for the moment the still earlier and shattering experiences of failure of the environment–mother, I would say that the traumatic experiences that lead to the organization of primitive defences belong to the threat to the isolated core, the threat of its being found, altered, communicated with. The defence consists in a further hiding of the secret self, even in the extreme to its projection and to its endless dissemination. Rape, and being eaten by cannibals, these are mere bagatelles as compared with the violation of the self's core, the alteration of the self's central elements by communication seeping through the defences. For me this would be the sin against the self. We can understand the hatred people have of psycho-analysis which has penetrated a long way into the human personality, and which provides a threat to the human individual in his need to be secretly isolated. The question is: how to be isolated without having to be insulated?

What is the answer? Shall we stop trying to understand human beings? The answer might come from mothers who do not communicate with their infants except in so far as they are subjective objects. By the time mothers become objectively perceived their infants have become masters of various techniques for indirect communication, the most obvious of which is the use of language. There is this transitional period, however, which has specially interested me, in which transitional objects and phenomena have a place, and begin to establish for the infant the use of symbols.

I suggest that an important basis for ego development lies in this area of the individual's communicating with subjective phenomena, which alone gives the feeling of real.

In the best possible circumstances growth takes place and the child now possesses three lines of communication: communication that is *for ever silent*, communication that is *explicit*, indirect and pleasurable, and this third or *intermediate* form of communication that slides out of playing into cultural experience of every kind.

Is silent communication related to the concept of primary narcissism?

In practice then there is something we must allow for in our work, the patient's non-communicating as a positive contribution. We must ask ourselves, does our technique allow for the patient to communicate that he or she is not communicating? For this to happen we as analysts must be ready for the signal: 'I am not communicating', and be able to distinguish it from the distress signal associated with a failure of communication. There is a link here with the idea of being alone in the presence of someone, at first a natural event in child-life, and later on a matter of the acquisition of a capacity for withdrawal without loss of identification with that from which withdrawal has occurred. This appears as the capacity to concentrate on a task.

My main point has now been made, and I might stop here. Nevertheless I wish to consider what are the opposites of communication.

OPPOSITES

There are two opposites of communication, simple non-communication, and active non-communication. Put the other way round, communication may simply arise out of not-communication, as a natural transition, or communication may be a negation of silence, or a negation of an active or reactive not-communicating.

In the clear-cut psycho-neurotic case there is no difficulty because the whole analysis is done through the intermediary of verbalization. Both the patient and the analyst want this to be so. But it is only too easy for an analysis (where there is a hidden schizoid element in the patient's personality) to become an infinitely prolonged collusion of the analyst with the patient's negation of non-communication. Such an analysis becomes tedious because of its lack of result in spite of good work done. In such an analysis a period of silence may be the most positive contribution the patient can make, and the analyst is then involved in a waiting game. One can of course interpret movements and gestures and all sorts of behavioural details, but in the kind of case I have in mind the analyst had better wait.

More dangerous, however, is the state of affairs in an analysis in which the analyst is permitted by the patient to reach to the deepest layers of the analysand's personality because of his position as subjective object, or because of the dependence of the patient in the transference psychosis; here there is danger if the analyst interprets instead of waiting for the patient to creatively discover. It is only here, at the place when the analyst has not changed over from a subjective object to one that is objectively perceived, that psycho-analysis is dangerous, and the danger is one that can be avoided if we know how to behave ourselves. If we wait we become objectively perceived in the patient's own time, but if we fail to behave in a way that is facilitating the patient's analytic process (which is the equivalent of the infant's and the child's maturational process) we suddenly become not-me for the patient, and then we know too much, and we are dangerous because we are too nearly in communication with the central still and silent spot of the patient's ego-organization.

For this reason we find it convenient even in the case of a straightforward psycho-neurotic case to avoid contacts that are outside the analysis. In the case of the schizoid or borderline patient this matter of how we manage extra-transference contacts becomes very much a part of our work with the patient.

Here one could discuss the purpose of the analyst's interpreting. I have always felt that an important function of the interpretation is the establishment of the *limits* of the analyst's understanding.

INDIVIDUALS AS ISOLATES

I am putting forward and stressing the importance of the idea of the *permanent isolation of the individual* and claiming that at the core of the individual there is no communication with the not-me world either way. Here quietude is linked with stillness. This leads to the writings of those who have become recognized as the world's thinkers. Incidentally, I can refer to Michael Fordham's very interesting review of the concept of the Self as it has appeared in Jung's writings. Fordham writes: 'The over-all fact remains that the primordial experience occurs in solitude.' Naturally this that I am referring to appears in Wickes's *The Inner World of Man* (1938), but here it is not always certain that a distinction is always drawn between pathological withdrawal and healthy central self-communication (cf. Laing, 1961).

Among psycho-analysts there may be many references to the idea of a 'still, silent' centre to the personality and to the idea of the primordial experience occurring in solitude, but analysts are not usually concerned with just this aspect of life. Among our immediate colleagues perhaps Ronald Laing is with most deliberation setting out to state the 'making patent of the latent self' along with diffidence about disclosing oneself (cf. Laing, 1961, p. 117).

This theme of the individual as an isolate has its importance in the study of infancy and of psychosis, but it also has importance in the study of adolescence. The boy and girl at puberty can be described in many ways, and one way concerns *the adolescent as an isolate*. This preservation of personal isolation is part of the search for identity, and for the establishment of a personal technique for communicating which does not lead to violation of the central self. This may be one reason why adolescents on the whole eschew psycho-analytic treatment, though they are interested in psycho-analytic theories. They feel that by psycho-analysis they will be raped, not sexually but spiritually. In practice the analyst can avoid confirming the adolescent's fears in this respect, but the analyst of an adolescent must expect to be tested out fully and must be prepared to use communication of indirect kind, and to recognize simple non-communication.

At adolescence when the individual is undergoing pubertal changes and is not quite ready to become one of the adult community there is a strengthening of the defences against being found, that is to say being found before being there to be found. That which is truly personal and which feels real must be defended at all cost, and even if this means a temporary blindness to the value of compromise. Adolescents form aggregates rather than groups, and by looking alike they emphasize the essential loneliness of each individual. At least, this is how it seems to me.

With all this is bound up the crisis of identity. Wheelis, who has struggled with identity problems, states (1958) clearly and crudely the problem of the analyst's vocational choice, and links this with his loneliness and need for intimacy which, in analytic work, is doomed to lead nowhere. The analyst who seems to me to be most deeply involved in these matters is Erik Erikson. He discusses this theme in the epilogue of his book, *Young Man Luther* (1958), and he reaches to the phrase 'Peace comes from the inner space' (i.e. not from outer space exploration and all that).

Before ending I wish to refer once more to the opposites that belong to negation. Melanie Klein used negation in the concept of the manic defence, in which depression that is a fact is negated. Bion (1962) referred to denials of certain kinds in his paper on thinking, and de Monchaux (1962) continued with the theme in her comment on Bion's paper.

If I take the idea of liveliness, I have to allow for at least two opposites, one being deadness, as in manic defence, and the other being a simple absence of liveliness. It is here that silence is equated with communication and stillness with movement. By using this idea I can get behind my rooted object to the theory of the Life and Death Instincts. I see that what I cannot accept is that Life has Death as its opposite, except clinically in the manic-depressive swing, and in the concept of the manic defence in which depression is negated and negatived. In the development of the individual infant living arises and establishes itself out of not-living, and being becomes a fact that replaces not-being, as communication arises out of silence. Death only becomes meaningful in the infant's living processes when hate has arrived, that is at a late date, far removed from the phenomena which we can use to build a theory of the roots of aggression.

For me therefore it is not valuable to join the word death with the word instinct, and less still is it valuable to refer to hate and anger by use of the words death instinct.

It is difficult to get at the roots of aggression, but we are not helped by the use of opposites such as life and death that do not mean anything at the stage of immaturity that is under consideration.

The other thing that I wish to tie on to the end of my paper is an altogether different opposite to aliveness or liveliness. This opposite is not operative in the majority of our cases. Usually the mother of an infant has live internal objects, and the infant fits into the mother's preconception of a *live* child. Normally the mother is not depressed or depressive. In certain cases, however, the mother's central internal object is dead at the critical time in her child's early infancy, and her mood is one of depression. Here the infant has to fit in with a role of *dead* object, or else has to be lively to counteract the mother's preconception with the idea of the child's deadness. Here the opposite to the liveliness of the infant is *an anti-life factor* derived from the mother's depression. The task of the infant in such a case is to be alive and to look alive and to communicate being alive; in fact this is the ultimate aim of such an individual, who is thus denied that which belongs to more fortunate infants, the enjoyment of what life and living may bring. To be alive is all. It is a constant struggle to get to the starting point and to keep there. No wonder there are those who make a special business of existing and who turn it into a religion. (I think that Ronald Laing's (1960, 1961) two books are attempting to state the predicament of this nature that many must contend with because of environmental abnormalities.) In healthy development the infant (theoretically) starts off (psychologically) without life and becomes lively simply because of being, in fact, alive.

As I have already said at an earlier stage, this being alive is the early communication of a healthy infant with the mother-figure, and it is as unselfconscious as can be. Liveliness that negates maternal depression is a communication designed to meet what is to be expected. The aliveness of the child whose mother is depressed is a communication of a reassuring nature, and it is unnatural and an intolerable handicap to the immature ego in its function of integrating and generally maturing according to inherited process.

You will have observed that I have brought the subject back to that of communication, but I do recognize that I have allowed myself a great deal of freedom in following trains of thought.

SUMMARY

I have tried to state the need that we have to recognize this aspect of health: the non-communicating central self, for ever immune from the reality principle, and for ever silent. Here communication is not non-verbal; it is, like the music of the spheres, absolutely personal. It belongs to being alive. And in health, it is out of this that communication naturally arises.

Explicit communication is pleasurable and it involves extremely interesting techniques, including that of language. The two extremes, explicit communication that is indirect, and silent or personal communication that feels real, each of these has its place, and in the intermediate cultural area there exists for many, but not for all, a mode of communication which is a most valuable compromise.

Note

1. Differing versions of this paper were given to the San Francisco Psychoanalytic Society, October 1962, and to the British Psycho-Analytical Society, May 1963.

10 FEAR OF BREAKDOWN (1963?)

EDITORS' INTRODUCTION

This, one of Winnicott's most famous and most quoted papers, was probably written around 1963 – its precise date of composition is unknown – and was published in the *International Review of Psycho-Analysis* in 1974. A paper of 1965, 'The Psychology of Madness', takes up the same themes and develops them further. The editors of *Psychoanalytic Explorations* point out that the same material was used in the postscript to the 1964 paper on classification (1989: 87, note 1). 'Fear of Breakdown' concentrates on three areas: the development of the infant ego organization, the consequences if this has not taken place, the application of this knowledge in the analytic situation and its use in the transference. The paper again highlights the mutually illuminating aspects of thinking about the analytic situation and the infant–mother couple.

Although imprecise uses of terms such as 'breakdown' and indeed 'madness' itself are familiar in everyday language, the discussion here is of a very particular situation, the fear of breakdown in an analysis. Winnicott subscribes to the view that some aspects of madness are known to us all, but it is the one that may arise in an ongoing treatment that is the focus of this paper. A fear of breakdown in analysis is the fear felt by *some* patients, not all. Winnicott states simply that this fear of clinical breakdown is the fear of a breakdown that has already been experienced, a fear of an original agony which produced the defence organization the patient displays as an illness syndrome. The fear arises in relation to the organization of the defences, and, in turn, to dependence. The organization of the defences and dependence are the basis for what is new in this paper.

'The Psychology of Madness' was partly a response to this paper's reception, and partly a further clarification of Winnicott's own thinking about what is being claimed and what is not in 'Fear of Breakdown'. In the second paper he discusses psychiatry and psychiatric accounts of madness, the physical and heredity aspects of madness, and the psychoanalytic concern with 'environmental distortion at the phase of the individual's absolute dependence' (Winnicott *et al.*, 1989: 122). He clarifies his claims about early mental organization and the ego, and what it is or is not possible for the clinician to say and know, and he again refers to the substantial basic work in the area presented in 'Psychoses and Child Care' (1952a).

Winnicott proposes that the fear is of a breakdown that happened at a time when the ego was not sufficiently formed to gather what was happening into the area of personal omnipotence, that is, before the establishment of unit status recognition and any rudimentary awareness of any 'I' capacity. The patient did not experience it because he could not, lacking the conceptual and perceptual apparatus to do so. Fundamental to the account is the link between 'more psychotic phenomena . . . [and] a breakdown of the establishment of the unit self' (p. 201). Emotional growth and infantile development depend upon environmental/maternal provision to provide ego support when the infant is without an ego. The stages of holding, of the mother and infant living together and the mother, father and infant living together, and the conditions of dependence that accompany each of these stages, are fundamental to how an infant can begin to be or to exist in his own right, that is, to realize inherited potential for growth and development, acquire an ego, come to have a personal existence as a unit, recognize the distinction between inside and outside, develop object relationships, negotiate id impulses, and endure impingement. The infant acquires the resources for the development of sufficient ego organization to withstand instinctual impulses both from inside and from an outside that either accepts him or impinges upon him.

It is in these early processes or their failure that the roots of psychosis reside, and they are fundamental for understanding the psychopathology of madness.

Winnicott is interested in the establishment of an ego that can undertake a defensive action, an ego that he insists is not there from the start. It is the successful negotiation of the conditions for the establishment of that ego that creates the situation of psychoneurosis that Freud treats as a point of departure in the 1890s. The breakdown Winnicott is referring to concentrates on the preceding primitive state and failures of development there. Psychotic illness is understood as a defence which returns to this early period and to the links between dependence and the defences. Breakdown signals a failure of a defence organization, that is, the failure of a secondary structure developed to defend against an *unthinkable* state of affairs. The strength of the adjective 'unthinkable' captures what is crucial to this fear that emerges in some patients. Winnicott identifies five states he calls 'primitive agonies', a term giving some sense of the catastrophic state of affairs he is attempting to understand. Much of the paper proposes that a psychotic illness can be a defence against precisely these states: a return to an unintegrated state, falling for ever, loss of psycho-somatic collusion, failure of indwelling, loss of sense of the real, loss of capacity to relate to objects. Each has a typical defence: disintegration, self-holding, depersonalization, exploitation of primary narcissism, autistic states.

Beginning from 'Primitive Emotional Development' (Chapter 2, this volume), where he described his primary interest in the child patient and the infant as requiring the study of psychosis in analysis, Winnicott began to formulate his position that the clues to the psychopathology of psychosis are to be found in 'the early . . . development of the infant before the infant knows himself (and therefore others) as the whole person that he is and . . . they are' (p. 61). The interest is in how the establishment of ego psychology is interrelated with dependence and maternal care, and itself depends upon them. This account of ego psychology is chronologically prior to the more conventional account of an ego psychology which is concerned with instinctual impulse accommodation, and provides the basis of classical psychoanalysis. For Winnicott, ego psychology grows out of, and is secondary to, the dependence on maternal care.

The importance of time and timing is a consistent theme. Winnicott is interested not just in the impact of the past, of something that has already happened, but in why it comes to dominate a present and a future, why it cannot be assimilated and left behind, if not in life, then in analysis. In this specific context Winnicott uses the unconscious to mean that the ego integration is too immature to gather all the phenomena into the area of personal omnipotence. The experience has happened, although the patient could not experience it; this means that, until he has experienced it, he is condemned to search for it, and be disturbed by it. Whether this symptom is there from the outset, or whether it emerges in the course of treatment, both situations offer information about infant development and its connections to emotional early experience.

If the patient can experience what was not previously experienced, the transference provides the means for re-experiencing the environmental/maternal failure which was part of a period when, to all intents and purposes, environment mother and infant were one and the same. In cases of this kind a distinction between them was experienced too early through a violation of the holding environment in which the baby, in its own time, could come to incorporate the world, and then allow world and self to be separate, with all the joys and alarm entailed. In the analysis, this thing of past and future *has to become* a thing of the here and now. Experiencing is the equivalent of remembering, of the lifting of repression of the classical Freudian account. The work through which this can be effected is time-consuming and painful for the patient, and for the clinician it involves an acceptance of slowing down and adjusting to the patient's pace.

According to fellow analyst Dr Margaret Little who, more than 30 years later in 1990, wrote about her analysis in *Psychotic Anxieties and Containment*, Winnicott arrived at this realization in the course of her treatment. She recalls a particular interpretation that had the force of a 'revelation'. Winnicott told her that the fear of annihilation which she felt at that moment belonged to 'annihilation' that had already happened when she was an infant. Considerations of confidentiality and discretion probably contributed to Winnicott's reticence about the contents of the paper at the time.

Winnicott describes three other states, fear of death, emptiness, and non-existence, for which the hypothesis he advances provides further understanding. Each is an experience that occurred at a time when the ego was too immature to experience it and the patient continues to seek out that experience. Fear of death, he proposes, involves 'death as a phenomenon, not as the sort of fact that we observe' (p. 205), again, something that happened when the patient could not experience it and which then amounts to annihilation. Wondering about suicide in these cases, he says, is about 'sending the body to death which has already happened to the psyche'.

Emptiness he associates not with direct trauma but with the absence of something, the wish to fill up or take in, that could not at the time be known anyway. The patient may establish forms of controlling this by not gathering in things such as food or learning, or by compulsive greed. The pleasure of taking things in is absent. In non-existence projection is employed to create a state in which there is no personal self to take or recognize responsibility.

Fear of Breakdown
(Written in 1963?[1])

PRELIMINARY STATEMENT

My clinical experiences have brought me recently to a new understanding, as I believe, of the meaning of a fear of breakdown.

It is my purpose here to state as simply as possible this which is new for me and which perhaps is new for others who work in psychotherapy. Naturally, if what I say has truth in it, this will already have been dealt with by the world's poets, but the flashes of insight that come in poetry cannot absolve us from our painful task of getting step by step away from ignorance towards our goal. It is my opinion that a study of this limited area leads to a restatement of several other problems that puzzle us as we fail to do as well clinically as we would wish to do, and I shall indicate at the end what extensions of the theory I propose for discussion.

INDIVIDUAL VARIATIONS

Fear of breakdown is a feature of significance in some of our patients, but not in others. From this observation, if it be a correct one, the conclusion can be drawn that fear of breakdown is related to the individual's past experience, and to environmental vagaries. At the same time there must be expected a common denominator of the same fear, indicating the existence of universal phenomena; these indeed make it possible for everyone to know empathetic-ally what it feels like when one of our patients shows this fear in a big way. (The same can be said, indeed, of every detail of the insane person's insanity. We all know about it, although this particular detail may not be bothering us.)

EMERGENCE OF THE SYMPTOM

Not all our patients who have this fear complain of it at the outset of a treatment. Some do; but others have their defences so well organised that it is only after a treatment has made considerable progress that the fear of break-down comes to the fore as a dominating factor.

For instance, a patient may have various phobias and a complex organisation for dealing with these phobias, so that dependence does not come quickly into the transference. At length dependence becomes a main feature, and then the analyst's mistakes and failures become direct causes of localised phobias and so of the outbreak of fear of breakdown.

MEANING OF 'BREAKDOWN'

I have purposely used the term 'breakdown' because it is rather vague and because it could mean various things. On the whole the word can be taken in this context to mean a failure of a defence organisation. But immediately we ask: a defence against what? And this leads us to the deeper meaning of the term, since we need to use the word 'breakdown' to describe the unthinkable state of affairs that underlies the defence organisation.

It will be noted that whereas there is value in thinking that in the area of psycho-neurosis it is castration anxiety that lies behind the defences, in the more psychotic phenomena that we are examining it is a breakdown of the establishment of the unit self that is indicated. The ego organises defences against breakdown of the ego-organisation, and it is the ego-organisation that is threatened. But the ego cannot organise against environmental failure in so far as dependence is a living fact.

In other words, we are examining a reversal of the individual's maturational process. This makes it necessary for me briefly to reformulate the early stages of emotional growth.

EMOTIONAL GROWTH, EARLY STAGES

The individual inherits a maturational process. This carries the individual along in so far as there exists a facilitating environment, and only in so far as this exists. The facilitating environment is itself a complex phenomenon and needs special study in its own right; the essential feature is that it has a kind of growth of its own, being adapted to the changing needs of the growing individual.

The individual proceeds from absolute dependence to relative dependence and towards independence. In health the development takes place at a pace that does not outstrip the development of complexity in the mental mechanisms, this being linked to neuro-physiological development.

The facilitating environment can be described as *holding*, developing into *handling*, to which is added *object-presenting*.

In such a facilitating environment the individual undergoes development which can be classified as *integrating*, to which is added *indwelling* (or *psycho-somatic collusion*) and then *object-relating*.

This is a gross over-simplification but it must suffice in this context. It will be observed that in such a description forward movement in development corresponds closely with the threat of retrograde movement (and defences against this threat) in schizophrenic illness.

ABSOLUTE DEPENDENCE

At the time of absolute dependence, with the mother supplying an auxiliary ego-function, it has to be remembered that the infant has not yet separated out the 'not-me' from the 'me' – this cannot happen apart from the establishment of 'me.'

PRIMITIVE AGONIES

From this chart it is possible to make a list of primitive agonies (anxiety is not a strong enough word here).

Here are a few:

1. A return to an unintegrated state. (Defence: disintegration.)
2. Falling for ever. (Defence: self-holding.)
3. Loss of psycho-somatic collusion, failure of indwelling. (Defence: depersonalisation.)
4. Loss of sense of real. (Defence: exploitation of primary narcissism, etc.)
5. Loss of capacity to relate to objects. (Defence: autistic states, relating only to self-phenomena.)

And so on.

PSYCHOTIC ILLNESS AS A DEFENCE

It is my intention to show here that what we see clinically is always a defence organisation, even in the autism of childhood schizophrenia. The underlying agony is unthinkable.

It is wrong to think of psychotic illness as a breakdown, it is a defence organisation relative to a primitive agony, and it is usually successful (except when the facilitating environment has been not deficient but tantalising, perhaps the worst thing that can happen to a human baby).

STATEMENT OF A MAIN THEME

I can now state my main contention, and it turns out to be very simple. I contend that clinical fear of breakdown is *the fear of a breakdown that has already been experienced*. It is a fear of the original agony which caused the defence organisation which the patient displays as an illness syndrome.

This idea may or may not prove immediately useful to the clinician. We cannot hurry up our patients. Nevertheless we can hold up their progress because of genuinely not knowing; any little piece of our understanding may help us to keep up with a patient's needs.

There are moments, according to my experience, when a patient needs to be told that the breakdown, a fear of which destroys his or her life, *has already been*. It is a fact that is carried round hidden away in the unconscious. The unconscious here is not exactly the repressed unconscious of psycho-neurosis, nor is it the unconscious of Freud's formulation of the part of the psyche that is very close to neuro-physiological functioning. Nor is it the unconscious of Jung's which I would call: all those things that go on in underground caves, or (in other words) the world's mythology, in which there is collusion between the individual and the maternal inner psychic realities. In this special context the unconscious means that the ego integration is not able to encompass something. The ego is too immature to gather all the phenomena into the area of personal omnipotence.

It must be asked here: why does the patient go on being worried by this that belongs to the past? The answer must be that the original experience of primitive agony cannot get into the past tense unless the ego can first gather it into its own present time experience and into omnipotent control now (assuming the auxiliary ego-supporting function of the mother [analyst]).

In other words the patient must go on looking for the past detail which is *not yet experienced*. This search takes the form of a looking for this detail in the future.

Unless the therapist can work successfully on the basis that this detail is already a fact, the patient must go on fearing to find what is being compulsively looked for in the future.

On the other hand, if the patient is ready for some kind of acceptance of this queer kind of truth, that what is not yet experienced did nevertheless happen in the past, then the way is open for the agony to be experienced in the transference, in reaction to the analyst's failures and mistakes. These latter can be dealt with by the patient in doses that are not excessive, and the patient can account for each technical failure of the analyst as counter-transference. In other words, gradually the patient gathers the original failure of the facilitating environment into the area of his or her omnipotence and the experience of omnipotence which belongs to the state of dependence (transference fact).

All this is very difficult, time-consuming and painful, but it at any rate is not futile. What is futile is the alternative, and it is this that must now be examined.

FUTILITY IN ANALYSIS

I must take for granted an understanding and acceptance of the analysis of psycho-neurosis. On the basis of this assumption I say that in cases I am discussing the analysis starts off well, the analysis goes with a swing; what is happening, however, is that the analyst and the patient are having a good time colluding in a psycho-neurotic analysis, when in fact the illness is psychotic.

Over and over again the analysing couple are pleased with what they have done together. It was valid, it was clever, it was cosy because of the collusion. But each so-called advance ends in destruction. The patient breaks it up and says: So what? In fact the advance was not an advance; it was a new example of the analyst's playing the patient's game of postponing the main issue. And who can blame either the patient or the analyst? (Unless of course there can be an analyst who plays the psychotic fish on a very long psycho-neurotic line, and hopes thereby to avoid the final catch by some trick of fate, such as the death of one or other of the couple, or a failure of financial backing.)

We must assume that both patient and analyst really do wish to end the analysis, but alas, there is no end unless the bottom of the trough has been reached, unless *the thing feared has been experienced*. And indeed one way out is for the patient to have a breakdown (physical or mental) and this can work very well. However, the solution is not good enough if it does not include analytic understanding and insight on the part of the patient, and indeed, many of the patients I am referring to are valuable people who cannot afford to break down in the sense of going to a mental hospital.

The purpose of this paper is to draw attention to the possibility that the breakdown has already happened, near the beginning of the individual's life. The patient needs to 'remember' this but it is not possible to remember something that has not yet happened, and this thing of the past has not happened yet because the patient was not there for it to happen to. The only way to 'remember' in this case is for the patient to experience this past thing for the first time in the present, that is to say, in the transference. This past and future thing then becomes a matter of the here and now, and becomes experienced by the patient for the first time. This is the equivalent of remembering, and this outcome is the equivalent of the lifting of repression that occurs in the analysis of the psycho-neurotic patient (classical Freudian analysis).

FURTHER APPLICATIONS OF THIS THEORY

Fear of Death

Little alteration is needed to transfer the general thesis of fear of breakdown to a specific fear of death. This is perhaps a more common fear, and one that is absorbed in the religious teachings about an after-life, as if to deny the fact of death.

When fear of death is a significant symptom the promise of an after-life fails to give relief, and the reason is that the patient has a compulsion to look for death. Again, it is the death that happened but was not experienced that is sought.

When Keats was 'half in love with easeful death' he was, according to my idea that I am putting forward here, longing for the ease that would come if he could 'remember' having died; but to remember he must experience death now.

Most of my ideas are inspired by patients, to whom I acknowledge debt. It is to one of these that I owe the phrase 'phenomenal death.' What happened in the past was death as a phenomenon, but not as the sort of fact that we observe. Many men and woman spend their lives wondering whether to find a solution by suicide, that is, sending the body to death which has already happened to the psyche. Suicide is no answer, however, but is a despair gesture. I now understand for the first time what my schizophrenic patient (who did kill herself) meant when she said: 'All I ask you to do is to help me to commit suicide for the right reason instead of for the wrong reason.' I did not succeed, and she killed herself in despair of finding the solution. Her aim (as I now see) was to get it stated by me that she died in early infancy. On this basis I think she and I could have enabled her to put off body death till old age took its toll.

Death, looked at in this way as something that happened to the patient but which the patient was not mature enough to experience, has the meaning of annihilation. It is like this, that a pattern developed in which the continuity of being was interrupted by the patient's infantile reactions to impingement, these being environmental factors that were allowed to impinge by failures of the facilitating environment. (In the case of this patient troubles started very early, for there was a premature awareness awakened before birth because of a maternal panic, and added to this the birth was complicated by undiagnosed placenta praevia.)

Emptiness

Again my patients show me that the concept of emptiness can be looked at through these same spectacles.

In some patients emptiness needs to be experienced, and this emptiness belongs to the past, to the time before the degree of maturity had made it possible for emptiness to be experienced.

To understand this it is necessary to think not of trauma but of nothing happening when something might profitably have happened.

It is easier for a patient to remember trauma than to remember nothing happening when it might have happened. At the time the patient did not know what might have happened, and so could not experience anything except to note that something might have been.

Example

A phase in a patient's treatment illustrates this. This young woman lay uselessly on the couch, and all she could do was to say: 'Nothing is happening in this analysis!'

At the stage that I am describing the patient had supplied material of an indirect kind so that I could know that she was probably feeling something. I was able to say that she had been feeling feelings, and she had been experiencing these gradually fading, according to her pattern, a pattern which made her despair. The feelings were sexual and female. They did not show clinically.

Here in the transference was myself (nearly) being the cause now of her female sexuality fizzling out; when this was properly stated we had an example in the present of what had happened to her innumerable times. In her case (to simplify for the sake of description) there was a father who at first was scarcely ever present, and then when he came to her home when she was a little girl he did not want his daughter's female self, and had nothing to give by way of male stimulus.

Now, emptiness is a prerequisite for eagerness to gather in. Primary emptiness simply means: before starting to fill up. A considerable maturity is needed for this state to be meaningful.

Emptiness occurring in a treatment is a state that the patient is trying to experience, a past state that cannot be remembered except by being experienced for the first time now.

In practice the difficulty is that the patient fears the awfulness of emptiness, and in defence will organise a controlled emptiness by not eating or not learning, or else will ruthlessly fill up by a greediness which is compulsive and which feels mad. When the patient can reach to emptiness itself and tolerate this state because of dependence on the auxiliary ego of the analyst, then, taking in can start up as a pleasurable function; here can begin eating that is not a function dissociated (or split off) as part of the personality; also it is in this way that some of our patients who cannot learn can begin to learn pleasurably.

The basis of all learning (as well as of eating) is emptiness. But if emptiness was not experienced as such at the beginning, then it turns up as a state that is feared, yet compulsively sought after.

Non-Existence

The search for personal non-existence can be examined in the same way. It will be found that non-existence here is part of a defence. Personal existence is represented by the projection elements, and the person is making an attempt to project everything that could be personal. This can be a relatively sophisticated defence, and the aim is to avoid responsibility (at the depressive position) or to avoid persecution (at what I would call the stage of self-assertion [i.e. the stage of I AM with the inherent implication I REPUDIATE EVERYTHING THAT IS NOT ME. It is convenient here to use in illustration the childhood game of 'I'm the king of the castle – you're the dirty rascal').

In the religions this idea can appear in the concept of one-ness with God or with the Universe. It is possible to see this defence being negatived in existentialist writings and teachings, in which existing is made into a cult, in an attempt to counter the personal tendency towards a non-existence that is part of an organised defence.

There can be a positive element in all this, that is, an element that is not a defence. It can be said that *only out of non-existence can existence start*. It is surprising how early (even before birth, certainly during the birth process) awareness or a premature ego can be mobilised. But the individual cannot develop from an ego root if this is divorced from psycho-somatic experience and from primary narcissism. It is just here that begins the intellectualisation of the ego-functions. It can be noted here that all this is a long distance in time prior to the establishment of anything that could usefully be called the self.

SUMMARY

I have attempted to show that fear of breakdown can be a fear of a past event that has not yet been experienced. The need to experience it is equivalent to a need to remember in terms of the analysis of psycho-neurotics.

This idea can be applied to other allied fears, and I have mentioned the fear of death and the search for emptiness.

Note

1. This paper was published in the *International Review of Psycho-Analysis* (1974). The date of its composition is uncertain. There is some evidence that it was written as a lecture to be given at the Davidson Clinic in Edinburgh in 1963, but that another paper was given instead; it was around this time that Winnicott used the same material in the postscript to his paper 'Classification' (1964[b]), in *The Maturational Processes and the Facilitating Environment* (1965[a]). In the paper 'The Psychology of Madness' (1965[c]), Winnicott further addresses a difficulty that he encountered in the idea behind 'Fear of Breakdown': namely, whether or not it is possible for a complete breakdown of defences *to be experienced. – Eds.*

Developing ideas: capacity for concern; guilt and the healthy life; handling; lack of the sense of guilt; primitive love impulse; environment-mother and object-mother; the spontaneous gesture; joy of being found, disaster of not; paradox of the right not to communicate; creating the good object out of need; the objectively perceived object; fear of breakdown; absolute dependence, relative dependence, towards independence; immorality and compliance

11 A CLINICAL STUDY OF THE EFFECT OF A FAILURE OF THE AVERAGE EXPECTABLE ENVIRONMENT ON A CHILD'S MENTAL FUNCTIONING (1965)

OTHER WRITINGS

The major papers of the early 1960s include 'Ego Distortions in Terms of True and False Self' (1960a), and 'The Concept of the False Self' (1964d). The case for this concept had been accumulating in Winnicott's work as he contemplated the impact of impingements upon the developing infant. It is already present in his consideration of Klein's depressive position (1954) where he talks about a false restitution in the child who has to take care of her mother's mood. These papers register significant advances in his own thinking.

He wrote about adolescence in 'Struggling Through the Doldrums' published in *New Society* in 1963 (see 1965d). He remained interested in thinking about adaptations to the psychoanalytic setting in 'Psychotherapy of Character Disorders' given at the European Congress of Child Psychiatry in Rome 1963, and 'Dependence in Infant-Care, in Child-Care and in the Psycho-Analytic Setting', given to the BPAS in 1962 (see 1963c). He was gathering his accounts of his Squiggle technique in his work with children and they were posthumously published as *Therapeutic Consultations in Child Psychiatry* in 1971.

During this period other significant contributions to child analysis, psychotherapy, and child development were published. The IPA hosted its first symposium on child analysis at the Edinburgh congress in 1962. In the published contributions there is no indication that Winnicott attended although he did give his paper on the parent–infant relationship at that congress. Melanie Klein's treatment of 'Richard' which she had conducted during the war was published posthumously in *Narrative of a Child Analysis* (1961). Child psychotherapists in the UK began to publish their work in the *Journal of Child Psychotherapy*; they included Edna O'Shaughnessy 'The Absent Object' (1964), Martha Harris 'Depression and the Depressive Position in an Adolescent Boy' (1965), and Irma Pick 'On Stealing' (1967). It was dominated by graduates of the training in child psychotherapy in the children's department at the Tavistock Clinic, which began in 1947 under the joint auspices of Esther Bick (a Kleinian) and John Bowlby (an Independent). Bick was to make several major contributions to the psychoanalytic treatment of children and is particularly known for her ideas about the function of the skin as a metaphor in early development (Bick, 1968). Anna Freud, who had established the training in child analysis at the Hampstead Clinic in 1947, was prolific in her writings. In 1965 she published *Normality and Pathology in Childhood* (A. Freud, 1965) which emphasizes understanding healthy development as the starting point for understanding pathology in children. She is appreciative of Winnicott's contribution, particularly the significance he gave to maternal provision in early development and the theory of transitional phenomena. Both Anna Freud and Esther Bick's trainings had infant and young child observation at their centre, a tradition that goes back to Winnicott's 'Set Situation' paper (1941) and Freud's earlier experiences in the Jackson Nursery in Vienna and in the Hampstead War Nurseries. Child psychotherapy training in the Independent tradition in the UK was not set up until the 1980s when the British Association of Psychotherapists established their child section. All three trainings were established outside the BPAS but there was considerable overlap of personnel from that institution to each of the psychotherapy trainings.

EDITORS' INTRODUCTION

This little-read paper conveys in a highly condensed form Winnicott's clinical thinking about his work with children. It is an account of a 'therapeutic consultation' with a 6-year-old child, 'Bob', published in the *IJPA* in 1965 as part of the IPA's celebration of Heinz Hartmann's 70th birthday. A shorter version of the case appears in *Therapeutic Consultations in Child Psychiatry* (1971b). Hartmann, with Kris and Lowenstein, were the proponents of ego psychology, the principal theoretical paradigm then current in the United States. In the UK, it was the tradition of Anna Freud that was closely aligned with it, and Anna Freud and her close collaborators Joseph Sandler and Walter Joffe all contributed papers to this issue.

The title of the paper indicates Winnicott's sympathy with one of Hartmann's principal concepts, the 'average expectable environment', the context within which the ego develops. Although the 'average expectable environment' of the title was Hartmann's, Winnicott gives it a different sense. For Hartmann the 'environment' referred to was what Winnicott thought of as the external or objective environment, whereas for him it meant primarily the 'subjective environment' as experienced by the child. Hartmann used 'adaptation' to signify how the child progressively adjusts through this 'average environment' to external demands at the same time as mitigating internal instinctual demands, but for Winnicott adaptation can also signify unhealthy compliance based on the formation of a false self. In the case presented he addresses the subjective, experiential reality of the child, demonstrating how this can be seen to accord with external failures and interruptions of maternal care.

Winnicott's own interest in ego functioning and the experience of 'ego-relatedness' are fundamental to his ideas about the emergence of a sense of self and subjectivity, and 'ego-relatedness' in the relationship with the good-enough mother is the theoretical link between Winnicott and the American ego psychologists although their perspectives are somewhat different. For Winnicott, ego-relatedness is linked implicitly with the environment mother who 'holds' the baby physically and psychically, lending her own good ego support to the young baby who has no ego capacity. He first introduces the term in his paper 'Primary Maternal Preoccupation' in 1956 where he examines the states of mind of the mother in late pregnancy and the early months of the infant's life. Out of this experience of the mother's ego adaptation, 'the infant may eventually build an idea of a person in the mother . . . in a positive way normally, and not out of the experience of the mother as a symbol of frustration' (1956b: 304). In 'The Antisocial Tendency' (1956c), Winnicott again refers to ego-relatedness, this time as the context within which id impulses must be experienced, and implying the necessity of both the 'environment mother' and the 'object mother' for integration to occur. In its absence, as in children who become antisocial, the 'environment must give new opportunity for ego relatedness' (1956c: 315).

The concept is central to the ideas developed in 'The Capacity to be Alone' (1958d) where Winnicott writes about the conditions where life can feel real. There he takes the idea further through his concept of 'ego orgasm' (ecstasy), perhaps echoing Lacan's *jouissance* (1960 Quoted in J. Abram 2007) and taken up by Bollas (1989) and White (2006).

This paper shows his close engagement with the child and his quite extraordinary empathy with children. It describes the provision of a receptive clinical setting where 'Bob' can communicate his experience, beginning when he was 14 months old, of his mother's depression. The treatment relies on Winnicott's psychoanalytic sensibility to elaborate the representation of the original trauma with the child. He uses the squiggle game, the technique he developed where therapist and child take turns to extend a squiggle into a drawing, which enables the child's pressing preoccupations to become manifest and to be addressed therapeutically.

The therapeutic consultation, an example of what Winnicott referred to as 'how little need be done' (Winnicott, 1962a: 166), was firmly rooted in his psychoanalytic training, which also furnished him with the tools to do 'something else and do it usefully'. He used it primarily in his child psychiatric practice but in his private child analytic practice, in certain cases, it provided an intervention that could re-establish ordinary development without the need for full analysis.

Bob's parents first consulted Winnicott because of a diagnosis of a 'primary defect' (learning difficulties). The child could not be seen for analysis but the consultation enabled 'this complex organization round a traumatic event [to] become transformed into material that can be forgotten because it has been remembered' (p. 224). In locating the child in his family history, and making sense of the boy's experience of his primary relationships, Winnicott again demonstrates the importance of an attention to the relation between inner and external reality.

Both the process and the content of Bob's engagement with the squiggle game contribute to Winnicott's diagnostic thinking about whether the child is capable of whole object-functioning. From the start (see Drawing 1, p. 226 he doubts the diagnosis of primary defect, and describes his own understanding of Bob's internal predicament as it emerges in the game. The theme of Humpty Dumpty which appeared suggested 'disintegration, related to premature reliance on an ego organization' (p. 217), and Bob's repeated drawing of eyes is later linked to fear aroused by the witch who makes him disappear (smudged-in eyes), to being lost, and then of falling, and the terror and night-mare associated with these themes. The boy's representation of '[the holding mother's] withdrawal of cathexis' (p. 221) emerges, and it is later corroborated by the mother's account. She had suffered a postnatal depression following the birth of her second child, and a primary symptom was her falling asleep (closing eyes). This is the stuff of primitive anxieties which arise as a feature of the infant's lived experience consequent upon the 'failure of the average expectable environment'. In such circumstances the baby is faced with annihilation anxiety (see Chapter 8, this volume), 'falling forever' (Winnicott, 1967c: 99). Winnicott changes the diagnosis 'from one of relative mental defect to one of recovery from infantile schizophrenia' (p. 215) but proposes that there is evidence 'for a psycho-neurotic organization set up and maintained in defence against the unthinkable or archaic or psychotic anxiety produced in the child by the failure of the mother's holding function' (p. 221).

The impact of the mother who de-cathects (loses interest in) her child has been taken up in France, where André Green's thinking was heavily influenced by Winnicott. In 1974 Green proposes what he calls 'the dead mother com-plex', the core of which is the child's experience of being de-cathected by a depressed mother (Green, 1986). Although Green does not cite this paper, his concern is with the consequences for development and psychopathology of the child who suffers a sudden and profound de-cathexis by the mother who becomes psychically dead to him. The 14-month-old Bob has his depressed mother and a new baby to contend with, reflecting the magnitude of the potential impingements upon his development.

Winnicott's methods and style of work with children reflect his concern as an analyst to facilitate his patients' elaboration of their 'true self'. He does this by limiting his verbal interpretations of a child's play and by providing an appropriate setting for the work. He says several times here that he is not interpreting what might be an underlying communication from the child; instead, he waits, observes, ponders and puts together what he can from the movement of the material. The interpretation addresses the fantasy material arising out of the squiggle game, without the need to spell out the direct link to the child's own experience. His view is that 'the important thing is not my talking so much as the fact that the child has reached to something' (p. 217).

Later he observes that it was unlikely that the child could have put into words what he conveyed in the game, but through it he was able to communicate his ego dysfunction. Winnicott assumes the communication will reverberate through the child's being and sponsor the impetus towards healthy development.

The re-presentation of traumatic experiences in the preverbal period is of great interest to developmentalists and clinicians, and recent research on early memory has been very controversial. In a paper which does not reference Winnicott, Gaensbauer (1995) describes his work with children who have suffered different kinds of early trauma, some extreme. His conclusions are similar to Winnicott's, that the child conveys in the manner available to him or her the memories that have been encoded in what is now termed implicit or procedural memory. 'As words became available, each of the children was able to superimpose verbal description on the nonverbal representations in ways which facilitated understanding and communication of the experience' (Gaensbauer, 1995: 142).

According to Brafman (2001: 5) the therapeutic consultation and the use of the squiggle technique in *Therapeutic Consultations* reflected Winnicott's awareness that 'his psychoanalytic colleagues viewed with suspicion if not outright disapproval his claims of therapeutic results in the course of brief clinical interviews'. Phillips (1988; cited in Brafman, 2001) writes of the 'magical' quality Winnicott's critics saw in these clinical descriptions, but Brafman's view is that the cases Winnicott presented were 'examples of *communication with children* [emphasis in the original]' (Brafman, 2001: 5, quoting Winnicott, 1971b: 8). Winnicott is interested in the child's experience of his problem rather than in fitting him into any diagnostic category. Despite Bob's referral apparently being concerned with diagnosis, it is Winnicott's interest in understanding his patient's lived experience that is notable. Brafman describes how Winnicott and the child would 'isolate themselves from the people and things around them and were . . . engaged in close intimate relationship where words and drawings complemented each other' (Brafman, 2001: 8). This would be the context for the emergence of a dream usually containing the kernel of the unconscious fantasy at the heart of the child's difficulties. In Winnicott's view he had become a subjective object for the child, represented in his unconscious world as one who could be of help. Brafman says, 'I imagine Winnicott was surprised when he first discovered that the articulation of this unconscious fantasy brought about such a dramatic improvement in the child but it seems he came to expect similar results with later cases' (2001: 8).

Winnicott was keenly aware of a child's parents as a source of either help or hindrance in his ongoing development. In many of his clinical accounts he recognizes their therapeutic potential in adapting to the changing needs of their children. He comments in the introduction to *The Piggle* (Winnicott, 1977: 2): 'It is possible for the [psychoanalytic] treatment of a child actually to interfere with a very valuable thing which is the ability of the child's home to tolerate and to cope with the child's clinical states that indicate emotional strain and temporary holdups in emotional development, or even the fact of development itself.' The child for whom analysis is not possible is even more dependent upon the home environment to sustain the therapeutic benefits of the consultation. Brafman quotes Winnicott (1971b: 5–6) as relying on the 'average expectable environment' to foster the changes that could indicate a loosening of a 'knot in the developmental process' that might have taken place in the consultation. In circumstances where the parents could not be relied upon to fulfil this possibility, Winnicott wrote about either exploring what could be done by 'management' or else by instituting 'a therapy which would give the child the opportunity for a personal relationship of the kind that is generally known as transference' (Brafman, 2001: 9), by which he meant a psychoanalytic treatment.

A Clinical Study of the Effect of a Failure of the Average Expectable Environment on a Child's Mental Functioning
(1965)

In order to illustrate a 6-year-old child's comment on his own infancy I offer an example of what may be called a *therapeutic consultation*.

The therapeutic consultation is a kind of clinical work which psycho-analysis makes possible. It is a diagnostic interview which is at the same time a piece of deep therapy. It is particularly applicable where a child can (for financial or location reasons) only attend once or perhaps three times; but there is also a place for this kind of work in the child psychiatry of private practice, where there is no team to complicate the procedure.

In this work the motto is: How little need be done? Here use is made of the psychiatrist's position as a subjective object of the child. This condition only lasts for a few interviews, after which the child uses the psychiatrist in a complex and essentially changing way, which the psycho-analyst knows as the transference. The psychiatrist is more free to be natural than he or she is in psycho-analysis proper, and indeed countertransference phenomena are not a threat. This matches the absence of transference movement. The psychiatrist finds it easy to be objective in this work of limited scope.

The aim is to 'unhitch' a developmental catch, so that the environmental influences may resume their function of facilitating the process of maturation in the child. When such a result is not reached then the case changes auto-matically over into one in which psycho-analysis is appropriate, and indeed necessary. This outcome is not to be reckoned a failure. It should be reckoned a failure, however, if a case is handed on to a psycho-analyst which could have been 'unhitched' in one to three interviews by this method that I am describing, in this and a series of similar cases.

The therapeutic consultation is not difficult to conduct, but experience is needed for it, and a knowledge of the theory of all aspects of individual emotional development, including the early stages that are characterized by very great dependence which is met by environmental adaptation to need [see Chapter 7, this volume].

The case I have chosen illustrates the way in which a child of limited intelligence can communicate a significant detail, if given opportunity. Unfortunately it is necessary to give all the steps that lead up to drawing No. 26, but any method that can be devized for relieving the reader of the need to follow the work of the consultation through tends to make the process obscure. In actual fact the process is a quite natural phenomenon and depends on the fact that when a child comes to see me there is a need in the child which will show in the course of time in the setting that I can provide. This setting is directly derived from what I have learned to provide as a psycho-analyst. It is like a first session of an analysis except that here I am doing all I know how to do, whereas in an analysis I choose to allow the material to unfold in the course of time, in samples of transference neurosis and psychosis.

When the reader reaches drawing No. 26 there will be a reward, in that the child will be found to tell me the way in which his mother's depression started when he was 14 to 16 months old. The information he gave me was found to be correct. Because the information was given me by the child I was able to use it, and in so doing I was able to release in the child the processes of development. Incidentally, this had an importance in that it changed the diagnosis from one of relative mental defect to one of recovery from infantile schizophrenia.

THE CASE: BOB (6 YEARS OLD)

Preliminary Contact

> First I saw Bob with his father and mother. I learned that in the household there was Bob aged 6 years, a brother aged 5 years, and another brother aged one year. There was also a girl of 15, the adopted daughter of the mother's parents. Bob's father worked in a factory. In the house there were three bedrooms, which were not enough. Bob and the next boy slept together, often in the same bed.

By this time I had reached the point in the consultation when I was finding out what Bob was like. His words were shortened and many of them were difficult to understand. Nevertheless he communicated freely. He had come in an excited state and he took up his position in one of the little chairs, eager for whatever should happen. It could really be said that he was full of some vague kind of hope.

> The mother had been for some years in the care of Dr Y, a psychiatric colleague who is also an analyst, on account of panics and depression. She had obviously been a very ill patient and had been treated by psychotherapy. The father had also had depressions and both parents had attended for group therapy. They said they felt that the existence of the family depended on the help given over the years by the psychiatrist Dr Y.

At this point in the preliminary contact the parents went to the waiting room and I had Bob alone with me in my room for 45 minutes.

Interview with Bob

Bob was easy to meet. He expected friendliness and helpfulness. I had provided paper and pencils and I suggested that we should play a game and I proceeded to show him what I meant. He was talking in an excited way and on one occasion there was a stammer, on the word punch (p . . . p . . . p . . . punch) when he was talking about the first drawing.

Drawing No. 1[1]

I made a squiggle for him to do something with. He knew what he wanted to do and he carefully filled it in with shading and called it a bull. It took me a long time to realize that the word bull meant ball, but to help me he gave me a long story about pumping (? bumping) up and down, and punching. I already made a mental note of this boy's capacity to conceive of a whole object, and I began to doubt the diagnosis that had been assumed to be correct – 'Primary Defect'.

I now suggested that he should make a squiggle for me to turn into something, but either he did not understand or else he could not make a squiggle. He said: 'Can I make a car?'

Drawing No. 2

This is his drawing of a car.

---

[1] Drawings are reproduced at the end of this paper.

Drawing No. 3

I offered him a squiggle and he seemed bewildered. He said it was a hand, but he added: 'It's too hard', meaning he could not play this game.

Drawing No. 4

He chose to draw the sun.

This was the end of a very cautious first phase in which he used the aspect of his self that tries to comply and to conform, but which does not carry feeling nor does it employ impulse.

The *second phase* started with

Drawing No. 5

His version of a squiggle. It was a drawing by use of a wavy line, and it may have been a person or a ghost. I added the moon.

It was now my turn and I did

Drawing No. 6

My squiggle. He put in the eyes and called it Humpty Dumpty.

The theme of Humpty Dumpty alerted me to the idea of disintegration, related to premature reliance on an ego organization. At this stage I had no idea that his putting in the eyes had significance, but in the critical drawing (No. 26) this Humpty Dumpty theme and the eyes came to make sense.

It should be noted that in this work I do not usually make interpretations, but I wait until the essential feature of the child's communication has been revealed. Then I talk about the essential feature, but the important thing is not my talking so much as the fact that the child has reached to something.

Drawing No. 7

Bob made a new characteristic squiggle composed of a wavy line; he quickly saw what he wanted to do with it and turned it into a snake, dangerous because it stings.

Here was now a drawing of Bob's own, based on his own squiggle, and very different from the drawings of the objectively perceived car and sun (Nos. 2 and 4). He was pleased with his own drawing.

(At this point he became interested in the numbers that I was putting on the drawings, and he told me all along the number of the next drawing.)

Drawing No. 8

My squiggle which he said was a hair. Then he said it was an 'ephelant' with a big mouth. He put in the eyes. (Eyes again!)

(I am not attempting to reproduce the curious distortion of speech which made it very hard for me to understand what he was saying. It was always possible to understand in the end.)

Drawing No. 9

This was his squiggle, done by the same technique of the wavy line. He said it was a 'roundabout', a 'puzzle place'. I found that he meant a maze, but he could not use this word. It was horrid. He went with his Daddy. In fast speech he told a story of this visit to a maze, and he was anxious while remembering it.

Here I made another mental note of the idea of a reaction to environmental failure. In this case the idea was of a failure on the part of the father, who had not realized that a maze would touch on archaic anxiety in Bob. I had got in touch with Bob's threatened confusional state, his potential disorientation. Naturally I was building up in my mind an idea of his illness as one of infantile schizophrenia, showing a tendency to recover spontaneously.

Drawing No. 10

This was my squiggle, and he went over it and emphasized everything. He said it was a 'roundabout like mine'.

It was clear in the context that by this Bob meant 'a roundabout like *nine*'. He did not mean '*mine*'. This illustrates the peculiar language distortion to which I needed to adapt myself, in order to receive his very clear communication. (I assume that this language distortion corresponds with the glass or perspex (or whatever) that the schizophrenic often reports as a something between the self and the actual world.)

Drawing No. 11

Bob now chose to draw. He drew the sun in his characteristic way and a jet plane by the other technique (after he had made its outline by the wavy lines method). Bob said: 'Twelve comes after it.' He was now numbering the drawings, and was correctly using the words 'he' and 'me' which I put next to the numbers to denote the order of events. He was able to call himself 'he', and me 'me', allowing for my having my own point of view, or identifying himself with me in the game.

Talking about No. 11, I asked Bob if he would like to go in a jet plane. He said: 'No, because they may go upside down.'

From this I gathered further evidence that Bob was letting me know of his experience of environmental unreliability during the period of his own near-absolute dependence. I continued with my policy of not making interpretations.

I seem to have asked at this point: 'Do you remember being born?' He replied: 'Well, that was a long time ago.' Then he added: 'Mummy showed me where I did be a baby.' (I found afterwards that his mother had recently taken him to see the home where he was born.)

While we were talking in this way we had continued with the drawings.

Drawing No. 12

My squiggle which he turned into a fish. He put in *the eye* and mouth.

Drawing No. 13

Here was one of his characteristic squiggles, which he turned into a boat. He told me a long story of someone who had gone in a big boat to Australia. He than said: 'My lines are all wiggly, wiggly.'

Drawing No. 14

My squiggle, which went off the page onto another sheet of paper (see No. 18). This amused him very much. He turned the squiggle into a hand.

Drawing No. 15

He made a wavy squiggle, and I squiggled all over his, and we were deliberately making a hopeless mess and muddle. Then he saw it as a Donald Duck and *put in the eyes*.

Drawing No. 16

My squiggle, which he turned into a 'lephelent'. He added: 'It has a beak and it can catch me.' He dramatized this.

Drawing No. 17

He turned his own squiggle into a shoe.

Drawing No. 18

Here I developed the theme of spines which came from the spilt-over parts of No. 14. He made this into 'an animal that will eat you'. At this point he put his hand to his penis, feeling danger there. I pointed this out to him, else he would not have noticed that he had made this gesture.

Drawing No. 19

His drawing of a tiger.

He had now mastered his immediate anxiety about retaliation based on oral sadism, and he talked about numbers: 'Shall we go up to 100?' Actually he was only capable of counting to 20, and a little further with effort.

We were now in a doldrums area, between the second phase and the next phase. I did not know, of course, whether there would be another phase.

Drawing No. 20 (not shown)

He wrote his name at my request, putting one letter round the wrong way. He wrote the number six (his age), because he could not spell it.

Drawing No. 21

His squiggle, which he said was 'a mountain; you walk all round it and get lost.'

Now we had entered the third phase, and we began to get down to the significant detail. The content of No. 21 made me prepared for a new version of environmental failure producing threat of primitive anxiety of the type of falling, depersonalization, confusion, disorientation, etc.

Drawing No. 22

My squiggle. I said, in a challenging voice: 'I bet you can't make anything of that.' He said: 'I'll try', and rather quickly he turned it into a 'glub' (glove).

(Bob now asked for a bigger sheet of paper. He obviously had something important to draw, and he used the larger sheets until the end.)

Drawing No. 23

His deliberate drawing of 'a big hill, a very big one, a big mountain.' 'You climb up there and you slip; it's all ice.' He added: 'Have you a car?'

From this I felt sure he was telling me about being held, and about being affected by someone's withdrawal of cathexis, and, of course, I wondered if this could be a picture of his mother's depression, and its effect on him when he was a baby. I continued to refrain from making comment, and asked him if his dreams were about this sort of thing.

He said: 'I forget them.' Then, remembering one: 'Oh, an awful dream about a witch.' I said: 'What awful dream?' He said: 'It was last night or another night. If I see it I cry. I don't know what it is. It is a witch.' (And here he started dramatizing.) 'It's horrid, and has a wand. It makes you pee. You can talk but you can't be seen and you can't see yourself. Then you say "one, one, one" and you come back.'

The word 'pee' here does not mean micturate. 'No, not wee-wee!' It means disappear. When the witch 'pees you' he 'makes you vanish.' The witch has a hat and soft shoes. It's a man witch.

Drawing No. 24

While all this was going on Bob was drawing an illustration (No. 24) of what he wanted to tell me at this point. He was dramatizing horror and his penis got excited and he screwed himself up because of anxiety.

Drawing No. 25

Shows himself in bed having the nightmare. When he saw the big stairs he said: 'Oh! oh! oh!' and he was very much in the event he was describing.

He now told me that the drawing was about two things. The awful one was the nightmare; but there was a real incident which was not horrid, it was nice. He really fell downstairs, and there was daddy at the bottom of the stairs, and he cried, and daddy carried him to mummy, and she took him and made him well.

I now had the clearest possible evidence of Bob's wish to tell me about a lapse in the environmental provision which had been 'good' in a general way. I therefore started to talk, and I drew

Drawing No. 26

A mother figure holding a baby. I scribbled out the baby in arms; and while I was starting to put into words the baby's danger of being dropped, Bob took the paper and *smudged in the woman's eyes.* (See No. 6.)

At the same time he said: 'She goes to sleep.'

This was the significant detail in the total communication. I now had his drawing illustrating the holding mother's withdrawal of cathexis.

I now put the baby on the floor, wondering how Bob would deal with the archaic anxiety associated with falling for ever.

Bob said: 'No, the witch came when the mother shut her eyes. I just screamed. I saw the witch. Mummy saw the witch. I shouted: "My mummy will get you!" Mummy saw the witch. Daddy was downstairs and he took his penknife and stuck it into the witch's tummy so it got killed for ever, and so the wand went too.'

In this fantasy can be seen the material for a psycho-neurotic organization set up and maintained in defence against the unthinkable or archaic or psychotic anxiety produced in the child by the failure of the mother's holding function.

Drawing No. 27

His drawing showing himself in bed and the male witch along with the wand which 'makes you pee' (disappear).

★   ★   ★

The communication having been made, Bob was ready to go. He seemed to be very satisfied with what had happened, and his excited state had calmed down.

Bob now went to his father in the waiting-room while his mother gave me the following account of the family problem.

Mother's Description given me after my Interview with Bob, with Bob and his Father in the Waiting-Room

At 2½ years Bob was taken to a children's hospital because of continuous crying. At the time the mother was depressed. A paediatrician said he was frustrated. After brain examination and various tests the parents were told that there was no disease but that Bob was six months behind in development. The parents were told they must expect him to be *simple*.

A year later, at 3½ years, Bob was taken again and the parents were told once more that he was 'simple'. At 3 years Bob did not speak at all. To help things forward the mother started a day nursery. Bob showed up as the slowest in the class and he was obviously tied to his mother. The parents had accepted the fact that Bob would be 'simple', but recently Dr Y (the mother's psychiatrist) had suggested that they ought to question this diagnosis because of the wide range of Bob's interests as reported by the mother in her sessions. He was always talking about space and God and life and death. He was very sensitive and obviously the word 'simple' did not cover the whole of the diagnosis.

On Intelligence Test Bob had scored 93 (Stanford-Binet).

There had been thumb-sucking throughout. A period of masturbation, erections, and day-dreaming seemed to have passed. At times he would get his penis out both at school and at home, but everyone tried not to make too much of this.

The mother herself remembers being unhappy at home at the time of her secondary school; she felt picked upon. It was better at a grammar-school, when she got on to dressmaking and cooking. She does not give the impression of high intelligence but evidence seems to show that she herself is not by any means limited. She passed her School Certificate examination.

The father, an only son, 'spent his childhood in dreamland' (mother's description), being unhappy at home. His parents were difficult people and indeed the mother ascribes the beginning of her depression to her having to be in contact with her in-laws. The father's mother had died a year ago.

Bob's mother did not suffer from panics any longer, and Bob's father had settled down to being a quiet personality. The family had times when there was a shortage of money. It was a severe blow to the father that his son should be 'simple', whereas the mother did not mind much. The father is an engineer.

Bob's Early History

Bob's birth had not been difficult. Breast feeding was complicated by what the mother called a 'doctor's mistake'. The mother had said: 'I know this baby is ill.' Then at two weeks it was discovered that he had pyloric stenosis and he was operated on immediately, being away a fortnight. The mother had tried to forgive the doctor for not believing her that the child was ill.

At 4 years 9 months the boy underwent tonsillectomy; here it was very evident to the parents that he was backward because they knew that although they could tell any other child what to expect they could not find a way of telling Bob. Bob had five days in hospital, with daily visiting. He was distressed during this period.

The mother said that she had this first baby in hospital but decided to have the others at home. In the third pregnancy the mother used the National Childbirth Trust (Dr Vellay). The birth was 'absolutely painless'. The father was present. They found the experience 'inspiring and lovely.' It was possible to detect here in this positive statement one side of the mother's illness, the idealization, which all the time carries with it the threat of the opposite. Contained in all this is her potential depression.

At the time of Bob's birth the mother feared hospital although the pregnancy was all right. The labour was in fact a short and easy one. *It was after the second birth, when Bob was 14 months old, that she started her panics and psychotherapy. I asked: 'How did you first become ill? In what way did your depression show itself?' She answered: 'I kept finding myself going to sleep while I was engaged in doing something.'*

It was when Bob was 14–16 months old that she was starting to get sleepy and this was the beginning of not being able to cope; and later the panics supervened. This information coming at the very end of the consultation interested me very much because of the evidence that I had already got of this from the material supplied by Bob himself.

As Bob left my house he said to his mother: 'Did you see how I rubbed in the lady's eyes?' This had obviously been the high-light, for him, of the therapeutic interview.

★   ★   ★

The parents visited me three weeks later, not bringing Bob. Here I learned much detail about each parent, and also more about Bob. At home his difficulties were compatible with a diagnosis of infantile schizophrenia, tending to spontaneous recovery. His main trouble was a learning difficulty.

Follow-up (After 7 months)

Learning at school has seemed to be released since the time of the consultation. At home, Bob makes steady growth in spite of father's illness (hospital) and mother's hospitalization with the baby, who had an illness.

COMMENT

It would seem that this boy retained a clear idea of the beginning of his illness, or of the organization of his defences into a personality pattern. He was able to communicate this, and he did so with some urgency once he had felt that I might possibly understand and therefore make effective his communication.

The work of this therapeutic consultation is made more interesting by the fact that this boy did not use words at 3 years, and that he had a learning difficulty, and that he was generally considered to be 'simple' by paediatricians and by school authorities and by the parents. It is unlikely that Bob could have told me what he did by verbal reply to verbal questions. Gradually, however, he unfolded the aetiology of his ego dysfunction.

The diagnosis became changed during the consultation from one of relative (mental) defect to one of infantile schizophrenia, with the patient tending to make spontaneous recovery.

It is interesting to note that schizophrenia, or the psychotic condition that resulted here in a learning difficulty, is in fact a highly sophisticated defence organization. The defence is against primitive, archaic ('unthinkable') anxiety produced by environmental failure in the stage of the child's near-absolute dependence. Without the defence there would be a breakdown of mental organization of the order of disintegration, disorientation, depersonalization, falling for ever, and loss of sense of real and of the capacity for relating to objects. In the defence the child isolates what there is of himself, and attains a position of invulnerability through introversion. In the extreme of this defence the child cannot be traumatized, and at the same time cannot be induced to regain vulnerability and dependence.

In the case of Bob the ego has known a certain limited type of disaster, limited in quantity, and has experienced breakdown, has reorganized against being retraumatized by developing the feeling of being traumatized all the time except when withdrawn. All details of experience have been retained and have been subjected to classification, categorization, and collation, and to primitive forms of thinking. It is to be presumed that as a result of the work of the therapeutic consultation this complex organization round a traumatic event has become transformed into material that can be forgotten because it has been remembered, that is to say, has become available for a sophisticated thinking process that is relatively detached from psychosomatic functioning.

Conclusion

In this clinical description I have tried to show the effect on a child of a specific example of failure in the area of what Hartmann (1939) has called 'the average expectable environment.'

> **Developing ideas:** true and false self; adolescent doldrums; therapeutic consultation; reaching to the failure situation

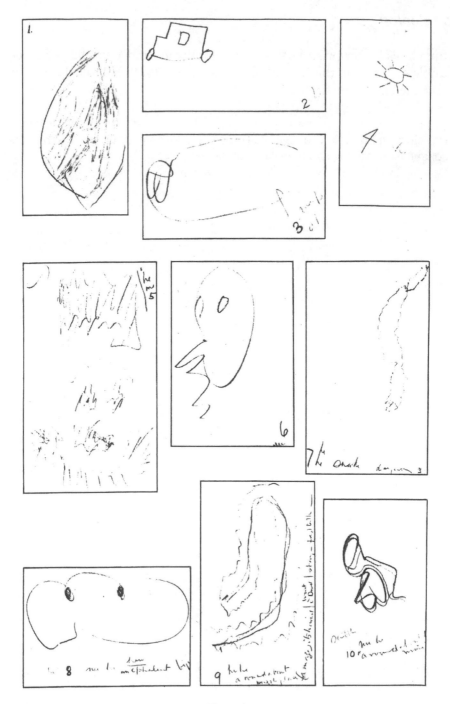

Figure 1

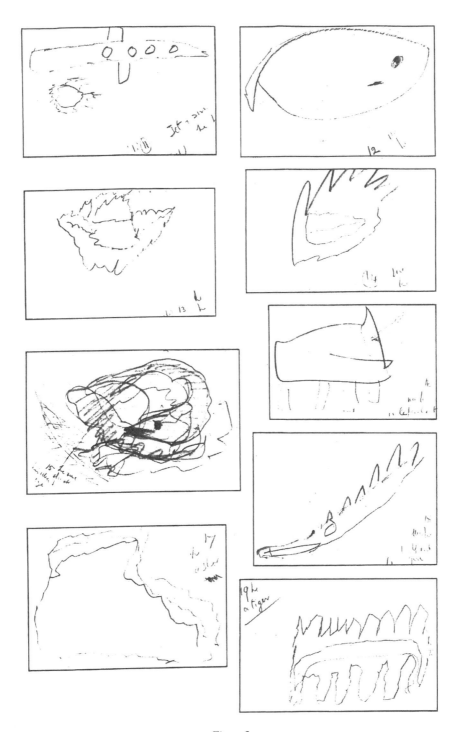

Figure 2

Omitted. Bob's writing of his name (one consonant reversed) and the figure 6 (he could not spell 'six'), his age.

20

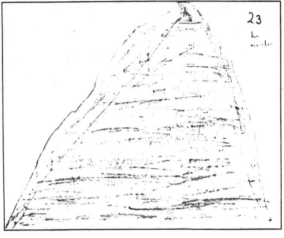

Figure 3

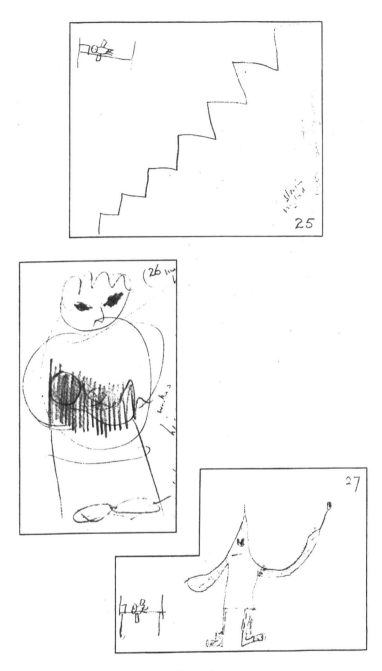

Figure 4

12 PLAYING: A THEORETICAL STATEMENT (1968)

OTHER WRITINGS

The remaining papers in this collection were published in *Playing and Reality* (1971a) after Winnicott's death. The last years of his life saw no reduction in his productivity despite his failing health. He continued to give talks and to work on short pieces many of which were posthumously published by the Winnicott Trust. These writings, recognizably the culmination of concerns evident throughout his work, are creative and fresh. He remained interested in ordinary living, 'The Ordinary Devoted Mother' (1966c), and health, 'The Concept of a Healthy Individual' (1967d) but he also wrote a remarkable new paper about masculinity and femininity in 1966, 'The Split-off Male and Female Elements to be found in Men and Women', published as part of 'Creativity and its Origins' in *Playing and Reality*. He wrote further about the mother's role in the 'Mirror-role of Mother and Family in Child Development' (1967b) and papers on creativity and culture.

Contemporaries of Winnicott in the Middle Group (renamed the Independent Group) elaborated many of the themes that pre-occupied him, particularly creativity, the work of the imagination and its links with the unconscious and dreams. Ella Freeman Sharpe, one of Winnicott's supervisors in the 1920s, had written a major work on dreams (Sharpe, 1937/1988). Her interest in metaphor and dreams took Freudian conceptualization into new territory and influenced the Independents to focus on the creative aspects of dreaming. Klauber took this up in the 1960s and linked it to the function of the dream in the analytic process (1967). Paula Heimann (1956) had written about the shaping of dreams as communication from the patient to the analyst. She left the Klein group in the mid 1950s like Winnicott before her, joining the Middle Group to become 'a leading influence within the British Independents for many years' (Rayner, 1991: 19). In the early 1960s Masud Khan wrote about the functioning of the ego in dreaming and he later pursued Winnicott's distinction between 'fantasying' and dreaming and its links with the distinction between 'object relating' and 'object usage' (1976). The following generation of Independents developed these themes further. Christopher Bollas and Michael Parsons, two of the best known contemporary British Independents have written about creativity, illusion and the true self. Bollas especially, has been interested in the way the true self creates its own 'idiom', an expression of the spontaneity from which it derives, that, with the contribution from the 'transformational object' (1989), transforms the ego. He sees this as essentially an aesthetic movement. Parsons has written about creativity and paradox, drawing on Greek tragedy and the martial arts as his focus of exploration (2000).

EDITORS' INTRODUCTION

This paper, first published in the *IJPA* and reproduced as Chapter 3 of *Playing and Reality*, contains Winnicott's most extended statement on the nature and significance of play and playing. The idea of Winnicott as the theorist of play derives particularly from his final papers and from the success of *Playing and Reality*, which gathers together the changing emphases of his work. While the origins of the approach described there are clearly present earlier, they are particularly a development of the original argument of the paper on transitional objects and phenomena. The discussion of play itself develops from the interest in transitional space. Winnicott is not concerned with play as functional to the organism or play as a masturbatory activity, though he agrees that the fantasies accompanying play may be of interest. He is far more interested in playing as a fundamental component of creative living.

The set situation paper (1941), the earliest paper presented in this volume, describes a child at play in a situation that Winnicott was able to observe many times. That account anticipates some of his later formulations about the conditions in which play becomes possible. The first article recorded by Abram, 'Why Children Play' (1942a), contains two statements that are developed in the transitional objects paper and the work of the 1960s: playing is the continuous evidence of creativity, which means aliveness (quoted in Abram, 2007: 150), and play links the individual's relation to inner personal reality with his relation to external or shared reality (Abram, 2007: 151). Both, especially the latter, inform the approach of the 1941 paper. Taken together, these emphases shape Winnicott's approach and his insistence that play and playing must be considered in their own right, rather than as part of a technique of therapy or a sublimatory activity that reveals an underlying fantasy and anxiety.

Despite these early mentions, playing was not notably present in his theorizations until the 1960s, and Greenacre's 1959 paper, 'Play in Relation to the Creative Imagination', an important early statement, mentions Winnicott only in relation to transitional objects, which suggests that a topic that has come to be almost synonymous with him was one in which he still had to establish his position. Greenacre herself makes the distinction between play therapy and play in relation to the creative imagination (Greenacre, 1959: 68) that is central for Winnicott, who insists that play and playing are far bigger topics than the basis for a therapeutic method which concentrates on interpreting its content.

Playing has a general significance as a creative experience in the space–time continuum. It occurs in the transitional space that emerges in the developmental processes through which the child begins to relate, psychologically and somatically, with objects in the external world. To arrive at a capacity to inhabit the transitional area and, later, to play, and later still to dream, involves those processes of illusion and disillusion that, for Winnicott, form the basis of the mother–child relation. Playing in Winnicott's usage involves a relation with, and a care of, the self. It is a form of living well (Winnicott, 1971a: 50).

In his book *Homo Ludens* (1950), Huizinga describes play as fundamental to the human species, a voluntary activity, executed within certain fixed limits of time and place, bound by freely accepted rules, having its aim in itself, and accompanied by a feeling of tension, joy and consciousness different from ordinary life. It is a cultural phenomenon, a continuing creation of the mind that can be returned to as a treasure retained in the memory, and for which repetition is an essential quality (Huizinga, 1950: 10). Winnicott echoes Huizinga in this chapter and its companion piece, Chapter 4 of *Playing and Reality*, 'Playing: Creative Activity and the Search for the Self'. The essential components of the Winnicottian account are creativity, play as voluntary, primary, related to a particular condition of the mind, to the self, and to the relations between them. Play happens in the intermediate area of experience and the possibility of its existence '*there*', the possibility of someone being able to play *there* (and therefore elsewhere) grows out of the *potential* space between child and mother which emerges 'when experience has produced in the child a high degree of confidence in the mother that she will not fail to be there if suddenly needed' (Winnicott *et al.*, 1990: 36). The processes that begin in this space, created on the basis of experience – initially the space of illusion – make it possible for a person to live creatively, to participate in and make use of the arena loosely demarcated by the term 'culture', and to engage in psychoanalysis, that 'highly specialized form of playing in the service of communication with oneself and others' (p. 237).

Once again Winnicott privileges the evolution of the infant's and child's relation with another, the mother, as the context for the development of the capacity for playing. He eschews the explanation of instincts as the source of excitement in playing, instead appealing to the 'precariousness of magic itself' derived from the infant's experience of illusion through the mother's adaptations at the beginning. The magic of this experience of illusion is embedded in the interstitial arena between the internal world of the self and the external world of objects; it is inherently precarious and exciting, and possible because of the reliability of the intimacy created by the mother's love–hate for the baby.

This reliability becomes the context for a further development which Winnicott refers to here as 'the stage of being alone in the presence of someone'. Another much-quoted paradox, which he explored in a 1958 paper entitled 'The Capacity to Be Alone' (Winnicott, 1958d), is invoked here to indicate the emergence of 'object constancy' in the baby, as the internal representation of the mother who can thus be held in mind in her absence. First the baby is alone in the presence of another and later can be alone with that reliable presence as an internal resource. The mother, first as external, then as internal playmate, allows playing, with all its magical excitement and precariousness, to be risked, without compliance but rather with a connection in the potential space, that is, playing together in a relationship. A mature capacity for playing is different from the physical activity of play; it depends on an ability to distinguish reality from fantasy, past from present, and to give playful rein to the creative imagination which is neither delusional nor literal. Patients who display the restrictions and the impoverishments that are the result of pathologies stemming from problems in very early processes must first learn to play before the analysis proper can begin.

The insistence on the ordinary processes of infant care, and the theory of the early conditions that lead to health and the healthy individual and that construct the place of art and intermediate experience in facilitating an ongoing encounter with the self, make Winnicott's work, as it developed from 1951 to 1971, distinctive.

And it is a particular approach to what an analysis is about. According to Green (1986) Winnicott sees psychoanalysis as preparing the patient for ongoing self-analysis. 'Play' and even more 'playing', are to be understood as extending the understanding of what happens in the consulting room. This reorients the very basis of analytic work since, for Winnicott, the capacity to play is *the* condition for being able to engage in depth in the process of analysis and for being able to use and enjoy the world of art *and* the ordinary world and its pleasures. As Parsons (2007) insists, Winnicott's complexity here depends on the paradoxical status of the analytic situation and the sense in which it is both real and not real. These ideas contribute to Winnicott's evolving attitude to psychoanalytic technique, in which he becomes more sceptical about the analyst's interpreting function and increasingly interested in the provision of a setting, analogous to potential or transitional space, where the patient, child or adult, can surprise himself with a new self-awareness. This is an emphasis on experiencing, and hence he can assert that 'playing is itself a therapy', valuable in and of itself.

Winnicott's work offers the basis for a psychoanalytic investigation of aesthetic experience and a revaluation of ordinary life and ordinary satisfactions. It is an interrogation of the existence of a sustaining self, able to engage with and make use of the world and of relationships with both persons and things within it, that grows out of the earliest contacts between mother and baby. The 'third area' has a structural as well as a developmental instrumentality, in that it informs all kinds of adult cultural experience, linking the world of infantile experience and the world of art and culture, making the later forms depend upon and grow out of the earliest. Cultural experience, he suggested, is located in 'the *potential space* between the individual and the environment', a space of 'maximally intense experiences' (1967a; but see 1971a: 100).

Playing
A Theoretical Statement
(1971)

In this chapter I am trying to explore an idea that has been forced on me by my work, and also forced on me by my own stage of development at the present time, which gives my work a certain colouring. I need not say that my work, which is largely psychoanalysis, also includes psychotherapy, and for the purpose of this chapter I do not need to draw a clear distinction between the uses of the two terms.

When I come to state my thesis I find, as so often, that it is very simple, and that not many words are needed to cover the subject. *Psychotherapy takes place in the overlap of two areas of playing, that of the patient and that of the therapist. Psychotherapy has to do with two people playing together. The corollary of this is that where playing is not possible then the work done by the therapist is directed towards bringing the patient from a state of not being able to play into a state of being able to play.*

Although I am not attempting to review the literature I do wish to pay tribute to the work of Milner (1952, 1957, 1969), who has written brilliantly on the subject of symbol-formation. However, I shall not let her deep comprehensive study stop me from drawing attention to the subject of playing in my own words. Milner (1952) relates children's playing to concentration in adults:

> When I began to see . . . that this use of me might be not only a defensive regression, but an essential recurrent phase of a creative relation to the world. . . .

Milner was referring to a '*prelogical fusion of subject and object*'. I am trying to distinguish between this fusion and the fusion or defusion of the subjective object and the object objectively perceived.[i] I believe that what I am attempting to do is also inherent in the material of Milner's contribution. Here is another of her statements:

> Moments when the original poet in each of us created the outside world for us, by finding the familiar in the unfamiliar, are perhaps forgotten by

most people; or else they are guarded in some secret place of memory because they were too much like visitations of the gods to be mixed with everyday thinking.

(Milner, 1957)

Play and Masturbation

There is one thing that I want to get out of the way. In psychoanalytic writings and discussions, the subject of playing has been too closely linked with masturbation and the various sensuous experiences. It is true that when we are confronted with masturbation we always think: what is the fantasy? And it is also true that when we witness playing we tend to wonder what is the physical excitement that is linked with the type of play that we witness. But playing needs to be studied as a subject on its own, supplementary to the concept of the sublimation of instinct.

It may very well be that we have missed something by having these two phenomena (playing and masturbatory activity) so closely linked in our minds. I have tried to point out that when a child is playing the masturbatory element is essentially lacking; or, in other words, that if when a child is playing the physical excitement of instinctual involvement becomes evident, then the playing stops, or is at any rate spoiled (Winnicott, 1968[a]). Both Kris (1951) and Spitz (1962) have enlarged the concept of auto-erotism to cover data of a similar kind (also cf. Khan, 1964).

I am reaching towards a new statement of playing, and it interests me when I seem to see in the psychoanalytic literature the lack of a useful statement on the subject of play. Child analysis of whatever school is built around the child's playing, and it would be rather strange if we were to find that in order to get a good statement about playing we have to go to those who have written on the subject who are not analysts (e.g. Lowenfeld, 1935).

Naturally one turns to the work of Melanie Klein (1932), but I suggest that in her writings Klein, in so far as she was concerned with play, was concerned almost entirely with the use of play. The therapist is reaching for the child's communication and knows that the child does not usually possess the command of language that can convey the infinite subtleties that are to be found in play by those who seek. This is not a criticism of Melanie Klein or of others who have described the use of a child's play in the psychoanalysis of children. It is simply a comment on the possibility that in the total theory of the personality the psychoanalyst has been too busy using play content to look at the playing child, and to write about playing as a thing in itself. It is obvious that I am making a significant distinction between the meanings of the noun 'play' and the verbal noun 'playing'.

Whatever I say about children playing really applies to adults as well, only the matter is more difficult to describe when the patient's material appears mainly in terms of verbal communication. I suggest that we must expect to find playing just as evident in the analyses of adults as it is in the case of our work with children. It manifests itself, for instance, in the choice of words, in the inflections of the voice, and indeed in the sense of humour.

TRANSITIONAL PHENOMENA

For me the meaning of playing has taken on a new colour since I have followed up the theme of transitional phenomena, tracing these in all their subtle developments right from the early use of a transitional object or technique to the ultimate stages of a human being's capacity for cultural experience.

I think it is not out of place to draw attention here to the generosity that has been shown in psychoanalytic circles and in the general psychiatric world in respect of my description of transitional phenomena. I am interested in the fact that right through the field of child care this idea has caught on, and sometimes I feel that I have been given more than my due reward in this area. What I called transitional phenomena are universal and it was simply a matter of drawing attention to them and to their potential for use in the building of theory. Wulff (1946) had already, as I discovered, written about fetish objects employed by babies or children, and I know that in Anna Freud's psycho-therapy clinic these objects have been observed with small children. I have heard Anna Freud speak of the use of the talisman, a closely allied phenomenon (cf. A. Freud, 1965). A A. Milne, of course, immortalized Winnie the Pooh. Schulz and Arthur Miller,[ii] among other authors, have drawn on these objects that I have specifically referred to and named.

I am encouraged by the happy fate of the concept of transitional phenomena to think that what I am trying to say now about playing may also be readily acceptable. There is something about playing that has not yet found a place in the psychoanalytic literature.

In 'The Location of Cultural Experience' (1967[a]) I make my idea of play concrete by claiming that *playing has a place* and a time. It is not *inside* by any use of the word (and it is unfortunately true that the word inside has very many and various uses in psychoanalytic discussion). Nor is it *outside*, that is to say, it is not a part of the repudiated world, the not-me, that which the individual has decided to recognize (with whatever difficulty and even pain) as truly external, which is outside magical control. To control what is outside one has to *do* things, not simply to think or to wish, and *doing things takes time*. Playing is doing.

PLAYING IN TIME AND SPACE

In order to give a place to playing I postulated a *potential space* between the baby and the mother. This potential space varies a very great deal according to the life experiences of the baby in relation to the mother or mother-figure, and I contrast this potential space (*a*) with the inner world (which is related to the psychosomatic partnership) and (*b*) with actual, or external, reality (which has its own dimensions, and which can be studied objectively, and which, however much it may seem to vary according to the state of the individual who is observing it, does in fact remain constant).

I can now restate what I am trying to convey. I want to draw attention away from the sequence psychoanalysis, psychotherapy, play material, playing, and to set this up again the other way round. In other words, *it is play that is the universal*, and that belongs to health: playing facilitates growth and therefore health; playing leads into group relationships; playing can be a form of communication in psychotherapy; and, lastly, psychoanalysis has been developed as a highly specialized form of playing in the service of communication with oneself and others.

The natural thing is playing, and the highly sophisticated twentieth-century phenomenon is psychoanalysis. It must be of value to the analyst to be constantly reminded not only of what is owed to Freud but also of what we owe to the natural and universal thing called playing.

It is hardly necessary to illustrate something so obvious as playing; nevertheless I propose to give two examples.

Edmund, Aged Two and a Half Years

The mother came to consult me about herself and she brought Edmund with her. Edmund was in my room while I was talking to his mother, and I placed among us a table and a little chair which he could use if he wished to do so. He looked serious but not frightened or depressed. He said: 'Where's toys?' This is all he said throughout the hour. Evidently he had been told to expect toys and I said that there were some to be found at the other end of the room on the floor under the bookcase.

Soon he fetched a bucketful of toys and he was playing in a deliberate way while the consultation between the mother and me proceeded. The mother was able to tell me the exact significant moment at two years five months when Edmund had started stammering, after which he gave up talking 'because the stammer frightened him'. While she and I were going through with a consultation situation about herself and about him, Edmund placed some small train parts on the table and was arranging them and making them join up and relate. He was only two feet away from his mother. Soon he got onto her lap and had a short spell as a baby. She responded naturally and adequately. Then he got down spontaneously and took up playing again at the table. All this happened while his mother and I were heavily engaged in deep conversation.

After about twenty minutes Edmund began to liven up, and he went to the other end of the room for a fresh supply of toys. Out of the muddle there he brought a tangle of string. The mother (undoubtedly affected by his choice of string, but not conscious of the symbolism) made the remark: 'At his most non-verbal Edmund is most clinging, needing contact with my *actual* breast, and needing my *actual* lap.' At the time when the stammer began he had been starting to comply, but he had reverted to incontinence along with the stammer, and this was followed by abandonment of talking. He was beginning to cooperate again at about the time of the consultation. The mother saw this as being part of a recovery from a setback in his development.

By taking notice of Edmund's playing I was able to maintain communication with the mother.

Now Edmund developed a bubble in his mouth while playing with the toys. He became preoccupied with the string. The mother made the comment that as a baby he refused all except the breast, till he grew up and went over to a cup. 'He brooks no substitute', she said, meaning that he would not take from a baby's bottle, and a refusal of substitutes had become a permanent feature in his character. Even his mother's mother, of whom he is fond, is not fully accepted because she is not the actual mother. All his life he has had his mother herself to settle him at night. There were breast troubles when he was born, and he used to cling on with his gums in the first days and weeks, perhaps as an insurance against mother's sensitive protection of herself, she being in a tender state. At ten months he had a tooth, and on one occasion he bit, but this did not draw blood.

'He was not quite so easy a baby as the first had been.'

All this took time, and was mixed up with the other matters that the mother wished to discuss with me. Edmund seemed here to be concerned with the one end of the string that was exposed, the rest of the string being in a tangle. Sometimes he would make a gesture which was as if he 'plugged in' with the end of the string like an electric flex to his mother's thigh. One had to observe that although he 'brooked no substitute' he was using the string as a symbol of union with his mother. It was clear that the string was simultaneously a symbol of separateness and of union through communication.

The mother told me that he had had a transitional object called 'my blanket' – he could use any blanket that had a satin binding like the binding of the original one of his early infancy.

At this point Edmund quite naturally left the toys, got onto the couch and crept like an animal towards his mother and curled up on her lap. He stayed there about three minutes. She gave a very natural response, not exaggerated. Then he uncurled and returned to the toys. He now put the string (which he seemed fond of) at the bottom of the bucket like bedding, and began to put the toys in, so that they had a nice soft place to lie in, like a cradle or cot. After once more clinging to his mother and then returning to the toys, he was ready to go, the mother and I having finished our business.

In this play he had illustrated much of that which the mother was talking about (although she was also talking about herself). He had communicated an ebb and flow of movement in him away from and back to dependence. But this was not psychotherapy since I was working with the mother. What Edmund did was simply to display the ideas that occupied his life while his mother and I were talking together. I did not interpret and I must assume that this child would have been liable to play just like this without there being anyone there to see or to receive the communication, in which case it would perhaps have been a communication with some part of the self, the observing ego. As it happened I was there mirroring what was taking place and thus giving it a quality of communication (cf. Winnicott, 1967[b]).

Diana, Aged Five Years

In the second case, as with the case of Edmund, I had to conduct two consultations *in* parallel, one with the mother, who was in distress, and a play relationship with the daughter Diana. She had a little brother (at home) who was mentally defective and who had a congenital deformity of the heart. The mother came to discuss the effect of this brother on herself and on her daughter Diana.

My contact with the mother lasted an hour. The child was with us all the time, and my task was a threefold one: to give the mother full attention because of her own needs, to play with the child, and (for the purpose of writing this paper) to record the nature of Diana's play.

As a matter of fact it was Diana herself who took charge from the beginning, for as I opened the front door to let in the mother an eager little girl presented herself, putting forward a small teddy. I did not look at her mother or at her, but I went straight for the teddy and said: 'What's his name?' She said: 'Just Teddy.' So a strong relationship between Diana and myself had quickly developed, and I needed to keep this going in order to do my main job, which was to meet the needs of the mother. In the consulting-room Diana needed all the time, naturally, to feel that she had my attention, but it was possible for me to give the mother the attention she needed and to play with Diana too.

In describing this case, as in describing the case of Edmund, I shall give what happened between me and Diana, leaving out the material of the consultation with the mother.

When we all three got into the consulting-room we settled down, the mother sitting on the couch, Diana having a small chair to herself near the child table. Diana took her small teddy bear and stuffed it into my breast pocket. She tried to see how far it would go down, and examined the lining of my jacket, and from this she became interested in the various pockets and the way that they did not communicate with each other. This was happening while the mother and I were talking seriously about the backward child of two and a half, and Diana gave the additional information: 'He has a hole in his heart.' One could say that while playing she was listening with one ear. It seemed to me that she was able to accept her brother's physical disability due to the hole in his heart while not finding his mental backwardness within her range.

In the playing that Diana and I did together, playing without thera-peutics in it, I felt free to be playful. Children play more easily when the other person is able and free to be playful. I suddenly put my ear to the teddy bear in my pocket and I said: 'I heard him say something!' She was very interested in this. I said: 'I think he wants someone to play with', and I told her about the woolly lamb that she would find if she looked at the other end of the room in the mess of toys under the shelf. Perhaps I had an ulterior motive which was to get the bear out of my pocket. Diana went and fetched the lamb, which was considerably bigger than the bear, and she took up my idea of friendship between the teddy bear and the lamb. For some time she put the teddy and the lamb together on the couch near where the mother was sitting. I of course was continuing my interview with the mother, and it could be noted that Diana retained an interest in what we were saying, doing this with some part of herself, a part that identifies with grown-ups and grown-up attitudes.

In the play Diana decided that these two creatures were her children. She put them up under her clothes, making herself pregnant with them. After a period of pregnancy she announced they were going to be born, but they were 'not going to be twins'. She made it very evident that the lamb was to be born first and then the teddy bear. After the birth was complete she put her two newly born children together on a bed which she improvised on the floor, and she covered them up. At first she put one at one end and the other at the other end, saying that if they were together they would fight. They might 'meet in the middle of the bed under the clothes and fight'. Then she put them sleeping together peacefully, at the top of the improvised bed. She now went and fetched a lot of toys in a bucket and in some boxes. On the floor around the top end of the bed she arranged the toys and played with them; the playing was orderly and there were several different themes that developed, each kept separate from the other. I came in again with an idea of my own. I said: 'Oh look! You are putting on the floor around these babies' heads the dreams that they are having while they are asleep.' This idea intrigued her and she took it up and went on developing the various themes as if dreaming their dreams for the babies. All this was giving the mother and me time which we badly needed because of the work we were doing together. Somewhere just here the mother was crying and was very disturbed and Diana looked up for a moment prepared to be anxious. I said to her: 'Mother is crying because she is thinking of your brother who is ill.' This reassured Diana because it was direct and factual, and she said 'hole in the heart' and then continued dreaming the babies' dreams for them.

So here was Diana not coming for a consultation about herself and not being in any special need of help, playing with me and on her own, and at the same time caught up in her mother's state. I could see that the mother had needed to bring Diana, she being herself too anxious for a direct confrontation with myself because of the very deep disturbance she felt on account of having an ill boy. Later, the mother came to me by herself, no longer needing the distraction of the child.

When at a later date I saw the mother alone we were able to go over what happened when I saw her with Diana, and the mother was then able to add this important detail, that Diana's father exploits Diana's forwardness and likes her best when she is just like a little grown-up. There can be seen in the material a pull towards premature ego development, an identification with the mother and a participation in the mother's problems that arise out of the fact that the brother is actually ill and abnormal.

Looking back on what happened I find it possible to say that Diana had prepared herself before she set out to come, although the interview was not arranged for her benefit. From what the mother told me I could see that Diana was organized for the contact with me just as if she knew she was coming to a psychotherapist. Before starting out she had collected together the first of her teddy bears and also her discarded transitional object. She did not bring the latter but came prepared to organize a somewhat regressive experience in her play activities. At the same time the mother and I were witnessing Diana's ability to be identified with her mother not only in respect of the pregnancy but also in respect of taking responsibility for the management of the brother.

Here, as with Edmund, the play was of a self-healing kind. In each case the result was comparable with a psychotherapeutic session in which the story would have been punctuated by interpretations from the therapist. A psychotherapist might perhaps have refrained from actively playing with Diana, as when I said I heard the teddy say something, and when I said what I said about

Diana's children's dreams being played out on the floor. But this self-imposed discipline might have eliminated some of the creative aspect of Diana's play experience.

I choose these two examples simply because these were two consecutive cases in my practice that came one morning when I was engaged in the writing of the paper on which this chapter is based.

THEORY OF PLAY

It is possible to describe a sequence of relationships related to the developmental process and to look and see where playing belongs.

★   ★   ★

A. Baby and object are merged in with one another. Baby's view of the object is subjective and the mother is oriented towards the making actual of what the baby is ready to find.

★   ★   ★

B. The object is repudiated, re-accepted, and perceived objectively. This complex process is highly dependent on there being a mother or mother-figure prepared to participate and to give back what is handed out.

This means that the mother (or part of mother) is in a 'to and fro' between being that which the baby has a capacity to find and (alternatively) being herself waiting to be found.

If the mother can play this part over a length of time without admitting impediment (so to speak) then the baby has some *experience* of magical control, that is, experience of that which is called 'omnipotence' in the description of intrapsychic processes (cf. Winnicott, 1962[b]).

In the state of confidence that grows up when a mother can do this difficult thing well (not if she is unable to do it), the baby begins to enjoy experiences based on a 'marriage' of the omnipotence of intrapsychic processes with the baby's control of the actual. Confidence in the mother makes an intermediate playground here, where the idea of magic originates, since the baby does to some extent *experience* omnipotence. All this bears closely on Erikson's work on identity-formation (Erikson, 1956). I call this a playground because play starts here. The playground is a potential space between the mother and the baby or joining mother and baby.

Play is immensely exciting. It is exciting *not primarily because the instincts are involved*, be it understood! The thing about playing is always the precariousness of the interplay of personal psychic reality and the experience of control of actual objects. This is the precariousness of magic itself, magic that arises in intimacy, in a relationship that is being found to be reliable. To be reliable the relationship is necessarily motivated by the mother's love, or her love-hate, or her object-relating, not by reaction-formations. When a patient cannot play the therapist must attend to this major symptom before interpreting fragments of behaviour.

★   ★   ★

C. The next stage is being alone in the presence of someone. The child is now playing on the basis of the assumption that the person who loves and who is therefore reliable is available and continues to be available when remembered after being forgotten. This person is felt to reflect back what happens in the playing.[iii]

★   ★   ★

D. The child is now getting ready for the next stage, which is to allow and to enjoy an overlap of two play areas. First, surely, it is the mother who plays with the baby, but she is rather careful to fit in with the baby's play activities. Sooner or later, however, she introduces her own playing, and she finds that babies vary according to their capacity to like or dislike the introduction of ideas that are not their own.

Thus the way is paved for a playing together in a relationship.

★   ★   ★

As I look back over the papers that mark the development of my own thought and understanding I can see that my present interest in play in the relationship of trust that may develop between the baby and the mother was always a feature of my consultative technique, as the following example from my first book shows (Winnicott, 1931). And further, ten years later, I was to elaborate it in my paper 'The Observation of Infants in a Set Situation' [see Chapter 1, this volume].

Illustrative Case

A girl first attended hospital when six months old, with moderately severe infective gastro-enteritis. She was the first baby, breast-fed. She had a tendency to constipation till six months, but not after.

At seven months she was brought again because she began to lie awake, crying. She was sick after food, and did not enjoy the breast feeds. Supplementary feeds had to be given and weaning was completed in a few weeks.

At nine months she had a fit, and continued to have occasional fits, usually at 5 a.m., about a quarter of an hour after waking. The fits affected both sides and lasted five minutes.

At eleven months the fits were frequent. The mother found she could prevent individual fits by distracting the child's attention. In one day she had to do this four times. The child had become nervy, jumping at the least sound. She had one fit in her sleep. In some of the fits she bit her tongue, and in some she was incontinent of urine.

At one year she was having four to five a day. It was noticed she would sometimes sit down after a feed, double up, and go off. She was given orange juice, then went off. She was put to sit on the floor, and a fit started. One morning she woke and immediately had a fit, then slept; soon she woke again and had another fit. At this time the fits began to be followed by a desire to sleep, but even at this severe stage the mother could often stop a fit in the early stage by distracting the child's attention. I made at the time this note:

> 'Taken on my knees she cries incessantly, but does not show hostility. She pulls my tie about in a careless way as she cries. Given back to her mother she shows no interest in the change and continues to cry, crying more and more pitifully right on through being dressed, and so till carried out of the building.'

At this time I witnessed a fit, which was marked by tonic and clonic stages and followed by sleep. The child was having four to five a day, and was crying all day, though sleeping at night.

Careful examinations revealed no sign of physical disease. Bromide was given in the day, according to need.

At one consultation I had the child on my knee observing her. She made a furtive attempt to bite my knuckle. Three days later I had her again on my knee, and waited to see what she would do. She bit my knuckle three times so severely that the skin was nearly torn. She then played at throwing spatulas on the floor incessantly for fifteen minutes. All the time she cried as if really unhappy. Two days later I had her on my knee for half an hour. She had had four convulsions in the previous two days. At first she cried as usual. She again bit my knuckle very severely, this time without showing guilt feelings, and then played the game of biting and throwing away spatulas; *while on my knee she became able to enjoy play.* After a while she began to finger her toes, and so I had her shoes and socks removed. The result of this was a period of experimentation which absorbed her whole interest. It looked as if she was discovering and proving over and over again, to her great satisfaction, that whereas spatulas can be put to the mouth, thrown away and lost, toes cannot be pulled off.

Four days later the mother came and said that since the last consultation the baby had been 'a different child'. She had not only had no fits, but had been sleeping well at night – happy all day, taking no bromide. Eleven days later the improvement had been maintained, without medicine; there had been no fits for fourteen days, and the mother asked to be discharged.

I visited this child one year later and found that since the last consultation she had had no symptom whatever. I found an entirely healthy, happy, intelligent and friendly child, fond of play, and free from the common anxieties.

PSYCHOTHERAPY

Here in this area of overlap between the playing of the child and the playing of the other person there is a chance to introduce enrichments. The teacher aims at enrichment. By contrast, the therapist is concerned specifically with the child's own growth processes, and with the removal of blocks to development that may have become evident. It is psychoanalytic theory that has made for an understanding of these blocks. At the same time it would be a narrow view to suppose that psychoanalysis is the only way to make therapeutic use of the child's playing.

It is good to remember always that playing is itself a therapy. To arrange for children to be able to play is itself a psychotherapy that has immediate and universal application, and it includes the establishment of a positive social attitude towards playing. This attitude must include recognition that playing is always liable to become frightening. Games and their organization must be looked at as part of an attempt to forestall the frightening aspect of playing. Responsible persons must be available when children play; but this does not mean that the responsible person need enter into the children's playing. When an organizer must be involved in a managerial position then the implication is that the child or the children are unable to play in the creative sense of my meaning in this communication.

The essential feature of my communication is this, that playing is an experience, always a creative experience, and it is an experience in the space-time continuum, a basic form of living.

The precariousness of play belongs to the fact that it is always on the theoretical line between the subjective and that which is objectively perceived.

It is my purpose here simply to give a reminder that children's playing has everything in it, although the psychotherapist works on the material, the content of playing. Naturally, in a set or professional hour a more precise constellation presents than would present in a timeless experience on the floor at home [see Chapter 1, this volume]; but it helps us to understand our work if we know that the basis of what we do is the patient's playing, a creative experience taking up space and time, and intensely real for the patient.

Also, this observation helps us to understand how it is that psychotherapy of a deep-going kind may be done without interpretative work. A good example of this is the work of Axline (1947) of New York. Her work on psychotherapy is of great importance to us. I appreciate Axline's work in a special way because it joins up with the point that I make in reporting what I call 'therapeutic consultations', that the significant moment is that at which *the child surprises himself or herself*. It is not the moment of my clever interpretation that is significant (Winnicott, 1971[b]).

Interpretation outside the ripeness of the material is indoctrination and produces compliance (Winnicott, 1960[a]). A corollary is that resistance arises out of interpretation given outside the area of the overlap of the patient's and the analyst's playing together. Interpretation when the patient has no capacity to play is simply not useful, or causes confusion. When there is mutual playing, then interpretation according to accepted psychoanalytic principles can carry the therapeutic work forward. *This playing has to be spontaneous, and not compliant or acquiescent*, if psychotherapy is to be done.

SUMMARY

(*a*) To get to the idea of playing it is helpful to think of the *preoccupation* that characterizes the playing of a young child. The content does not matter. What matters is the near-withdrawal state, akin to the *concentration* of older children and adults. The playing child inhabits an area that cannot be easily left, nor can it easily admit intrusions.

★   ★   ★

(*b*) This area of playing is not inner psychic reality. It is outside the individual, but it is not the external world.

★   ★   ★

(*c*) Into this play area the child gathers objects or phenomena from external reality and uses these in the service of some sample derived from inner or personal reality. Without hallucinating the child puts out a sample of dream potential and lives with this sample in a chosen setting of fragments from external reality.

★   ★   ★

(*d*) In playing, the child manipulates external phenomena in the service of the dream and invests chosen external phenomena with dream meaning and feeling.

★   ★   ★

(*e*) There is a direct development from transitional phenomena to playing, and from playing to shared playing, and from this to cultural experiences.

★   ★   ★

(*f*) Playing implies trust, and belongs to the potential space between (what was at first) baby and mother-figure, with the baby in a state of near-absolute dependence, and the mother-figure's adaptive function taken for granted by the baby.

★   ★   ★

(*g*) Playing involves the body:

  (i) because of the manipulation of objects;
  (ii) because certain types of intense interest are associated with certain aspects of bodily excitement.

★   ★   ★

(*h*) Bodily excitement in erotogenic zones constantly threatens playing, and therefore threatens the child's sense of existing as a person. The instincts are the main threat to play as to the ego; in seduction some external agency exploits the child's instincts and helps to annihilate the child's sense of existing as an autonomous unit, making playing impossible (cf. Khan, 1964).

★   ★   ★

(*i*) *Playing is essentially satisfying.* This is true even when it leads to a high degree of anxiety. There is a degree of anxiety that is unbearable and this destroys playing.

★   ★   ★

(*j*) The pleasurable element in playing carries with it the implication that the instinctual arousal is not excessive; instinctual arousal beyond a certain point must lead to:

  (i)   climax;
  (ii) failed climax and a sense of mental confusion and physical discomfort that only time can mend;
  (iii) alternative climax (as in provocation of parental or social reaction, anger, etc.).

Playing can be said to reach its own saturation point, which refers to the capacity to contain experience.

★   ★   ★

(*k*) Playing is inherently exciting and precarious. This characteristic derives *not* from instinctual arousal but from the precariousness that belongs to the interplay in the child's mind of that which is subjective (near-hallucination) and that which is objectively perceived (actual, or shared reality).

Notes

i. For further discussion of this the reader may consult my papers 'Ego Integration in Child Development' (1962[b]) and 'Communicating and Not Communicating leading to a Study of Certain Opposites' [Chapter 9, this volume].
ii. Miller (1963): This story does eventually tail off into a sentimental ending, and therefore, as it seems to me, abandons the direct link with childhood observation.
iii. I have discussed a more sophisticated aspect of these experiences in my paper 'The Capacity to be Alone' [1958d].

13 THE USE OF AN OBJECT AND RELATING THROUGH IDENTIFICATIONS (1968)

EDITORS' INTRODUCTION

This paper was given at a meeting of the New York Psychoanalytic Society in November 1968. Its unsympathetic reception there was probably related to its roots in British object relations theory, at that time something of a 'foreign language' to American psychoanalysts. A revised version was published in the *IJPA* in 1969 and subsequently as Chapter 6 of *Playing and Reality*. In 1989, together with a number of previously unseen notes about the paper, the Winnicott Trust published the clinical material that had been given in New York *Psychoanalytic Explorations* (Winnicott *et al.*, 1989). A short discussion of Freud's *Moses and Monotheism* and its relationship to Winnicott's thesis (Winnicott, 1969/1989) was also included.

This paper contains Winnicott's most mature views about psychic development, the evolution of the human subject and the role of the (m)other (and subsequently the father); about the nature and function of aggression and destructiveness; about psychoanalytic technique and the aims of psychoanalysis itself. Many commentators (Eigen, 1993; Goldman, 1998; Phillips, 1988; Rappaport, 1998) have seen this paper as one of his most important contributions to psychoanalysis, but others, though sympathetic, see Winnicott as overreaching himself rather as Freud did in his search for a general theory of human psychology (Reeves, 2007).

The paper's central concern is with how the infant comes to know external reality and becomes able to benefit from it. Winnicott describes this as the capacity to 'use' it. From the paradoxical unity in early life of the 'environment–individual set-up' (Winnicott, 1952a: 99), the infant's own developmental achievement consists in emerging as a separate entity, capable of 'finding' a world and others outside himself. Winnicott's radical conceptualization of the processes involved emphasizes that this step, which relies on a two-person (mother and infant) view, cannot be taken for granted. In his account of Freud's *Moses and Monotheism*, the father is introduced as the essential third in the baby's establishing a sense of self: '. . . here I suggest that the baby is likely to make use of the father as a blue-print for his or her own integration when just becoming at times a unit' (Winnicott, 1969: 243).

The central problem is that of the individual coming to experience reality in a non projective way, to be himself in a world of experiencing others. The period of the 'subjective object' is that of primary creativity, of the illusion of omnipotence, in Winnicott's idiosyncratic use, of 'object-relating'. 'Object-relating' would usually suggest a person's differentiation and separateness from the object, but Winnicott subverts this by making the term refer to a prior stage, where the object exists only as a 'bundle of projections' (p. 254). Scarfone (2005) discusses the confusing double use of the term 'projection' in Winnicott's initial suggestion of an awareness, albeit primitive, of separateness. Projection in the era of the subjective object refers to 'the indistinctness between the emotion and the object', where the experience of the object resides in the infant's sense of the emotion felt 'within the subject–object compound' and where 'relating really means "being in a given emotional state"' with the object (Scarfone, 2005: 40). It is only later, in the differentiated stage, the 'I' stage, a stage that follows object-relating, that the more conventional use of projection as getting rid of something unwanted into the other becomes applicable. Winnicott himself says, these 'two ideas are by no means identical. It is exactly here that we direct our study' (p. 256).

Scarfone's commentary also clarifies the nature of 'identifications' as they appear in the second half of the title. In the state of 'object-relating' the infant is not differentiated from the object and the experience is of identification/being merged-in-with/sameness. The object is not an other into whom qualities are put, but represents the quality of emotion that the infant experiences, for instance pleasure or pain, in the non-differentiated state. The concept of projective identification refers to a later stage.

The 'use of the object' stage occurs when the sense of 'I' emerges from the stage of non-differentiation. It is an achievement predicated upon the environmental provision that remains available through the young child's development. Some commentators (Rappaport, 1998; Rayner, 1986) have stressed the dawning recognition in the infant of the dependency involved in separateness that creates the aggression in this process. But in fact in Winnicott's account this belongs to a later stage when anger and hate can be said to be experienced. The destructiveness of this point in development is seen as potential and dependent upon the response of the mother. It is her propensity to retaliate that is the danger. The actual role of the external object is vital to this process of 'being found instead of placed by the subject in the world' (p. 259). The 'I' of the infant subject is constituted through the same set of processes as is the subjectivity of the object. Perhaps one of the confusions in the paper is in Winnicott's use of the term 'object', classically used to denote the internal object whereas he is also describing the 'other' of the mother in external reality whose role is to survive. Ogden (1992: 621) points out that it is here that the mother as separate and existing in her own right is fully confronted by the infant for the first time and, as a result, he can be concerned about her. This is critically different from Melanie Klein's concept of reparation in which the infant *internally* restores the mother whom he feels he has damaged.

'The Use of an Object in the Context of *Moses and Monotheism*' (Winnicott, 1969) proposes that the father is first apprehended and recognized by the infant as an integrated whole, in contrast to the mother, who, in the baby's mind and experience, is first created and then found to be 'other'. The actual presence of the father, together with his role as a structuring figure in the mother's mind, is ascribed a central function in the baby's move from experiencing the object subjectively to perceiving it objectively: 'there is a great deal too to be taken into account that has to do with the imago of the father in the mother's inner reality and its fate there' (Winnicott, 1969: 242). 'Thirdness' alludes to the Oedipal situation as a future development, but its significance is as an outcome of the move from subjective to objective objects. It emphasizes the significance of how the real mother actually behaves with her child and the presence or otherwise of the real father, but it also includes the mother's mental experiences of 'the father' and their roots in her experiences of her own father and that of the baby. For Winnicott the infant's sense of 'thirdness' is not collapsed into the early Oedipus complex, which is a substantive difference from Klein's view.

The assertion that the otherness of the object, the recognition of external reality, is created out of the infant's (subject's) destroying it is among Winnicott's most challenging paradoxes. By making the child's destructiveness the agent of transformation rather than its outcome he inverts the usual version of how reality is apprehended (p. 256). The destruction involved is that of the (internal) object as the omnipotent creation of the infant. Scarfone (2005) describes this as the object being unbound from the bundle of projections, while Ogden refers to the infant destroying a part of himself as 'his own omnipotence as projected on to the omnipotent internal object' (Ogden, 1992: 622). For Winnicott this 'destruction' is not anger or hate, contrasting with Klein's view that love and hate are there from the beginning and it is only 'the aggressive reaction to the encounter with the reality principle' that leads painfully to the appreciation of external reality and therefore to separateness.

The survival capacity of the mother allows the infant to find her in the world after first having omnipotently created her there. The mother's non-retaliatory presence enables the baby to discover the limits of his omnipotence and hence the beginnings of his sense of 'I' and 'you'. In discovering the otherness of the (m)other, the child is able to find her of use and interest in her own right. The world as other becomes a resource of possibilities to be used. This could include being able to use the (m)other projectively in the more conventional sense.

This evolution in the infant's capacity for self-reflection in the intersubjective realm has internal consequences. Winnicott proposes that the infant, and later the adult, goes on continually 'destroying' the subjective object in unconscious fantasy, and that both repression and the beginning of unconscious conflict profoundly enrich the internal life of the developing individual.

These ideas have immense consequences for psychoanalytic technique and the aims of psychoanalysis. With a patient who is unable to engage in external reality 'objectively', the task of the analyst becomes one of surviving repetition in the transference of the original failure situation where this developmental stage was not accomplished: 'We now find all these matters coming along for revival and correction in the transference relationship, matters which are not so much for interpretation as for experiencing' (Winnicott, 1969: 242). Through this repetition in this new situation of analysis, the patient moves from the era of the subjective object to placing/finding the analyst in the external world, and the analyst can come to be experienced as the source of something other, not created out of the individual's illusion of omnipotence (see Chapter 2).

Winnicott also talks about 'the *making* of interpretations and not about interpretations as such' (p. 253, emphasis added). This characteristically quixotic statement could mean that interpretation be limited to trying to understand the patient's experience of the analyst's technique and of the setting itself. That is, interpretation reminds the patient that the analyst's mind is functioning to hold and manage the patient's destructive attacks (David Riley, personal communication). And what model of the mind/development informs the analyst's thinking is less important than the fundamental fact of his or her survival. The analysis of a neurotic analysand, by contrast, would range around the tensions between the externalization in the transference of their subjective objects and the capacity to perceive the differentiated separateness of the analyst in their otherness. The analyst can be used and experienced by the patient as having something of their own to contribute to the analytic couple. The analyst is not a solipsistic creation of the analysand.

The Use of an Object and Relating through Identifications[1]
(1969)

In this chapter I propose to put forward for discussion the idea of the use of an object. The allied subject of relating to objects seems to me to have had our full attention. The idea of the use of an object has not, however, been so much examined, and it may not even have been specifically studied.

This work on the use of an object arises out of my clinical experience and is in the direct line of development that is peculiarly mine. I cannot assume, of course, that the way in which my ideas have developed has been followed by others, but I should like to point out that there has been a sequence, and the order that there may be in the sequence belongs to the evolution of my work.

What I have to say in this present chapter is extremely simple. Although it comes out of my psychoanalytical experience I would not say that it could have come out of my psychoanalytical experience of two decades ago, because I would not then have had the technique to make possible the transference movements that I wish to describe. For instance, it is only in recent years that I have become able to wait and wait for the natural evolution of the transference arising out of the patient's growing trust in the psychoanalytic technique and setting, and to avoid breaking up this natural process by making interpretations. It will be noticed that I am talking about the making of interpretations and not about interpretations as such. It appals me to think how much deep change I have prevented or delayed in patients *in a certain classification category* by my personal need to interpret. If only we can wait, the patient arrives at understanding creatively and with immense joy, and I now enjoy this joy more than I used to enjoy the sense of having been clever. I think I interpret mainly to let the patient know the limits of my understanding. The principle is that it is the patient and only the patient who has the answers. We may or may not enable him or her to encompass what is known or become aware of it with acceptance.

By contrast with this comes the interpretative work that the analyst must do, which distinguishes analysis from self-analysis. This interpreting by the analyst, if it is to have effect, must be related to the patient's ability *to place the analyst outside the area of subjective phenomena*. What is then involved is the patient's ability to use the analyst, which is the subject of this paper. In teaching, as in the feeding of a child, the capacity to use objects is taken for granted, but in our work it is necessary for us to be concerned with the development and establishment of the capacity to use objects and to recognize a patient's inability to use objects, where this is a fact.

It is in the analysis of the borderline type of case that one has the chance to observe the delicate phenomena that give pointers to an understanding of truly schizophrenic states. By the term 'a borderline case' I mean the kind of case in which the core of the patient's disturbance is psychotic, but the patient has enough psychoneurotic organization always to be able to present psycho-neurosis or psychosomatic disorder when the central psychotic anxiety threatens to break through in crude form. In such cases the psychoanalyst may collude for years with the patient's need to be psychoneurotic (as opposed to mad) and to be treated as psychoneurotic. The analysis goes well, and everyone is pleased. The only drawback is that the analysis never ends. It can be ter-minated, and the patient may even mobilize a psychoneurotic false self for the purpose of finishing and expressing gratitude. But, in fact, the patient knows that there has been no change in the underlying (psychotic) state and that the analyst and the patient have succeeded in colluding to bring about a failure. Even this failure may have value if both analyst and patient acknowledge the failure. The patient is older and the opportunities for death by accident or disease have increased, so that actual suicide *may* be avoided. Moreover, it has been fun while it lasted. If psychoanalysis could be a way of life, then such a treatment might be said to have done what it was supposed to do. But psycho-analysis is no way of life. We all hope that our patients will finish with us and forget us, and that they will find living itself to be the therapy that makes sense. Although we write papers about these borderline cases we are inwardly troubled when the madness that is there remains undiscovered and unmet. I have tried to state this in a broader way in a paper on classification (Winnicott, 1959a).

It is perhaps necessary to prevaricate a little longer to give my own view on the difference between object-relating and object-usage. In object-relating the subject allows certain alterations in the self to take place, of a kind that has caused us to invent the term cathexis. The object has become meaningful. Projection mechanisms and identifications have been operating, and the subject is depleted to the extent that something of the subject is found in the object, though enriched by feeling. Accompanying these changes is some degree of physical involvement (however slight) towards excitement, in the direction of the functional climax of an orgasm. (In this context I deliberately omit reference to the aspect of relating that is an exercise in cross-identifications. This must be omitted here because it belongs to a phase of development that is subsequent to and not prior to the phase of development with which I am concerned in this paper, that is to say, the move away from self-containment and relating to subjective objects into the realm of object-usage.)

Object-relating is an experience of the subject that can be described in terms of the subject as an isolate ([see Chapter 9, this volume] and Winnicott, 1958[b]). When I speak of the use of an object, however, I take object-relating for granted, and add new features that involve the nature and the behaviour of the object. For instance, the object, if it is to be used, must necessarily be real in the sense of being part of shared reality, not a bundle of projections. It is this, I think, that makes for the world of difference that there is between relating and usage.

If I am right in this, then it follows that discussion of the subject of relating is a much easier exercise for analysts than is the discussion of usage, since relating may be examined as a phenomenon of the subject, and psychoanalysis always likes to be able to eliminate all factors that are environmental, except in so far as the environment can be thought of in terms of projective mechanisms. But in examining usage there is no escape: the analyst must take into account the nature of the object, not as a projection, but as a thing in itself.

For the time being may I leave it at that, that relating can be described in terms of the individual subject, and that usage cannot be described except in terms of acceptance of the object's independent existence, its property of having been there all the time. You will see that it is just these problems that concern us when we look at the area that I have tried to draw attention to in my work on what I have called transitional phenomena.

But this change does not come about automatically, by maturational process alone. It is this detail that I am concerned with.

In clinical terms: two babies are feeding at the breast. One is feeding on the self, since the breast and the baby have not yet become (for the baby) separate phenomena. The other is feeding from an other-than-me source, or an object that can be given cavalier treatment without effect on the baby unless it retaliates. Mothers, like analysts, can be good or not good enough; some can and some cannot carry the baby over from relating to usage.

I should like to put in a reminder here that the essential feature in the concept of transitional objects and phenomena (according to my presentation of the subject) is *the paradox, and the acceptance of the paradox*: the baby creates the object, but the object was there waiting to be created and to become a cathected object. I tried to draw attention to this aspect of transitional phenomena by claiming that in the rules of the game we all know that we will never challenge the baby to elicit an answer to the question: did you create that or did you find it?

I am now ready to go straight to the statement of my thesis. It seems I am afraid to get there, as if I fear that once the thesis is stated the purpose of my communication is at an end, because it is so very simple.

To use an object the subject must have developed a *capacity* to use objects. This is part of the change to the reality principle.

This capacity cannot be said to be inborn, nor can its development in an individual be taken for granted. The development of a capacity to use an object is another example of the maturational process as something that depends on a facilitating environment.[2]

In the sequence one can say that first there is object-relating, then in the end there is object-use; in between, however, is the most difficult thing, perhaps, in human development; or the most irksome of all the early failures that come for mending. This thing that there is in between relating and use is the subject's placing of the object outside the area of the subject's omnipotent control; that is, the subject's perception of the object as an external phenomenon, not as a projective entity, in fact recognition of it as an entity in its own right.[3]

This change (from relating to usage) means that the subject destroys the object. From here it could be argued by an armchair philosopher that there is therefore no such thing in practice as the use of an object: if the object is external, then the object is destroyed by the subject. Should the philosopher come out of his chair and sit on the floor with his patient, however, he will find that there is an intermediate position. In other words, he will find that after 'subject relates to object' comes 'subject destroys object' (as it becomes external); and then may come '*object survives* destruction by the subject'. But there may or may not be survival. A new feature thus arrives in the theory of object-relating. The subject says to the object: 'I destroyed you', and the object is there to receive the communication. From now on the subject says: 'Hullo object!' 'I destroyed you.' 'I love you.' 'You have value for me because of your survival of my destruction of you.' 'While I am loving you I am all the time destroying you in (unconscious) *fantasy*.' Here fantasy begins for the individual. The subject can now *use* the object that has survived. It is important to note that it is not only that the subject destroys the object because the object is placed outside the area of omnipotent control. It is equally significant to state this the other way round and to say that it is the destruction of the object that places the object outside the area of the subject's omnipotent control. In these ways the object develops its own autonomy and life, and (if it survives) contributes-in to the subject, according to its own properties.

In other words, because of the survival of the object, the subject may now have started to live a life in the world of objects, and so the subject stands to gain immeasurably; but the price has to be paid in acceptance of the ongoing destruction in unconscious fantasy relative to object-relating.

Let me repeat. This is a position that can be arrived at by the individual in early stages of emotional growth only through the actual survival of cathected objects that are at the time in process of becoming destroyed because real, becoming real because destroyed (being destructible and expendable).

From now on, this stage having been reached, projective mechanisms assist in the act of *noticing what is there*, but they are not *the reason why the object is there*. In my opinion this is a departure from theory which tends to a conception of external reality only in terms of the individual's projective mechanisms.

I have now nearly made my whole statement. Not quite, however, because it is not possible for me to take for granted an acceptance of the fact that the first impulse in the subject's relation to the object (objectively perceived, not subjective) is destructive. (Earlier I used the word cavalier, in an attempt to give the reader a chance to imagine something at that point without too clearly pointing the way.)

The central postulate in this thesis is that, whereas the subject does not destroy the subjective object (projection material), destruction turns up and becomes a central feature so far as the object is objectively perceived, has autonomy, and belongs to 'shared' reality. This is the difficult part of my thesis, at least for me.

It is generally understood that the reality principle involves the individual in anger and reactive destruction, but my thesis is that the destruction plays its part in making the reality, placing the object outside the self. For this to happen, favourable conditions are necessary.

This is simply a matter of examining the reality principle under high power. As I see it, we are familiar with the change whereby projection mechanisms enable the subject to take cognizance of the object. This is not the same as claiming that the object exists for the subject because of the operation of the subject's projection mechanisms. At first the observer uses words that seem to apply to both ideas at one and the same time, but under scrutiny we see that the two ideas are by no means identical. It is exactly here that we direct our study.

At the point of development that is under survey the subject is creating the object in the sense of finding externality itself, and it has to be added that this experience depends on the object's capacity to survive. (It is important that 'survive', in this context, means 'not retaliate'.) If it is in an analysis that these matters are taking place, then the analyst, the analytic technique, and the analytic setting all come in as surviving or not surviving the patient's destructive attacks. This destructive activity is the patient's attempt to place the analyst outside the area of omnipotent control, that is, out in the world. Without the experience of maximum destructiveness (object not protected) the subject never places the analyst outside and therefore can never do more than experience a kind of self-analysis, using the analyst as a projection of a part of the self. In terms of feeding, the patient, then, can feed only on the self and cannot use the breast for getting fat. The patient may even enjoy the analytic experience but will not fundamentally change.

And if the analyst is a subjective phenomenon, what about waste-disposal? A further statement is needed in terms of output.[4]

In psychoanalytic practice the positive changes that come about in this area can be profound. They do not depend on interpretative work. They depend on the analyst's survival of the attacks, which involves and includes the idea of the absence of a quality change to retaliation. These attacks may be very difficult for the analyst to stand,[5] especially when they are expressed in terms of delusion, or through manipulation which makes the analyst actually do things that are technically bad. (I refer to such a thing as being unreliable at moments when reliability is all that matters, as well as to survival in terms of keeping alive and of absence of the quality of retaliation.)

The analyst feels like interpreting, but this can spoil the process, and for the patient can seem like a kind of self-defence, the analyst parrying the patient's attack. Better to wait till after the phase is over, and then discuss with the patient what has been happening. This is surely legitimate, for as analyst one has one's own needs; but verbal interpretation at this point is not the essential feature and brings its own dangers. The essential feature is the analyst's survival and the intactness of the psychoanalytic technique. Imagine how traumatic can be the actual death of the analyst when this kind of work is in process, although even the actual death of the analyst is not as bad as the development in the analyst of a change of attitude towards retaliation. These are risks that simply must be taken by the patient. Usually the analyst lives through these phases of movement in the transference, and after each phase there comes reward in terms of love, reinforced by the fact of the backcloth of unconscious destruction.

It appears to me that the idea of a developmental phase essentially involving survival of object does affect the theory of the roots of aggression. It is no good saying that a baby of a few days old envies the breast. It is legitimate, however, to say that at whatever age a baby begins to allow the breast an external position (outside the area of projection), then this means that destruction of the breast has become a feature. I mean the actual impulse to destroy. It is an important part of what a mother does, to be the first person to take the baby through this first version of the many that will be encountered, of attack that is survived. This is the right moment in the child's development, because of the child's relative feebleness, so that destruction can fairly easily be survived. However, even so it is a tricky matter; it is only too easy for a mother to react moralistically when her baby bites and hurts.[6] But this language involving 'the breast' is jargon. The whole area of development and management is involved, in which adaptation is related to dependence.

It will be seen that, although destruction is the word I am using, this actual destruction belongs to the object's failure to survive. Without this failure, destruction remains potential. The word 'destruction' is needed, not because of the baby's impulse to destroy, but because of the object's liability not to survive, which also means to suffer change in quality, in attitude.

The way of looking at things that belongs to my presentation of this chapter makes possible a new approach to the whole subject of the roots of aggression. For instance, it is not necessary to give inborn aggression more than that which is its due in company with everything else that is inborn. Undoubtedly inborn aggression must be variable in a quantitative sense in the same way that every- thing else that is inherited is variable as between individuals. By contrast, the variations are great that arise out of the differences in the experiences of various newborn babies according to whether they are or are not carried through this very difficult phase. Such variations in the field of experience are indeed immense. Moreover, the babies that have been seen through this phase well are likely to be more aggressive *clinically* than the ones who have not been seen through the phase well, and for whom aggression is something that cannot be encompassed, or something that can be retained only in the form of a liability to be an object of attack.

This involves a rewriting of the theory of the roots of aggression since most of that which has already been written by analysts has been formulated with- out reference to that which is being discussed in this chapter. The assumption is always there, in orthodox theory, that aggression is reactive to the encounter with the reality principle, whereas here it is the destructive drive that creates the quality of externality. This is central in the structure of my argument.

Let me look for a moment at the exact place of this attack and survival in the hierarchy of relationships. More primitive and quite different is annihilation. Annihilation means 'no hope'; cathexis withers up because no result completes the reflex to produce conditioning. On the other hand, attack in anger relative to the encounter with the reality principle is a more sophisticated concept, postdating the destruction that I postulate here. *There is no anger* in the destruc- tion of the object to which I am referring, though there could be said to be joy at the object's survival. From this moment, or arising out of this phase, the object is *in fantasy* always being destroyed. This quality of 'always being destroyed' makes the reality of the surviving object felt as such, strengthens the feeling tone, and contributes to object-constancy. The object can now be used.

I wish to conclude with a note on using and usage. By 'use' I do not mean 'exploitation'. As analysts, we know what it is like to be used, which means that we can see the end of the treatment, be it several years away. Many of our patients come with this problem already solved – they can use objects and they can use us and can use analysis, just as they have used their parents and their siblings and their homes. However, there are many patients who need us to be able to give them a capacity to use us. This for them is the analytic task. In meeting the needs of such patients, we shall need to know what I am saying here about our survival of their destructiveness. A backcloth of unconscious destruction of the analyst is set up and we survive it or, alternatively, here is yet another analysis interminable.

SUMMARY

Object-relating can be described in terms of the experience of the subject. Description of object-usage involves consideration of the nature of the object. I am offering for discussion the reasons why, in my opinion, a capacity to use an object is more sophisticated than a capacity to relate to objects; and relating may be to a subjective object, but usage implies that the object is part of external reality.

This sequence can be observed: (1) Subject *relates* to object. (2) Object is in process of being found instead of placed by the subject in the world. (3) Subject *destroys* object. (4) Object survives destruction. (5) Subject can *use* object.

The object is always being destroyed. This destruction becomes the unconscious backcloth for love of a real object; that is, an object outside the area of the subject's omnipotent control.

Study of this problem involves a statement of the positive value of destructiveness. The destructiveness, plus the object's survival of the destruction, places the object outside the area of objects set up by the subject's projective mental mechanisms. In this way a world of shared reality is created which the subject can use and which can feed back other-than-me substance into the subject.

Notes

1. Based on a paper read to the New York Psychoanalytic Society, 12 November 1968, and published in the *International Journal of Psycho-Analysis*, Vol. 50 (1969).
2. In choosing *The Maturational Processes and the Facilitating Environment* as the title of my book in the International Psycho-Analytical Library (1965), I was showing how much I was influenced by Dr Phyllis Greenacre (1960) at the Edinburgh Congress. Unfortunately, I failed to put into the book an acknowledgement of this fact.

3. I was influenced in my understanding of this point by W. Clifford M. Scott (personal communication, c. 1940).
4. The next task for a worker in the field of transitional phenomena is to restate the problem in terms of disposal.
5. When the analyst knows that the patient carries a revolver, then, it seems to me, this work cannot be done.
6. In fact, the baby's development is immensely complicated if he or she should happen to be born with a tooth, so that the gum's attack on the breast can never be tried out.

14 CREATIVITY AND ITS ORIGINS (1971)

EDITORS' INTRODUCTION

This paper, Chapter 5 of *Playing and Reality*, contains a summation of Winnicott's whole approach to psychoanalysis and to life and includes an example of a consummate clinician at work. His interest is in the creative impulse, in the creative apperception of life, and in the possibility of living creatively. Creativity, described as living fully and well, is linked with experience, with the importance of being able to live the life one has, and to be oneself. The discussion is approached from the baby's earliest encounters with the environment at the point of maximum dependence because either these encounters make possible a particular way of living and viewing the world or they impede it. Winnicott terms this encountering 'creative', but it could also be described as involved and aware. In this context it makes no sense to speak of the individual in isolation; from the beginning, what is fundamental is always the individual in relation with others, even when that individual/the baby, is not yet conscious of others as other.

Winnicott insists upon the difference between a creation and the process of creating it, between art and the idea of creation more generally, and he makes the case for the origins of both in the earliest encounters with the environment, when environment and mother are the same. The processes experienced then make possible a particular way of living and viewing the world. He contrasts healthy living and compliance, again proposes an approach to aggression that releases it from its links with anger and hate, and makes transitional phenomena the basis of the creative impulse as a universal capacity. The paper discusses the creative impulse itself, and what it means to live creatively. It invites comparison with Schiller's description of the aesthetic impulse as an impulse to play (*spieltrieb*) (1954). Much psychoanalytic work about art has foundered on its concern with describing the artistic product in terms of the management of internal anxiety, but Winnicott moves away from this although he does not develop any detailed account of the specific creativity of the artist.

The central section introduces a new area in Winnicott's work. It tackles the differences and similarities between men and women in terms of what precedes sexual difference. It was first given to the BPAS in February 1966 as a paper entitled 'The Split-Off Male and Female Elements', with the anthropologist Margaret Mead as discussant. It is reproduced in *Psychoanalytic Explorations* in an extended form with the addition of further clinical material and a series of comments from others (Winnicott *et al.*, 1989).

Winnicott makes three apparently contradictory claims about creativity: that it is universal, that it is a prerogative of women, and that it is a masculine feature. The first, the most general in its claims about the person and the self and in what it regards as the ultimate aims of psychoanalysis, is consistent with the general trajectory of his work. The second and third claims are the results of his thinking about, and decision to interpret, an incident with a patient in a long analysis, in terms of the early (maternal) environment, as Winnicott had experienced it in a session. The section builds upon earlier references to being and doing in his work but here they are linked with 'male' and 'female'. In the session discussed he had found himself hearing the male patient on the couch as a girl with penis envy; he had then gone further by locating the madness this seemed to indicate in himself in the transference, and interpreting on this basis to the patient. The material was neither new nor unfamiliar in the analysis, but *in that session* it had produced something new, which led to his discussion of male and female elements. The material was received unsympathetically and confusedly by his colleagues, with the exception of Mead herself, perhaps because the terms themselves – male/female, masculine/feminine – can lend themselves to confusion.

The discussion here extends beyond the parameters of creativity, play and transitionality to offer a set of statements linking creativity with both being and doing, but depending on being. It returns Winnicott to the conditions necessary for the attainment of unit status and the acceptance of separateness, with its consequent loss of omnipotence. In turn, this links with his approach to play as not primarily concerned with the instincts. It locates both creativity and what he is calling male and female elements in the earliest stages of life, the process of separation from the environment that establishes the bases for the self and the acquisition of gender. Winnicott himself was concerned with the central role of the mother as the environment upon which both developments depend. The female element is described as a state deriving from a primary identification with the breast, mother, environment. Following Freud, the male element, doing, is associated with activity and with the drives.

If the paper initially seems to address the arenas of difference between men and women, it actually concentrates on what is shared between them at the start, when the sexual divide evident to the world on the basis of genitalia is irrelevant for the baby. The confusions in this area arising from the variety of words relating to basic species division are perhaps contributed to by Winnicott's own terms, 'male and female elements' and their association (or not) with men and women, and 'masculine' and 'feminine'. The discussants at the paper's original reading fell into these areas of difficulty, conflating the sets of terms (this paper; Winnicott, 1971a).

But Winnicott's own thinking had originated in the clinical material he reports, where he assumed the position of the mad mother in the transference. From this realization he again identifies the environment mother and her centrality in the acquisition of identity through the acquisition of a self. Sexual difference belongs to a later moment. As a clinician, Winnicott was involved in listening and hearing in a particular way, and on this occasion he identified a dimension in himself through what he heard that assisted in understanding the patient's pathology in terms of his mother's desire for a girl.

Psychoanalysis generally emphasizes the body's significance for the psyche; the body is to be understood in relation to both conscious and unconscious experience, and since the body is always libidinally invested the experience of it is always mediated by unconscious and conscious perceptions. For the Winnicottian infant, body and world are undifferentiated at the start, and initial body image and awareness, when it first develops, is not *gendered*. But bodies are always *sexed*, in that the social ascription of a sex based on observation of bodily attributes precedes the baby's inhabiting of either gender (Mitchell, 2006). Winnicott links the idea of being with the kinds of bodily and emotional care that are increasingly understood, not least because of his work, as fundamental to health. In this discussion he emphasizes what he calls a 'dissociation' between male and female elements that was produced by the mother's pathology and contributed to this patient's continuing dissatisfaction. It is his different handling of 'the non-masculine element' in the transference that is new.

Clinically, the split-off dissociated part, whether male or female, tends to remain at a certain age – his words, 'man' and 'girl', make this clear. And for the analyst, there is always the issue of who, or which element/part, is being analyzed, that is, which elements are being presented at any one time, and why. He also raises the implications for object-relating. The male bit of the man (but it could equally be a woman), does both active relating and passive being related to; there is instinct in both, the drive, for Winnicott as for Freud, always being masculine/active.

In the case described, he proposes that the pure *female* element found *primary unity with him as the analyst*, and it was this which gave the patient the feeling of having started to live. He had found the basis for 'being', because the pure female element is related to the breast. At this stage baby and breast are synonymous, for Winnicott the condition on which the emergence of the self that must live in a world of sexual difference depends. The 'female element' involves a different, earlier conception of the relation with the object, an object-relating that is part of 'being' and, for Winnicott, non-instinctual. The male element is secondary, developmentally speaking, to the female element, which does not seek because the conditions of seeking – awareness of and desire for the other, absence, and loss – are not yet in place; the separateness that makes this possible has not happened. This is a further elaboration of his account of the development of the self, and how the individual comes to live life creatively, to live life to the full.

To think further about the implications for the adult man on the couch of Winnicott's recognizing his internalization of his mother's wish for something that he, the patient, is not, and the strength of that 'girl' and her desire to triumph, opens up a debate about the power of the mother as caregiver in structuring the unconscious of the child and the adult, and its transferential implications.

Creativity and its Origins
(1971)
THE IDEA OF CREATIVITY

I am hoping that the reader will accept a general reference to creativity, not letting the word get lost in the successful or acclaimed creation but keeping it to the meaning that refers to a colouring of the whole attitude to external reality.

It is creative apperception more than anything else that makes the individual feel that life is worth living. Contrasted with this is a relationship to external reality which is one of compliance, the world and its details being recognized but only as something to be fitted in with or demanding adaptation. Compliance carries with it a sense of futility for the individual and is associated with the idea that nothing matters and that life is not worth living. In a tantalizing way many individuals have experienced just enough of creative living to recognize that for most of their time they are living uncreatively, as if caught up in the creativity of someone else, or of a machine.

This second way of living in the world is recognized as illness in psychiatric terms.[1] In some way or other our theory includes a belief that living creatively is a healthy state, and that compliance is a sick basis for life. There is little doubt that the general attitude of our society and the philosophic atmosphere of the age in which we happen to live contribute to this view, the view that we hold here and that we hold at the present time. We might not have held this view elsewhere and in another age.

These two alternatives of living creatively or uncreatively can be very sharply contrasted. My theory would be much simpler than it is if one or other extreme could be expected to be found in any one case or situation. The problem is made obscure because the degree of objectivity we count on when we talk about external reality in terms of an individual is variable. To some extent objectivity is a relative term because what is objectively perceived is by definition to some extent subjectively conceived of.[2]

While this is the exact area under examination in this book we have to take note that for many individuals external reality remains to some extent a subjective phenomenon. In the extreme case the individual hallucinates either at certain specific moments, or perhaps in a generalized way. There exist all sorts of expressions for this state ('fey', 'not all there', 'feet off the ground', 'unreal') and psychiatrically we refer to such individuals as schizoid. We know that such persons can have value as persons in the community and that they may be happy, but we note that there are certain disadvantages for them and especially for those who live with them. They may see the world subjectively and be easily deluded, or else while being firmly based in most areas they accept a delusional system in other areas, or they may be not firmly structured in respect of the psychosomatic partnership so that they are said to have poor coordination. Sometimes a physical disability such as defective sight or hearing plays into this state of affairs making a confused picture in which one cannot clearly distinguish between a hallucinating state and a disability based ultimately on a physical abnormality. In the extreme of this state of affairs the person being described is a patient in a mental hospital, either temporarily or permanently, and is labelled schizophrenic.

It is important for us that we find clinically *no sharp line* between health and the schizoid state or even between health and full-blown schizophrenia. While we recognize the hereditary factor in schizophrenia and while we are willing to see the contributions made in individual cases by physical disorders we look with suspicion on any theory of schizophrenia that divorces the subject from the problems of ordinary living and the universals of individual development in a given environment. We do see the vital importance of the environmental provision especially at the very beginning of the individual's infantile life, and for this reason we make a special study of the facilitating environment in human terms, and in terms of human growth in so far as dependence has meaning (cf. Winnicott, 1963[a], 1965[a]).

People may be leading satisfactory lives and may do work that is even of exceptional value and yet may be schizoid or schizophrenic. They may be ill in a psychiatric sense because of a weak reality sense. To balance this one would have to state that there are others who are so firmly anchored in objectively perceived reality that they are ill in the opposite direction of being out of touch with the subjective world and with the creative approach to fact.

To some extent we are helped in these difficult matters by remembering that hallucinations are dream phenomena that have come forward into the waking life and that hallucinating is no more of an illness in itself than the corresponding fact that the day's events and the memories of real happenings are drawn across the barrier into sleep and into dream-formation.[3] In fact, if we look at our descriptions of schizoid persons we find we are using words that we use to describe little children and babies, and there we actually expect to find the phenomena that characterize our schizoid and schizophrenic patients.

The problems outlined in this chapter are examined in this book at the point of their origin, that is in the early stages of individual growth and development. In fact, I am concerned with a study of the exact spot at which a baby is 'schizoid' except that this term is not used because of the baby's immaturity and special state relative to the development of personality and the role of the environment.

Schizoid people are not satisfied with themselves any more than are extroverts who cannot get into touch with dream. These two groups of people come to us for psychotherapy because in the one case they do not want to spend their lives irrevocably out of touch with the facts of life, and in the other case because they feel estranged from dream. They have a sense that something is wrong and that there is a dissociation in their personalities, and they would like to be helped to achieve unit status [see Chapter 8, this volume] or a state of time-space integration in which there is one self containing everything instead of dissociated elements that exist in compartments,[4] or are scattered around and left lying about.

$$\star \quad \star \quad \star$$

In order to look into the theory that analysts use in their work to see where creativeness has a place it is necessary, as I have already stated, to separate the idea of the creation from works of art. It is true that a creation can be a picture or a house or a garden or a costume or a hairstyle or a symphony or a sculpture; anything from a meal cooked at home. It would perhaps be better to say that these things could be creations. The creativity that concerns me here is a universal. It belongs to being alive. Presumably it belongs to the aliveness of some animals as well as of human beings, but it must be less strikingly significant in terms of animals or of human beings with low intellectual capacity[5] than it is with human beings who have near-average, average, or high intellectual capacity. The creativity that we are studying belongs to the approach of the individual to external reality. Assuming reasonable brain capacity, enough intelligence to enable the individual to become a person living and taking part in the life of the community, everything that happens is creative except in so far as the individual is ill, or is hampered by ongoing environmental factors which stifle his creative processes.

In regard to the second of these two alternatives it is probably wrong to think of creativity as something that can be destroyed utterly. But when one reads of individuals dominated at home, or spending their lives in concentration camps or under lifelong persecution because of a cruel political régime, one first of all feels that it is only a few of the victims who remain creative. These, of course, are the ones that suffer (see Winnicott, 1968[b]). It appears at first as if all the others who exist (not live) in such pathological communities have so far given up hope that they no longer suffer, and they must have lost the characteristic that makes them human, so that they no longer see the world creatively. These circumstances concern the negative of civilization. This is looking at the destruction of creativity in individuals by environmental factors acting at a late date in personal growth (cf. Bettelheim, 1960).

What is being attempted here is to find a way of studying the loss by individuals of the creative entry into life or of the initial creative approach to external phenomena. I am concerned with aetiology. In the extreme case there is a relative failure *ab initio* in the establishment of a personal capacity for creative living.

As I have already indicated, one has to allow for the possibility that there cannot be a complete destruction of a human individual's capacity for creative living and that, even in the most extreme case of compliance and the establishment of a false personality, hidden away somewhere there exists a secret life that is satisfactory because of its being creative or original to that human being. Its unsatisfactoriness must be measured in terms of its being hidden, its lack of enrichment through living experience (Winnicott, 1968[b]).

Let us say that in the severe case all that is real and all that matters and all that is personal and original and creative is hidden, and gives no sign of its existence. The individual in such an extreme case would not really mind whether he or she were alive or dead. Suicide is of small importance when such a state of affairs is powerfully organized in an individual, and even the individual himself or herself has no awareness of what might have been or of what has been lost or is missing (Winnicott, 1960[a]).

The creative impulse is therefore something that can be looked at as a thing in itself, something that of course is necessary if an artist is to produce a work of art, but also as something that is present when *anyone* – baby, child, adolescent, adult, old man or woman – looks in a healthy way at anything or does anything deliberately, such as making a mess with faeces or prolonging the act of crying to enjoy a musical sound. It is present as much in the moment-by-moment living of a backward child who is enjoying breathing as it is in the inspiration of an architect who suddenly knows what it is that he wishes to construct, and who is thinking in terms of material that can actually be used so that his creative impulse may take form and shape, and the world may witness.

Where psychoanalysis has attempted to tackle the subject of creativity it has to a large extent lost sight of the main theme. The analytic writer has perhaps taken some outstanding personality in the creative arts and has tried to make secondary and tertiary observations, ignoring everything that one could call primary. It is possible to take Leonardo da Vinci and make very important and interesting comments on the relationship between his work and certain events that took place in his infancy. A great deal can be done interweaving the themes of his work with his homosexual trend. But these and other circum-stances in the study of great men and women by-pass the theme that is at the centre of the idea of creativity. It is inevitable that such studies of great men tend to irritate artists and creative people in general. It could be that these studies that we are tempted to make are irritating because they look as if they are getting somewhere, as if they will soon be able to explain why this man was great and that woman achieved much, but the direction of inquiry is wrong. The main theme is being circumvented, that of the creative impulse itself. The creation stands between the observer and the artist's creativity.

It is not of course that anyone will ever be able to explain the creative impulse, and it is unlikely that anyone would ever want to do so; but the link can be made, and usefully made, between creative living and living itself, and the reasons can be studied why it is that creative living can be lost and why the individual's feeling that life is real or meaningful can disappear.

One could suppose that before a certain era, say a thousand years ago, only a very few people lived creatively (cf. Foucault, 1966). To explain this one would have to say that before a certain date it is possible that there was only very exceptionally a man or woman who achieved unit status in personal development. Before a certain date the vast millions of the world of human beings quite possibly never found or certainly soon lost at the end of infancy or childhood their sense of being individuals. This theme is developed a little in Freud's *Moses and Monotheism* (1939) and is referred to in a footnote which I consider to be a very important detail in Freud's writings: 'Breasted calls him "the first individual in human history".' We cannot easily identify ourselves with men and women of early times who so identified themselves with the community and with nature and with unexplained phenomena such as the rising and setting of the sun, thunderbolts and earthquakes. A body of science was needed before men and women could become units integrated in terms of time and space, who could live creatively and exist as individuals. The subject of monotheism belongs to the arrival of this stage in human mental functioning.

A further contribution to the subject of creativity came from Melanie Klein (1957). This contribution results from Klein's recognition of aggressive impulses and destructive fantasy dating from very early in the life of the individual baby. Klein takes up the idea of the destructiveness of the baby and gives it proper emphasis, at the same time making a new and vital issue out of the idea of the fusion of erotic and destructive impulses as a sign of health. The Klein statement includes the concept of reparation and restitution. In my opinion, however, Klein's important work does not reach to the subject of creativity itself and therefore it could easily have the effect of further obscuring the main issue. We do need her work, however, on the central position of the guilt sense. Behind this is Freud's basic concept of ambivalence as an aspect of individual maturity.

Health can be looked at in terms of fusion (erotic and destructive drives) and this makes more urgent than ever the examination of the origin of aggression and of destructive fantasy. For many years in psychoanalytic metapsychology aggression seemed to be explained on the basis of anger.

I have put forward the idea that both Freud and Klein jumped over an obstacle at this point and took refuge in heredity. The concept of the death instinct could be described as a reassertion of the principle of original sin.

I have tried to develop the theme that what both Freud and Klein avoided in so doing was the full implication of dependence and therefore of the environmental factor [see Chapter 8, this volume]. If dependence really does mean dependence, then the history of an individual baby cannot be written in terms of the baby alone. It must be written in terms also of the environmental provision which either meets dependence needs or fails to meet them (Winnicott [see Chapter 2, this volume] and Winnicott, 1948[b], 1952[a]).

It is hoped that psychoanalysts will be able to use the theory of transitional phenomena in order to describe the way in which good-enough environmental provision at the very earliest stages makes it possible for the individual to cope with the immense shock of loss of omnipotence.[6] What I have called the 'subjective object' (Winnicott, 1962[b]) becomes gradually related to objects that are objectively perceived, but this happens only when a good-enough environmental provision or 'average expectable environment' (Hartmann, 1939) enables the baby to be mad in one particular way that is conceded to babies. This madness only becomes true madness if it appears in later life. At the stage of infancy it is the same subject as that to which I referred when I talked about the acceptance of the paradox, as when a baby creates an object but the object would not have been created as such if it had not already been there.

We find either that individuals live creatively and feel that life is worth living or else that they cannot live creatively and are doubtful about the value of living. This variable in human beings is directly related to the quality and quantity of environmental provision at the beginning or in the early phases of each baby's living experience.

Whereas every effort is made by analysts to describe the psychology of the individual and the dynamic processes of development and defence organization, and to include impulse and drive in terms of the individual, here at this point where creativity either comes into being or does not come into being (or alternatively is lost) the theoretician must take the environment into account, and no statement that concerns the individual as an isolate can touch this central problem of the source of creativity.

It seems important here to refer to a special complication that arises out of the fact that while men and women have much in common they are nevertheless also unalike. Obviously creativity is one of the common denominators, one of the things that men and women share, or they share distress at the loss or absence of creative living. I now propose to examine this subject from another angle.

THE SPLIT-OFF MALE AND FEMALE ELEMENTS TO BE FOUND IN MEN AND WOMEN[7]

There is nothing new either inside or outside psychoanalysis in the idea that men and women have a 'predisposition towards bisexuality'.

I try here to use what I have learned about bisexuality from analyses that have gone step by step towards a certain point and have focused on one detail. No attempt will be made here to trace the steps by which an analysis comes to this kind of material. It can be said that a great deal of work usually has had to be done before this type of material has become significant and calls for priority. It is difficult to see how all this preliminary work can be avoided. The slowness of the analytic process is a manifestation of a defence the analyst must respect, as we respect all defences. While it is the patient who is all the time teaching the analyst, the analyst should be able to know, theoretically, about the matters that concern the deepest or most central features of personality, else he may fail to recognize and to meet new demands on his understanding and technique when at long last the patient is able to bring deeply buried matters into the content of the transference, thereby affording opportunity for mutative interpretation. The analyst, by interpreting, shows how much and how little of the patient's communication he is able to receive.

As a basis for the idea that I wish to give in this chapter I suggest that creativity is one of the common denominators of men and women. In another language, however, creativity is the prerogative of women, and in yet another language it is a masculine feature. It is this last of the three that concerns me in what follows here.

CLINICAL DATA

Illustrative Case

I propose to start with a clinical example. This concerns the treatment of a man of middle age, a married man with a family, and successful in one of the professions. The analysis has proceeded along classical lines. This man has had a long analysis and I am not by any means his first psychotherapist. A great deal of work has been done by him and by each of us therapists and analysts in turn, and much change has been brought about in his personality. But there is still something he avers that makes it impossible for him to stop. He knows that what he came for he has not reached. If he cuts his losses the sacrifice is too great.

In the present phase of this analysis something has been reached which is new *for me*. It has to do with the way I am dealing with the non–masculine element in his personality.

On a Friday the patient came and reported much as usual. The thing that struck me on this Friday was that the patient was talking about *penis envy*. I use this term advisedly, and I must invite acceptance of the fact that this term was appropriate here in view of the material, and of its presentation. Obviously this term, penis envy, is not usually applied in the description of a man.

The change that belongs to this particular phase is shown in the way I handled this. On this particular occasion I said to him: 'I am listening to a girl. I know perfectly well that you are a man but I am listening to a girl, and I am talking to a girl. I am telling this girl: "You are talking about penis envy."'

I wish to emphasize that this has nothing to do with homosexuality.

(It has been pointed out to me that my interpretation in each of its two parts could be thought of as related to playing, and as far as possible removed from authoritative interpretation that is next door to indoctrination.)

It was clear to me, by the profound effect of this interpretation, that my remark was in some way apposite, and indeed I would not be reporting this incident in this context were it not for the fact that the work that started on this Friday did in fact break into a vicious circle. I had grown accustomed to a routine of good work, good interpretations, good immediate results, and then destruction and disillusionment that followed each time because of the patient's gradual recognition that something fundamental had remained unchanged; there was this unknown factor which had kept this man working at his own analysis for a quarter of a century. Would his work with me suffer the same fate as his work with the other therapists?

On this occasion there was an immediate effect in the form of intellectual acceptance, and relief, and then there were more remote effects. After a pause the patient said: 'If I were to tell someone about this girl I would be called mad.'

The matter could have been left there, but I am glad, in view of subsequent events, that I went further. It was my next remark that surprised me, and it clinched the matter. I said: 'It was not that *you* told this to anyone; it is *I* who see the girl and hear a girl talking, when actually there is a man on my couch. The mad person is *myself*.'

I did not have to elaborate this point because it went home. The patient said that he now felt sane in a mad environment. In other words he was now released from a dilemma. As he said, subsequently, 'I myself could never say (knowing myself to be a man) "I am a girl". I am not mad that way. But you said it, and you have spoken to both parts of me.'

This madness which was mine enabled him to see himself as a girl *from my position*. He knows himself to be a man, and never doubts that he is a man.

Is it obvious what was happening here? For my part, I have needed to live through a deep personal experience in order to arrive at the understanding I feel I now have reached.

This complex state of affairs has a special reality for this man because he and I have been driven to the conclusion (though unable to prove it) that his mother (who is not alive now) saw a girl baby when she saw him as a baby before she came round to thinking of him as a boy. In other words this man had to fit into her idea that her baby would be and was a girl. (He was the second child, the first being a boy.) We have very good evidence from inside the analysis that in her early management of him the mother held him and dealt with him in all sorts of physical ways as if she failed to see him as a male. On the basis of this pattern he later arranged his defences, but it was the mother's 'madness' that saw a girl where there was a boy, and this was brought right into the present by my having said 'It is I who am mad'. On this Friday he went away profoundly moved and feeling that this was the first significant shift in the analysis for a long time (although, as I have said, there had always been continuous progress in the sense of good work being done).[8]

I would like to give further details relative to this Friday incident. When he came on the following Monday he told me that he was ill. It was quite clear to me that he had an infection and I reminded him that his wife would have it the next day, which in fact happened. Nevertheless, he was inviting me to *interpret* this illness, which started on the Saturday, as if it were psychosomatic. What he tried to tell me was that on the Friday night he had had a satisfactory sexual intercourse with his wife, and so he *ought* to have felt better on the Saturday, but instead of feeling better he had become ill and had felt ill. I was able to leave aside the physical disorder and talk about the incongruity of his feeling ill after the intercourse that he felt ought to have been a healing experience. (He might, indeed, have said: 'I have 'flu, but in spite of that I feel better in myself.')

My interpretation continued along the line started up on the Friday. I said: 'You feel as if you ought to be pleased that here was an interpretation of mine that had released masculine behaviour. *The girl that I was talking to, however, does not want the man released*, and indeed she is not interested in him. What she wants is full acknowledgement of herself and of her own rights over your body. Her penis envy especially includes envy of you as a male.' I went on: 'The feeling ill is a protest from the female self, this girl, because she has always hoped that the analysis would in fact find out that this man, yourself, is and always has been a girl (and "being ill" is a pregenital pregnancy). The only end to the analysis that this girl can look for is the discovery that in fact you are a girl.' Out of this one could begin to understand his conviction that the analysis could never end.[9]

In the subsequent weeks there was a great deal of material confirming the validity of my interpretation and my attitude, and the patient felt that he could see now that his analysis had ceased to be under doom of interminability.

Later I was able to see that the patient's resistance had now shifted to a denial of the importance of my having said 'It is I who am mad'. He tried to pass this off as just my way of putting things – a figure of speech that could be forgotten. I found, however, that here is one of those examples of delusional transference that puzzle patients and analysts alike, and the crux of the problem of management is just here in this interpretation, which I confess I nearly did not allow myself to make.

When I gave myself time to think over what had happened I was puzzled. Here was no new theoretical concept, here was no new principle of technique. In fact, I and my patient had been over this ground before. Yet we had here something new, new in my own attitude and new in his capacity to make use of my interpretative work. I decided to surrender myself to whatever this might mean in myself, and the result is to be found in this paper that I am presenting.

Dissociation

The first thing I noticed was that I had never before fully accepted the complete dissociation between the man (or woman) and the aspect of the personality that has the opposite sex. In the case of this man patient the dissociation was nearly complete.

Here, then, I found myself with a new edge to an old weapon, and I wondered how this would or could affect the work I was doing with other patients, both men and women, or boys and girls. I decided, therefore, to study this type of dissociation, leaving aside but not forgetting all the other types of splitting.

Male and Female Elements in Men and Women[10]

There was in this case a dissociation that was on the point of breaking down. The dissociation defence was giving way to an acceptance of bisexuality as a quality of the unit or total self. I saw that I was dealing with what could be called a *pure female element*. At first it surprised me that I could reach this only by looking at the material presented by a male patient.[11]

A further clinical observation belongs to this case. Some of the relief that followed our arrival at the new platform for our work together came from the fact that we now could explain why my interpretations, made on good grounds, in respect of use of objects, oral erotic satisfactions in the transference, oral sadistic ideas in respect of the patient's interest in the analyst as part-object or as a person with breast or penis – why such interpretations were never mutative. They were accepted, but: so what? Now that the new position had been reached the patient felt a sense of relationship with me, and this was extremely vivid. It had to do with identity. The pure female split-off element found a primary unity with me as analyst, and this gave the man a feeling of having started to live. I have been affected by this detail, as will appear in my application to theory of what I have found in this case.

Addendum to the Clinical Section

It is rewarding to review one's current clinical material keeping in mind this one example of dissociation, the split-off girl element in a male patient. The subject can quickly become vast and complex, so that a few observations must be chosen for special mention.

⋆   ⋆   ⋆

(*a*) One may, to one's surprise, find that one is dealing with and attempting to analyse the split-off part, while the main functioning person appears only in projected form. This is like treating a child only to find that one is treating one or other parent by proxy. Every possible variation on this theme may come one's way.

⋆   ⋆   ⋆

(*b*) The other-sex element may be completely split off so that, for instance, a man may not be able to make any link at all with the split-off part. This applies especially when the personality is otherwise sane and integrated. Where the functioning personality is already organized into multiple splits there is less accent on 'I am sane', and therefore less resistance against the idea 'I am a girl' (in the case of a man) or 'I am a boy' (in the case of a girl).

⋆   ⋆   ⋆

(*c*) There may be found clinically a near-complete other-sex dissociation, organized in relation to external factors at a very early date, mixed in with later dissociations organized as a defence, based more or less on cross-identifications. The reality of this later organized defence may militate against the patient's revival in the analysis of the earlier reactive split.

(There is an axiom here, that a patient will always cling to the full exploit-ation of personal and *internal* factors, which give him or her a measure of omnipotent control, rather than allow the idea of a crude reaction to an environmental factor, whether distortion or failure. Environmental influence, bad or even good, comes into our work as a traumatic idea, intolerable because not operating within the area of the patient's omnipotence. Compare the melancholic's claim to be responsible for *all* evil.)

★   ★   ★

(*d*) The split-off other-sex part of the personality tends to remain of one age, or to grow but slowly. As compared with this, the truly imaginative figures of the person's inner psychic reality mature, interrelate, grow old, and die. For instance, a man who depends on younger girls for keeping his split-off girl-self alive may gradually become able to employ for his special purpose girls of marriageable age. But should he live to ninety it is unlikely that the girls so employed will reach thirty. Yet in a man patient the girl (hiding the pure girl element of earlier formation) may have girl characteristics, may be breast-proud, experience penis envy, become pregnant, be equipped with no male external genitalia and even possess female sexual equipment and enjoy female sexual experience.

★   ★   ★

(*e*) An important issue here is the assessment of all this in terms of psychiatric health. The man who initiates girls into sexual experience may well be one who is more identified with the girl than with himself. This gives him the capacity to go all out to wake up the girl's sex and to satisfy her. He pays for this by getting but little male satisfaction himself, and he pays also in terms of his need to seek always a new girl, this being the opposite of object-constancy.

At the other extreme is the illness of impotence. In between the two lies the whole range of relative potency mixed with dependence of various types and degrees. What is normal depends on the social expectation of any one social group at any one particular time. Could it not be said that at the patriarchal extreme of society sexual intercourse is rape, and at the matriarchal extreme the man with a split-off female element who must satisfy many women is at a premium even if in doing so he annihilates himself?

In between the extremes is bisexuality and an expectation of sexual experience which is less than optimal. This goes along with the idea that social health is mildly depressive – except for holidays.

It is interesting that the existence of this split-off female element actually prevents homosexual practice. In the case of my patient he always fled from homosexual advances at the critical moment because (as he came to see and to tell me) putting homosexuality into practice would establish his maleness which (from the split-off female element self) he never wanted to know for certain.

(In the normal, where bisexuality is a fact, homosexual ideas do not conflict in this way largely because the anal factor (which is a secondary matter) has not attained supremacy over fellatio, and in the fantasy of a fellatio union the matter of the person's biological sex is not significant.)

★   ★   ★

Creativity and its origins   275

(f) It seems that in the evolution of Greek myth the first homosexuals were men who imitated women so as to get into as close as possible a relationship with the supreme goddess. This belonged to a matriarchal era out of which a patriarchal god system appeared with Zeus as head. Zeus (symbol of the patriarchal system) initiated the idea of the boy loved sexually by man, and along with this went the relegation of women to a lower status. If this is a true statement of the history of the development of ideas, it gives the link that I need if I am to be able to join my clinical observations about the split-off female element in the case of men patients with the theory of object-relating. (The split-off male element in women patients is of equal importance in our work, but what I have to say about object-relating can be said in terms of one only of the two possible examples of dissociation.)

SUMMARY OF PRELIMINARY OBSERVATIONS

In our theory it is necessary to allow for both a male and a female element in boys and men and girls and women. These elements may be split off from each other to a high degree. This idea requires of us both a study of the clinical effects of this type of dissociation and an examination of the distilled male and female elements themselves.

I have made some observations on the first of these two, the clinical effects; now I wish to examine what I am calling the distilled male and female elements (not male and female persons).

PURE MALE AND PURE FEMALE ELEMENTS

Speculation about Contrast in Kinds of Object-relating

Let us compare and contrast the unalloyed male and female elements in the context of object-relating.

I wish to say that the element that I am calling 'male' does traffic in terms of active relating or passive being related to, each being backed by instinct. It is in the development of this idea that we speak of instinct drive in the baby's relation to the breast and to feeding, and subsequently in relation to all the experiences involving the main erotogenic zones, and to subsidiary drives and satisfactions. My suggestion is that, by contrast, the pure female element relates to the breast (or to the mother) in the sense of *the baby becoming the breast (or mother), in the sense that the object is the subject.* I can see no instinct drive in this.

(There is also to be remembered the use of the word instinct that comes from ethology; however, I doubt very much whether imprinting is a matter that affects the newborn human infant at all. I will say here and now that I believe the whole subject of imprinting is irrelevant to the study of the early object-relating of human infants. It certainly has nothing to do with the trauma of separation at two years, the very place where its prime importance has been assumed.)

The term subjective object has been used in describing the first object, the object *not yet repudiated as a not-me phenomenon*. Here in this relatedness of pure female element to 'breast' is a practical application of the idea of the subjective object, and the experience of this paves the way for the objective subject – that is, the idea of a self, and the feeling of real that springs from the sense of having an identity.

However complex the psychology of the sense of self and of the establishment of an identity eventually becomes as a baby grows, no sense of self emerges except on the basis of this relating in the sense of BEING. This sense of being is something that antedates the idea of being-at-one-with, because there has not yet been anything else except identity. Two separate persons can *feel* at one, but here at the place that I am examining the baby and the object *are* one. The term primary identification has perhaps been used for just this that I am describing and I am trying to show how vitally important this first experience is for the initiation of all subsequent experiences of identification.

Projective and introjective identifications both stem from this place where each is the same as the other.

In the growth of the human baby, as the ego begins to organize, this that I am calling the object-relating of the pure female element establishes what is perhaps the simplest of all experiences, the experience of *being*. Here one finds a true continuity of generations, being which is passed on from one generation to another, via the female element of men and women and of male and female infants. I think this has been said before, but always in terms of women and girls, which confuses the issue. It is a matter of the female elements in both males and females.

By contrast, the object-relating of the male element to the object pre-supposes separateness. As soon as there is the ego organization available, the baby allows the object the quality of being not-me or separate, and experiences id satisfactions that include anger relative to frustration. Drive satisfaction enhances the separation of the object from the baby, and leads to objectification of the object. Henceforth, on the male element side, identification needs to be based on complex mental mechanisms, mental mechanisms that must be given time to appear, to develop, and to become established as part of the new baby's equipment. On the female element side, however, identity requires so little mental structure that this primary identity can be a feature from very early, and the foundation for simple being can be laid (let us say) from the birth date, or before, or soon after, or from whenever the mind has become free from the handicaps to its functioning due to immaturity and to brain damage associated with the birth process.

Psychoanalysts have perhaps given special attention to this male element or drive aspect of object-relating, and yet have neglected the subject-object identity to which I am drawing attention here, which is at the basis of the capacity to be. The male element *does* while the female element (in males and females) *is*. Here would come in those males in Greek myth who tried to be at one with the supreme goddess. Here also is a way of stating a male person's very deep-seated envy of women whose female element men take for granted, sometimes in error.

It seems that frustration belongs to satisfaction-seeking. To the experience of being belongs something else, not frustration, but maiming. I wish to study this specific detail.

Identity: Child and Breast

It is not possible to state what I am calling here the female element's relation to the breast without the concept of the good-enough and the not-good-enough mother.

(Such an observation is even more true in this area than it is in the comparable area covered by the terms transitional phenomena and transitional objects. The transitional object represents the mother's ability to present the world in such a way that the infant does not at first have to know that the object is not created by the infant. In our immediate context we may allow a total significance to the meaning of adaptation, the mother either giving the infant the opportunity to feel that the breast is the infant, or else not doing so. The breast here is a symbol not of doing but of being.)

This being a good-enough purveyor of female element must be a matter of very subtle details of handling, and in giving consideration to these matters one can draw on the writing of Margaret Mead and of Erik Erikson, who are able to describe the ways in which maternal care in various types of culture determines at a very early age the patterns of the defences of the individual, and also gives the blueprints for later sublimation. These are very subtle matters that we study in respect of *this* mother and *this* child.

The Nature of the Environmental Factor

I now return to the consideration of the very early stage in which the pattern is being laid down by the manner in which the mother in subtle ways handles her infant. I must refer in detail to this very special example of the environmental factor. Either the mother has a breast that *is*, so that the baby can also *be* when the baby and mother are not yet separated out in the infant's rudimentary mind; or else the mother is incapable of making this contribution, in which case the baby has to develop without the capacity to be, or with a crippled capacity to be.

(Clinically one needs to deal with the case of the baby who has to make do with an identity with a breast that is active, which is a male element breast, but which is not satisfactory for the initial identity which needs a breast that *is*, not a breast that *does*. Instead of 'being like' this baby has to 'do like', or to be done to, which from our point of view here is the same thing.)

The mother who is able to do this very subtle thing that I am referring to does not produce a child whose 'pure female' self is envious of the breast, since for this child the breast is the self and the self is the breast. Envy is a term that might become applicable in the experience of a tantalizing failure of the breast as something that IS.

The Male and Female Elements Contrasted

These considerations have involved me then in a curious statement about the pure male and the pure female aspects of the infant boy or girl. I have arrived at a position in which I say that object-relating in terms of *this pure female element has nothing to do with drive (or instinct)*. Object-relating backed by instinct drive belongs to the male element in the personality uncontaminated by the female element. This line of argument involves me in great difficulties, and yet it seems as if in a statement of the initial stages of the emotional development of the individual it is necessary to separate out (not boys from girls but) the uncontaminated boy element from the uncontaminated girl element. The classical statement in regard to finding, using, oral erotism, oral sadism, anal stages, etc., arises out of a consideration of the life of the pure male element. Studies of identification based on introjection or on incorporation are studies of the experience of the already mixed male and female elements. Study of the pure female element leads us elsewhere.

The study of the pure distilled uncontaminated female element leads us to BEING, and this forms the only basis for self-discovery and a sense of existing (and then on to the capacity to develop an inside, to be a container, to have a capacity to use the mechanisms of projection and introjection and to relate to the world in terms of introjection and projection).

At risk of being repetitious I wish to restate: when the girl element in the boy or girl baby or patient finds the breast it is the self that has been found. If the question is asked, what does the girl baby do with the breast? – the answer must be that this girl element *is* the breast and shares the qualities of breast and mother and is desirable. In the course of time, desirable means edible and this means that the infant is in danger because of being desirable, or, in more sophisticated language, exciting. Exciting implies: liable to make someone's male element *do* something. In this way a man's penis may be an exciting female element generating male element activity in the girl. But (it must be made clear) no girl or woman is like this; in health, there is a variable amount of girl element in a girl, and in a boy. Also, hereditary factor elements enter in, so that it would easily be possible to find a boy with a stronger girl element than the girl standing next to him, who may have less pure female element potential. Add to this the variable capacity of mothers to hand on the desirability of the good breast or of that part of the maternal function that the good breast symbolizes, and it can be seen that some boys and girls are doomed to grow up with a lop-sided bisexuality, loaded on the wrong side of their biological provision.

I am reminded of the question: what is the nature of the communication Shakespeare offers in his delineation of Hamlet's personality and character?

Hamlet is mainly about the awful dilemma that Hamlet found himself in, and there was no solution for him because of the dissociation that was taking place in him as a defence mechanism. It would be rewarding to hear an actor play Hamlet with this in mind. This actor would have a special way of delivering the first line of the famous soliloquy: 'To be, or not to be . . .' He would say, as if trying to get to the bottom of something that cannot be fathomed, 'To be, . . . or . . .' and then he would pause, because in fact the character Hamlet does not know the alternative. At last he would come in with the rather banal alternative: '. . . or not to be'; and then he would be well away on a journey that can lead nowhere. 'Whether 'tis nobler in the mind to suffer / The slings and arrows of outrageous fortune, / Or to take arms against a sea of troubles, / And by opposing end them?' (Act III, Sc. I). Here Hamlet has gone over into the sado-masochistic alternative, and he has left aside the theme he started with. The rest of the play is a long working-out of the statement of the problem. I mean: Hamlet is depicted at this stage as searching for an alternative to the idea 'To be'. He was searching for a way to state the dissociation that had taken place in his personality between his male and female elements, elements which had up to the time of the death of his father lived together in harmony, being but aspects of his richly endowed person. Yes, inevitably I write as if writing of a person, not a stage character.

As I see it, this difficult soliloquy is difficult because Hamlet had himself not got the clue to his dilemma – since it lay in his own changed state. Shakespeare had the clue, but Hamlet could not go to Shakespeare's play.

If the play is looked at in this way it seems possible to use Hamlet's altered attitude to Ophelia and his cruelty to her as a picture of his ruthless rejection of his own female element, now split off and handed over to her, with his unwelcome male element threatening to take over his whole personality. The cruelty to Ophelia can be a measure of his reluctance to abandon his split-off female element.

In this way it is *the play* (if Hamlet could have read it, or seen it acted) that could have shown him the nature of his dilemma. The play within the play failed to do this, and I would say that it was staged by him to bring to life his male element which was challenged to the full by the tragedy that had become interwoven with it.

It could be found that the same dilemma in Shakespeare himself provides the problem behind the content of the sonnets. But this is to ignore or even insult the main feature of the sonnets, namely, the poetry. Indeed, as Professor L. C. Knights (1946) specifically insists, it is only too easy to forget the poetry of the plays in writing of the *dramatis personae* as if they were historical persons.

SUMMARY

1. I have examined the implications for me in my work of my new degree of recognition of the importance of dissociation in some men and women in respect of these male or female elements and the parts of their personalities that are built on these foundations.

★　　★　　★

2. I have looked at the artificially dissected male and female elements, and I have found that, for the time being, I associate impulse related to objects (also the passive voice of this) with the male element, whereas I find that the characteristic of the female element in the context of object-relating is identity, giving the child the basis for being, and then, later on, a basis for a sense of self. But I find that it is here, in the absolute dependence on maternal provision of that special quality by which the mother meets or fails to meet the earliest functioning of the female element, that we may seek the foundation for the experience of being. I wrote: 'There is thus no sense in making use of the word "id" for phenomena that are not covered and catalogued and experienced and eventually interpreted by ego functioning' (Winnicott, 1962[b]).

Now I want to say: 'After being – doing and being done to. But first, being.'

ADDED NOTE ON THE SUBJECT OF STEALING

Stealing belongs to the male element in boys and girls. The question arises: what corresponds to this in terms of the female element in boys and girls? The answer can be that in respect of this element the individual usurps the mother's position and her seat or garments, in this way deriving desirability and seductiveness stolen from the mother.

Notes

1. I have discussed this issue in detail in my paper 'Classification: Is there a Psycho-Analytic Contribution to Psychiatric Classification?' (1964[b]), and the interested reader can pursue this theme there.

2. See *The Edge of Objectivity* (Gillespie, 1960), among many works that deal with the creative element in science.
3. Though this is inherent in Freud's hypothesis of dream-formation, it is a fact that has often been overlooked (cf. Freud, 1900).
4. I have discussed a specific instance of this elsewhere (1966[b]), in terms of obsessional neurosis.
5. A distinction must be made between primary mental defect and clinical defect secondary to schizophrenia of childhood and autism, etc.
6. This antedates the relief that comes from such mental mechanisms as cross-identification.
7. Paper read to the British Psycho-Analytical Society, 2 February 1966, and revised for publication in *Forum*.
8. For a detailed discussion of the mirror-role of mother in child development see Winnicott, 1967[b].
9. It will be understood, I hope, that I am not suggesting that this man's very real physical illness, 'flu, was brought about by the emotional trends that coexisted with the physical.
10. I shall continue to use this terminology (male and female elements) for the time being, since I know of no other suitable descriptive terms. Certainly 'active' and 'passive' are not correct terms, and I must continue the argument using the terms that are available.
11. It would be logical here to follow up the work this man and I did together with a similar piece of work involving a girl or a woman patient. For instance, a young woman reminds me of old material belonging to her early latency when she longed to be a boy. She spent much time and energy willing herself a penis. She needed, however, a special piece of understanding, which was that she, an obvious girl, happy to be a girl, at the same time (with a 10 per cent dissociated part) knew and always had known that she was a boy. Associated with this was a certainty of having been castrated and so deprived of destructive potential, and along with this was murder of mother and the whole of her masochistic defence organization which was central in her personality structure.

Giving clinical examples here involves me in a risk of distracting the reader's attention from my main theme; also, if my ideas are true and universal, then each reader will have personal cases illustrating the place of dissociation rather than of repression related to male and female elements in men and women.

Developing ideas: mirror-role of mother; fantasying as primary dissociation; play; psychotherapy and play; the precariousness of play; destructive drive creates externality; object relating and object usage; split-off male and female elements; 'being' and 'doing'; creative living; paradox

REFERENCES

Standard Edition = Freud, S. (1966). *Standard Edition of the Complete Psychological Works of Sigmund Freud.* London: Hogarth.

Collected Papers = Winnicott, D. W. (1958a). *Collected Papers: Through Paediatrics to Psycho-Analysis.* London: Tavistock.

Maturational Processes = Winnicott, D. W. (1965a). *The Maturational Processes and the Facilitating Environment.* London: Hogarth Press and the Institute of Psycho-analysis.

Abram, J. (Ed.). (2000). *Andre Green at the Squiggle Foundation.* London: Karnac.

Abram, J. (2007). *The Language of Winnicott.* London: Karnac.

Aguayo, J. (2002). 'Reassessing the Clinical Affinity between Melanie Klein and D. W. Winnicott (1935–51)'. *International Journal of Psychoanalysis* 83: 1133–1152.

Aichhorn, A. (1925/1963). *Wayward Youth.* New York: Viking.

Aisenstein, M. (2006). 'The Indissociable Unity of Psyche and Soma: A View from the Paris Psychosomatic School'. *International Journal of Psychoanalysis* 87: 667–680.

Alvarez, A. (1996). 'The Clinician's Debt to Winnicott'. *Journal of Child Psychotherapy* 22: 377–382.

Ambrosiano, L. (2008). 'Plato was the Eldest'. In P. Campanile (Ed.), *The Italian Psycho-analytic Annual 2008: Theory and Observation: Redefining the Field: Rivista di Psicoanalisi – Journal of the Italian Psychoanalytic Society* (pp. 15–30). London: Karnac.

Astor, J. (1990). 'The Emergence of Fordham's Model of Development: A New Integration in Analytical Psychology'. *Journal of Analytical Psychology* 35: 261–278.

Axline, V. M. (1947). *Play Therapy: The Inner Dynamics of Childhood.* Boston, MA: Houghton Mifflin.

Bálint, A., and Bálint, M. (1939). 'On Transference and Counter-Transference'. *International Journal of Psychoanalysis* 20: 223–230.

Balint, M. (1939/1949). 'Early Developmental States of the Ego: Primary Object Love'. *International Journal of Psychoanalysis* 30: 265–273.

—— (1952). 'On Love and Hate'. *International Journal of Psychoanalysis* 33: 355–362.

—— (1959). *Thrills and Regressions.* London: Hogarth Press.

—— (1968). *The Basic Fault.* London: Tavistock.

Barkin, L. (1978). 'The Concept of the Transitional Object'. In S. Grolnick and M. Barkin (Eds.), *Between Fantasy and Reality* (pp. 511–536). New York: Jason Aronson.

Barnett, B. (2001). 'A Comparison of the Thought and Work of Donald Winnicott and Michael Balint'. In M. Bertolini, A. Giannakoulas, and M. Hernandez (Eds.), in collaboration with A. Molino, *Squiggles and Spaces: Revisiting the Work of D. W. Winnicott* (Vol. 2, pp. 185–188). London: Whurr.

Bertolini, M., Giannakoulas, A., and Hernandez, M. (2001). *Squiggles and Spaces: Revisiting the Work of D. W. Winnicott* (Vol. 2). London: Whurr.

Bettelheim, B. (1960). *The Informed Heart: Autonomy in a Mass Age.* New York: Free Press; London: Thames & Hudson, 1961.

Bick, E. (1968). 'The Experience of the Skin in Early Object-Relations'. *International Journal of Psychoanalysis* 49: 484–486.

Bion, W. R. (1962). 'The Psycho-Analytic Study of Thinking'. *International Journal of Psycho-analysis* 43: 306–310.

—— (1967). *Second Thoughts: Selected Papers on Psychoanalysis.* London: Karnac.

Bollas, C. (1987). *The Shadow of the Object.* London: Free Association Books.

—— (1989). *Forces of Destiny.* London: Free Association Books.

Bornstein, B. (1951). 'On Latency'. *The Psychoanalytic Study of the Child* 6: 279–285.

Bowlby, J. (1940). 'The Influence of the Early Environment in the Development of Neurosis and Neurotic Character'. *International Journal of Psychoanalysis* 21: 154–178.

—— (1944). 'Forty-Four Juvenile Thieves: Their Characters and Home-Life'. *International Journal of Psychoanalysis* 25: 19–52; 107–127.

—— (1953). *Child Care and the Growth of Love.* Harmondsworth, UK: Penguin.

—— (1960). 'Separation Anxiety'. *International Journal of Psychoanalysis* 41: 89–113.

—— (1969). *Attachment and Loss* (Vol. 1). London: Hogarth Press and the Institute of Psychoanalysis.

—— (1973). *Attachment and Loss* (Vol. 2). London: Hogarth Press and the Institute of Psychoanalysis.

—— (1980). *Attachment and Loss* (Vol. 3). London: Hogarth Press and the Institute of Psychoanalysis.

Brafman, A. H. (2001). *Untying the Knot: Working with Children and Parents.* London: Karnac.

Britton, R. (1998). *Belief and Imagination.* New Library of Psychoanalysis. London: Routledge.

Caldwell, L. (Ed.). (2002). *The Elusive Child,* London: Karnac.

—— (2005). *Sex and Sexuality: Winnicottian Perspectives.* London: Karnac.

—— (2007). *Winnicott and the Psychoanalytic Tradition.* London: Karnac.

Carvalho, R. (1992). 'Review of W. R. Bion *A Memoir of the Future.* 1991. London: Karnac Books'. *Journal of Analytical Psychology* 37: 110–115.

Casement, P. J. (1995). 'Review of D. Goldman. *In Search of the Real: The Origins and Originality of D. W. Winnicott.* 1993. New York: Aronson. *Journal of the American Psycho-analytic Association* 43: 223–227.

Clancier, L., and Kalmanovitch, J. (1987). *Winnicott and Paradox.* London: Tavistock.

Davis, M., and Wallbridge, D. (1981). *Boundary and Space: An Introduction to the Work of D. W. Winnicott.* New York: Brunner/Mazel.

Davis, M. (1987). 'The Writing of D. W. Winnicott'. *International Review of Psycho-Analysis* 14: 491–502.

—— (1993). 'Winnicott and the Spatula Game'. *Winnicott Studies* 8: 57–68.

de Monchaux, C. (1962). 'Thinking and Negative Hallucination'. *International Journal of Psychoanalysis* 43: 311–314.

Deri, S. (1978). 'Transitional Phenomena: Vicissitudes of Symbolization and Creativity'. In S. Grolnick and M. Barkin (Eds.), *Between Fantasy and Reality* (pp. 43–60). New York: Jason Aronson.

De Silvestris, P. (2001). 'Interminable Illusion'. In M. Bertolini, A. Giannakoulas, M. Hernandez (Eds.), in collaboration with A. Molino, *Squiggles and Spaces: Revisiting the Work of D. W. Winnicott* (Vol. 2, pp. 59–64). London: Whurr.

Drapeau, P. (2002). 'From Freud to Winnicott: An Encounter Between Mythical Children'. In L. Caldwell (Ed.), *The Elusive Child* (pp. 15–44). New York: Jason Aronson.

Dreyfus, P. (2001). 'A Discussion of Bernard Barnett's Comparison of D. W. Winnicott'. In M. Bertolini, A. Giannakoulas, and M. Hernandez (Eds.), in collaboration with A. Molino,

Squiggles and Spaces: Revisiting the Work of D. W. Winnicott (Vol. 2, pp. 236–241). London: Whurr.

Edgcumbe, R. (2000). *Anna Freud: A View of Development, Disturbance, and Therapeutic Techniques*. London: Routledge.

Eigen, M. (1993). *The Electrified Tightrope*. Northvale, NJ: Jason Aronson.

Emde, R. N., Klingman, D. H., Reich., J. H., and Wade, J. D. (1978). 'Emotional Expression in Infancy: 1. Initial Studies of Social Signaling and an Emergent Model'. In M. Lewis and L. Rosenblum (Eds.), *The Development of Affect*. New York: Plenum Press.

Erikson, E. (1950). *Childhood and Society*. London: Penguin.

—— (1956). 'The Problem of Ego Identity'. *Journal of the American Psychoanalytic Association* 4: 56–121.

—— (1958). *Young Man Luther*. London: Faber.

Etchegoyen, H. (1990). *The Fundamentals of Psychoanalytic Technique*. London: Karnac.

Fairbairn, W. R. D. (1952). *Psychoanalytic Studies of the Personality*. London: Tavistock (reprinted 1990, 1992, London: Routledge).

Farhi, N. (2001). 'Psychotherapy and the Squiggle Game: A Sophisticated Game of Hide-and-Seek'. In M. Bertolini, A. Giannakoulas, and M. Hernandez (Eds.), in collaboration with A. Molino, *Squiggles and Spaces: Revisiting the Work of D. W. Winnicott* (Vol. 2, pp. 65–75). London: Whurr.

Ferenczi, S. (1913). 'Stages in the Development of the Sense of Reality'. In *First Contributions to Psychoanalysis* (pp. 219–239). London: Hogarth, 1952.

—— (1933). 'Confusion of Tongues Between Adults and the Child: The Language of Tenderness and of Passion'. *Contemporary Psychoanalysis* 24: 196–206.

Flarsheim, A. (1978). 'Discussion of Antony Flew'. In S. Grolnick and M. Barkin (Eds.), *Between Fantasy and Reality* (pp. 503–510). New York: Jason Aronson.

Foucault, M. (1966). *Les Mots et les choses*. Paris: Éditions Gallimard. Published in English under the title *The Order of Things*. London: Tavistock; New York: Pantheon. 1970.

Freeman, T. (1962a). 'Narcissism and Defensive Processes in Schizophrenic States'. *International Journal of Psychoanalysis* 34: 415–425.

—— (1962b). 'The Psychoanalytic Observation of Chronic Schizophrenic Reactions'. In D. Richter et al. (Eds.), *Aspects of Psychiatric Research*. London: Oxford University Press.

—— (1965). *Studies in Psychosis*. London: Tavistock.

—— (1973). *A Psychoanalytic Study of Psychosis*. New York: International Universities Press.

—— (1988). *The Psychoanalyst in Psychiatry*. London: Karnac.

Freud, A. (1936). *The Ego and the Mechanisms of Defence*. London: Hogarth.

—— (1939–45). 'Infants without Families'. In *The Writings of Anna Freud* (Vol. 3). New York: International Universities Press, 1973.

—— (1953). 'Some Remarks on Infant Observations'. *The Psychoanalytic Study of the Child* 8: 9–19.

—— (1965). *Normality and Pathology in Childhood*. London: Hogarth Press and the Institute of Psychoanalysis.

Freud, S. (1900). 'The Interpretation of Dreams'. In *Standard Edition* (Vols 4 and 5).

—— (1909a). 'Notes upon a Case of Obsessional Neurosis'. In *Standard Edition* (Vol. 10).

—— (1909b). 'The Analysis of a Phobia in a Five-Year-Old Boy'. In *Standard Edition* (Vol. 10).

—— (1911). 'Formulations on the Two Principles of Mental Functioning'. In *Standard Edition* (Vol. 12, pp. 213–226).

—— (1915). 'Instincts and their Vicissitudes'. In *Standard Edition* (Vol. 14).

—— (1920). 'Beyond the Pleasure Principle'. In *Standard Edition* (Vol. 18).

—— (1923). 'The Ego and the Id'. In *Standard Edition* (Vol. 19).

—— (1926). 'Inhibitions, Symptoms and Anxiety'. In *Standard Edition* (Vol. 20).

—— (1927). 'The Future of an Illusion'. In *Standard Edition* (Vol. 21, pp. 5–58).

—— (1939). 'Moses and Monotheism'. In *Standard Edition* (Vol. 23).

Gaddini, R. with Gaddini, E. (1970). 'Transitional Objects and the Process of Individuation: A Study in Three Different Social Groups'. *Journal of the American Academy of Child Psychiatry* 9: 347–365.

Gaensbauer, T. J. (1995). 'Trauma in the Preverbal Period: Symptoms, Memories, and Developmental Impact'. *The Psychoanalytic Study of the Child* 50: 122–149.

Geissmann, C., and Geissmann, P. (1998). *A History of Child Psychoanalysis*. New Library of Psychoanalysis. London: Routledge.

Giannakoulas, A. (2005). 'Childhood Sexual Theories and Childhood Sexuality: The Primal Scene and Parental Sexuality'. In L. Caldwell (Ed.), *Sex and Sexuality: Winnicottian Perspectives* (pp. 55–68). London: Karnac.

Gillespie, W. H. (1960). *The Edge of Objectivity: An Essay in the History of Scientific Ideas*. Princeton, NJ: Princeton University Press.

Gillespie, W. (1971). 'Obituary'. *International Journal of Psychoanalysis* 52: 528.

Glover, E. (1943). 'The Concept of Dissociation'. *International Journal of Psychoanalysis* 24: 7–13.

Godley, W. (2001). *Saving Masud Khan*. London: London Review Books.

Goldman, D. (Ed.). (1993). *In One's Bones: The Clinical Genius of Winnicott*. New York: Jason Aronson.

—— (1998). 'Surviving as Scientist and Dreamer: Winnicott and "The Use of an Object"'. *Contemporary Psychoanalysis* 34: 359–367.

Gordon, R. (2001). 'Psychosomatics in Jung and Winnicott'. In M. Bertolini, A. Giannakoulas, and M. Hernandez (Eds.), in collaboration with A. Molino, *Squiggles and Spaces: Revisiting the Work of D. W. Winnicott* (Vol. 2, pp. 169–172). London: Whurr.

Green, A. (1986). 'The Dead Mother'. In *On Private Madness* (pp. 142–173). London: Hogarth. First published in French in 1972.

—— (2000). 'The Posthumous Winnicott: On *Human Nature*'. In Abram, J. (Ed.) *Andre Green at the Squiggle Foundation* (pp. 69–84). London: Karnac.

—— (2005). *Key Ideas for a Contemporary Psychoanalysis* (trans. A. Weller). New Library of Psychoanalysis. London: Routledge.

Greenacre, P. (1958). 'Early Physical Determinants in the Development of the Sense of Identity'. *Journal of the American Psychoanalytic Association* 6: 612–627

—— (1959). 'Play in Relation to the Creative Imagination'. *The Psychoanalytic Study of the Child* 14: 61–80.

—— (1960). 'Considerations regarding the Parent-Infant Relationship'. *International Journal of Psychoanalysis* 41: 571–584.

—— (1964). 'A Study on the Nature of Inspiration'. *Journal of the American Psychoanalytic Association* 12: 6–31.

—— (1969). 'The Fetish and the Transitional Object'. *The Psychoanalytic Study of the Child* 24: 144–164.

—— (1970). 'The Transitional Object and the Fetish with Special Reference to the Role of Illusion'. *International Journal of Psychoanalysis* 51: 447–456.

Greenberg, J., and Mitchell, S. (1983). *Object Relations in Psychoanalytic Theory*. Cambridge, MA and London: Harvard University Press.

Grolnick, S., and Barkin, M. (Eds.). (1978). *Between Fantasy and Reality*. New York: Jason Aronson.

Guntrip, H. (1975). 'My Experience of Analysis with Fairbairn and Winnicottt – (How Complete a Result Does Psycho-Analytic Therapy Achieve?).' *International Review of Psycho-Analysis* 2: 145–156.

—— (1996). 'My Experience of Analysis with Fairbairn and Winnicott'. *International Journal of Psychoanalysis* 77: 739–754.

Harris, M. (1965). 'Depression and the Depressive Position in an Adolescent Boy'. *Journal of Child Psychotherapy* 1(3): 33–40.

Hartmann, H. (1939). *Ego Psychology and the Problem of Adaptation*. London: Imago; New York: International Universities Press, 1958.

Heimann, P. (1950). 'On Counter-Transference'. *International Journal of Psychoanalysis* 31: 81–84.

—— (1956). 'Dynamics of Transference Interpretations'. *International Journal of Psychoanalysis* 37: 303–310; and in M. Tonnesmann (Ed.), *About Children and Children-No-Longer*. New Library of Psychoanalysis. London: Routledge, 1989.

Heimann, P., and Isaacs, S. (1943). 'Regression'. In P. King and R. Steiner (Eds.), *The Freud-Klein Controversies 1941–45*. New Library of Psychoanalysis. London: Routledge, 1991.

Hernandez, M., and Giannakoulas, A. (2001). 'On the Construction of Potential Space'. In M. Bertolini, A. Giannakoulas, and M. Hernandez (Eds.), in collaboration with A. Molino, *Squiggles and Spaces: Revisiting the Work of D. W. Winnicott* (Vol. 1, pp. 146–167). London: Whurr.

Hoffer, W. (1955). *Psychoanalysis: Practical and Research Aspects*. Baltimore, MD: Williams & Wilkins.

Hopkins, J. (1996). 'The Dangers and Deprivations of Too Good Mothering'. *Journal of Child Psychotherapy* 22 (3).

Hopkins, L. B. (2006). *False Self: The Life of Masud Khan*. New York: Other Press.

Huizinga, J. (1950). *Homo Ludens*. Boston, MA: Beacon Press.

Hurry, A. (1998). *Psychoanalysis and Developmental Therapy*. London: Karnac.

Inderbitzin, L., and Levy, S. (2000). 'Regression and Psychoanalytic Technique: The Concretization of a Concept'. *Psychoanalytic Quarterly* 69: 195–223.

Isaacs, S. (1943). 'The Nature and Function of Phantasy'. In P. King and R. Steiner (Eds.), *The Freud-Klein Controversies 1941–45* (pp. 199–243). New Library of Psychoanalysis. London: Routledge, 1991.

Isaacs Elmhirst, S. (1980). 'Transitional Objects in Transition'. *International Journal of Psychoanalysis* 61: 367–373.

James, M. (1960). 'Premature Ego Development'. *International Journal of Psychoanalysis* 41: 288–294.

—— (1962a). 'Infantile Narcissistic Trauma – Observations on Winnicott's Work in Infant Care and Child Development'. *International Journal of Psychoanalysis* 43: 69–79.

—— (1962b). 'The Theory of the Parent-Infant Relationship: Contribution to the Discussion'. *International Journal of Psychoanalysis* 43: 247–248.

Jaques, E. (1951). *The Changing Culture of the Factory*. London: Routledge and Kegan Paul.

Joffe, W. G., and Sandler, J. (1965). 'Notes on Pain, Depression, and Individuation'. *The Psychoanalytic Study of the Child* 20: 394–424.

Jones, E. (1946). 'A Valedictory Address'. *International Journal of Psychoanalysis* 27: 7–11.

Joyce, A. (2009). 'Infantile Psychosomatic Integrity and Maternal Trauma'. In T. Baradon (Ed.), *Relational Trauma in Infancy: Psychoanalytic, Attachment and Neuropsychological Contributions to Parent-Infant Psychotherapy*. London: Routledge.

Kahr, B. (1996). *Winnicott: A Biographical Portrait*. London: Karnac.

Kanter, J. (2004). *Face to Face with Children: The Life and Work of Clare Winnicott*. London: Karnac.

Khan, M. (1962). 'Dream Psychology and the Evolution of the Psychoanalytic Situation'. *International Journal of Psychoanalysis* 43: 21–31.

—— (1964). 'The Function of Intimacy in Acting Out in Perversions'. In R. Slovenko (Ed.), *Sexual Behaviour and the Law*. Springfield, IL: Thomas, 1965.

—— (1971). 'Infantile Neurosis as a False-Self Organization'. *Psychoanalytic Quarterly* 40: 245–263.

—— (1976). 'The Changing Use of Dreams in Psychoanalytic Practice'. *International Journal of Psychoanalysis* 57: 325–330.

—— (1987). 'Introduction'. In *Through Paediatrics to Psycho-Analysis* (pp. xi–xlviii). London: Hogarth.

King, P. (1953). 'Experiences of Success and Failure as Essential to the Process of Development'. In *Time Present and Time Past: Selected Papers of Pearl King* (pp. 41–52). London: Karnac, 2005.

—— (1978). 'Affective Responses of the Analyst to the Patient's Communication'. *International Journal of Psychoanalysis* 59: 329–334.

King, P., and Steiner, R. (Eds.). (1991). *The Freud–Klein Controversies 1941–1945*. New Library of Psychoanalysis. London: Routledge.

Klauber, J. (1967). 'On the Significance of Reporting Dreams in Psycho-Analysis'. *International Journal of Psychoanalysis* 48: 424–432.

—— (1986). 'The Relationship of Transference and Interpretation'. In *Difficulties in the Analytic Encounter* (pp. 25–44). London: Free Association Books.

—— (1987). *Illusion and Spontaneity in Psychoanalysis*. London: Free Association Books.

Klein, M. (1932). *The Psycho-Analysis of Children* (Rev. Edn.). London: Hogarth Press and the Institute of Psychoanalysis.

—— (1934). 'On Criminality'. In *Contributions to Psycho-Analysis 1921–1945*. London: Hogarth Press and the Institute of Psychoanalysis, 1948.

—— (1935). 'A Contribution to the Psychogenesis of Manic-Depressive States'. In *Love, Guilt and Reparation and Other Works 1921–1945* (Vol. 1., pp. 262–289). London: Hogarth Press, 1975.

—— (1940). 'Mourning and its Relation to Manic-Depressive States'. *International Journal of Psychoanalysis* 21: 125–153.

—— (1944). 'The Emotional Life and Ego-Development of the Infant with Special Reference to the Depressive Position'. In P. King and R. Steiner (Eds.), *The Freud–Klein Controversies 1941–45* (pp. 566–599). New Library of Psychoanalysis. London: Routledge, 1991.

—— (1946). 'Notes on Some Schizoid Mechanisms'. In M. Klein, P. Heimann, and S. Isaacs, with J. Riviere (Ed.), *Developments in Psycho-Analysis* (pp. 292–320). London: Hogarth, 1952.

—— (1952). 'On Criminality' (1934). In M. Klein, P. Heimann, and R. E. Money-Kyrle (Eds.), *New Directions in Psychoanalysis: The Significance of Infant Conflict in the Pattern of Adult Behaviour*. London: Karnac.

—— (1957). *Envy and Gratitude*. London: Tavistock.

—— (1959). 'Our Adult World and Its Roots in Infancy'. In *Envy and Gratitude and Other Works 1946–1963* (pp. 247–263). London: Hogarth Press, 1975.

—— (1961). 'Narrative of a Child Analysis'. In *Writings* (Vol. 4). London: Hogarth Press and the Institute of Psychoanalysis, 1975.

Klein, M., Heimann, P., and Money-Kyrle, R. E. (Eds.). (1955). *New Directions in Psychoanalysis: The Significance of Infant Conflict in the Pattern of Adult Behaviour*. New York: Basic Books.

Knights, L. C. (1946). *Explorations*. London: Chatto & Windus; Harmondsworth: Penguin Books (Peregrine series), 1964.

Kris, E. (1951). 'Some Comments and Observations on Early Autoerotic Activities'. *The Psychoanalytic Study of the Child* 6: 95–116.

Kristeva, J. (2001). *Melanie Klein*. New York: Columbia University Press.

Lacan, J. (1948). 'Aggressivity in Psychoanalysis'. In *Écrits: A Selection* (trans. A. Sheridan, pp. 8–29). London: Tavistock, 1977.

—— (1949a). 'The Mirror Stage as Formative Function of the I' [Le stade du miroir comme formateur de la fonction de Je]. *Revue Francaise de Psychanalyse* 4 (Oct–Dec): 449–455.

—— (1949b). 'The Mirror Stage as Formative of the Function of the I as Revealed in Psycho-analytic Experience'. In *Écrits: A Selection* (trans. A. Sheridan, pp. 1–7). London: Tavistock, 1977.

—— (1987 [*1960*]). 'Letter to D. W. Winnicott' (trans. Jeffrey Mehlman). *October* 40: 76–78. Published in 1985 as 'Lettre à D. W. Winnicott' *Ornicar?* 33: 7–10.

Laing, R. D. (1960). *The Divided Self*. London: Penguin.

—— (1961). *The Self and Others*. London: Penguin.

Lanyado, M. (2006a). 'Doing "Something Else": The Values of Therapeutic Communication when Offering Consultations and Brief Psychotherapy'. In M. Lanyado and A. Horne (Eds.), *A Question of Technique* (pp. 175–192). London: Routledge.

—— (2006b). 'Brief Psychotherapy and Therapeutic Consultations: How Much Therapy is "Good-Enough"'. In M. Lanyado and A. Horne (Eds.). *The Handbook of Child and Adolescent Psychotherapy* (pp. 233–246). London: Routledge.

Likierman, M. (2007). 'Donald Winnicott and Melanie Klein: Compatible Outlooks?'. In L. Caldwell (Ed.), *Winnicott and the Psychoanalytic Tradition* (pp. 112–127). London: Karnac.

Little, M. (1951). 'Counter-Transference and the Patient's Response to It'. *International Journal of Psychoanalysis* 32: 32–40.

—— (1957). ' 'R'—The Analyst's Total Response to his Patient's Needs'. *International Journal of Psychoanalysis* 38: 240–254.

—— (1990). *Psychotic Anxieties and Containment*. Northvale, NJ: Jason Aronson.

Lomas, P. (1961). 'Family Role and Identity Formation'. *International Journal of Psycho-analysis* 42: 371–380.

Lowenfeld, M. (1935). *Play in Childhood*. Bath, UK: Cedric Chivers, 1969.

Lucas, R. (2009). *The Psychotic Wavelength*. New Library of Psychoanalysis. London: Routledge.

MacAlpine, I. (1952). 'Psychosomatic Symptom Formation'. *Lancet*, 9 February.

Maffei, G. (2001). 'C. G. Jung's *Memories, Dreams, Reflections*: Notes on the Review by D. W. Winnicott'. In M. Bertolini, A. Giannakoulas, and M. Hernandez (Eds.), in collaboration with A. Molino, *Squiggles and Spaces: Revisiting the Work of D. W. Winnicott* (Vol. 2, pp. 196–203). London: Whurr.

Martin-Cabrè, L. (2001). 'Winnicott and Ferenczi: Trauma and the Maternal Analyst'. In M. Bertolini, A. Giannakoulas, and M. Hernandez (Eds.), in collaboration with A. Molino, *Squiggles and Spaces: Revisiting the Work of D. W. Winnicott* (Vol. 2, pp. 179–184). London: Whurr.

Marty, P. (1976). *Les mouvements individuels de vie et de mort [Individual movements of life and death]*. Paris: Payot.

—— (1980). *L'ordre psychosomatique [The psychosomatic order]*. Paris: Payot.

Marty, P., and De M'Uzan, M. (1963). 'La pensée opératoire' [Mechanical functioning]. *Rev. Franç Psychanal* 27: 345–356.

Marty, P., De M'Uzan, M., and David, C. (1994). *L'Investigation psychosomatique: Sept obser-vations cliniques [1963] [Psychosomatic investigations: Seven clinical observations]*. Paris: PUF.

McDougall, J. (1980). 'A Child is Being Eaten – I. Psychosomatic States, Anxiety Neurosis and Hysteria – A Theoretical Approach. II: The Abysmal Mother and the Cork Child – A Clinical Illustration'. *Contemporary Psychoanalysis* 16: 417–459.

Middlemore, M. (1941). *The Nursing Couple*. London: Hamish Hamilton.

Miller, A. (1963). *Jane's Blanket*. New York and London: Collier/Macmillan.

Milner, M. (1952). 'Aspects of Symbolism in Comprehension of the Not-Self'. *International Journal of Psychoanalysis* 33: 181–195.

—— [J. Field Pseud.]. (1957). *On Not Being Able to Paint* (Rev. Edn.). London: Heinemann.

—— (1969). *The Hands of the Living God*. London: Hogarth Press and the Institute of Psychoanalysis.

—— (1987a). 'The Role of Illusion in Symbol Formation'. In *The Suppressed Madness of Sane Men* (pp. 83–113). New Library of Psychoanalysis. London: Routledge, 1990.

—— (1987b). *The Suppressed Madness of Sane Men: Forty-Four Years of Exploring Psychoanalysis*. New Library of Psychoanalysis. London: Routledge.

Mitchell, S. (2006). 'Using Winnicott to Understand Gender/Social Sex'. Plenary presentation to Donald Winnicott Today.

Modell, A. H. (1985). 'The Works of Winnicott and the Evolution of his Thought'. *Journal of the American Psychoanalytic Association* 335: 113–137.

Money-Kyrle, R. (1951). *Psychoanalysis and Politics*. London: Duckworth.

—— (1956). 'Normal Counter-Transference and Some of its Deviations'. *International Journal of Psychoanalysis* 37: 360–366.

Muller, J. P., and Richardson, W. J., (1982). *Lacan and Language: A Reader's Guide to Ecrits*. New York: International Universities Press

Ogden, T. (1988). 'Misrecognitions and the Fear of Not Knowing'. *Psychoanalytic Quarterly* 57: 643–666.

—— (1989). *The Primitive Edge of Experience*. Northvale, NJ: Jason Aronson.

—— (1992). 'The Dialectically Constituted/Decentred Subject of Psychoanalysis. II: The Contributions of Klein and Winnicott'. *International Journal of Psychoanalysis* 73: 613–626.

—— (2001). 'Reading Winnicott'. *Psychoanalytic Quarterly* 70: 299–323.

—— (2005). 'On Holding and Containing, Being and Dreaming'. In *This Art of Psychoanalysis*. New Library of Psychoanalysis. London: Routledge.

O'Shaughnessy, E. (1964). 'The Absent Object'. *Journal of Child Psychotherapy* 1(2): 34–43.

—— (2008, December). *Where is Here? When is Now?* Paper presented at the Here and Now Today conference, UCL, London.

Padel, J. (1991). 'The Psychoanalytic Theories of Melanie Klein and Donald Winnicott and Their Interaction in the British Society of Psychoanalysis'. *Psychoanalytic Review* 78: 325–345.

Parsons, M. (2000). *The Dove that Returns, The Dove that Vanishes*. New Library of Psychoanalysis. London: Routledge.

—— (2007). 'Raiding the Inarticulate: The Internal Analytic Setting and Listening Beyond Countertransference'. *International Journal of Psychoanalysis* 88: 1141–1156.

Phillips, A. (1988). *Winnicott*. Modern Masters Series. London: Fontana.

Pick, I. (1967). 'On Stealing'. *Journal of Child Psychotherapy* 2(1): 67–79.

Racker, H. (1953). 'A Contribution to the Problem of Counter-Transference'. *International Journal of Psychoanalysis* 34: 313–324.

Ramzy, I. (Ed.). (1977). 'Introduction'. In *The Piggle: An Account of the Psychoanalytic Treatment of a Little Girl*. London: Hogarth.

Rappaport, D. (1998). 'Destruction and Gratitude: Some Thoughts on "The Use of an Object"'. *Contemporary Psychoanalysis* 34: 369–378.

Rayner, E. (1986). *Human Development: The Psychodynamics of Human Growth, Maturity and Ageing* (3rd Edn.). London: Routledge.

—— (1991). *The Independent Mind in British Psychoanalysis*. London: Free Association Books.

Reeves, C. (2005a). 'A Duty to Care: Reflections on the Influence of Bowlby and Winnicott on the 1948 Children Act'. In J. Issroff (Ed.), *Donald Winnicott and John Bowlby: Personal and Professional Perspectives*. London: Karnac.

—— (2005b). 'Singing the Same Tune'. In J. Issroff (Ed.), *Donald Winnicott and John Bowlby: Personal and Professional Perspectives*. London: Karnac.

—— (2006). 'The Anatomy of Riddance'. *Journal of Child Psychotherapy* 32(3): 273–94.

—— (2007). 'The Mantle of Freud: Was "The Use of an Object" Winnicott's *Todestrieb*?'. *British Journal of Psychotherapy*, 23(3): 365–382.

Reich, A. (1951). 'On Counter-Transference'. *International Journal of Psychoanalysis* 32: 25–31.

Ribble, M. (1943). *The Rights of Infants*. New York: Columbia University Press.

Riviere, J. (1936). 'On the Genesis of Psychical Conflict in Earliest Infancy'. *International Journal of Psychoanalysis* 17: 399–422.

Robertson, J. (1958). *Young Children in Hospital*. London: Tavistock.

Rodman, N. (1987). *The Spontaneous Gesture: Selected Letters of D. W. Winnicott*. London: Karnac.

Rodman, F. R. (2003). *Winnicott: Life and Work*. Cambridge, MA: Perseus.

Rosenfeld, H. (1947). 'Analysis of a Schizophrenic State with Depersonalization'. *International Journal of Psychoanalysis* 28: 130–139.

—— (1950). 'Note on the Psychopathology of Confusional States in Chronic Schizophrenia'. *International Journal of Psychoanalysis* 31: 132–137.

—— (1954). 'Considerations Regarding the Psycho-Analytic Approach to Acute and Chronic Schizophrenia'. *International Journal of Psychoanalysis* 35: 135–140.

—— (1965). *Psychotic States*. London: Hogarth.

—— (1987). 'On the Treatment of Psychotic States by Psychoanalysis: A Historical Approach'. In *Impasse and Interpretation* (pp. 281–311). New Library of Psychoanalysis.

Roudinesco, É. (1990). *Jacques Lacan & Co.: A History of Psychoanalysis in France, 1925–1985* (trans. J. Mehlman). Chicago, IL: University of Chicago Press.

Rycroft, C. (1955). 'On Idealisation, Illusion and Catastrophic Disillusion'. *International Journal of Psychoanalysis* 36: 469–472.

—— (1956). 'Symbolism and its Relationship to the Primary and Secondary Processes'. *International Journal of Psychoanalysis* 37: 137–146.

—— (1968). *Imagination and Reality: Psychoanalytic Essays 1951–61*. London: Hogarth.

—— (1972). 'D. W. Winnicott'. In P. Fuller (Ed.), *Psychoanalysis and Beyond*. London: Chatto and Windus, 1985.

Sandler, J. (1975). 'Countertransference and Role Responsiveness'. *International Review of Psycho-Analysis* 3: 43–47.

Scarfone, D. (2005). Laplanche and Winnicott Meet . . . and Survive'. In L. Caldwell (Ed.), *Sex and Sexuality: Winnicottian Perspectives* (pp. 33–54). London: Karnac.

Schiller, F. (1954). *On the Aesthetic Education of Man in a Series of Letters*. New Haven, CT: Yale University Press.

Scott, W. C. M. (1949). 'The Body Scheme in Psychotherapy'. *British Journal of Medical Psychology* 22.

Searles, H. F. (1960). *The Nonhuman Environment*. New York: International Universities Press.

—— (1962). 'Scorn, Disillusionment and Adoration in the Psychotherapy of Schizophrenia'. *Psychoanalytic Review* 49(3): 39–60.

—— (1963). *Collected Papers on Schizophrenia and Related Subjects*. London: Hogarth.

Sechehaye, M. (1951). *Symbolic Realization*. New York: International Universities Press.

Sedgwick, D. (1997). 'Some Images of the Analyst's Participation in the Analytic Process'. *Journal of Analytical Psychology* 42: 41–46.

Segal, H. (1950). 'Some Aspects of the Analysis of a Schizophrenic'. *International Journal of Psychoanalysis* 31: 268–278.

—— (1956). 'Depression in the Schizophrenic'. *International Journal of Psychoanalysis* 37: 339–343.

—— (1957). 'Notes on Symbol Formation'. *International Journal of Psychoanalysis* 38: 391–397.

—— (2006). 'Reflections on Truth, Tradition, and the Psychoanalytic Tradition of Truth'. *American Imago* 63: 283–292.

Sharpe, E. F. (1937). *Dream Analysis*. London: Karnac, 1988.

Sharpe, S. (1927). 'Contribution to Symposium on Child Analysis'. *International Journal of Psychoanalysis* 8: 380–384.

Shoenberg, P. (2001). 'Winnicott and the Psyche-Soma'. In M. Bertolini, A. Giannakoulas, and M. Hernandez (Eds.), in collaboration with A. Molino, *Squiggles and Spaces: Revisiting the Work of D. W. Winnicott* (Vol. 2). London: Whurr.

—— (2007). *Psychosomatics: The Uses of Psychotherapy*. London: Palgrave Macmillan.

Spezzano, C. (2004). 'Comments to *International Journal of Psychoanalysis* internet discussion group bulletin on paper 'A Missing Link in Psychoanalytic Technique: Psychoanalytic Consciousness' by Fred Busch, with rejoinder by Betty Joseph'. *International Journal of Psychoanalysis* 85: 567–578.

Spitz, R. (1962). 'Autoerotism Re-examined: The Role of Early Sexual Behaviour Patterns in Personality Formation'. *The Psychoanalytic Study of the Child* 17: 283–318.

Spurling, L. (2003). 'On Psychoanalytic Figures as Transference Objects'. *International Journal of Psychoanalysis* 84: 31–43.

—— (2008). 'Is There Still a Place for the Concept of "Therapeutic Regression" in Psychoanalysis?'. *International Journal of Psychoanalysis* 89: 523–540.

Stern, D. (1985). *The Interpersonal World of the Infant*. New York: Basic Books.

Stevenson, O. (1954). 'The First Treasured Possession'. *The Psychoanalytic Study of the Child* 2.

Stewart, H. (1992). *Psychic Experience and Problems of Technique*. New Library of Psychoanalysis. London: Routledge.

Tonnesmann, M. (1993). 'The Third Area of Experience in Psychoanalysis'. In *Winnicott Studies*, no. 8, Autumn.

—— (1989). *About Children and Children no Longer*. New Library of Psychoanalysis. London: Routledge.

—— (2002). 'Early Emotional Development: Ferenczi to Winnicott'. In L. Caldwell (Ed.), *The Elusive Child* (pp. 45–58). London: Karnac.

—— (2007). 'Michael Balint and Donald Winnicott: Contributions to the Treatment of Severely Disturbed Patients in the Independent Tradition'. In L. Caldwell (Ed.), *Winnicott and the Psychoanalytic Tradition* (pp. 129–140). London: Karnac.

Trevarthen, C., and Hubley, P. (1978). 'Secondary Intersubjectivity: Confidence, Confiding and Acts of Meaning in the First Year'. In A. Lock (Ed.), *Action, Gesture and Symbol: The Emergence of Language* (pp. 183–230). London: Academic Press.

Turner, J. (2002). 'Illusion in the Work of Winnicott'. *International Journal of Psychoanalysis* 83: 1051–1062.

Tyson, P., and Tyson, R. L. (1993). *Psychoanalytic Theories of Development: An Integration*. New Haven, CT: Yale University Press.

Usuelli Kluzer, A. (1992). 'The Significance of Illusion in the Work of Freud and Winnicott: A Controversial Issue'. *International Review of Psycho-Analysis* 19: 179–187.

—— (2001). 'Illusion and Reality in the Work of D. W. Winnicott'. In M. Bertolini, A. Giannakoulas, and M. Hernandez (Eds.), in collaboration with A. Molino, *Squiggles and Spaces: Revisiting the Work of D. W. Winnicott* (Vol. 2, pp. 49–58). London: Whurr.

Wheelis, A. (1958). *The Quest for Identity*. New York: Norton.

White, J. (2006). *Generation: Preoccupations and Conflicts in Contemporary Psychoanalysis*. London: Routledge.

Wickes, F. G. (1938). *The Inner World of Man*. New York: Farrar & Rinehart; London: Methuen, 1950.

Willoughby, R. (2002). 'Public, Private and Secret Narratives in The Life and Work of Masud

Khan'. Thesis submitted for the degree of Doctor of Philosophy, University of Kent at Canterbury.

—— (2004). *Masud Khan: The Myth and the Reality*. London: Free Association Books.

Winnicott, C. (1954). 'Casework Techniques in the Child Care Services'. In *Child Care and Social Work*. Hertfordshire: Codicote, 1964.

Winnicott, C., Shepherd, R., and Davis, M. (Eds.). (1984). *Deprivation and Delinquency*. New York: Methuen.

Winnicott, D. W. (1931). *Clinical Notes on Disorders of Childhood*. London: Heinemann.

—— (1935). 'The Manic Defence'. In *Collected Papers*.

—— (1936). 'Appetite and Emotional Disorder'. In *Collected Papers*.

—— (1939). *Aggression: In the Child and the Outside World*. London: Tavistock.

—— (1942a). 'Why Children Play'. In J. Hardenberg (Ed.), *The Child and the Outside World*. London: Tavistock, 1957.

—— (1942b). 'Review of M. Middlemore. *The Nursing Couple*. 1941. London: Hamish Hamilton'. *International Journal of Psychoanalysis* 23: 179–181.

—— (1945a). 'Getting to Know Your Baby' (Broadcast Talks). London: Heinemann for *The New Era in Home and School* 26: 1–5.

—— (1945b). 'Thinking and the Unconscious'. *Liberal Magazine* (March). Reprinted in D. W. Winnicott, *Home is Where we Start From: Essays by a Psychoanalyst* Eds. C. Winnicott, R. Shepherd, and M. Davis (pp. 169–171). Harmondsworth, UK: Penguin, 1986.

—— (1946). 'What Do We Mean by a Normal Child?'. In J. Hardenberg (Ed.), *The Child and the Outside World*. London: Tavistock, 1957.

—— (1947). 'Physical Therapy of Mental Disorder'. *British Medical Journal* correspondence, *British Medical Journal* 17 May: 688.

—— (1948a). 'Reparation in Respect of Mother's Organized Defence against Depression'. In *Collected Papers*.

—— (1948b). 'Paediatrics and Psychiatry'. In *Collected Papers*.

—— (1948c). 'Children's Hostels in War and Peace'. *British Journal of Medical Psychology* 21: 175–180. Reprinted in *The Child and the Outside World* (pp. 117–121). London: Tavistock, 1957.

—— (1949a). 'Leucotomy'. *British Medical Students' Journal*, Spring 3(2): 35.

—— (1949b). 'The Ordinary Devoted Mother and Her Baby'. Nine broadcast talks republished in *The Child and the Family*. London: Tavistock, 1957.

—— (1949c). 'Birth Memories, Birth Trauma, and Anxiety'. In *Collected Papers*.

—— (1950a). 'Growth and Development in Immaturity'. In *The Family and Individual Development* (pp. 21–29). London: Tavistock, 1965.

—— (1950b). 'The Deprived Child and how he can be Compensated for Loss of Family Life'. In *The Family and Individual Development* (pp. 132–145). London: Tavistock, 1965.

—— (1951). 'The Foundation of Mental Health'. *British Medical Journal* 1(4719). Also in *Deprivation and Deliquency* Eds. C. Winnicott, R. Shepherd, and M. Davis (pp. 168–171). New York: Methuen, 1984.

—— (1952a). 'Psychoses and Child Care'. In *Collected Papers*.

—— (1952b). 'Anxiety Associated with Insecurity'. In *Collected Papers*.

—— (1953). 'Symptom Tolerance in Paediatrics'. In *Collected Papers*.

—— (1954a). 'The Depressive Position in Normal Emotional Development'. In *Collected Papers*.

—— (1954b). 'Withdrawal and Regression'. In *Collected Papers*.

—— (1956a). 'On Transference', published as 'Clinical Varieties of Transference'. In *Collected Papers*.

—— (1956b). 'Primary Maternal Preoccupation'. In *Collected Papers*.

—— (1956c). 'The Antisocial Tendency'. In *Collected Papers* (1958a, pp. 306–315).

—— (1957a). 'Excitement in the Aetiology of Coronary Thrombosis'. In D. W. Winnicott, *Psychoanalytic Explorations* Eds. C. Winnicott, R. Shepherd, and M. Davis. London: Karnac, 1989.

—— (1957b). *The Child and the Family*. London: Tavistock.

—— (1957c). *The Child and the Outside World*. London: Tavistock.

—— (1958a). *Collected Papers: Through Paediatrics to Psycho-Analysis*. London: Tavistock.

—— (1958b). 'Child Analysis in the Latency Period'. In *Maturational Processes*.

—— (1958c). 'Psycho-Analysis and the Sense of Guilt'. In *Maturational Processes*.

—— (1958d). 'The Capacity to Be Alone'. In *Collected Papers*.

—— (1958e). 'The Family Affected by Depressive Illness in One or Both Parents'. In *The Family and Individual Development* (pp. 50–60). London: Tavistock, 1965

—— (1958f). 'The Fate of the Transitional Object'. In D. W. Winnicott, *Psychoanalytic Explorations* Eds. C. Winnicott, R. Shepherd, and M. Davis (pp. 53–58). London: Karnac.

—— (1959a). 'Classification: Is There a Psycho-Analytic Contribution to Psychiatric Classification?'. In *Maturational Processes* (1965a, pp. 124–139).

—— (1959b). 'Review of *Envy and Gratitude*'. In D. W. Winnicott, *Psycho-Analytic Explorations* Eds. C. Winnicott, R. Shepherd, and M. Davis (pp. 443–446). London: Karnac, 1989.

—— (1960a). 'Ego Distortion in Terms of True and False Self'. In *Maturational Processes*.

—— (1960b). 'Counter-Transference'. In *Maturational Processes*.

—— (1960c). 'String: A Technique of Communication'. In *Maturational Processes*.

—— (1960d). 'The Relationship of a Mother to her Baby at the Beginning'. In *The Family and Individual Development* (pp. 15–20). London: Tavistock, 1965.

—— (1960e). 'Aggression, Guilt and Reparation'. In *Deprivation and Delinquency* Eds. C. Winnicott, R. Shepherd, and M. Davis (pp. 106–112). London: Tavistock, 1984.

—— (1961a). 'Varieties of Psychotherapy'. In *Deprivation and Delinquency*. London: Tavistock, 1984.

—— (1961b, first presented 1959). 'The Effect of Psychotic Parents on the Emotional Development of the Child'. In *The Family and Individual Development* (pp. 69–78). London: Tavistock, 1965.

—— (1962a). 'The Aims of Psycho-Analytical Treatment'. In *Maturational Processes*.

—— (1962b). 'Ego Integration in Child Development'. In *Maturational Processes*.

—— (1962c). 'A Personal View of the Kleinian Contribution'. In *Maturational Processes*.

—— (1963a). 'Morals and Education'. In *Maturational Processes*.

—— (1963b). 'Psychotherapy of Character Disorders'. In *Maturational Processes* (1965a, pp. 203–216).

—— (1963c, first presented 1962). 'Dependence in Infant-Care, in Child-Care, and in the Psycho-Analytic Setting'. In *Maturational Processes* (1965a, pp. 249–259).

—— (1964a). *The Child, the Family and the Outside World*. London: Penguin.

—— (1964b). 'Psycho-Somatic Disorder'. In D. Winnicott, *Psychoanalytic Explorations*, Eds. C. Winnicott, R. Shepherd, and M. Davis. London: Karnac, 1989.

—— (1964c). 'The Concept of the False Self'. In C. Winnicott, R. Shepherd, and M. Davis (Eds.), *Home is Where We Start From: Essays by a Psychoanalyst* (pp. 65–70). Harmondsworth, UK: Penguin, 1986.

—— (1965a). *The Maturational Processes and the Facilitating Environment*. London: Hogarth Press and the Institute of Psychoanalysis.

—— (1965b). *The Family and Individual Development*. London: Tavistock.

—— (1965c). 'The Psychology of Madness: A Contribution from Psycho-Analysis'. In D. W. Winnicott, *Psychoanalytic Explorations* Eds. C. Winnicott, R. Shepherd, and M. Davis (pp. 118–129). London: Karnac, 1989.

—— (1965d, first presented in 1963). 'Struggling Through the Doldrums'. In *The Family and Individual Development* (pp. 79–87), London: Tavistock, 1965.

—— (1966a). 'Absence and Presence of a Sense of Guilt Illustrated in Two Patients'. In D. W. Winnicott, *Psychoanalytic Explorations* Eds. C. Winnicott, R. Shepherd, and M. Davis. London: Karnac, 1989.

—— (1966b). 'Comment on Obsessional Neurosis and "Frankie"'. *International Journal of Psychoanalysis* 47: 143–144.

—— (1966c). 'The Ordinary Devoted Mother'. Talk given to the Nursery Association of GB and N. Ireland, London Branch, 16 February 1966. Published in *Winnicott on the Child*. Cambridge, MA: Perseus.

—— (1966d). 'The Split-Off Male and Female Elements to be found in Men and Women'. Part of Chapter 5 'Creativity and its Origins' in *Playing and Reality* (pp. 65–85). London: Tavistock, 1971a.

—— (1967a). 'The Location of Cultural Experience'. *International Journal of Psychoanalysis* 48: 368–372.

—— (1967b). 'Mirror-role of Mother and Family in Child Development'. In P. Lomas (Ed.), *The Predicament of the Family: A Psycho-Analytical Symposium*. London: Hogarth Press and the Institute of Psychoanalysis.

—— (1967c). 'Delinquency as a Sign of Hope'. In C. Winnicott, R. Shepherd, and M. Davis (Eds.), *Home Is Where We Start From: Essays by a Psychoanalyst*. New York: Norton.

—— (1967d). 'The Concept of a Healthy Individual'. In C. Winnicott, R. Shepherd, and M. Davis (Eds.), *Home is Where We Start From: Essays by a Psychoanalyst* (pp. 21–34). Harmondsworth, UK: Penguin, 1986. [First published in J. D. Sutherland (Ed.). (1971). *Towards Community Mental Health*. London: Tavistock.]

—— (1968a). 'Playing: Its Theoretical Status in the Clinical Situation'. *International Journal of Psychoanalysis* 49: 591–599.

—— (1968b). 'La Schizophrénie infantile en termes d'échec d'adaptation'. In *Recherches* (special issue: 'Enfance aliénée', II), December, Paris.

—— (1969). 'The Use of an Object in the Context of *Moses and Monotheism*'. In D. W. Winnicott, *Psychoanalytic Explorations* Eds. C. Winnicott, R. Shepherd, and M. Davis (pp. 240–246), London: Karnac, 1989.

—— (1970a). 'Basis for Self in Body'. In D. W. Winnicott, *Psychoanalytic Explorations* Eds. C. Winnicott, R. Shepherd, and M. Davis. London: Karnac, 1989.

—— (1970b). 'Cure'. In D. W. Winnicott, C. Winnicott, R. Shepherd, and M. Davis, *Home Is Where We Start From: Essays by a Psychoanalyst*. New York: Norton, 1990.

—— (1970c). 'Residential Care as Therapy'. In C. Winnicott, R. Shepherd, and M. Davis (Eds.), *Deprivation and Delinquency*. New York: Methuen, 1984.

—— (1971a). *Playing and Reality*. London: Tavistock, republished by Routledge, 1991.

—— (1971b). *Therapeutic Consultations in Child Psychiatry*. London: Hogarth Press and the Institute of Psychoanalysis.

—— (1971c). 'Playing: Creative Activity and the Search for the Self'. In *Playing and Reality* (pp. 53–64). London: Tavistock.

—— (1971d). 'Dreaming, Fantasying and Living'. In *Playing and Reality*. London: Tavistock.

—— (1971e). 'Interrelating Apart from Instinctual Drive and in Terms of Cross-Identifications'. In *Playing and Reality*. London: Tavistock.

—— (1977). *The Piggle*. London; Hogarth Press and the Institute of Psychoanalysis.

—— (1986). 'Cure'. In D. W. Winnicott, C. Winnicott, R. Shepherd, and M. Davis (Eds.), *Home is Where We Start From: Essays by a Psychoanalyst* (pp. 112–121). Harmondsworth, UK: Penguin. (See also 1970b.)

Winnicott, D. W. (author), Winnicott, C., Shepherd, R., and Davis, M. (Eds.). (1986), *Home is Where We Start From: Essays by a Psychoanalyst*. Harmondsworth, UK: Penguin.

—— (1988). *Human Nature*. London: Free Association Books.

Winnicott, D. W. (author), Winnicott, C., Shepherd, R., and Davis, M. (Eds.). (1989). *Psychoanalytic Explorations*. London: Karnac.

—— (1990). *Home Is Where We Start From: Essays by a Psychoanalyst.* New York: Norton.

Winnicott, D. W., Brazelton, T.B., Greenspan, S. I., and Spock, B. (2002). *Winnicott on the Child.* London: Perseus.

Winnicott, D. W., and Britton, C. (1947). 'Residential Management as Treatment for Difficult Children: The Evolution of a Wartime Hostels Scheme'. *Human Relations* 1 (June): 87–97.

Winnicott, D. W., and Gibbs, N. (1926). 'Varicella Encepalitis and Vaccinia Encephalitis'. *British Journal of Children's Diseases* 23: 107–122.

Winnicott, D., and Khan, M. (1953). 'Review of *Psychoanalytic Studies of the Personality*'. *International Journal of Psychoanalysis* 34: 329–333.

Winnicott, D., with Khan, M. (1986). *Holding and Interpretation. Fragment of an Analysis.* London: Hogarth.

Wright, K. (1991). *Vision and Separation Between Mother and Baby.* Northvale, NJ: Jason Aronson.

—— (2007). 'The Suppressed Madness of Sane Analysts'. In L. Caldwell (Ed.). *Winnicott and the Psychoanalytic Tradition* (pp. 165–173). London: Karnac.

Wulff, M. (1946). 'Fetishism and Object Choice in Early Childhood'. *Psychoanalytic Quarterly* 15: 450–471.

INDEX

auxiliary ego 175, 202, 203; analyst's 207; functioning 177

average expectable environment, failure of, effect of, on child's mental functioning [clinical example: Bob] 214–225

Axline, V. M. 245

B Group 4

baby: *see* infant(s)/baby(ies)

Balint, A. 70

Balint, M. 1, 23, 55, 70–71, 127–130, 148; and Winnicott, theoretical links between 9–10

Barkin, L. 20, 100, 102

Barnett, B. 9

'basic fault' 129

being, continuity of 11, 55, 88–89, 91, 97, 149, 160, 165–167, 205

Bettelheim, B. 267

Bick, E. 209, 210

Bion, W. R. 1, 6, 12, 15–16, 23–24, 70, 84, 150, 170, 195

birth symbolism 81

bisexuality 270, 273, 275, 280

bladder functions 93

body: image 263; mind and psyche, interrelation of 17; scheme 87, 96, 156, 159–160, 175

Bollas, C. 1, 16, 211, 230

borderline patient(s) 22, 23, 25, 70, 86, 130, 153, 156, 164, 167, 193, 253, 254; analysis of 253

boundary: formation 20, 102; violations 25, 130

Bowlby, J. 3, 27, 32, 60, 147, 148, 209

BPAS: *see* British Psychoanalytical Society

BPS: *see* British Psychological Society

Brafman, A. H. 213, 214

breakdown 6, 24, 63, 140, 224; as failure of defence organization 201; fear of 197–208; meaning of 201

breast (*passim*): absent 49, 84; attack on 63, 64, 258, 260; baby as 276, 278–280; creative hallucination for baby 6, 19, 56, 112, 113; deintegration contained by 13; envy of 257, 279; first object 125; good 280; magically introjected 115; primary identification with 262; as self 279; and transitional object 107, 110, 111

breathing 41, 46, 47, 93–95

British Association of Psychotherapists 210

British object relations theory 1, 249

British Psychoanalytical Society (BPAS) 1–4, 9, 31–33, 54, 55, 71, 100, 127, 147–148, 170, 209–210, 262

British Psychological Society (BPS) 4, 12, 32, 83, 98

Britton, C.: see Winnicott, C.

Britton, R. 3, 4, 83, 99

bronchial spasm and anxiety 43

Bullard, D. M. 24

Busch, F. 8

Cambridge University 2

Carvalho, R. 13

Casement, P. J. 13

castration: anxiety 76, 77, 134, 156, 201; dream 76

cataloguing 91, 94, 96, 97

cathexis 186, 254, 258; withdrawal of 212, 220–221

central or true self, concept of 160

Chestnut Lodge, Washington, CD 70

child(ren) (*passim*): analysis of 26, 27, 209, 235; antisocial 190 [chronically disturbed 30]; autistic 123; development 83, 170, 209; evacuated 7, 27, 34, 54, 71, 78 [see also evacuation, in World War II]; psychiatry 1–4, 26, 27, 214; psychoanalysis with, and Winnicott's theories 20–30; psychotherapy 26, 209; sexual fantasies of 28; Winnicott's work with 26–28, 209–213, 236

Child Guidance Clinic, London 3

Children's Act (1948) 4

Clancier, L. 5

classification 101, 131–132, 197, 224, 253–254

clinical regression 130, 143

Coleridge, S. T. 20

colic 38

communicating/communication: capacity for 185; cul-de-sac 188, 189; explicit 182, 196 [indirect, pleasurable 192]; failure of 192; false and empty 183; implicit 182; non-verbal 183; opposites of 188, 193–194; pathological 184; preverbal forms of 182; and right not to communicate 182–196; with self 182, 183; silent 184, 192; symbolic 183; theory of 182, 187–188; verbal 183, 236

compliance 16, 90, 183, 210, 233, 246, 261, 264, 267

Fordham, M. 12–14, 184, 194
fort/da (cotton-reel) game 35, 51–53, 153
Foucault, M. 268
fragmentation 83
free association 143
Freeman, T. 70
Freud, A. 1–5, 14, 26–27, 60, 148, 209–210, 236; Controversial Discussions 2
Freud, S. (*passim*): ambivalence, basic concept of 268; analysis [of psychotics 24; choice of cases for 136; technique and setting of 137, 138]; anxiety 43; breast, absence of 84; classical technique 2, 5; cotton-reel (*fort/da*) game 35, 51–53, 153; countertransference 71; drive as masculine 263; father, role of 249; and Ferenczi 1, 23, 33; fixation points in psychosexual development 128; hate 79; illusion 56; infantile sexuality 167; internalized danger 44; and Jung, disagreement between 31; metapsychology 5; on narcissism 9, 15; object relations theory 1; obsessional neurosis, theory of 98; Oedipus complex 22; pleasure principle 149, 154; primary repression 152; psychic reality [concept of 189; inner 175]; psychological meanings, theory of 20; psychosomatic disorders 85; regression 131; self, division of 16; self-analysis of 137; sexuality 16, 17 [pre-genital 155]; and Winnicott, theoretical links between 1, 5–6
Fromm Reichmann, F. 24
fusion 159, 175, 176, 187, 268; prelogical, of subject and object 234

Gaddini, E. 101
Gaddini, R. 101
Gaensbauer, T. J. 213
Garma, A. 148
generations, continuity of 277
genital and pregenital stages 135
Giannakoulas, A. 19, 28
Gibbs, N. 32
Gillespie, W. 4, 282
Glover, E. 57
God, one-ness with, concept of 207
Godley, W. 25
Goldman, D. 5, 249
good-enough adaptation 130
good-enough environment 89, 173, 175
Gordon, R. 13
greed 18, 36, 48, 49, 50, 140 [compulsive 200]

Green, A. 1, 5, 6, 7, 212, 233
Greenacre, P. 100, 148, 231
Greenberg, J. 171
Grolnick, S. 100
guilt: capacity for 22; sense of 171, 173, 174, 177
Guntrip, H. 10

hallucination(s)/hallucinosis 64, 65, 106, 178, 247, 265; creative, for baby, breast as 6, 19, 56, 112–113
hallucinatory magic omnipotence, stage of 6
Hamlet 280
Hampstead Clinic 210
Hampstead War Nurseries 3, 210
Harris, M. 209
Hartmann, H. 210, 225, 269
hate/hatred 49, 178, 192; in analyst 74–75, 78, 81–82; in countertransference 70–82; in infant 72; in mother 72; ways of expressing 76
Hayward, S. T. 24
Heimann, P. 54, 71, 73, 127, 147, 230
Hernandez, M. 19
hesitation 37, 40, 44, 46, 50, 52, 85; period of 34, 38, 47; stage of 38; as superego manifestation 43
history-taking, value of 109
Hoffer, W. 168
holding: concept of 21, 148, 150, 157–158, 161; environment 160, 161, 167, 199; function, maternal 15–16, 149, 212, 221; self- 198, 202
homosexuality 119, 135, 267, 271, 275
honeymoon period, in analysis 190
Hopkins, J. 151
Hopkins, L. B. 25
Horder, T. 2
Hubley, P. 35
Huizinga, J. 232
Humpty Dumpty 212, 217; stage 175
Hungarian school 71
hypnosis 91, 136
hypo-manic patients 74
hypochondria 46, 58, 59, 97
hysterical phenomena 92

id: drives 176, 177, 181; gratification 18; impulses 198, 211; manifestations, pregenital 156; regression 128; satisfactions 277

Middle Group 2, 4, 9, 230
Middlemore, M. 55
Miller, A. 236
Miller, E. 3
Milne, A. A. 236
Milner, M. 1, 20, 99, 127, 234, 235; and
    Winnicott, theoretical links between
    10–11
mind: and body [relation 84; and psyche,
    interrelation of 17]; concept of 87; false
    entity 87; false localization 87, 96;
    localization of, in head 96–97; and psyche-
    soma 83–98; theory of 35, 84, 88–91
    [clinical illustration 92–95]
mirror(ing) 15, 239; role, mother's 11
Mitchell, S. 171, 263
Modell, A. H. 100
Money-Kyrle, R. E. 127, 147
monotheism 268
mood, analysis of 132
morality 171, 173
mother(s) (passim): adaptation of to baby/
    infant 6, 14, 19, 84, 89, 90, 111–115, 130,
    151, 166, 213, 232, 247, 278; angry 44;
    attachment to 108; and baby/infant,
    separate 55; containing function of 15, 16,
    150, 170; depressed 118, 120, 196, 211, 215,
    220 [analyst as 57]; dreaming their babies'
    dreams for them 241; empathy of 158, 162;
    environment- 18, 171, 172, 176, 177, 178,
    180, 182, 187, 188, 192, 199, 211, 263;
    good-enough 14, 111, 127, 211 [and not-
    good-enough, concept of 278]; holding
    function of 15, 149, 212, 221; identification
    with infant 166; imaginative elaboration of
    84, 88, 96, 97, 104, 150; –infant/baby/child
    relationship (passim); inner reality of 251;
    internal 35, 51, 52 [object– 21]; mad, in
    transference, analyst as 263; mirror role of
    15; not-good-enough 278; object– 18, 171,
    176, 178, 180, 182, 188, 211; ordinary
    devoted 14; reverie of 84; unreliability of
    188
mothering, good-enough 114, 175
motility 18, 83, 102
Muller, J. P. 12
muscle erotism 18, 110, 159, 175, 186

'nameless dread' 150
narcissism 9, 15, 86, 89, 130, 136, 139, 149,
    158, 183, 184, 207; primary [concept of
    192; exploitation of 198, 202]

National Health Service (NHS) 26, 170
negation 193, 195
negative transference 7, 24, 140
neurosis 29, 40, 135, 215; obsessional 98
neurotic(s)/neurotic patient(s) 23, 48, 72, 74,
    77, 140, 141, 145; analysis of 22, 71, 252
New York Psychoanalytic Society 249
non-communicating/non-communication
    184, 187, 192, 196; active 188, 189, 193 [or
    reactive 183]; simple 183, 193, 194
non-differentiation, initial, for baby 14, 250
non-integration 57
nonexistence: as defence 207; fear of 200
nostalgia 123
not-communicating: active or reactive 188;
    simple 188
not-me 103, 105, 106, 153, 158, 159, 175, 187,
    193, 194, 202, 236, 277; possession 103, 106
    [transitional object as 102]

O'Shaughnessy, E. 129, 209
object(s): capacity to use 253, 255, 259;
    cathexis 186; constancy 172, 233, 259, 275;
    external, pathological uses of 100; fetish
    100, 236; internal 115, 195 [concept of
    111]; internalized 35; love, primary 9; –
    mother 18, 171, 176, 178, 180, 182, 188,
    211; objectification of 277; objectively
    perceived 183, 188–193; presenting 202; –
    relating/relation(s)/relationship(s) (passim)
    [infant–mother 9; school, British 1, 249;
    theories 8, 129, 255, 276]; transformational
    231; use of/-usage 230, 250, 254, 255, 259
objective reality 65, 102
observation, infant 32–52
observing ego 141, 146, 239
obsessional neurosis 98
obsessional rituals 107
Oedipus complex 14, 22, 134, 135, 146, 155,
    167, 173, 174, 181, 251
Oedipus situation 49
Ogden, T. 1, 16, 20, 21, 55, 56, 151, 250, 251
omnipotence: area of 161, 187; as defence 15;
    experience of, infant's 185, 204, 242;
    hallucinatory magic, stage of 6; illusion of
    6, 12, 15, 19, 151, 250, 252; infantile 14, 15,
    112, 152, 160, 185, 186, 242, 251; loss/
    abrogation of 106, 262, 269; magic 6;
    patient's 152, 275; personal 198, 199, 203
omnipotent control 203, 255, 256, 257, 259,
    274; magical 110
omnipotent fantasy 18

oral aggression 179
oral erotism 104, 132, 279
oral erotogenic zone 103
oral sadism 176, 220, 279
original self 13

Paddington Green Children's Hospital 2, 26, 33, 36, 116
Padel, J. 8
paediatrics 1, 2, 4, 21, 26, 133, 222
pallor 45, 63
panic, maternal 206
paradox 87, 102, 115, 153, 186, 231, 233; acceptance of 255, 269
paranoid anxieties 77
parent(s): –infant relationship, theory of 147–168; therapeutic capacity of 29
Parsons, M. 1, 230, 231, 233
pathological withdrawal 136, 184, 194
patient(s) (*passim*): 'as-if' 99; borderline 22, 23, 25, 70, 86, 130, 153, 156, 164, 167, 193, 254 [analysis of 253]; depressed/depressive 59, 140; experience of as central 13; hypo-manic 74; neurotic 23, 48, 72, 74, 77, 140, 141, 145 [analysis of 22, 71, 252]; psychoneurotic 136, 193, 253 [analysis of 22, 204, 205, 207]; psychosomatic 85, 97; psychotic (regressive) 140 [analysis of 23, 57, 58, 62, 64, 73, 74, 75, 76, 78, 80]; regressed 9, 23, 130, 140; schizophrenic 72, 205, 265
Payne, S. 4
penis 35, 47, 219, 221, 222, 279; envy 262, 271–275
perception vs. apperception 15
period of hesitation 34, 38, 47
persecutory anxiety, infantile 171
personality: disintegration of 62; false 267; psychoneurotic aspects of 187; schizoid aspects of 187; split 184, 191; theory of 235
personalization 55, 61, 62, 63, 83, 86; satisfactory 63
perversion(s) 119, 120; sexual 100
phallus, maternal, delusion of 100
phenomenal death 205
Phillips, A. 84, 149, 171, 172, 173, 213, 249
phobia(s) 201
Pick, I. 209
Pierce Clark, L. 24
Piggle 27, 28, 29
play/playing (*passim*): –analysis 52; capacity to 12, 28, 233, 246; importance of 6;

precariousness of 245; significance of 231; theory of (clinical example) 243–245; in time and space (clinical examples) 237–242; use of 28, 102, 235
pleasure principle 111, 149, 153, 154, 156, 185
possession, first 103
postnatal depression 212
potential space between mother and baby 99, 232, 233, 234, 237, 242, 247
pre-concern, stage of 66–67
pre-frontal leucotomy 54
precocious ego development 84
pregenital id-manifestations 156
pregenital sexuality 155
pregenital stage and genital stage 135
premature ego 207; development 86, 241
'pre-ruth': infant's earliest relation to mother as 18; self 18
primary aggression 18; and libido, fusion of 19
primary creativity 15, 16, 99, 102, 107, 112, 250
primary defect 211, 212
primary emptiness 206
primary envy 170
primary identification 12, 111, 158, 262, 277; false 12
primary identity 277
primary maternal preoccupation 147, 149, 185, 211
primary narcissism 9, 15, 86, 130, 136, 139, 149, 158, 183, 184, 207; concept of 192; exploitation of 198, 202
primary object love, theory of 9
primary process 102, 149, 158
primary repression 152
primary unintegration/unintegrated state 55, 57, 62, 66
primitive agony(ies) 198, 202, 203
primitive anxiety(ies) 150, 151, 156, 163, 212, 220, 224
primitive ego 149
primitive emotional development 58, 59, 65, 129, 132
primitive love 67, 179; impulse 18, 22, 75, 172, 173
primitive mental mechanisms 167
primitive relationship(s) 59; analysis of 59
primitive retaliation 67
primitive ruthlessness 56, 66–67
primitive superego 35, 173